the
treasury
of

Great
Canadian
Humour

the treasury of Great Canadian Humour

edited and introduced by alan walker

McGRAW-HILL RYERSON LIMITED

Toronto   Montreal   New York   London

The Treasury of Great Canadian Humour

A list of sources is printed on pp. v to ix

ISBN 0-07-077627-x

Library of Congress Catalog Card Number 74-11914

1 2 3 4 5 6 7 8 9 0   BP—74   32 10 9 8 7 6 5 4

Printed and bound in Canada

Acknowledgements

The editor wishes to make grateful acknowledgement for permission to reprint the following copyright material:

THE CONJURER'S REVENGE, from *Literary Lapses*, by Stephen Leacock, reprinted by permission of The Canadian Publishers, McClelland and Stewart Limited, Toronto. In Britain, acknowledgement is made to The Bodley Head for permission to include THE CONJURER'S REVENGE from *Literary Lapses* by Stephen Leacock.

THE HITCH-HIKER, from *A Barr'l of Apples*, by Gregory Clark, reprinted by permission of Canada Wide Feature Service.

WHAT HAPPENED TO TEEN-AGERS? from the book *We Gave You the Electric Toothbrush*, by Robert Thomas Allen. Reprinted by permission of Doubleday & Company, Inc.

THE PRIZE FISH, by Jack Scott, is reprinted from *From Our Town*.

HOW TO LOSE AN EAR is reprinted from *Sackcloth and Splashes* by Keith Crombie & J. E. McDougall, McClelland and Stewart Limited, Toronto.

Excerpts from THE INCOMPARABLE ATUK, by Mordecai Richler, reprinted by permission of The Canadian Publishers, McClelland and Stewart Limited, Toronto.

CRIME AND PUNISHMENT, by Richard Needham, from *The Hypodermic Needham*, Macmillan of Canada, 1970. Reprinted by permission of The Globe and Mail.

Excerpts reprinted from *Neighbourly News* by Andy Clarke.

SPFFFLTT! SPLITCH! HUT! KAK! HOOT! by Earl McRae, reprinted by permission of The Canadian Magazine.

Excerpt reprinted from *There Goes MacGill* by Ronald Hambleton, by permission of the author.

THANK YOU, UNCLE BEN, FOR THE NICEST WHATEVER-IT-IS THAT EVER RUINED A HOUSE, by Maggie Grant, reprinted by permission of The Canadian Magazine.

THERE'S INTRIGUE WHEN "MEESTAIR ROSS" IS ON ASSIGNMENT, by Alexander Ross. Reprinted with permission Toronto Star.

SHE WAS SO YOUNG TO DIE! is reprinted from *Sackcloth and Splashes* by Keith Crombie and J. E. McDougall, McClelland and Stewart Limited, Toronto.

Excerpts from CHARLIE FARQUHARSON'S HISTRY OF CANADA by Don Harron. Reprinted by permission of McGraw-Hill Ryerson Limited.

DOWN, PTE. ENGLEBY, DOWN, AND KINDLY STOP LICKING MY HAND, from *I've Been Around and Around and Around and Around* ... by George Bain. © 1964 by Clarke, Irwin & Company Limited. Used by permission.

LORD OF THE FLEAS, from *Saturday Night at the Bagel Factory*, by Don Bell, reprinted by permission of The Canadian Publishers, McClelland and Stewart Limited, Toronto.

THE GREAT DETECTIVE, by Stephen Leacock. © Dodd, Mead & Company, Inc. Reprinted by permission of Dodd, Mead & Company Inc.

from *Laugh With Leacock* by Stephen Leacock. Copyright 1930 by Dodd, Mead & Company, Inc. Copyright renewed 1958 by George Leacock. In Britain, acknowledgement is made to The Bodley Head for permission to include THE GREAT DETECTIVE by Stephen Leacock from *Short Circuits*.

THE RELUCTANT SPECIALIST, by Harry Symons, from *The Bored Meeting*, Ryerson Press, 1951, reprinted by permission of the Symons family.

FISCHER WINS! by Ben Wicks, reprinted by permission of Weekend Magazine, Montreal.

IN THE MALEMUTE SALOON, by Joan Walker, from *Pardon my Parka*, reprinted by permission of The Canadian Publishers, McClelland and Stewart Limited, Toronto.

THEY KNOW WHEN A MAN ANSWERS, from *Still a Nicol*, by Eric Nicol. Reprinted by permission of McGraw-Hill Ryerson Limited.

Excerpts from THE LUCK OF GINGER COFFEY, by Brian Moore, reprinted by permission of Little, Brown and Company (Canada) Limited. In the United States, reprinted by permission of Collins–Knowlton–Wing, Inc. Copyright © by Brian Moore.

Excerpts from NURSERY RHYMES TO BE READ ALOUD BY YOUNG PARENTS WITH OLD CHILDREN, by George Bain. © 1965 by Clarke, Irwin & Company Limited. Used by permission.

THE COMMON MAN, by Joseph Schull, reprinted from *Saturday Night*, by permission of the author.

Excerpts from AND NOW ... HERE'S MAX, by Max Ferguson. Reprinted by permission of McGraw-Hill Ryerson Limited.

CANADA AS SHE IS MISUNDERSTOOD, by Peter McArthur, is reprinted from *To Be Taken with Salt*, Limpus Baker & Company, London, 1903.

LET ME CALL YOU, SWEETHEART, by Richard J. Needham, reprinted by permission of The Globe and Mail.

MICE IN THE BEER, from *Mice in the Beer*, by Norman Ward, reprinted by permission of Longman Canada Limited.

Excerpt from JUPITER EIGHT, by Francis Pollock, reprinted by permission of Jonathan Cape Limited, London.

THIS HERE BALLET, from *Still a Nicol*, by Eric Nicol. Reprinted by permission of McGraw-Hill Ryerson Limited.

Excerpts from SEX AND SECURITY, by Dave Broadfoot. Reprinted by permission of McGraw-Hill Ryerson Limited.

Excerpt from THE GRASS IS NEVER GREENER, by Robert Thomas Allen, reprinted by permission of The Canadian Publishers, McClelland and Stewart Limited, Toronto.

Excerpts from THE GREAT FUR OPERA, by Kildare Dobbs, reprinted by permission of the Hudson's Bay Company.

PAY ATTENTION, NOW, by Doug Fetherling, printed by permission of Doug Fetherling.

Excerpt from TEMPEST-TOST by Robertson Davies. © 1951 by Clarke, Irwin & Company Limited. Used by permission.

THE INSTRUCTION, from *Homebrew and Patches*, by Harry J. Boyle, © 1972 Harry J. Boyle, reprinted by permission of the Canadian Speakers' & Writers' Service.

NOT JUST ANY DAMP CANDIDATE ACCEPTED BY STATE DEPARTMENT, from *I've Been Around and Around and Around and Around* ... by George Bain. © 1964 by Clarke, Irwin & Company Limited. Used by permission.

Excerpts from THE CLOCKMAKER; OR, THE SAYINGS AND DOINGS OF SAM SLICK, OF SLICKVILLE, by Thomas Chandler Haliburton, reprinted by permission of The Canadian Publishers, McClelland and Stewart Limited, Toronto.

Excerpt from BARTLEBY. Permission granted : House of Anansi Press Limited, from *Bartleby*, by Chris Scott, © 1971.

THE NIGHT THE THING GOT IN, reprinted from *The Salt-Box* by Jan Hilliard. By permission of W. W. Norton & Company, Inc. Copyright 1951 by Jan Hilliard.

A JAMES BOND STORY, from *Lady Chatterley, Latterley*, by Walter O'Hearn, reprinted by permission of The Canadian Publishers, McClelland and Stewart Limited, Toronto.

THE DAY JAKE MADE HER RAIN, from *Jake and the Kid*, by W. O. Mitchell, reprinted by permission of The Macmillan Company of Canada Limited. In the United States, reprinted by permission of Collins–Knowlton–Wing, Inc. Copyright © 1961 by W. O. Mitchell.

FINDING A COFFIN FOR A DEAD SNAKE IS NO EASY MATTER, by Alexander Ross. Reprinted with permission Toronto Star.

A RESERVATION, from *Boobs in the Woods*, by Merrill Denison, reprinted by permission of the author.

Excerpts from THE MAYOR OF UPPER UPSALQUITCH, by John S. Crosbie. Reprinted by permission of McGraw-Hill Ryerson Limited.

GOLF LESSON, by Jack Scott, is reprinted from *From Our Town*.

FIFI AND HER FIRST-CLASS MAN, from *Needham's Inferno* by Richard J. Needham, Macmillan of Canada, 1966. Reprinted by permission of The Globe and Mail.

TURVEY ATTENDS A COURT-MARTIAL, from *Turvey: A Military Picaresque*, by Earle Birney, reprinted by permission of The Canadian Publishers, McClelland and Stewart Limited, Toronto.

HAIR DOES NOTHING FOR PEOPLE, by E. U. Schrader, from *Dateline: Gloucester Pool*, compiled and edited by Dick MacDonald, Content Publishing Limited, Montreal.

Excerpt from WHY ROCK THE BOAT? by William Weintraub, reprinted by permission of Little, Brown & Company (Canada) Limited, Toronto.

THE FIRE, from *A Barr'l of Apples*, by Gregory Clark, reprinted by permission of Canada Wide Feature Service.

WHY CULLODEN WAS LOST, from *More Candid Chronicles*, by Hector Charlesworth, reprinted by permission of The Macmillan Company of Canada Limited.

IF SEYMOUR CAN DUMP THE RAGS, BENNY WILL ORDER THE PANTS, by Tom Alderman, reprinted by permission of The Canadian Magazine.

GOD HELP THE YOUNG FISHMAN, by Ethel Wilson, from *Mrs. Golightly and Other Stories*, by permission of The Macmillan Company of Canada Limited.

A NIGHT IN THE OPERA HOUSE, from *The Night We Stole The Mountie's Car*, by Max Braithwaite, reprinted by permission of The Canadian Publishers, McClelland and Stewart Limited, Toronto.

THE RATS ARE KEPT OUT OF THE RAT-RACE SO THEY ARE OUT TO TAKE OVER THE WORLD, by Maggie Grant, reprinted by permission of The Canadian Magazine.

ZOOLOGY, from *Mortgage Manor*, by Lex Schrag. Reprinted by permission of McGraw-Hill Ryerson Limited.

88 KEYS TO TROUBLE, from *The Great Canadian Lover*, by Mervyn J. Huston, Musson, 1964. Reprinted by permission of Hurtig Publishers, Edmonton.

Excerpt from WILLOWS REVISITED, by Paul Hiebert, reprinted by permission of The Canadian Publishers, McClelland and Stewart Limited, Toronto.

Excerpts from SAY, UNCLE from *Still a Nicol*, by Eric Nicol. Reprinted by permission of McGraw-Hill Ryerson Limited.

PERRY MASON AND THE CASE OF THE DAPPER DETECTIVE, from *Just Add Water and Stir*, by Pierre Berton, reprinted by permission of The Canadian Publishers, McClelland and Stewart Limited, Toronto. In the United States, reprinted from *My War with the Twentieth Century* by Pierre Berton. Reprinted by Doubleday & Company Inc.

Excerpts from THE EYE OPENER, by Bob Edwards, reprinted by permission of Grant McEwan.

BORROWING A MATCH, by Stephen Leacock, from *Literary Lapses*, reprinted by permission of The Canadian Publishers, McClelland and Stewart Limited, Toronto. In Britain, acknowledgement is made to The Bodley Head for permission to include BORROWING A MATCH from *Literary Lapses* by Stephen Leacock.

TWENTIETH CENTURY ARTIFACTS AWAY BACK IN 1959, by Pierre Berton, from *Adventures of a Columnist*, reprinted by permission of The Canadian Publishers, McClelland and Stewart Limited, Toronto. In the United States, reprinted from *My War with the Twentieth Century* by Pierre Berton. Copyright © 1965 by Pierre Berton. Reprinted by Doubleday & Company, Inc.

Selections from 3 CHEERS FOR ME by Donald Jack. Copyright © 1962, 1963 by Donald L. Jack. Reprinted by permission of Doubleday & Company, Inc.

AUNT MATILDA'S BED-TIME STORY is reprinted from *Sackcloth and Splashes* by Keith Crombie & J. E. McDougall, McClelland and Stewart Limited, Toronto.

THE TYPICAL MORON, by Mary Lowrey Ross, reprinted from *Saturday Night* by permission of the author.

Selections from HIMIE KOSHEVOY'S TREASURE JEST OF BEST PUNS, by Himie Koshevoy, reprinted by permission of Graydonald Graphics Limited, Vancouver.

A SHORT STORY, by C. B. Pyper, is reprinted from *One Thing After Another*, J. M. Dent & Sons Ltd., 1948, by permission of the author.

LADDERS, by Norris Hodgins, from *The Parsleys and the Sage*, reprinted by permission of the author.

BRUTALLY EXPLICIT! ROSSI'S EROTIC TOUR DE FORCE, by Alexander Ross. Reprinted with permission Toronto Star.

AFTERNOON OF AN ART CRITIC, by Norman Ward, from *The Fully Processed Cheese*, reprinted by permission of Longman Canada Limited.

ON OUR CULTURAL RENAISSANCE by Doug Fetherling, printed by permission of Doug Fetherling.

"MOMMA ISN'T HOME NOW," from *Still a Nicol*, by Eric Nicol. Reprinted by permission of McGraw-Hill Ryerson Limited.

THE OLD MAN EARNS HIS DRINK, by Farley Mowat, from *The Boat Who Wouldn't Float*, reprinted by permission of The Canadian Publishers, McClelland and Stewart Limited, Toronto.

THEN I REMEMBERED is reprinted from *Sackcloth and Splashes* by Keith Crombie & J. E. McDougall, McClelland and Stewart Limited, Toronto.

A CHILD'S GARDEN OF CLICHÉS, by Pierre Berton, from *Adventures of a Columnist*, reprinted by permission of The Canadian Publishers, McClelland and Stewart Limited, Toronto. In the United States, reprinted from *My War with the Twentieth Century* by Pierre Berton. Copyright © 1965 by Pierre Berton. Reprinted by Doubleday & Company, Inc.

STEPHEN GIVES ME A MAN-TO-MAN TALK – ON DRAGON-FLIES, by Gary Lautens. Reprinted with permission Toronto Star.

FLATTERY is reprinted from *Sackcloth and Splashes* by Keith Crombie & J. E. McDougall, McClelland and Stewart Limited, Toronto.

THE BEE FIGHT, by Billy Bock, from *The Best of Billy Bock*, edited by John Archer and Robert Peterson, Modern Press, 1967. Reprinted by permission of Western Producer Book Service.

MAN, YOU'RE A GREAT PLAYER! from *Laughing with Lautens*, by Gary Lautens. Reprinted by permission of McGraw-Hill Ryerson Limited.

GERALDE AND THE GREEN, GREEN GRASS, by Robert Fontaine, is reprinted from *Maclean's Magazine*.

COULD I SEE A GOOD MURDER? from *My Life as a Rose-Breasted Grosbeak*, by Stuart Trueman, reprinted by permission of The Canadian Publishers, McClelland and Stewart Limited, Toronto.

Excerpt from CANAJAN, EH? by Mark M. Orkin. Copyright © 1973 Mark M. Orkin. Illustrations © General Publishing Company Limited. Used by permission of General Publishing Company Limited, Don Mills, Ontario.

THE DOG EXPLOSION, by Hugh Hood, is reprinted from *The Fruit Man, the Meat Man & the Manager* by permission of Oberon Press.

Excerpts from THE SHORT HAPPY WALKS OF MAX MACPHERSON, by Harry Bruce, reprinted by permission of The Macmillan Company of Canada Limited.

ANGLO-SAXON AND I, by Margaret Atwood, reprinted from *Acta Victoriana* by permission of the author.

OFFICER, ARREST THAT BOOK! from *Laughing with Lautens*, by Gary Lautens. Reprinted by permission of McGraw-Hill Ryerson Limited.

BREVITY, by Maggie Grant, reprinted by permission of The Canadian Magazine.

YES, SANTA, THERE IS A VIRGINIA, from *Needham's Inferno*, by Richard J. Needham, Macmillan of Canada, 1966. Reprinted by permission of The Globe and Mail.

"OF *COURSE* IT'S A NITWIT COUNTRY," by Jack McIver, reprinted from *The Canadian Magazine*.

Table of Contents

Appendix

Introduction

In 1956, I hated to get up in the morning almost as much as I do now. So at 9:01 a.m. on that long-ago day I was groggy when the earnest woman at the front of the classroom told us to open our "red" books — red for Lit. and green for Comp. — to page whatever-it-was and announced: "Today we are going to learn about humour."

That woke me up. What was there to "learn" about humour? In Zoology the day before, when Gary Kellam threw half a worm at Patti Campbell and she screamed and Gary got two Ds, *that* was funny. We'd all gone into hysterics when the gym teacher ruptured himself on the pommel-horse. And we knew that Joy Buzzers and Whoopee Cushions were the funniest inventions since the square wheel.

We opened our red books to Stephen Leacock's essay called "My Financial Career" — the one where he goes into the bank and gets rattled. For forty minutes the teacher dissected it and put it back together, and then we had to answer fifteen dumb questions to help us remember the right "points" for the examination that was coming up in six months. To this day, "My Financial Career" remains the least funny piece I have ever read, with the exception of *Jude the Obscure*.

That teacher was one of many people who ruin humour by examining it too closely and explaining it too well. Leacock himself made a mess of things in his painfully thorough book *Humour: Its Theory and Techniques*. He published it in 1935 — about ten years after he'd stopped being funny.

There are definitions and philosophies of humour, but the only profitable one conforms to the maxim that brevity is the soul of wit; humour is either funny or it isn't. No explanations are necessary or even forgivable.

In compiling *The Treasury of Great Canadian Humour* I read several hundred newspaper and magazine pieces, and about 300 books. It was great fun discovering how many funny writers Canada has, and has had over the years. I laughed so much that once I even told my publisher I couldn't possibly accept any money for editing this book. On really funny days, I felt guilty because I wasn't paying *him*.

You will not find any Joy Buzzers or Whoopee Cushions in the pages that follow. There aren't many worms, and I don't think there's a pommel-horse. There are three of Stephen Leacock's funniest pieces. But "My Financial Career" is not one of them.

Most people I know are writers or editors and they're supposed to know something about writing and editing. But even they, when I told them I was going to compile *The Treasury of Great Canadian Humour*, giggled and said things like, "Gonna be a pretty thin book i'nt it?" (Writers can't talk very well.)

I admit that had crossed my mind. The first thing I'd done was start a list from memory: "CANADIAN HUMOUR." . . . Well, I had edited a volume of Eric Nicol's work the year before (*Still A Nicol*), so I wrote his name down first. Then Stephen Leacock of course. And slowly they came: The Big Ones. Robert Thomas Allen . . . Greg Clark . . . Mordecai Richler . . . George Bain . . . Richard Needham . . . Pierre Berton (back then, anyway) . . . Max Ferguson, so funny I cried . . . *Paul Hiebert* — how could I have forgotten him? . . .

And, after a lot of research, I came up with the ones less known today. Soon I had more than a hundred. I showed the list to my gonna-be-a-thin-book-i'nt-it friends, and they repented and said it would be a pretty thick book after all.

Their problem, and mine, had been that nobody really takes humorous writers seriously — in the sense that they don't consider them real Writers, like all those people you read about in the *Times Literary Supplement*. You read a funny book and thank-you-very-much, now on to something that's Good For You. And you forget who made you laugh.

The problem is compounded because Canada has had so many one-book authors, who are so easy to forget. Most of them were journalists or schoolteachers or housewives who muttered their way through the idiocies of their fellows, then could stand it no longer, wrote a funny book, got it out of their systems and retired on their copious royalties. Here today, gone the next, as others of their breed replaced them, relieving their frustrations in the same way.

As I rediscovered so many of these undeservedly forgotten funny men and women, it became clear that my problem wasn't what to put into *The Treasury of Great Canadian Humour*, but what to leave out.

Verse was the first to go (except for snippets of Bain, Needham and the special effects of Paul Hiebert) because Canadian poetry on the whole is a humourless business — occasionally attaining cynicism but practically never wit.

I ruled out translations, which are a risky business in any literary form and especially so in Canadian humour because so many English Canadians and French Canadians find each other automatically hilarious at exactly the wrong time.

Cartoons? There have been a few great political cartoonists in Canada but few purely funny ones because we have so few magazines that will print their stuff. One of the funniest cartoonists in the world, Fons Van Woerkom, arrived in Canada about six years ago, made it into a few magazines — and the next thing I knew he sent me a letter from New York.

There's no audible humour in this book either. How can I do a book of Canadian humour and leave out Wayne and Shuster? I didn't think I'd have to, but radio, TV and theatre scripts I read just didn't work in print. Even ones I'd heard and laughed at just lay on the printed page like finnan haddie.

There is no Underground humour in this book. Not because I'm a literary snob, but I have read Canadian satire magazines as they have come and gone over the years, and now I read what passes for topical satire in the Underground press, and I am depressed at so much that is specious and badly crafted. Wouldn't it be nice if we had a *Private Eye* or a *National Lampoon?* In an appendix to this book there is an article from *The Canadian Magazine* by Jack McIver about *National Lampoon.* I include it partly because McIver is a funny man, but also because it in turn includes healthy chunks of *Lampoon* satire on Canada. An unusually high proportion of *Lampoon* writers and editors are Canadian. They manage to write funny and pungent satire about Canada presumably because they live in New York.

Finally, some readers might wonder why there isn't more *old* Canadian humour in this book. There's some, and it stands up well (or it wouldn't be here). Thomas Chandler Haliburton will be funny forever. Leacock of course. But not everyone wears so well. Take Thomas McCulloch, the Nova Scotia clergyman who has been credited with inventing Canadian humour (surely Cabot or Cartier must have done that when they met their first three-pound mosquito). McCulloch began writing letters in the Halifax Acadian Recorder in 1821 and he signed them "Mephibosheth Stepsure". Today they read about as humorously as Pilgrim's Progress, which I'm sure McCulloch must have greatly admired.

So I read everybody and made some heart-rending decisions, because I couldn't put in everything and everybody I liked. Naturally, I won't please you all. I have even dared to omit a few writers who have won the Stephen Leacock Memorial Medal for Humour — because, in 1974, they can't stand up to the competition. I'm not the only one who thinks so. One Leacock medal winner's book is in the Metropolitan Toronto Central Library and it isn't classified under Humour. It isn't even classified under *Literature*. It's in Sociology, which is exactly where it belongs.

I promised not to dissect the funny pieces you're about to read, but since I plowed through so much, a couple of general comments about Canadian humour might do somebody some good. Preferably forthcoming humourists.

The few critical commentaries on Canadian humour or on individual writers, and many newspaper and magazine reviews, use the same phrase, "gentle humour." Canadians write "gentle humour." Nobody includes Mordecai Richler in that, or *National Lampoon*'s Canadians, but on the whole we don't have much satire and what we do have is rarely hard-hitting — which is to say it seems calculated not to upset anybody. The primary categories into which Canadian humour falls are Domestic (how Daddy bruised his thumb while getting Tabby out of the eavestrough); Academic/Journalistic (how Daddy bruised his thumb cleaning his typewriter); and Nostalgic (how Daddy bruised his thumb cleaning a butter churn). A lot of it *is* soft . . . reminiscent . . . gentle. And yet, charming — and funny.

I'll settle for it any day.

—Alan Walker, 1974

The Conjurer's Revenge

Stephen Leacock

"Now, ladies and gentlemen," said the conjurer, "having shown you that the cloth is absolutely empty, I will proceed to take from it a bowl of goldfish. Presto!"

All around the hall people were saying, "Oh, how wonderful! How does he do it?"

But the Quick Man on the front seat said in a big whisper to the people near him, "He — had — it — up — his — sleeve."

Then the people nodded brightly at the Quick Man and said, "Oh, of course"; and everybody whispered round the hall, "He — had — it — up — his — sleeve."

"My next trick," said the conjurer, "is the famous Hindostanee rings. You will notice that the rings are apparently separate; at a blow they all join (clang, clang, clang) — Presto!"

There was a general buzz of stupefaction till the Quick Man was heard to whisper, "He — must — have — had — another — lot — up — his — sleeve."

Again everybody nodded and whispered, "The — rings — were — up — his — sleeve."

The brow of the conjurer was clouded with a gathering frown.

"I will now," he continued, "show you a most amusing trick by which I am enabled to take any number of eggs from a hat. Will some gentleman kindly lend me his hat? Ah, thank you — Presto!"

He extracted seventeen eggs, and for thirty-five seconds the audience began to think that he was wonderful. Then the Quick Man whispered along the front bench, "He — has — a — hen — up — his — sleeve," and all the people whispered it on. "He — has — a — lot — of — hens — up — his — sleeve."

The egg trick was ruined.

It went on like that all through. It transpired from the whispers of the Quick Man that the conjurer must have concealed up his sleeve, in addition to the rings, hens, and fish, several packs of cards, a loaf of bread, a doll's cradle, a live guinea-pig, a fifty-cent piece, and a rocking-chair.

The reputation of the conjurer was rapidly sinking below zero. At the close of the evening he rallied for a final effort.

"Ladies and gentlemen," he said, "I will present to you, in conclusion, the famous Japanese trick recently invented by the natives of Tipperary. Will you, sir," he continued, turning toward the Quick Man, "will you kindly hand me your gold watch?"

It was passed to him.

"Have I your permission to put it into this mortar and pound it to pieces?" he asked savagely.

The Quick Man nodded and smiled.

The conjurer threw the watch into the mortar and grasped a sledge hammer from the table. There was a sound of violent smashing. "He's – slipped – it – up – his – sleeve," whispered the Quick Man.

"Now, sir," continued the conjurer, "will you allow me to take your handkerchief and punch holes in it? Thank you. You see, ladies and gentlemen, there is no deception, the holes are visible to the eye."

The face of the Quick Man beamed. This time the real mystery of the thing fascinated him.

"And now, sir, will you kindly pass me your silk hat and allow me to dance on it? Thank you."

The conjurer made a few rapid passes with his feet and exhibited the hat crushed beyond recognition.

"And will you now, sir, take off your celluloid collar and permit me to burn it in the candle? Thank you, sir. And will you allow me to smash your spectacles for you with my hammer? Thank you."

By this time the features of the Quick Man were assuming a puzzled expression. "This thing beats me," he whispered, "I don't see through it a bit."

There was a great hush upon the audience. Then the conjurer drew himself up to his full height and, with a withering look at the Quick Man, he concluded:

"Ladies and gentlemen, you will observe that I have, with this gentleman's permission, broken his watch, burnt his collar, smashed his spectacles, and danced on his hat. If he will give me the further permission to paint green stripes on his overcoat, or to tie his suspenders in a knot, I shall be delighted to entertain you. If not, the performance is at an end."

And amid a glorious burst of music from the orchestra the curtain fell, and the audience dispersed, convinced that there are some tricks, at any rate, that are not done up the conjurer's sleeve.

from Literary Lapses

The Hitch-Hiker

Gregory Clark

The old boy on the side of the road, thumbing, was possibly a Character. Maybe even a Philosopher.

As a rule, I don't pick up hitch-hikers any more, unless they are in uniform. The last few times I have had fleas, it was due to having picked up Characters.

But this old boy, as I rapidly approached him, had an Interesting look. He might well be an Interesting Character. And when, at about forty yards, I detected at his feet a nice, clean, fresh-looking haversack, and when I perceived he had a fine, red, tanned face, and that his wispy white hair blowing in the wind could hardly be sticky, I threw overboard my prejudices and began to slacken speed. An Interesting Character is always a welcome pick-up. And sometimes you catch the top bracket of hitch-hikers, who are Philosophers.

"Hi!" I called out the window, noting with delight that he was carrying a gnarled walking stick.

He opened the door and lifted in his haversack.

In his wind-blown old face he had bright, sharp eyes; and all the wrinkles about them were from good nature.

Slowly he reached out and closed the door, glancing behind.

"Careful," he said. "Cars coming."

"I'll be careful," I assured him cheerily. "You've picked a careful driver."

"That I noticed," he said, "when I seen you coming in the distance."

"Aha! You pick your cars, eh?"

He was still turned to watch rearward.

"Yes, sir," he agreed. "I avoid these new-model cars."

"Well, heck," I protested. "This one isn't so ancient — 1950."

"It's O.K. now," said the old boy. "Nothing coming."

So I steered back off the shoulder and stepped on the gas.

He continued to watch back.

"You're not nervous are you?" I inquired, to get the ball rolling. "You can't be a hitch-hiker and nervous."

"No, sir, I ain't nervous," he said, turning and making himself comfortable. "And I am a regular, you might say a practising, hitch-hiker."

I knew I had a Philosopher.

"Well, sir," I said, "how far am I to have the pleasure of your company?"

"To Porter's Corners, if you're going that far," he replied. "Twenty-six mile. You come over a rise, and there's a big swamp spread out below . . ."

"I know it well," I assured him.

"Full of rabbits," he said. "Cottontail and swamp hare, both. AND foxes."

"I don't doubt that," I said.

A car whipped past us from behind, and the driver and the woman beside him both glared at us.

Indeed, they turned to glare back, after they had passed.

"What's eating them?" I put in.

"Oh, it's hard to say," said my Philosopher. "No accounting for manners on the highway, is there?"

Another car overtook us and swished past. The driver turned and motioned with his thumb, backwards.

"What's the matter with him?" I snorted.

"Guess he wants you to speed up," suggested the Philosopher.

"I'm hitting fifty," I stated. "That's my speed. And also the law's."

"They're always in a rush," admitted the old boy, turning to glance behind. "Nobody behind you. You ain't forming no queue."

"I agree," I said, "that people who dawdle on the highway are the cause of more accidents than anybody else. A man going forty is bound to build up a tail of half a dozen or a dozen cars behind him. And trying to pass him results in more accidents than all the speed in the world. But tell me. About foxes. What is your interest in foxes and the big swamp at Porter's Corners? Are you a sportsman?"

"Well, no," said my kindly old passenger. "I guess I am what you might call a naturalist or something. I just like to set in the swamp and look and listen."

"Well, now!" I exclaimed, delighted. "Orchids? Birds?"

"Yes and no," said my Philosopher. "They're all part of it. Just setting and listening and watching."

"You a farmer?"

"No, I spent my life as a sawmill hand," said the old boy. "But I been retired now twenty years or so. Living on my daughter, a fine woman."

"You interest me," I declared. "How about this business of sitting in a swamp, looking and listening? Tell me about this."

Two cars from behind overtook us and sped past. The first was driven by a man who had three women passengers. They all glared back at me, and waved their hands in a menacing fashion. The second car was full of small children in the rear window, and they, wide-eyed, waved and yelled and pressed their noses against the glass.

"For goodness' sake," I announced, looking at my speedometer.

"This craze for speed," said my companion.

So I put on five miles and brought her up to fifty-five.

"Not too fast," cautioned my Philosopher, taking a gander out the back window as I accelerated.

But I held it at fifty-five, as we chatted about swamps and orchids and screech owls and foxes; and presently we overtook a thin-necked gentleman with large ears going about forty.

"Look at this," I pointed out to my passenger. "Dawdling along at his own sweet pace."

We swished past him.

In a moment, I became aware that the dawdling gentleman was right on my tail. He moved out to pass.

"Just look at that!" I cried. "We pass him and right away..."

The dawdler shot past me. And hardly had he passed me before he began to slacken speed.

"Why, the son of a gun!" I gritted. "Imagine that! Going forty or less, and now . . ."

I veered out and leaped past him. He gave a couple of toots on his horn, put on speed, passed me, and hardly had he passed before he again slackened speed so that I nearly ran him down.

"One of these here traffic evangelists," commented my Philosopher, "trying to teach others how to drive, eh?"

I veered out and passed him, and as I did so I turned to give him an indignant glare. He was motioning energetically toward the back of my car.

I drew over to the shoulder. He pulled up behind me.

I got out.

"You got a dog," he called from his window, "on your back bumper."

Sure enough, there was a hound squatted cosily on my back bumper, slapping his tail.

"Well," explained my old Philosopher, as he bailed out. "Nobody will pick me up with a hound. So I trained him to hide in the bushes, and jump on whenever I get aboard."

"Old-model cars . . ." I reflected.

"I pick 'em," said he, "for their bumpers. I know my models."

The hound's name was Bojangles. We took him in the car. A fine, wise Redbone he was. And I let the Philosopher and Bojangles out at their favourite entry to the Porter's Corners swamp.

And I wished to God I could have gone with them.

from A Bar'l of Apples

What Happened to Teen-agers?

Robert Thomas Allen

We were all taken by surprise when our children grew up. A father, right in the middle of telling his son he'd toss him right over the garden fence if he didn't do something, would look up and notice for the first time that the kid was six feet high and had muscles and an intrigued smile as if he'd enjoy a bit of exercise. (It's even worse when you suddenly realize you can't lick your teen-aged *daughters*.)

I notice that we never hear of teen-agers any more. We have students, youths, young people, but no teen-agers. Back in the days when our kids were still at home we had all kinds of them. Magazines wrote about them endlessly and TV writers invented them until the "typical" teen-ager of TV or movie was about as close to anything real as Roy Rogers was to a cowboy. They were portrayed by talented, well-groomed, accomplished young Broadway actresses in their mid-twenties who wore blue jeans and pony tails and leaped a lot and said things like "real cool" and figured that was close enough. I often used to sit watching them and trying to relate them to the teen-age daughters around me, whose main drive in life was to wear spike heels and French perfume, dress like a $25,000-a-year fashion model out of *Seventeen* magazine, give as much lip as the traffic would bear, stay up till two in the morning (which they claimed every kid of normal parents was allowed to do), and to avoid all work, which they claimed all normal parents did themselves.

They began to take strange courses at school, like how to tear an automobile engine apart, and my own daughters believed that anyone — me, for instance — who thought English would be more useful, was some weird sort of peasant who was dying out.

"What would you do," they'd ask me with scorn, "if your car broke down, say, in the middle of the Sahara Desert? Just stand there and look at it I suppose."

The truth is that's just what I would do. What I couldn't get across to them was that it was just what they would have done, too, except that they would look at it from inside the car. Already they could stand and look at an unmade bed all Saturday morning without even seeing it.

In those days there were often TV conversations on programs like *Mother Knows Best* between a teen-age daughter curled up on the rug and a wise and understanding mother who explained things like how to recognize true love when it came along. I used to wonder where TV writers did their research. The conversations in my house were all about hair, clothes, and jobs that my daughters were trying not to do.

"Why aren't you at the dishes?"

"I have to do my hair."

"Why didn't you do it this morning?"

"I had to do my homework this morning."

"You had time to do it last night."

"I was looking at *Gunsmoke* last night."

"You were supposed to be ironing your blouse last night for the Twirp Dance."

"It doesn't need ironing."

"Which one are you going to wear?"

"The one with the blue trim."

"You'd better press your blue skirt, too."

"I have to do my hair."

"Are you going to let it grow or have it shaped?"

"I'm going to have it the same length all over."

"You should wash it. It's beginning to look dull."

"I have to clean my room."

"You should have thought of that last Friday."

"My hair wasn't dull last Friday."

Often conversations like this took place at the supper table. I used to sit looking from one to the other like someone at a tennis match, and finally roar: "*NOBODY IS EVER TO MENTION HAIR AT THIS TABLE AGAIN!*" There were more fights about hair in our house than anything else. Forbidding three females to talk about hair was typical of some of the rules I used to make. I'd be suddenly in the position of Captain Queeg of *The Caine Mutiny* who said no sailor was to go on leave until they found the man who stole his fresh strawberries. All of us, including my wife, would sit in absolute silence looking at one another's hair. The new hillbilly look has a lot to be said for it.

While TV writers kept writing about mothers telling their daughters how to recognize real love when it came along, real daughters couldn't have cared less whether they recognized it or not as long as they were wearing the clothes they wanted when it arrived. They spent about three quarters of their home life fighting for them with their mothers, who just wanted them to be clean, and dressed so that adults wouldn't laugh, and so that they'd be warm on cold days.

I used to live near the school-bus stop and could watch the teen-agers gathering in the morning, sneering in the direction of their homes, indignantly showing one another the socks, sweaters, coats, mitts, and mufflers their mothers made them wear.

"Look what *my* mother made me wear!" they would say, holding things as if they were at a rummage sale. "You'd think I lived at the NORTH POLE!" Meanwhile their mothers, judging by what was going on in my house, were sitting at the table biting their knuckles and sobbing, "You'd think I had Hong Kong flu or something."

Their daughters would all come home at 3:30 on the same bus, waving to their mothers, all on the honour roll for citizenship, co-operation, and neatness. They'd make cottage-cheese sandwiches, leave the cheese, breadknife and crumbs where they dropped, and walk right out of their shoes, sweaters, and books and leave them in the middle of the kitchen floor.

Anything they walked away from they forgot, even things they paid for themselves, and this in spite of a strong sense of property. When they went to parties they all came in clutching their own records, even though they all had the same ones, which they all lost. The Beatles hadn't arrived but Elvis Presley had, and I remember one time one of my kids had a party; when it broke up six girls were all going around saying soberly, "Who's got my 'Hound Dog'?"

At midnight I was still finding "Hound Dogs" under chairs, along with forgotten shoes, books, and handbags, and by the time I found the last one I was so sleepy I looked like an old hound dog myself.

All that doesn't seem long ago but it was before young people decided that man was a cosmic accident. A lot of girls then were violently religious and my own daughters used to go around praying for me and getting me to drive them to church affairs arranged by some indefatigable woman named Mrs. Henshaw who evidently lived in church basements and either had the most confused mind in the world or my daughters got everything she said wrong.

"We're to be at the church tonight at 7:30," they'd say. "You're to bring some nuts."

This would be the first I'd heard of it. "What kind of nuts?"

"I don't know," they'd say, from behind a *TV Guide.* "Coconuts, I guess. You're to bring your old glasses too."

"My what?"

"Your old glasses. They're for the needy."

"Who needs them?"

"Poor people who aren't as privileged as you. We're to have them there before our rehearsal for the Lonely Wanderer. At the church — I think — or somebody's house. Maybe it's Mrs. Henshaw's."

My wife and I spent some weekends snapping out instructions like cab dispatchers. "I'll drive them in as soon as I've had my bath and pick up the halos for them on the way back so they have them for the pageant at 3:30 unless there's a meeting of the Junior Citizenship League," I'd yell, trying to catch up to the schedule of one particularly active minister who kept needling me by telling my daughters to ask me some night at supper if I'd heard God's voice lately.

I used to meet other fathers outside the wrong churches, houses, and youth centres, who were as confused as I was. One time a tall thin father was parked outside the Sunday school, wearing a ski cap and dozing. As I came on the scene he woke up, leaned out and called, "Is this where I was to bring the bagpipes?"

Another father, backing up slowly and leaning out his door, said, "I thought they said 'gas pipes'."

One time I arrived with a car full of props and found nobody around but an old gent walking on his heels on the church lawn and muttering, "Angels! Angels! Every blessed one of them!" He was evidently referring to my daughters and their friends who were taking part in the last act of a pageant, which I'd thought was going to take place the next night. Oddly, I knew what he meant. I'd sat on hard Sunday school benches watching my daughters, who were wearing wings and lit by candlelight, with tears pouring down my cheeks, just fifteen minutes after I'd been telling them that I'd written for the procedure for getting them into reform school. Like most parents, I sometimes wish I had the chance to sit on the same hard benches now.

from We Gave You the Electric Toothbrush

The Prize Fish

Jack Scott

Henry Pludge had a fool-proof plan to win the fishing-derby. It was ludicrously simple. He decided that he would catch a salmon, keep it alive in a tank in his basement, fatten it up for a year, and walk away with the first prize.

Henry built a large steel tank in his basement, swore his wife to secrecy, and went fishing. After several days he landed a small, eight-pound spring salmon. He kept it alive in a large wash-tub which he carried to his home under the cloak of darkness. He dumped the salmon into the tank, started the system of constantly changing water, and went upstairs to bed.

For the first few days it was touch and go with the fish. He was finding the change from salt to fresh water too sudden. He sulked unhappily in one corner of the tank, looking up at Henry with brooding, baleful eyes. What's more, the salmon refused to eat and began wasting away. Once, when Henry dangled a fresh herring in front of his nose, the salmon wheeled and bit Henry sharply on the wrist. Henry cursed the fish and shook his fist at the tank. "It'll be a pleasure to conk you come next August," he cried.

The next morning when he returned to the tank, the herring was gone. The salmon was finning at the surface obviously looking for breakfast.

Once the salmon started eating he proved to be a glutton. Henry soon discovered that the fish would eat almost anything.

He was looking into the tank one day, munching on an apple, when he dropped the core. The salmon took it at a gulp.

The fish proved more than co-operative with Henry's plan to force-feed it. It ate watermelon, corn-on-the-cob, hash, cigarette butts, cheese and crackers, chile con carne, and several other un-likely items including roast beef, which it preferred well done.

Henry began spending more and more time in the basement. He liked to watch the salmon making its swift, effortless circles in the tank. He had taken to calling it "Sam" and sometimes he caught himself talking to it, as men talk to dogs.

Sam the Salmon responded to this affection. When Henry spoke to him by name he answered with bubbles. His powerful tail wagged whenever Pludge's face appeared over the rim of the tank.

Like a goldfish in a small bowl, Sam adapted himself to his close quarters and, though he grew bigger by the day, he appeared to be getting enough exercise. He looped and circled, darted in swift triangles.

It was only in the spring that he appeared unhappy, and the sound of him leaping and slapping the surface kept the Pludges awake many nights. Once they had to go down and carry him back to the tank from the sawdust bin where a prodigious leap had carried him.

"The poor fish is probably wanting a mate," Henry said to his wife.

"So will I if you stay in this basement much longer," his wife replied.

On the morning of the great fishing derby Henry put Sam on the scales and watched the indicator go up to sixty-four pounds, eight ounces. "Wow!" he exclaimed. Sam wagged his tail.

In the dawn Henry placed Sam in a smaller tank, drove to an isolated cove and loaded the tank into a rowboat. Then he headed out into the sound. The plan was simple. He would bait a hook with fresh herring. Poor, trusting Sam would take it. Then Henry would conk him on the skull, jettison the smaller tank, and go in to claim his reward.

Far out in the sound Henry shipped his oars, carefully readied the gigantic club with which to dispatch Sam, and began to bait the hook. Sam rose to the surface and peered over the rim of the tank, his tail wagging eagerly.

Henry's hands fumbled with the herring. "The poor fish," he was thinking to himself. "I have denied him a whole year of freedom, kept him locked in a basement far from deep water and girl salmon and now . . . now I am going to kill him when he trusts me." His eyes clouded over. His lips began to tremble. Sam looked at him inquiringly.

Suddenly Henry Pludge lifted the tank with a mighty effort and tipped it over the side. There was a great splash and Sam appeared at the surface, shaking his massive head. He began to swim in small circles, as if in the basement tank, but gradually they widened out until Henry lost sight of him. Then, far out now, Sam leaped joyously, his great silver body arching above the water.

"Farewell, Sam," Henry shouted. Then the fish was gone.

from From Our Town

How to Lose an Ear

Keith Crombie & J. E. McDougall

The street car was crowded. I was tired. I was seated. Before me stood an amazon of about thirty, clinging to a strap. Should I surrender my seat? As I said, I was tired. She did not look the least fatigued. If women are to have equal rights with men, why should not men have equal rights with women? And yet I was uncomfortable. With a burst of gallantry I arose.

"Madam," said I, "won't you be seated?"

She smiled at me.

"Young man," she said in a thunderous voice that attracted the attention of every passenger, "Young man, this is splendid of you! This is the sort of thing that makes one believe that the age of chivalry is not dead. I regret that I am unable to accept your offer. I am quite as able to stand as you. You look tired, whereas I am as fresh as a daisy. Moreover, I am getting off here."

She left. Under the burning gaze of a car-full of eyes I

turned to sit down. A nondescript individual had slipped into my place and was securely ensconced behind a newspaper.

When they finally pulled us apart it was discovered that he had lost an ear.

from Sackcloth and Splashes

from The Incomparable Atuk

Mordecai Richler

. . . The Twentyman Fur Co., a vastly misunderstood enterprise, was, at the time, suffering from a run of foul newspaper publicity and questions in Parliament because, it was claimed, the Eskimo was dying of consumption, malnutrition, and even frostbite, all because of what the white man had done to make his accustomed way of life unfeasible. Peel, the brightest young advertising man in Toronto, was flown north to see if he could come up with an idea. And so, to the everlasting consternation of Sgt. Wilson, he gave Atuk two electric blankets, a sack of flour, his cigarette lighter, and twelve bars of chocolate in exchange for a sheaf of his verse. The poems, as everybody knows, later ran in a series of advertisements in magazines all across Canada. A professor from Eglinton University, Norman Gore, sought out Atuk at Baffin Bay, and came back with the ingredients of the now famous volume of poems.

The success of Atuk's book was such that he was flown to Toronto for a literary party at the Park Plaza Hotel. His thoughtful publisher laid in a supply of chocolate bars and put some raw salmon on ice. A press conference was arranged. Atuk was interviewed on television. He was taken to see a midget wrestling match, a striperama, Rabbi Glenn Seigal's Temple, and other wonders of Toronto. Afterwards Atuk simply refused to return to the Bay. Instead he turned to Professor Norman Gore for help.

The front door to Gore's house was ajar and Atuk, following a native practice, walked right in.

"Hallo?"

A scuffle in the living-room. Sounded like a lamp being knocked over. Atuk entered just in time to find Nancy Gore, the professor's nicely plump wife, doing up the top two buttons of her blouse. Her face was flushed.

"Sorry to intrude. I seek the professor."

A tall, muscular Negro began hastily to dust a table.

"Ah, that will be all, Joseph."

"Thank you, m'am," the Negro said; and he fled.

"The professor will be home, ah, shortly . . . if you care to wait. Em, excuse me."

When Gore turned up an hour later Atuk came right to the point.

"I wish to stay in Toronto," Atuk said.

"You've had a quick *succès d'éstime*," Gore said, "so you think it's easy. Actually, the writer's path in this country is a thorny one."

"Maybe I will be lucky."

But Gore was troubled. Though he adored the chunky little primitive, he was not blind to the sly side of his nature. A certain un-Presbyterian shiftiness. It would be enlightening, he thought, to see what might come of a savage innocent in Toronto. No — too cruel.

"Go back to the Bay, Atuk. You will only be corrupted here."

"No. I stay. Maybe I'll be lucky."

So Gore, although still apprehensive, sent Atuk to see Harry Snipes.

Harry Snipes was a protégé of Buck Twentyman's. Always interested in *kitsch*, he had recently accepted the editorship of *Metro, the magazine for cool canucks*, and in fact wrote most of that immensely popular journal under such pseudonyms as Hilda Styles (Why Women from Halifax to Vancouver Menstruate Monthly), Hank Steele, Jr. (I Married An Intellectual Cockroach in Calgary), Sir Horace Simcoe-Taylor, Our Correspondent to the Royal Court (Tony — Lucky Chump or Plucky Champ), and so forth.

Atuk was shown into Snipe's office.

"Well, well, lemme see," Snipes consulted a typewritten sheet on his desk. "Uh-huh ... mm ... Gore says you're quite a poet."

Atuk lowered his eyes modestly.

"Well, I've read your stuff, old chap. It's Georgian. Cornpoke." Snipes reached quickly into his desk, brought out a copy of his own most recent book of poems, *Ejaculations, Epiphanies, et etc*, signed it, and handed it to Atuk. "You want to get with it. You want to make your poetry more gutsy."

Atuk promised he would try.

"That'll be three seventy-five, please."

Atuk paid up immediately.

"Good. Now lemme see ... Are you familiar with the *Metro* image?"

"Yes."

"We're fighting for our life here. We stand for a Canadian national identity and the American mags are trying to drive us out of business. Like fiction?"

"Yes."

"Good. Now lemme see." Snipes lifted a copy of the Aug. 4, 1940 issue of *Collier's* off a stack of old magazines and neatly razored out a short story. "Here's a good one. I want you to re-set it in Moose Jaw 1850. We haven't any Western yarns for the May issue. But please remember to change more than the names. Play around with the physical descriptions and details. Use your imagination, Atuk. That's what we're paying you for." ...

Bette Dolan was Canada's Darling.

She was not the biggest TV star in the country, our only beauty queen or foremost swimmer; neither was she the first Canadian girl to make a film. But Bette Dolan, while in the same tradition as such diverse Canadian talents as, say, Deanna Durbin, Marilyn Bell, Barbara Ann Scott, and Joyce Davidson, surpassed all of them in appeal. Bette Dolan was a legendary figure. A Canadian heroine.

Bette's beginnings were humble. She came from a small town in southern Ontario, the neighbourly sort of place where retired people live. Her fierce father, Gord Dolan, was a bodybuilding enthusiast, a devotee of the teachings of Doc Burt Parks. Once Mr. Best Developed Biceps of Eastern Canada he still retained the title of Mr. Niagara Fruit Belt Sr. His wife, May, was a long thin woman with a severe mouth. Formerly a school teacher, she was still active in the church choir. The Dolans would have ended their days predictably; he, enjoying an afternoon of manly gossip in the barber's and his sessions in the gym; and she, planning the next meeting of the Supper-of-the-Month Club, if only their surprisingly lovely daughter had not lifted them out of decent obscurity with one superhuman stroke.

Bette Dolan was the first woman to swim Lake Ontario in less than twenty hours.

As if that weren't sufficiently remarkable, she was only eighteen at the time, an amateur, and she beat three others, all professionals, while she was at it: an American, an Egyptian, and a celebrated Australian marathon swimmer. The American and the Egyptian woman gave up early on and even the much heralded Australian was pulled out of the lake and rushed to the hospital after only fourteen hours in the black icy water. But the incredibly young, luscious, then unknown Canadian girl, coached by her own father, swam on and on and on. True, she had sobbed, puked, and pleaded to be pulled out of the water, but, the very first time that happened, Gord Dolan, ever-watchful in the launch ahead, spurred his daughter on by holding up a blackboard on which he had written,

DADDY DON'T LIKE QUITTERS

The young girl's effort in the face of seemingly invincible odds caught the imagination of Toronto as nothing had before. It's true the much-admired Marilyn Bell had already swum the lake, but it had taken *her* twenty hours and fifty-one minutes, and it was much as if her accomplishment, remarkable as it was, redoubled interest in Bette Dolan's attempt to better it. Anyway, the fact is that by six o'clock in the morning a crowd, maybe the largest, certainly the most enthusiastic, ever known in the history of Toronto, had gathered on the opposite shore to wait for Bette. They lit bonfires and sang hymns and cheered each half mile gained by the girl. Television technicians set up searchlights and cameras. Motor-cycle policemen and finally an ambulance arrived.

Back in Toronto, as morning came and radio and television newscasters spoke feverishly of twelve-foot waves, some people prayed, others hastily organized office pools or phoned their bookies, and still more leaped into their cars and added to the largest known traffic jam in Toronto's history. Sunny Jim Woodcock, The People's Prayer For Mayor, spoke on Station CKTO. "I told you when I was elected that I would put Toronto on the map. Bette Dolan is setting an example here for youth all over the free world. *More power to your elbows, kid!*" The *Standard*, never a newspaper to be caught off the mark, printed two sets of their late morning edition. One with a headline, SHE MAKES IT, WOW!, the other, TOUGH LUCK, SWEETHEART!

On the launch, Gord Dolan watched anxiously, he prayed, kissed his rabbit's foot, and spat twice over his left shoulder, as his daughter struggled against the oncoming waves.

"Please pull me in," she called. "Please ... I can't make it ..."

He scrawled something hurriedly on the blackboard and held it up for Bette to see again.

THE OTHER BROADS HAVE QUIT. PARK AVE. SWIMWEAR OFFERS $2,500, IF YOU FINISH. DON'T DROWN NOW. DADDY.

But Bette had already been in the lake for sixteen hours. The plucky girl had come thirty-four miles. Thrashing about groggily, her eyes glazed, she began to weep. "... can't feel my legs any more ... can't ... think ... going to drown ..."

"All right," Dolan said, gesturing his girl towards the launch, "we'll pull you in now, kid."

But as Bette, making an enormous effort, swam to within inches of the launch Gord Dolan pulled ahead a few more yards.

"Come on, honey. Come to Daddy."

Again she started for the launch and again Gord Dolan pulled away. "You see," he shouted to her. "You can do it."

(When Gord Dolan spoke on television several weeks later, after accepting the Canadian-Father-of-the-Year Award, he said, "That was the psychology bit. I've made a study of people, you know.")

Initially, the prize money being offered was five thousand dollars, but once the last of the foreign competitors pulled out, as soon as it became obvious that Toronto had taken the surviving Canadian youngster to its heart and, what's more, that she was on the brink of collapse, Buck Twentyman made a phone call. Minutes later a helicopter idled over Gord Dolan's battered launch, a uniformed man descended a rope ladder, and Dolan was able to chalk up on his board,

TWENTYMAN HISSELF OFFERS TEN MORE GRAND. — IF YOU MAKE IT. DADDY IS MIGHTY PROUD. GO, BABY.

When Bette Dolan finally stumbled ashore at seven p.m., after nineteen hours and forty-two minutes in the lake, she was greeted by a frenzied crowd. Newsreel cameramen, reporters, advertising agents, some who had prayed and others who had won bets at long odds, swarmed around her. Souvenir-crazed teen-agers pulled eels off Bette's thighs and back. The youngster collapsed and was carried off to a waiting ambulance. When she woke the next afternoon it was to discover that her life had been irredeemably altered. Bette Dolan was a national heroine.

As was to be expected, she was immediately inundated with offers to endorse bathing suits, health foods, beauty lotions, chocolate bars, and so forth, but Bette turned down everything. "I did not swim the lake for personal gain," she told reporters. "I wanted to show the world what a Canadian girl could do."

SHE SWAM THE LAKE — BECAUSE IT WAS THERE, was the title of Jean-Paul McEwen's prize-winning column. Seymour Bone's approach, in his column on the next page, was considerably more intellectual. Quoting Frazer, Jung, Hemingway, and himself from a previous column, he elaborated on man's historical-psychological need to best nature. While he was able to accept Bette as a symbol, Bone reserved judgement on the girl and her motives. He needn't have bothered. The rest is part of the Dolan legend. Surely everybody now knows how she turned the bulk of her prize money over to her town council to build a fantastically well-equipped gym as a challenge to the crippled children; how the Red Feather, the United Appeal, the White Cane, and innumerable other worthy organizations all profited from Bette's television, film, and public appearances. Bette Dolan was incorruptible.

Harry Snipes wrote in *Metro*, The Girl With All The Curves Has No Angles.

She has a heart, Jean-Paul McEwen observed in his column, bigger than Alberta.

Bette was also lovely, unspoilt, radiant, and the most sought-after public personage in the dominion. In earlier times she would have come forth to bless churches, but in Canada, things being what they were, she pulled the switch on new power projects and opened shopping centres here, there, and everywhere.

Wherever Bette went she was instantly recognized. Ordinary people felt better just for having seen her. But if Canada loved Bette Dolan it was also true that she so loved her country that she felt it would be unfair, sort of favouritism, for her to give herself to any one man. So although many, including cabinet ministers, actors, millionaires, and playboys, had tried, Bette remained, in her mother's words, a clean girl. Until, that is, she met Atuk.

Bette first met Atuk at the party for him at the Park Plaza Hotel and saw him again at another party a couple of months later. Atuk was enthralled and promptly asked if he could meet Bette again. To his amazement, she said yes. Actually, Bette was more grateful than he knew because, by this time, nobody bothered to ask her for a date any more. Bette made dinner for Atuk at her apartment. Carrot juice, followed by herb soup and raw horse steak with boiled wild rice. Atuk, thoughtful as ever, had scraped together some money and brought along a bottle of gin. Bette, lithe and relaxed in her leotards, told Atuk about her father and how his life had been changed by the teachings of Doc Burt Parks. She sensed Atuk felt depressed, maybe even defeated by Toronto, and tried her best to encourage him. "You'll be a success here yet," she said.

"I don't know. It is so difficult."

"But success doesn't depend on the *size* of your brain," she assured him.

Atuk hastily added some gin to the carrot juice.

"Dr. Parks has always said," Bette continued, too absorbed to protest, "that if you want to succeed you must always shoot for the bull's-eye."

Atuk promised to try.

"You're as good as the next fellow. You simply must believe that, Atuk. You see, the most successful men have the same eyes, brain, arms, and legs as you have."

"I drink now. You too."

"I'll bet," she said, narrowing her eyes, "that you envy some people."

"Many, many people."

"*But still more people envy you.*"

"Do they?"

"Sure. Some are bald — you have a head full of hair. Some are blind — you can see. *Everybody envies somebody else.* You must learn to have faith in yourself."

Soon they were sipping gin and carrot juice together nightly and Bette continued to do her utmost to fill Atuk with confidence.

"Why go to so much trouble?" he once asked her.

"Because I have to help people. That's me." Her long, powerful, Lloyd's-insured legs curled under her on the sofa, a lock of blonde hair falling over her forehead, Bette smiled and said, "Do you realize you're just about the only male who has never — never tried the funny stuff with me?"

"Don't you admire me for it?" he asked hopefully.

"Yes. Certainly I do." She got down on the floor and began a lightning series of chin-ups. A sure sign she was troubled. "But don't you love me?" She rolled over on her back, supporting her buttocks with her hands and revolving her legs swiftly. "Everyone loves Bette Dolan," she insisted. . . .

As Atuk stepped on to the platform everybody began to chatter. Most of them, it's safe to say, were familiar with Atuk's best-loved poem, the one that had appeared in his book, the national advertisements, and that he had read in the same cellar shortly after he had first come to Toronto.

> *I go hunt bear in white dawn,*
> *good spirit come with me.*
> *I go fish in silver twilight,*
> *good spirit come with me.*
> *Over the white crust soon comes*
> *forever night*
> *good spirit,*
> *O, spirit,*
> *stay with me.*

Press photographers bore down on the small squat hunter.

"This night will go down in literary history. Like the time Leacock . . ."

Panofsky squinted, trying to roll a cigarette in the dim light. "You think I ought to go up to say hello to Bone?"

"Endsville," Goldie said. "I don't want you to invite him. I —"

"Quiet, Everybody!"

His gesture modest but firm, Atuk indicated that there would be no more pictures.

Atuk.

Gore warned the party at his table not to expect too much from the reading. Continued exposure to Toronto had not done the Eskimo any good. The poet had, he said, fallen in with Harry Snipes, the most notorious of Canada's middle-aged angries, and, as a result, his latest work, though not without an impact of its own, had lost a certain Arctic simplicity.

Atuk retreated a little from under the spotlight, smiled shyly, coughed, and began to read.

> *Twentyman Fur Company,*
> *I have seen the best seal hunters of my generation*
> *putrefy raving die from tuberculosis,*
> *Massey, you square,*
> *eskimos don't rub noses any more and the cats*
> *around Baffin Bay dig split-level houses.*
> *Listen to me, Pearson,*
> *a house is not a home,*
> *an igloo is not a pad.*
> *And you, Diefenbaker, can kiss my ass*
> *where holy most holy pea-soup hockey players have*
> *rumbled.*
> *Canada, wake up, you're all immigrants to me:*
> *my people are living like niggers.*

"You disgusting son-of-a-bitch," Rory said, "from now on you clear every poem with me."

"But listen, listen to them, will you."

The applause was deafening.

"That's not the point," Rory said. "You took Twentyman's name in vain."

Still protesting, Rory was thrust back as admirers gathered round to congratulate Atuk.

"Is much good you all like," Atuk said. "My heart fills."

Crime and Punishment

Richard J. Needham

Once upon a time, there was a country whose federal authorities confined their activity to the deportation of industrious Greeks. In this country, there was a province whose politicians hid under the bed at the mention of wine, women, or weed. In this province, there was a city where instead of burying the dead, people elected them to high municipal office. And in this city there was a high school named Jugglemarks C.I., where you might have found a student named Roman Raskolnikov.

Raskolnikov was an agreeable young man who did well in such subjects as elementary mumbling, intermediate profanity and advanced cheating, thus preparing himself for a successful career in the business world or the political world or the academic world or indeed any other world. One day, however, he committed a terrible act in the history classroom. When the teacher, Mr. Force-pump Feedback, read out loud from the textbook that Jacques Cartier reached Canada in 1934, Raskolnikov shot up his hand. "Sir, shouldn't that be 1534?" The teacher turned purple with rage, the students green with alarm and embarrassment.

Mr. Feedback cried, "Do you mean to tell me, young man, that you have the insolence to question the holy sacred truth as contained in the holy sacred textbook?"— at which all the students reverently bowed their heads in worship; all save Raskolnikov, who stood his ground. "Perhaps, sir, it is a misprint." Mr. Feedback was furious. "Raskolnikov, you will report immediately to the office of the vice-principal, Mr. Oliver Cramwell, and tell him of your unspeakable conduct. May Almighty God have mercy upon your soul."

After Raskolnikov had confessed his vile deed, Mr. Cramwell played with the model guillotine which he used to sharpen pencils. Then he said, "We at Jugglemarks C.I. have always prided ourselves on turning out a product — male or female, as the case may be — that will be acceptable to the personnel managers of Pow Chemical or the Glum Life or the Natural Bust. What will happen if word gets about that we have students so irresponsible"— at which he frowned and Raskolnikov shuddered —"as to question the Holy Word promulgated by the Department of Education? There is a hard bench outside my office on which you will sit every day from 7 a.m. to 9 a.m. and from 3:30 p.m. to 5 p.m., thus bringing upon yourself the sneers, jeers and general contumely of decent, responsible students who are working toward Ontario dullardships."

Reacting with anger at what he deemed a cruel punishment, Raskolnikov wandered along to the boys' washroom, where — finding himself alone — he pulled out a black crayon and wrote with it on the wall, "The vice-principal is a fink." Having done so, he returned to his classroom. The next day, Jugglemarks C.I. was in a dreadful uproar. The school authorities had offered a generous reward for anybody identifying the miscreant — a hand-woven copy of *The Modern Age*. The halls teemed with policemen in and out of uniform. Questions were asked in Parliament, and the bureaucrats in the Departure of Education were so upset they had only four martinis for lunch.

Raskolnikov wondered if he should confess, but decided against it, and went through his twice-daily detention. One evening, as he walked down Yonge Street, he saw an attractive young lady smiling at male passersby and trying to engage them in conversation. "Who are you?" he asked, "and how have you fallen to this life of shame?"

She replied, "My name is Sonia Samovar, and I used to attend Madame Tussaud C.I. here in Toronto. But on my eighteenth birthday, I decided to take the afternoon off and purchase a recording of Sgt. Pepper's Homely Tarts Club Band or maybe Ludy Beethoven and the Moonlighters. I told the school it was for a dental appointment, they phoned my home to check up on me and, well, you know the rest of the story. I can never go back."

The young man nodded. "But do you have to do this?" Sonia answered, "It is not so bad as it looks. Most men who pick up girls on the street are really looking for someone to whom they can tell their troubles — that their wives don't understand them or, what is worse, do. When a man responds to my alluring glances, I steer him down to the Honey Dew, get coffee for us both, and settle in to listen, cluck sympathetically, and occasionally pat his hand. For the first half-hour, I charge $5, for the second $10, and so on up the scale, with a 10-per-cent surcharge for those who insist on showing me colour pictures of their children taken on the Antique Carrousel at Expo 67."

Raskolnikov decided to reveal his own terrible secret to her, and her eyes widened as his grisly tale unfolded. She told him, "You must turn yourself in to the police and tell them it was you who did it. Perhaps, if you confess, you'll be let off with a merciful sentence such as having to read the collected speeches of Tommy Stanfield, Pierre Douglas and Robert Trudeau. Perhaps they will let you pay off your debt to society by drinking Carleton University coffee, or by being deported to Fredericton, where you will work at hard labour in the Lord Beaverbrook Memorial Car Wash, Shoeshine Parlour and Quick Lunch."

Raskolnikov shook his head, saying, "They will have to come and get me," at which Sonia seized his hand and led him to the office of an immense newspaper called the *Mop and Pail*. "Somewhere in this impenetrable bungle," she told Raskolnikov, "is a gentleman of advanced years named Rasputin J. Novgorod, who dishes out worthless advice to all and Sundridge. Perhaps he can persuade you to confess your heinous deed."

As they entered the old man's office, he was snarling and cackling at his secretary, Luscious Lindy, who paid no attention but continued to paint flowers on her earlobes. "Atheism is the opiate of the people. One man's Mede is another man's Persian. Can a wet nurse find happiness with a dry cleaner? Vice is its own reward. That microskirt makes you look like a refugee from Canada Packers. What's this ugly talk of Quebec breaking away from France? Santa is an acidhead. Gad, sir, now that family allowances have been introduced, you'll see an end to poverty in our fair land of Canada."

As Sonia hovered anxiously at the door, Raskolnikov made his entrance and blurted out, "I have committed a terrible crime." Novgorod chuckled, "Don't tell me, let me guess. You look to me like a high-school student. Perhaps you made a pass at one of the women teachers. Don't worry over it, my boy, she will cherish the golden moment in her memory for as long as she lives. Perhaps you were caught·reading poetry when you should have been studying algebraic equations; that's how I spent most of my own time in school. Perhaps you knocked off two little old ladies with an axe; well, that's one approach to the world population problem."

"It was worse than that," said Raskolnikov, and told him the story. The old man blenched, and lit a fresh cigarette from one of the five smouldering on the edge of the desk. "There's no hope or help for it, young man, you will simply have to turn yourself in and ask for clemency. Perhaps they will let you off with four years of Flop and Swill at the University of Toronto or that popular new course, Creative Rioting."

Raskolnikov walked to the nearest police station, where he told the desk sergeant, "It was I who wrote that sign on the wall at Jugglemarks C.I." The sergeant made him repeat it, then cried out an order. Policemen came rushing from all sides, and in no time at all Raskolnikov was on his way to the cells. "Keep up your courage," cried Sonia. "I will bring you food parcels containing such delicacies as Arctic charwoman, peasant-under-glass, Danish wastrels, and Bonanza cream pie."

After a brief trial, the court announced its sentence, eight years in Etobicoke, at which Sonia let out a piercing scream and fainted. The judge continued, "You will wear a grey flannel soup at all times, shave twice a day, and keep your chastity belt fastened until the plane comes to a complete flop at the interminable building. You will refrain from walking in the park, parking in the walk, dancing in the dark, singing in the rain, or walking your baby back home on a leash longer than six feet. Once a year, you will be allowed to have a bath at a temperature of 78.1 degrees."

Sonia told him afterwards, "The eight years will go fast, and I will be faithful to you in my own fashion." So they did, and so she was, and now they are happy together in Toronto. With their high-school background, they have built up a prosperous little business faking notes for unscrupulous students, such as, "Dere Mr. Procrustes: The reason Lucrezia didn't kum to skule yisterday is becus she wuz atacked by a grisly bear, thanking you, Mrs. Borgia."

from The Hypodermic Needham

from Neighbourly News

Andy Clarke

Everybody loves Aunt Tib, who is Mrs. Elizabeth Goudey of Port Maitland and has just passed her ninety-fourth birthday. She lives alone and likes it. Recently, when a load of wood was delivered, the pieces were too long for her stove, so she bought a bucksaw. In her next trip to the store, the merchant asked her how she was getting along with the bucksaw. "I don't have any trouble with the saw," she said, "but I have quite a job to get my leg up to hold the wood down."

The Colborne *Enterprise* tells about an old gentleman who was sitting at the side of the road, laughing. A passerby stopped and inquired the reason for his mirth. "I will be ninety-eight years old tomorrow," was the answer, "and I haven't an enemy in the world."

"How come?" asked the stranger.

Well, it's like this: I've outlived all of 'em and I'm not making any new ones."

The Fort Frances *Times* throws a little light on the subject of red flannel underwear. "Red paint for barns, red flannel for winter wear — such things are among the traditions of this continent, now apparently slowly fading out under the impact of modern living. But how did they originate? The red barns have been with us since early settlers found they could protect their property against Canada's weather conditions by use of a paint made from readily available pigments which happened to have a red hue. Red barns are still common, but the paint now used is superior in quality to that employed by the early settlers. The red flannels would appear to have an even longer background, which some people believe extends back to Biblical times. They base their claim on a quotation from Proverbs 31: 21: 'She is not afraid of the snow for her household; for all her household are clothed with scarlet'."

The Burk's Falls *Arrow* no doubt can vouch for this story which has come to us direct from Mrs. Norman McGirr of Sundridge in the Parry Sound district. She writes that she has found a most remarkable clover plant and transplanted it into a can. On it she found: ten four-leaved clovers; four five-leaved; one six-leaved; one seven-leaved and one nine-leaved. "Neighbourly News" has recorded several seven-leaved clovers in the past, but in 181 broadcasts to date we have never before encountered a clover sprig of more than seven leaves. If nine leaves means an extra dose of good luck, I congratulate Mrs. McGirr, and if her good fortune overflows sufficiently, I hope some of it is spilled in this direction.

That parsnip thirty inches long dug from the garden of John Shier of Newmarket, held its top rating only one week, because another resident, Ivo Ramm, walked into the editor's office and heaved a forty-two-inch parsnip across the desk. Nuff sed.

I don't know whether J. Ollier of the Shelburne *Free Press* was aiming this way or not, but he says: "Among the things we should be thankful for is that a man's voice hasn't the same power in proportion to his weight as that of a canary. If it had, his ordinary conversation could be heard 800 miles away." I like that man's writing. His range of observation seems to be limitless. For instance, he asks: "How many squirts make a gallon of milk?" Then, he has dug up an authority who says there are from 340 to 350 squirts in a gallon of milk, for he has counted 'em so many times in milking ten to seventeen cows a day for fifteen years that this mathematically-inclined dairyman figures he's milked 109,500 gallons, or 37,777,500 squirts.

Spffflltt! Splitch! Hut! Kak! Hoot!

Earl McRae

"How can you possibly win?" asks my wife. "You have trouble calling the dog."

"Ducks are different," I tell her. "Maybe they'll like me."

"But you don't know what to *say* to them."

"Quack, quack! What else have you heard a duck say?"

"There *must* be more to it than that."

I head for the library to find out. The Canadian Duck Calling Championship is less than twenty-four hours away and I've never called a duck in my life. I've never hunted a duck, eaten a duck, or touched a duck. The only ducks I've seen are Donald and Daffy and a few floating around in parks. Ducks don't bother me and I don't bother ducks. But the shotgun is different. The shotgun bothers me very much. I think about it all the time. The shotgun is a Winchester 1200 and it's first prize in the contest. I've always wanted a shotgun but I've never wanted to pay for one. Maybe I won't have to.

"We don't have any books on how ducks quack," says the lady at the library, "but maybe you can find something in here under Duck."

She hands me the Basic Everyday Encyclopedia. I look up Duck. It tells how a duck swims, flies, eats, looks and who his relatives are, but it doesn't say how a duck quacks.

I try three record stores but they have nothing either.

I'm getting panicky when I'm zapped by a brainwave.

Phone Daffy and Donald.

"You've gotta spit when you talk," says Mel Blanc from Los Angeles. Mel Blanc is Daffy Duck's private name. Mel Blanc is sixty-five years old and he's been Daffy Duck's voice since 1937. He's also the voices of Porky Pig, Petunia Pig, Tweety, Sylvester

Cat, Yosemite Sam, Leghorn, Foghorn, Speedy Gonzales and Barney Rubble, to name several. "Like this — *spffflltt! Spluttooey!* Get your tongue out over your lips and blow. Keep the lips tight and make sure your mouth is moist so you get a good splatter. *Spffflltttt!* Try it."

"*Spiltch....*"

"Not bad, not bad. Get that tongue out there. Then do a little hu-*hoo*, hu-*hoo*, hu-*hoo* at the end. Daffy is really Sylvester speeded up. You know, a doctor once x-rayed my throat and he said I have the same muscular construction as Caruso had. *Spluttooey! Spliffittle!*"

"*Spiltch....*"

"Keep at it."

Clarence Nash talks from his home in Glendale, Calif. He's sixty-eight years old and he's really Donald Duck. He's been Donald Duck since 1935. He's also Jiminy Cricket and Mickey Mouse.

"*Kwack! Kwack!* Get your tongue on the left side of your mouth and then kinda give it a little twist while squirting some air up to the roof — *kwack!* — like that. Poke, twist and squirt. That's what it is. Let's hear it."

"*Kwenk!* (Cough, cough.)"

"Is your tongue up there? Squirt. *Kwack, kwack, kwack!*"

"*Kwok, kwoink!* (Hack, cough!)"

"Keep on working on it. You've definitely got something there. Try a little brandy every now and then to lubricate the cords."

Clarence Nash leaves me with these words of inspiration.

"Me and some friends were up at Gould Swamp on Lake Almanor in northern California duck hunting a few years back and I said how funny it was that I could always call ducks using Donald's voice in the summer when it wasn't duck-hunting season but I could never call them in the fall when it *was* the season. Just as I said that — we were sitting in a boat — these ducks flew overhead. I stood up in the boat and started Donald's quack — *kwack, kwack, KWACK, KWACK, KWACK, kwack, kwack!* — and do you know those darned ducks turned around and came back? Yes sir! I was so excited I forgot to use my shotgun. My friends shot 'em instead. So keep working on it and you just might surprise everybody."

I spent the rest of the night in the basement doing Donald and Daffy into my tape recorder. By dawn, I'm not bad on Donald but very bad on Daffy. After a light breakfast of Donald Duck orange juice, and a few practice quacks on my wife, I leave for the southern Ontario city of Orillia. I'm wearing my special Donald Duck T-shirt and on the seat beside me is my tape recorder with Donald and Daffy quacks blaring away. I roll up the windows. It's cool and overcast in Orillia but the streets are packed and banners span the streets announcing the championship. I phone Earl Newhall, a member of the Central Ontario Retriever Club which is sponsoring the event, to find out entry details. He says the preliminaries are at 2 p.m., the finals at 7 and the entry fee is $5.

"What kind of call are you using?" asks Newhall.

"Oh, a bit of Daffy and a bit of Donald. How about you?"

"I'm using an Olt 66."

"I've never seen him. Is he Disney Studios or Warner Brothers?"

"What are you talking about?"

"Pardon?"

"Where do you buy a Daffy and a Donald? I've never seen them in the stores."

"Stores? What stores?"

Newhall drops a bombshell. He says the Olt 66 is a wooden device known as a duck call, that it costs about $6 and if I haven't got one of these duck calls, I haven't got a chance of winning. There are eleven contestants in the event and they'll all be using their favourite duck calls. Calling a duck without a duck call, says Newhall, is like shooting a puck with a broomstick. It can be done but not very well. Nobody told me. And the national quacking title is only an hour and a half away. Panic.

"Try the sporting-goods stores for a duck call," suggests Newhall. "I recommend an Olt 66. Don't get anything under $6 because they're no good. Lousy reeds. If you get one, call me back. I'll give you a crash course in how to use it. I shouldn't help the competition like this but, in your case, I will."

"Are you any good?" I ask.

"I'm okay. I used to play trumpet in a high school band and the mouthpiece is the same as that on the Olt 66. Quacking technique is the same too. I also have an album called Hunters' Duck Calls and I've tape recorded ducks in the swamps so I'd say I'm fair. But you've gotta forget Daffy and Donald. The judges will shoot you down for sure."

"Will the judges be ducks?"

Newhall laughs until he realizes I'm serious.

"No, they'll be three humans. Experts in duck quacks."

"Will we be calling in real, live ducks?"

Newhall sighs. "There are *no* ducks on the grounds of the Orillia Community Centre. Listen, are you *sure* you really want to enter this thing?"

"This is the only one I got," says the guy behind the counter in Barnett's Surplus Store. He blows the dust off a little red box with "Stag Lubricant Company Limited, Rockwood, Ont." printed on the side. He opens it and pulls out a brown wooden thing with "Chieftain No. 7 Duck Call" printed on it. He says it is $2.95. I remember Newhall's warning about the cost of calls but I'm desperate. I've tried three sporting-goods shops and none had duck calls. They had crow calls, goose calls, turkey calls and squirrel calls but no duck calls. Not the season.

I jump in my car and drive down to the shores of Lake Couchiching. I only have an hour until the championship. Since it's not duck-hunting season, I wrap a hanky around my Chieftain No. 7 and stand on the shore pretending I'm blowing my nose. Just maybe some ducks are hanging around out there. *SKWARRRNK! SKANNNK!* A crow takes off out of a tree. I consult the instruction pamphlet.

Place the burnished mouthpiece against your upper lip covering most of the hole. The lower lip is hooked over the swell of the mouthpiece. Then breathe or grunt gently, never blow like a horn. When you do this correctly, your Adam's apple will move up and down. It is absolutely necessary that you learn to control the call, practise on scales, simple tunes, etc.

I try again, one hand on my Adam's apple. *SKOINNNK!* My Adam's apple doesn't move. *SKWANNNK!* A slight tremble. *SKWARNNNK!* Nothing. I just don't sound like a duck. I sound like·a guy standing all alone on the shore of Lake Couchiching blowing the daylights out of a nose that's been blocked for ten years. I consult the instructions again.

You cannot hope to call ducks unless you memorize their various calls. In other words, owning a horn does not make one eligible to play in the band.

The pamphlet doesn't say what their various calls are. I put my Chieftain No. 7 back in its box, go to a pay phone and call Earl Newhall.

"There's only forty-five minutes to go," he says. "Forget the Chieftain. You need an Olt 66."

"But I couldn't *find* one!"

"Elwood Epps out on the highway has them."

"I don't know the various calls."

"The judges will be asking each contestant for three calls: the highball, the greeting call and the feeding chuckle. Then a combined call. Each one is different but I can give you the idea."

Twenty minutes later I have my Olt 66. Burnished walnut with a vinylite reed and a lovely cord to hang it around my neck. I'm in the basement of Al Taylor's home. Taylor is president of the Central Ontario Retriever Club. There are guys quacking all around me. It's very noisy. Only twenty-five minutes to quacking time.

"Okay," shouts Earl Newhall over the cacophony. "First call will be the highball. That's what you use when the ducks are beyond 500 yards. The highball is three fairly loud quacks and then about seven softer quacks, falling off about three or four notes to zero. You blow from the stomach, not the throat. *KWACK! KWACK! KWACK! Kwack, kwack, kwack, kwack, kwack.*

"What you are saying into the mouthpiece is 'hoot, hoot, hoot' to get that quacking sound. Some guys prefer 'hut, hut, hut' or 'kak, kak, kak'. Me? I've had great success with 'hoot, hoot, hoot'." He lays another highball on me. I try it. He says it's good. I smile and polish off my Olt 66 on my Donald Duck T-shirt.

"Now the greeting call. This is when the ducks are at about 200 yards. You want to call them down. The greeting call is like the highball only more excitable and a little louder." He shows how. I try it. He says it's good but force those "hoots" up from the stomach, not the throat. Maybe a "kak" would have been better.

"The last one is the feeding chuckle," shouts Newhall. "The ducks are coming down now and you're saying 'hey, fellas, there's food here, come and get it.' You cup your fingers over the end like this and then you waggle them over the opening while saying 'ducka, ducka, ducka' over and over again. Some guys say 'ticka, ticka, ticka' and 'docka, docka, docka' but, again, I prefer 'ducka, ducka, ducka.' By waggling your fingers over the end, you change the tone of the chuckle."

"Newhall has a real good chuckle," says Brian Hewlett.

"Thanks," smiles Newhall. "I just wish I could highball like Munro Blackwell and Gary Cook."

"Some of them Indians can highball by slapping their feet up and down in the mud," says Hewlett.

"Take the Crees," says Taylor. "You can't beat them at calls."

"Just use their hands and nothing else," says Newhall.

With fifteen minutes to go we leave in a convoy of cars for the Community Centre. I drive with one hand and quack with the other. My highball sounds good but I change my feeding chuckle from "ducka, ducka, ducka" to "ticka, ticka, ticka" for smoother performance.

The faded wooden grandstand is packed with men, women, children, cats and dogs. Music blares from loudspeakers and an ambulance is parked off to one side of the field. There's a smattering of applause as we pile out of the cars and huddle along the fence waiting for the contest to start. It's cold and drizzling now. Everybody who's anybody in Canadian quacking is here, including Ray Baldakin, the Canadian champion for three consecutive years. He's leaning against one end of the fence, a little bearded guy of forty-one, and he has *four* different duck calls hanging around his neck. He has them under his windbreaker so nobody can see them. Gary Cook is here too. He's thirty-one, a maintenance man for an Orillia bakery, and a heavy favourite. He keeps popping peppermints into his mouth and gulping from a big orange-juice jar filled with cold water. Cook is using a Stubble King, a new duck call made by Munro Blackwell, a manufacturer from Simcoe, Ont. The Stubble King, many say, is the duck call of tomorrow, will revolutionize the game. It sounds more like a duck than a duck, say its admirers. Six of the eleven contestants will be quacking on a Stubble King. Many of the fans have come only to hear the new sensation.

"Ray," says a fan to Baldakin, "can I have your autograph for my son?"

"Sure," says Baldakin, scribbling his name on a piece of rain-soaked paper. The man tears back to the grandstand.

"What you using?" Baldakin asks Newhall, standing beside him.

"Olt 66."

"Olt eh? Not bad. Good really."

"I like the mouthpiece but sometimes I find it hard to get my lips in place."

"Should shave it down," says Baldakin, as heads lean in for a tip from the master.

"What you using, Ray?" ventures Newhall.

Baldakin shifts his weight, as all eyes stare at the bulge beneath his windbreaker. "I got a Faulk's WA33, a Mallard Tone M-245 and a couple of others."

"Gentlemen," a voice booms over the loudspeakers, "will you please line up at the caravan to draw your starting numbers from a bag."

A murmur goes through the grandstand as we line up. I draw No. 7. To keep their edge, the contestants amble aimlessly around the field quacking away like a bunch of flute players in search of a band. I'm too embarrassed to quack. These guys are *good!* The start is delayed for some reason and the tension increases. Realizing I need even more help, I summon my courage and approach the champ. I ask him if he says "hoot, hoot" or "kak, kak."

"Neither. I just use air. When you're *learning* you say those things but not when you're experienced. Look, I've slept in the marshes with ducks, made recordings of their quacks and nobody can tell me what a duck sounds like."

A twenty-minute delay is announced. Groans from the grandstand and curses from the quackers. The rain beats down harder. I run for the nearest pay phone and place a call to Pekin, Illinois, home of the Philip S. Olt Co., makers of the Olt 66, oldest (1904) and largest bird-call firm in North America. Arthur Olt, the president himself, comes on the line.

"There's not much I can say to help you at this late hour," he says. "We make some thirty different models and the 66 is certainly one of our best. Of course, you know about blowing from the stomach I assume. Good."

"Do you say 'hoot, hoot' or 'kak, kak' or what?" I ask.

"No, I say 'quack, quack' and on the chuckle I say 'ticketa, ticketa'. It really works for me. It's too bad Al Sonderman isn't in. He's our duck-calling expert, been with us forty years. If it makes a sound, Al can do it."

I gallop back to the Community Centre. The contest still hasn't started. Someone says they can't find one of the judges. The starting time has been put off to three o'clock.

"Ray, who's the *world* duck-calling champion?"

"Guy named Butch Richenback of Stuttgart, Arkansas,"

says Baldakin. "Won it last December."

I race back to the pay phone, place a call to Stuttgart, Arkansas.

"Do you say 'hoot, hoot' or 'kak, kak' or what?" I ask Richenback.

"I say 'hut, hut, hut' and on the chuckle I say 'tooka, tooka, tooka'. Took me sixteen years to perfect them and I'm only twenty-six now. I was junior champ of the U.S. in '57 and I came second five times in the Arkansas State championship. In '71, I took the Mississippi Delta Regional title. All I can tell you is to keep cool, don't panic and don't go too fast on the chuckle. You'll trip up your tongue. Too bad you can't use a Chick Majors Dixie Mallard. That's what won me the world championship. Named after Chick himself. He's retired now but he still tunes my call for me. Best tune-up man in the business. Anyway, I hope you win!"

What's good enough for Butch Richenback is good enough for me. It will be "hut, hut, hut" and "tooka, tooka, tooka".

"Don't feel bad," says judge Murray Martin, outdoors editor of the Orillia daily paper. "You gave it a brave try."

"You just didn't *sound* much like a duck," says judge Don Simpkin, a wildlife biologist for the Ontario Ministry of Natural Resources.

"You've got to *think* duck to *do* a duck," says judge Jim Cridland, duck hunter, duck caller and duck-decoy carver.

On the highball, greeting call and feeding chuckle — each for a total of five points — I scored two, one, one (highball), one, one and one (greeting call) and one, two, one (chuckle).

On the combined, out of ten points, I chalked up one, three and zero.

I came tenth out of the eleven contestants.

An Orillia denturist named Doug Robertson saved me from total disgrace. He just used his hands and vocal cords and sounded like Donald Duck with a smoker's rasp.

Even Ray Baldakin was toppled, eliminated in the afternoon preliminaries with me. There was some consolation in that.

The new champion is Ron Lockhart, a thirty-eight-old art director with a Toronto advertising agency.

He says "kak, kak, kak" and "tooka, tooka, tooka," thinks like a duck and has a very mobile Adam's apple.

from The Canadian Magazine

from There Goes MacGill

Ronald Hambleton

In the air-conditioned coach of the transcontinental train out of Sudbury, MacGill had chosen the double seat at the far end of the smoking section; and although he did not object to company in his little four-seat section, he was damn sure he was going to weed out the passengers. He did not expect to sleep much, for he had only just wakened up in mid-afternoon, but just in case, he laid out thirty-five cents for a rented pillow, stocked up on cigarettes, changed his shoes for slippers, and at last felt the expansive leisure of the traveller steal over him. He put his mackinaw — too thick to pack — over one seat, and scattered a couple of magazines beside him, to be removed instantly if a fellow-traveller of congenial appearance should appear.

It was past ten before the train pulled out of Sudbury, beginning the long, slow curve, over thirteen miles long, to Ottawa. From his vantage point, MacGill looked right down the car, the seat tops making their regular pattern diminishing into the distance, the little glowing spotlights, some lit and some not, shining on heads blonde, brunette, and bald. He sat, facing the engine, his feet up on the seat opposite, symbolically riding into the future.

Before the train started, other passengers stiffly made their way between the rows of seats, selecting, regaining places, making themselves comfortable. A family of five, one of whom had to sit with strangers, conducted their debate which of them was to be the exile. A couple of lovers or newlyweds instantly curled up into one another's arms, like mice, and appeared to go to sleep. A tired and stumbling old man with white hair, passed back and forth twice, clutching in his hand the cardboard envelope issued by the steamship line. Some poor sucker lost his old lady, said MacGill without sympathy.

Much to his surprise, he fell into a doze not long after the train pulled out, his pillow unused on the seat opposite, and when he came to again, most of the spotlights were out, and the general guidelights down the middle were at their dimmest. No one had invaded his corner, and this he regretted for a moment while he strove to banish the stiffness from his legs and neck. His mouth always fell open in sleep, and particularly when he slept half-erect as now, the ache was intolerable. The membranes of his throat and palate were dry and sticky, and this angered him, unreasonably, and suddenly he took a dislike to the whole coachful of passengers, who slept on indifferent to his suffering, gliding like a derelict ship. Far down the car, a man got up, still half-asleep, stuffed his shirt back into his pants, turned once or twice around like a dog, and curled up again into the seat. A baby snarled at the soother that had been crammed into its mouth. A woman raised two white arms to the ceiling, made rigid fists, and yawned like a cry. Everyone slept or wooed sleep, except Patrick MacGill. He felt like shouting at them, but he couldn't do that in cold sobriety. He got to his feet, and without so much as a backward look at his belongings, started blundering down the aisles, knocking into elbows and heads at almost every seat. When he noticed that he was heading toward the door marked "Women" he turned round and went back towards the "Men." This was "Engaged," so the little red light said, so he went through the connecting doors into the next coach, a coach full of compartments and sleepers. It was a new world of muffled sound. The hidden sleepers behind their green curtains spoke to one another; the lowers snored softly upwards, and the uppers bowed downwards in return. Then MacGill knew at last that he was en route for an unknown land. Beneath his feet, the wheels pounded the rails that lay upon Canada, but here in the timeless world of sleep, there was scarcely any motion. It was as if he had already arrived somewhere, and he drugged himself with the possibility of standing forever in this green swaying world.

One of the sleepers meaninglessly cried out Makearoise and soonersh — or so it sounded; and MacGill passed on into the lighted part where the porter sat cleaning shoes all night long, and past that and into the next racketing link between coaches and so into the next coach, a deserted de luxe dining room car, and through that and through the next air lock into the club car.

Here was another whole new world, another transformation, one so shockingly different that MacGill stopped to blink at it. The conversation, a mixture of French and English, hit him like a gust of wind, stunning him momentarily. On his right hand was the door to another "Men's," "Vacant," so he popped in and turned the key on himself.

Rather absentmindedly, he lowered his pants and sat down, but rose quickly again when he felt the biting cold of naked porcelain. He had forgotten to lower the plastic seat. He lowered it and took his place again, and while the motion of the train gently and soothingly ground his behind into the oval, he read yet once again the warnings against gambling, the regulations excerpted from the Transportation Act, and the assorted admonitions "To Flush Press Here," but "Please Do Not Flush While Train Is Standing In Station," and "Leave This Toilet As You Would Have Had It Left By Others." He fingered but did not press the alarm bell and the light switch; he took a paper cup and gave his ears the pleasure of hearing the point ponk against the sink, and so he fell into a reverie. Through the slit of unfrosted window beside him, lights flashed by, giving the illusion of tremendous speed, but within him and within the train, the calm of a hurricane's eye.

The handle rattled, turned, and then, frustrated, turned back. A voice asked *Occupé?* and another replied *Oui, mais pour si longtemps.* Then there was a knock at the door, gentle, inquisitive, but MacGill ignored it. A question came through the door, which MacGill answered by a sardonic kick at the flush pedal. The voice outside gave a satisfied, victorious exclamation and spoke no more.

MacGill muttered, "Here I sit broken-hearted paid a nickel and only farted," got up, adjusted his clothing, but before leaving combed his greying hair in the small square mirror, recognizing once again the thin, lean face of the man he knew so well. The rattle at the door came again and a voice said "You come?" MacGill said roughly, "You bet I come, Frenchy," and gave a hitch to his pants. He strode out so quickly that he all but collided with a short, stout, rather anxious man acting as aide-de-camp to another about the same age but who carried the assurance of authority.

Once MacGill was out of the way, the flunkey held the door open for his friend or master, who stepped through. MacGill stared right into the other man's eye and said, "And I bet you'd do it for him too if you could, eh, sonny?"

The other backed away without moving, raised his eyes and arms together in a dramatic shrug and retreated backwards into the club car. Now, MacGill was awake, and interested, and he had not forgotten that the aide-de-camp had said "You come?" so he strolled a step or two into the club car and saw that it was not quite as full, though quite as noisy, as he had thought at first.

There were about half a dozen men and two women; or three, he thought, if you count the marathon sock-knitter who quite precisely raised her head at the end of every row to look intently and severely at everyone in the car, and to sip the lemon-coloured drink beside her. MacGill excluded her from the party, as he did also a self-contained little figure in a corner, whom he now recognized as the rather doddery white-haired old man who had passed through the coach earlier in the night. Seated here, although he was about MacGill's age, he looked not nearly so doddery — in fact, almost possible as a companion. He was casually dressed, but everything about him was clean and well kept, in contrast with MacGill's checked shirt, oil-stained gaberdine pants and heavy pullover. MacGill sat down in the seat beside him and said, "You can't sleep either?"

A head-shake, and then, without raising eyes from the magazine, "I tried to the first night, but I just tossed and turned. So I decided to have my insomnia out here tonight."

MacGill pointed to the book, "Can you read through all this racket?"

Deprecatingly, "This doesn't take any reading." A pause, then he turned his blue eyes to MacGill. "Friends give you things you'd never read any other time but on trains."

MacGill shrugged. "Me, I don't read. But I drink." He waved a hand over to the steward. "What about you?"

"I better say no. I've not been all that fit, and I've learned what to do and what not to do."

"Well, that's quite a lesson, but don't try teaching me, 'cause I don't learn easy."

This produced not the least response, though MacGill waited out a measurable interval. The other man allowed himself to shrink away from the contact, which aroused in MacGill a faint disapproval, a sense of unfamiliarity. He was watching a turtle slide back under its house, and he tried giving the shell one last tap. "My name's MacGill, by the way."

The turtle's eye did not wink, but the voice replied, "And mine's Peavey, Daniel Peavey."

They bent towards one another, moving a formal greeting, and then MacGill gave him up, though not without some regret.

He turned to catch the waiter's eye, but instead only met the anxious eye of the aide-de-camp. He grinned to himself, and almost dug an elbow into Peavey's rib. "Sometimes," he said, "you got to make your fun."

He got up and approached the other man, and said, as if sharing a common anxiety, "Been in there quite a time, eh? What do you think we better do?"

The aide seemed to believe that MacGill was actually interested. MacGill said, nodding towards the toilet, "He the big push?" and when the man looked puzzled, said, "This his party?"

A nod. "We are all friends from Saint Vital to Ottawa." And then, "Labiche."

This threw MacGill, so the man explained by pointing to himself. "Labiche," he explained.

MacGill, enlightened, said, "Oh, you're Labiche," and noted the shaft of pain through the man's eyes at the mispronunciation. He then tapped himself and said, "MacGill," and winced in his turn as Labiche said, "Ah, Mageel!"

That exhausted their small talk, and MacGill was about to seek another conversationalist, when a member of the party glided toward them with a cardboard box containing mixed nuts. It was huge, and even now it was over half full. Although the box was not exactly offered to him, MacGill dipped his hand in, and helped himself so generously that the nut man stared astonished, so MacGill said "Mageel" and the man replied "Tarratine."

MacGill held the nuts with his left hand as if looking for somewhere to put them, and with his right, he made an encircling motion as if around a glass. There was a glass three-quarters full of liquid nearby which he picked up and sipped carefully. It tasted wonderful, so to the astonishment again of both Labiche and Tarratine, he tossed it off as if it were water.

"That tastes like another," he said.

Labiche said, hurt, "You have drunk the drink of the minister."

"Minister?" And just then the long-awaited big push came out of the toilet, and MacGill recognized consciously the face and manner of the public figure so important that he had a man trained to usher him into a toilet. So he said to Labiche, "I get it. It's a political party," and reassured by a nod, went boldly forward to the table where the drinks were set out, and poured himself another one.

The party had been going on since the train left Sudbury. MacGill learned that Labiche was the head salesman of a large chain grocery in Manitoba, and the "minister" was not in fact a cabinet minister, but a local member of the dominion Parliament, though he never did get it clear whether or not the man was a member of the government. Whatever he was, he was important enough to have a private coach, and an entourage to take him back from his constituency in Ottawa.

The group did not exactly welcome MacGill, for by his clothes and the fact that he spoke no French, he was proven to be a stranger and an interloper; but the club car was public ground, and since the drinks were more than enough and all paid for, they tolerantly allowed him to elbow his way in, listen when he could to the conversation, and even at times lapsed into English out of consideration for him. Neither the white-haired old gentleman named Peavey nor the marathon knitter tried to include themselves in the party, although they discreetly accepted nuts when Tarratine offered them.

MacGill never again had to help himself to a drink, for he had established himself as a member of the party, and the waiter naturally held out the tray to him as he did to the others. Once, when MacGill found himself staring at an empty glass, he parodied Labiche's nervous manner and shouted to the waiter, "Don't wait for order; bring it five minutes ago!"

Somewhere in a gap between drinks he told them long stories about himself and his various jobs in mining and logging camps in Ontario and British Columbia, allowed them to believe that half a lifetime of industrious application had allowed him at last to return to the old country, and in particular gave them a most convincing if inaccurate account of his recent adventures in the uranium district north of Lake Superior. At first, they pricked their ears up at this, especially the minister, to whom this bordered on political talk, but his interest petered out when he realized that MacGill really knew nothing that mattered.

MacGill tried for a long time to lure either of the two women into conversation, but they were sitting rather awkwardly behind a thin table that stuck out from the wall, and they were further hemmed in by the bulk of the silent man of the group, a cattle exporter, Guérard by name, who every week shipped several hundred thousand dollars' worth of cattle from Manitoba to South America, principally to Guatemala, by train to New Orleans and from there by air. Silent he was, but when he started to tell his one anecdote of the evening, he spoke quickly and vigorously, as one accustomed to a number of listeners.

Labiche whispered audibly to MacGill that Guérard was a very big breeder, at which MacGill smiled wryly, and added that they were trying to promote a trade in cattle between Canada and Russia.

"Already," said Guérard in his loud confident tone, "we have had two provisional orders. I imagine that our trouble will be over if we can sell to Russia the right kind of bull."

It was clearly an old, familiar witticism, and none of them laughed as loud as MacGill. In fact, he kept up his laughter so long that in a moment he was laughing alone, and that made him trail off; and that, in turn, made the others realize suddenly that the whole of the merriment was being reflected by a man who was not a member of the party at all, and that they were beginning to feel like interlopers. Instinctively, they drew together and began to speak French to one another, excluding MacGill.

This did not affect him much, because he was pretty tight. In fact, on hearing the French, he caught the eye of one of the two women and said "Alouette!" and she had to half-smile at him, for it was after all a French word, but she did not realize that he had been asking permission to sing. He began, in fact:

"Alouette, gentille alouette,
Alouette, je te plumerai.
Je te plu —"

But then he broke off, because Labiche quickly rose to his feet, though MacGill was right beside him, and began to shush him, putting a hand on his shoulder which MacGill tried to brush off as if it were a beetle by a series of very light strokes. Then Labiche was leaning over him like a dentist, and MacGill staring up, mouth open. He said, faintly, "*Je te plumerai le — le —*"

At which Labiche replied, between his teeth, "*Moi, je vous plumerai!*"

Then MacGill opened his mouth to the full, and cried out "Louette, gentille alouette. Old Macdonald had a farm, E I E I O!" and waved his arms asking the others to join in. As he turned, he saw Peavey miles away looking at him, but as soon as their eyes met, Peavey dropped his back to his magazine, and MacGill thought "Patronizing bastard." He could no longer bear Labiche towering over him, so he rose too, and suddenly everyone was on his feet except the two women who were impregnably safe behind the little table. Behind the crowd, the marathon knitter went implacably on, the sock turning in her hands as in a machine, with the streamers of red, yellow and green wool growing out of a small basket on her lap. She seemed to MacGill to be plucking or stroking a blossom rather than knitting, and he launched out towards her what he fancied was a smile but which when it arrived seemed to her to be a grimace in the worst possible taste.

Somehow, the coach was not riding as steadily as it should. MacGill found himself alone in the centre of the coach, and when he turned, there was the man Labiche and the man Tarratine talking to Peavey, waving their arms like semaphores, but Peavey was shrugging himself out of the situation. The waiter stopped by him, with his arms full of little bottles of whisky, and warned him that others were asleep in their roomettes, but MacGill only stared him down, and began slipping the little bottles into his pocket, one after another, until the waiter backed away. Then MacGill did the unpardonable thing. He strode up to Tarratine and wrenched the box of nuts from his hand. Some of them spilled out as he waved them crying, "Don't keep them to yourself, sonny."

He began to pass from one to another, saying, "Take only the nuts you need, only two to a lady, only two to a lady." The implication was unmistakable, unforgivable. With a uniform yelp, all the French Canadians, Labiche, Tarratine, and Guérard, leaving only the minister safely out of it, surrounded him. One removed the nuts from his hand, another reached into his pocket to retrieve the cache of little bottles, but Guérard restrained him by saying, *Nous avons pas à nous abaisser comme cet ivrogne,* and Labiche stood on tiptoe to cry into MacGill's ear, "We gave you our friendship and you must have been taking our drinks from us but we cannot give you our acceptance of these gross insults!"

It was a loud and clear cry. MacGill stood stolidly, like an ox surrounded by ponies. Guérard said firmly, "We welcome you to stay and listen and joke with us, but if one of us is breaking into one of your English parties, would you be patient as we have been with you?"

This puzzled MacGill because he was not conscious either of bursting into a party, or of a noticeable degree of patience being needed or given, on either side. He swept them to one side, without violence, and made straight for Peavey, perhaps with some idea of finding an ally in the other English-speaking man in the room, certainly forgetting for the moment that he had only a few minutes before written off Mr. Peavey as any kind of companion. He planted himself in the direction of the other three men, and said, "What do you think, chum?"

Mr. Peavey looked up, as it were lifting a weight of weariness to look through a window at a storm outside, retreat and noninvolvement written all over his face. "I don't know," he said. "I wasn't looking."

This was almost insulting. "Weren't looking! You mean you had your nose buried in —"

Mr. Peavey shook his head. "I don't mean anything, but it's not my affair. If they think you're abusing their hospitality —"

"That's not what I said. I said what do you think? Just trying to be sociable."

Mr. Peavey shrugged. "It's not my affair," but even as he said it, his mind changed, and he tried to improve matters by saying, "I'd rather not come into it," and saw how unpractised he was at the art of withdrawal.

MacGill stood there a while, trying to force him by will to raise his eyes, but when he could not, all he said was "Agh!" and turned away, but saying to himself I'll see you again, somewhere, sometime.

The three Frenchmen were still guarding the approaches behind which the minister and the two women put up a display of indifference. All around him the train cried in the night, miles sped by, and time sped by, and yet the tableau persisted. The four Frenchmen made themselves into a living communiqué, at which to show his disdain, MacGill shrugged and sat down, put his crossed legs as far as he could into the walkway, and then having made this gesture, curled them up under his seat, and stared at himself mirrored in the flickering window. Slowly, the phalanx dissolved, and beside MacGill, the knitter, as if called upon to make a comment to include them all, made a four-pronged weapon of her sock-needles, and drove them without mercy into the heart of the wool.

Thank You, Uncle Ben, for the Nicest Whatever-It-Is That Ever Ruined a House

Maggie Grant

I usually manage to finish writing my Christmas thank-you notes by Jan. 31 at worst, but this year I've bogged down on Uncle Ben. That's my rich uncle, the one who's going to leave me a nice legacy if I survive him. Which seems doubtful at the moment.

There is also this about Uncle Ben: he's the type who would cut a person out of his will if that person failed to thank him for a Christmas present, or even failed to be adequately enthusiastic about it. My problem this year is that — well, just glance at these unfinished notes and perhaps you'll understand.

December 28

Dear Uncle Ben,

We had a lovely Christmas with all sorts of exciting presents, particularly yours. At first we were puzzled about its use, since no instruction sheet was enclosed, but suddenly light dawned — an electric bean pot, what a marvelous idea! To be able to plug in and bake old-fashioned beans right at the table is such an innovation we've invited a few friends in to participate in your gift's debut. At this very moment the feast is hissing away in the dining room and . . .

January 3

Dear Uncle Ben,

I know you'll be amused to learn that when we opened your lovely present we jumped to the conclusion it was a bean pot.

We realized the error of our ways when some beans we were cooking exploded all over the dining room. The pattern they made on the ceiling looked exactly like Santa Claus and his eight tiny reindeer! Fortunately our insurance covers the cost of repainting the room and repairing the chandelier.

Now our neighbor has told us your present is actually a bed-warmer and we're pleased as punch because both John and I suffer from cold feet these winter nights and as a matter of fact he is now snoring peacefully abed with the warmer toasting his . . .

January 5

Dear Uncle Ben,

Excuse the scribble, but I'm writing this in my lap so I can stay close to John's bed in case he needs anything. He's under sedation after burning both his feet (I won't bother you with the details of how it happened) but will soon be able to get about on crutches. Luckily a personal injury clause in our insurance policy will pay his salary while he's off work.

I must delay no longer in thanking you for the lovely humidifier, it was so generous of you. About an hour ago I set it going in the living room and already . . .

January 20

Dear Uncle Ben,

At last a peaceful moment to write you! We've been higgledy-piggledy lately due to the living room broadloom having to be torn up and taken away to be dyed. It got badly stained in a foolish little mishap we had with steam and boiling water and my Sheraton table had to be refinished. But it's an ill wind, etc., because I love the rug's new color and insurance paid for everything.

Now to business! We are simply delighted with your Christmas present though I'm going to confess that at first we were unsure about its function. Then John's office manager dropped in and told us it's an outdoor barbecue. How silly of us not to realize it at once! To celebrate the new look in the living room we're going to prepare dinner there tonight, with John acting as chef. As I write he is fussing around with steaks and things . . .

January 31

Dear Uncle Ben,

As you can see by this letterhead, we are staying at a hotel.
We had a fire at the house, but don't be alarmed, it wasn't too bad,
mostly smoke damage. A marvellous cleaning crew is at work
busily washing walls, shampooing furniture and so forth. I understand this is a frightfully costly operation so thank goodness we
were covered by insurance. In connection with this, I am expecting
the company's adjuster to call at any moment, but meanwhile am
dashing this off to thank you for . . .

February 1

Dear Uncle Ben,

If a Mr. Smither, an insurance adjuster, should try to get in
touch with you in any way, I do beg you to disregard him — I'm
afraid he's mentally ill. He called in to see me about some claims
we've had recently and suddenly started screaming and shouting
dreadful things about the lovely Christmas present you sent us.
Well, really! No man in his right mind would act that way about
an inanimate object! The only think to do is ignore him. And now,
my darling uncle, I hope you are going to forgive the long delay
in writing to thank you for the . . . for the . . .

from   The Canadian Magazine

There's Intrigue when "Meestair Ross" Is on Assignment

Alexander Ross

The Orient Express hurtled through the black night, the lights from its steaming windows casting weird, transient shadows on the slumbering landscape of central Europe. Inside one of its first-class compartments sat a tall, devilishly handsome young man in a blue pin-stripe suit. A black attaché case was handcuffed to his wrist. His eyes were closed. But even in repose, a sardonic smile flickered on his full, sensuous lips.

Suddenly, the door of the compartment opened, and a stunning blonde woman stepped inside. She was, as the French say, of *une age certaine*. But her eyes were smouldering, and her tawny hair cascaded down over the black cloak she wore, shimmering like burnished gold. With a sinuous whisper of silk, she insinuated herself into the seat beside the sleeping man, who wore a tiny plastic maple leaf in his faultlessly tailored lapel. Her full, ripe lips stole toward his earlobe.

"Meestair Ross," she whispered. "Meestair Ross! You must help me. You are zee only one who can help me!"

The handsome Canadian awoke and was instantly alert, the sardonic smile still playing on his finely chiselled features.

"Excuse me Miss," he said, "but I believe you addressed me as Mr. Ross. You must be mistaken." From an extravagantly slim wallet, he produced a business card. "As you can see from my card," he said, "my name is Hector Smeeth, and I am the eastern Europe representative for General Foods.

"I am on my way to Sofia to see some officials from the Bulgarian Ministry of Nutrition. I'm on the trail of a big order, actually — 50,000 cases of Captain Crunch, the breakfast cereal for Young Pioneers . . ."

The woman peered beneath his shaggy eyebrows, and gazed

deeply into his sensitive gray eyes. "My name is Natasha," she murmured, "and I know your real mission!" She leaned forward as she spoke, and her full, ripe bosom strained against the fabric of her diaphanous blouse. "You must help me," she whispered. "In my handbag I am carrying documents of the utmost urgency, and I am being followed. Unless they are delivered by midnight to the Tanzanian embassy in Sofia, my life is forfeit!

"Only you can help me," she breathed. "You must . . ."

Ross — for that was indeed his name — suspected a trick. As a special operative for MC-5, the super-secret counter-espionage arm of the External Affairs Department, he was no stranger to international intrigue. The world knew him only as a mild-mannered newspaper columnist who was paid a pittance by his employers in Toronto to report the mouthings of colourless municipal politicians. But that was only his "cover." In reality, Ross was an underground legend in the shadowy world of counter-espionage. Frequently, his daily column failed to appear. In its place would be inserted a notice: Ross on Assignment, it would say, or Ross will return Soon.

Unwary readers assumed this meant that Ross was drunk, depressed, or indisposed. Only a trusted few in the chancelleries of various foreign capitals knew it as a signal — the clear assurance that, no matter how desperate the crisis, help was on the way.

Which was why, on this murky night in September, Ross found himself speeding across Central Europe on the Orient Express, neck-deep in danger, in the middle of the most crucial assignment of his brilliant career.

It was Mitchell Sharp himself who had briefed him before his departure. "It's in your h-h-h-h-hands," said the external affairs minister. "D-d-d-don't fail your c-c-c-country."

And now here he was in the darkened train compartment, with the beautiful blonde breathing passionately into his shell-pink ear. Only a saint could have resisted her blandishments, but Ross remained unmoved.

"I know you'd like to hear about Toronto," he said, straightening his foulard tie. "Perhaps you have relatives there . . ."

"Kiss me, my fool," she murmured.

"You see," he responded, "Toronto has a Metropolitan form of government, which makes our subways the cleanest in the world. And the place is changing, you know. We're getting very cosmopolitan. . . ."

"Take me, you savage," she breathed, as her hand stole towards the combination lock on his attaché case.

"... and, by golly, I wish you could meet our mayor. His name's Bill Dennison, and is he ever colourful! We've got the fastest-rising property values in North America, the downtown core is booming, and ..."

Abruptly the woman arose from her seat, breathing heavily, and stormed out of the compartment. She raced to the next car, and reported to a heavy-set man in a woollen overcoat: "Zee man is made of stone! He ees incorruptible!"

"Very well," said her superior, who was an agent of Comintprop, the dread Soviet espionage unit, "we must take sterner measures. There is an old Russian proverb that says, 'If honey won't work, there's always the fly-swatter.'"

Revolver drawn, he raced towards the compartment that Ross had occupied only moments before — and found it empty. The scarlet pimpernel of Canadian espionage had eluded his hunters once again!

By the time the train arrived in Sofia, Ross was safely at his destination. He'd leaped from the train window, skilfully rolled down an embankment, swum several miles up a tributary of the Danube, jogged five miles to a hidden airfield, boarded a waiting helicopter that he piloted himself, touched down on the heliport on the roof of the Canadian embassy in Moscow, been spirited in a black limousine to a nearby hotel, and ushered into a suite that was full of large, beefy men who were drinking Labatt's beer and singing "Roll Me Over in the Clover."

"Thank God you've arrived!" said one of them, who was none other than Harry Sinden, the coach of Team Canada. "Have you got them?"

"Don't worry chief," said Ross, a cool smile playing about his devilishly handsome face. "Eagleson's latest instructions are right here in my attaché case."

from The Toronto Star

She Was So Young to Die!

Keith Crombie & J. E. McDougall

My host introduced me to her and then departed with a curiously relieved air.

"It's colder to-day, isn't it?" she said.

"Yes," I replied. "Though not so cold as yesterday."

A silence ensued.

"It must be twenty minutes after — or twenty minutes to," she remarked.

"Do you play bridge?" I asked quickly.

"Oh, I think bridge is simply *wonderful*," she responded.

"Yes, I suppose it is," I said. "It never struck me in exactly that way before."

Again there was a silence. "It must be twenty minutes after — or twenty minutes to," she ventured.

I winced. "Do you do any tobogganing?"

"Oh, yes," she said.

"Do you like it?" I inquired.

"Oh," she answered, "I think all forms of winter sports are simply *wonderful*."

There was another silence.

She cleared her throat. "It must be twenty minutes after — or twenty minutes to," she said, brightly.

I groaned.

"Did you hear Heifetz the other night?" I asked.

She: "Oh, yes, Heifetz is simply *wonderful*."

I: "Where do you spend your summers?"

She: "In Muskoka."

I: "How do you like it, there?"

She: "Oh, I think Muskoka is simply *wonderful*."

I: "Have you been reading about the excavations at Luxor?"

She: "Oh, yes. I think they are simply *won* ———"

I: "We had a very busy time at the office to-day. Burglars robbed the safe, the office boy fell out of a second-story window and six stenographers went home with influenza."

She: "Oh, I think business is simply *won* ———."

I: "Do you like oysters, Mark Twain, vacuum cleaners, Niagara Falls, woollen underwear, gin, monkeys and maple syrup?"

She: "Oh, I think they are all simply *wonderful.*"

I had to confess myself beaten. I stopped. There was another silence.

Suddenly she turned on me a glowing smile. "It must be twenty minutes after — or twenty min ——"

They arrested my host for the murder. As a matter of fact it was his fault. He never should have introduced me to her.

from Sackcloth and Splashes

from Charlie Farquharson's Histry of Canada

Don Harron

Yer Fore-Word

Well sir, Billy, I s'pose you'd like to know how Charlie Farquharson come to be all of a sudden one day historical.

I mind it was last spring. I was out with the tractor jist this side of my hardwood bush. I'd finished up the spring ploughin' so I was havin' kind of a harrowin' day. It's not too bad when you plough her, but my gol when yer on the harrows you have to stop all the time fer to git them big stones outen the way.

Well sir, I'd jist gotten offa my Allis Chalmers...that's the name of my tractor fer you city folks...and was jist startin' to pry a fair-size piece of granite outen the path of the harrows, when I seen this fella leanin' fernenst the fence. He was there watchin' me heave my stones.

Now you take yer av'rage stranger leanin' fernenst a fence and that's all he's doin', means one of two things: either he's one of yer unemployables or he's workin' fer the guvermint.

Turns out this fella's a genial-ologist workin' fer the Department of Mind yer Resources. He was goin' 'round the country collectin' samples of rock. That's all he was doin', and gittin' paid fer it too. And he was jist waitin' till I got offa my tractor before he asked me if I minded him gittin' his rocks offa my farm.

"My gol," I said, "you can jist folley along in front of the harrows and take all of 'em. But what in the Sam Hill do you want with all that rock anyways?"

And do you know what this sibilant servant told me? He told me that the rocks hard by my hardwood bush was over two billion five hundert million year old. Now I know them guvermint fellas is fond of yer inflation, but my gol, even if you cut her in haff, that's still old.

He called my stones by a funny name too. Now you take yer av'rage rock on the farm, I'd purty well allus taken 'em fer granite. But this fella says, take away yer top soil and when you git right down to it, the Farquharson farm is just a lotta schist. That's what she's called, yer pre-Cambrian schist, what was dropped off by them glacy-ears jist after yer last Ice Age.

Now when I say yer last Ice Age I'm not talkin' 'bout yer Winter of '71 when we had twelve foot of snow. If yer gonna look at this thing real historical yer gonna have to go way back beyond yer behind of that.

'Sides, I don't wanta say too much about yer winter here in Canada. I figger if you don't say too much mebbe it'll go away like it did once between Ice Ages and ev'rythin' got cam and bammy fer a time. Yer climate is a main factor of yer histry, and most of Canada is even today out doors. And that makes fer an offal lotta hoppin', jumpin', and runnin' about jist to keep warm, 'stead of gittin' down to bizness. I figger the hole histry of our country woulda bin differnt if yer temperchure had bin razed jist a few degrees of Fornheat. You take yer av'rage temperchure even today, it's purty mean.

Anyways, if yer ready, put yer feet in the stove and we'll git started with my oriole histry of Canada . . . that jist means it was took down by the wife Valeda, writin' fast as Billy-yo jist as it come outta my mouth. I woulda writ it down myself, but Valeda says nobody's gonna read writin' when it's written rotten. Seems there's two kinds of histry, yer oriole and yer annual, but I ain't got the time to do this ev'ry year.

Yer Universal

Histry is somethin' you can't never finish, so you might jist as well git started at the beginnin'.

I guess Adam and Eve is about the oney ones what really know how the hole thing git started. I'm talkin' 'bout yer Earth when she was jist settin' out . . . oh . . . musta bin neons ago.

Of course yer Earth, she's jist part of yer Universal. That's the hole rang-dang-do rolled into one — per Spiro Nebulous, yer assteroids, yer Big Dippy, and the rest of yer heavenly constella-pations.

Now even the scientificks and assterologists don't seem to agree on how this hole rig got a shove fer to git it started. There's some as says yer Universal never got begun at all. They say she's allus bin there in yer solid state, and it's there she's goin' to stay through yer light years and yer dark.

On the other hands, there's some scientificks as says the hole thing started with a ring-tailed snorter of a spondiferous decom-bustin'. In other words, things got off to a Big Bang and the intire proceedin's bin goin' downhill ever since.

Now there you have yer two differnt theces to play with. You can b'leeve in yer solid state if you like, but the wife and myself is kinda parshul to yer Big Bang.

Yer Pre-Historic Man

Gol darnit, it's time to git offa the land and onto yer lively stock. I guess ev'rybody knows that we never coulda begun stand-in' on our hind legs with our thumbs up in the air.

I b'leeve it was hard onto four-score and seven thousand year ago our fore-paws walked upon this earth.** Before man was Man, he was jist another Mammyal,*** and fer quite some time he felt purty much like a fish . . . outta water.

Let's face it, yer old-time man warn't too differnt from the

**Fore-Feetnote: And if we'd never had got up 'offa them, we might be better off in yer lumber regions today, accordin' to yer Osterpaths and Cairo-practicers.

***Teat Note: Yer Mammyal was so called 'cause he'd breast feed 'stead of suckin' eggs, and was all the time yellin' fer his Mammy.

rest of yer apish gibberons, orange-utangs, and bassoons. I mean you put 'em all together and none of 'em stuck out much. They was all pretty hairy and walkin' low to the ground on all floors. And they all of 'em lived by yer Law of the Jungle — Let Us Prey (still inforce today).

But the main differnce 'tween yer monkey incesters and yer Prime-evil man was yer tool. You take yer av'rage mammyal, they wasn't too much on brains altho' offal high on the in-stinks. But durin' yer gorilla warfare, yer early man had enough scents to pick somethin' up offa the ground and bash the other prime mates brains around with it. And all that brain-bashin' was the start of yer civilly-eyezation.

Yer Voyeurs

Not ev'ry one of them French phesants wanted to git married and keep their feat parrylel to the ground while they raised a few hectors of land by the river with yer coloniac irrigation. There was a buncha pups wanted to raise more'n hectors! They wanted to whoop it up all night long in yer northern bushes and debotch things up with the Injians. I don't think they was out fer more'n a furry canew trip and a darn good time. But them Voyeurs (as they called the old-time bunny chasin' Hugh Heffers of that time) without knowin' what they was doin' had made their way acrost North 'Merka uncoverin' most of the continence.

The first of them'd be the young lad worked fer Sam Plain as Chief Boy Scout, Etenny Groolay. Young Et, he was the Great Laker of his time, bein' the first whitey to pass Ureon, Speerier, and Ontaryo altho' you can't blame him fer what happen to Eery.

He was oney a young slip of a tad when he started out, but he never got over playin' Injian. They finely got fed up with him one night hard by Lake Simcoe when he was first course on a menyou mainly made up of Cannibal's Soup.

A coupla Three Riverers name of Rattysun and Grossyears got further afeeled into the inferior. They come back to Montreal fuzzy to the gunnels with more skins than Holt Renfrew, but not havin' a huntin' license they was both fined fer bein' gamey and off-season.

Well, sir, them two swamp-swingers was so mad they flipped. And they flipped right over to the Anglish side of the fence where they was welcomed as the first French seprators will-in' to help skim the cream offa the top of Canada.

Yer Second Whirl at War

You take yer av'rage war, it's an offal price to pay fer gittin' outen a bizness slump and into yer holycost. There warn't so many uniform fellas knocked off as yer '14-'18 ruckus, but a turble lotta plainclothes people. Fifty millyun. This kinda post-naval berth control is cuttin' off yer nose to spike yer drink.

How it started was yer Germin, yer Eyetalian, and yer Jap all had Axes 'tween them. Yer Germin started first, stuck his nose into Pole-land. The first six months or so was called yer "phoney war," 'cause nothin' really happened; both sides was jist phonin' it in behind their lines. Yer French was behind their Maggynose Line, and as fer yer Germin, well you must remember us singin' "We're gonna hang out Warshin'ton yer Ziegfeld line."

But all that stopped when Germins bliss-creaked their way into our Netherglands. After that yer Eyetalian dick-tater Muscle Eeny stabbed someone's back in France, and yer Axes was in.

Yer Birtish hadda evaccinate theirselves hard by Dumcurk, and Bungle fer Breton. That's when Never Chamberlinen folded like his umbrella. In come Winsome Church-hill to give us yer two fingers up and told yer Naztys to bring on their Pansy Divisions. But my gol, they never come. Twenty miles of Chanel and they never set a goosed foot on yer White Cleft Dover.

Her man Goring thought he'd conker by airmales. He ordered yer Berlitz on London and his Lustwafflers kept droppin' bums over St. Pall's and other sites fer sore eyes. But when we sent up a few Spittlefires, them Germin Junkies went scurvyin' back to their Fodderland.**

Well sir, after yer Big Berlitz come yer Long Sitz. Ev'rybody sat around on the end of their Lendleash.

Next thing happen was way out in yer High-wayin' Islands hard by Honeylooloo, when a buncha Bananzy Jap pilots committed Mata Harry on yer U.S. Navel. This was a dirty trick and so was what we done to our Canadian Japs right after. Our Japs

**Flyin' Feetnote: Valeda says how could them Germins teach Junkies fer to fly. I told her it was the names of their airplanes, and now she won't let me mention them other Fokkers and Messyschitz.

was mostly Vancoover-born, never seen yer Nip-on. Jist the same, they was round-up, confiscated of their homes, and sent deep into Canada to be inturd.

Now this ain't histry to me. I 'member it at the time. I was by now one of yer Privates in yer Royl Muskoka Dismounted Foot. We started in yer bull-pen at yer Colossalinoleum in Tronto, moved to Camp Boredem, and on to Petaweewee. I felt like one of yer Kellogg Reg'lars 'cause I was allus on the go. I finely ended up at yer Hamilton Trades Scool as a Second Class Artifice. I spent mosta my leaves in London, Paris, and Brantford.

I never got over-seized tho'. I got the Spam Medal without yer Armor Star, but b'leeve me, I'da gone ... with all them Seagram Hylanders and Guvner General's Mudguards. ... I wasn't one of them Zombies fightin' King to stay in our Country.

Now you mind in yer First Whirl of War, I synthesized with yer insolationists. But not this time, no sirree Bob, and I'll tell you why. This time it wasn't no Kyzer itchin' fer a fight fer want of nothin' better to do. This time it was that Nazty cyclepath, Hitler, was wantin' to put the kybosh on a hole buncha people ... namely yer Jew. Now before I joined up I don't think I'd met more'n one Jew in my life. He was a little truck-drivin' sheeny name of Lipman, used to buy chickens offa me mebbe twice a month fer cash. He never tried to jew me down and I never tried to gentle him up. It was just bizness doin' bizness with him ... cut and dry ... but allus above yer board.

And it made me mad to think that Hymie Himmler and his S.S. Gepasto was tryin' to send the likes of Lipman and his fambly to camp fer the summer where none of 'em wouldn't git back.

We hadda lotta French fellas from Cuebec couldn't see goin' over to fight when yer prescription finely come out. They din't wanta fight somebody else's battles, and fer that I don't blame 'em. But yer Airy-huns — yer Goring and yer Goballs — was after the hole rang-dang-doo of us fer to be slaves fer their Massa Rates. And we'd all have to be "stricken-yer-Doytch" and mebbe after a time git wiped right outta yer race. That'd be yer Jenny-side.

Now yer Cuebecwas (as yer Seprator calls hisself) fellas today is worried 'bout the same thing; mebbe some of 'em understand better now what that war was all about.

Down, Pte. Engleby, Down and Kindly Stop Licking My Hand

George Bain

Sometimes, in those quiet moments before sleep comes, a time I usually give up to meditations on the bomb and the probability of one's coming down with yaws, I spare a moment to wonder whatever became of the beagles in the Canadian Army.

It was the *Canadian Army Journal* that brought us together, the beagles and me. A captain who was stationed at Camp Borden — ah, those distant, carefree days — wrote a piece which he was pleased to title "Beagling as Training for War." It was an awakening, I can tell you.

The captain was moved to put pen to paper, the *Journal* said, as a consequence of his having been given the management of a pack of beagles at the School of Infantry. (They can't have been drafted, since we don't go in for that sort of thing. It hardly seems likely they enlisted. To be quite candid, I don't know how the hell the beagles came to be at the School of Infantry.) In any event, the captain made quite a case for beagling. Hunting and soldiering have gone hand in hand for centuries, he said, and he cited a number of for-instances, including the following:

"Queen Boadicea encouraged her warriors to hunt before going into battle, subsequently leading them to victory on the heels of their successes in the hunting field."

Over the centuries there has come down to us a quatrain composed by one of the Queen's court which tells the story rather tersely (but well):

> Fresh from hunting down the boar,
> Bo would lead her troops to war;
> This, plus frequent draughts of mead,
> Made her men quite brave indeed.

(Actually, it was the mead that did it. After they had been into that for a couple of hours they'd tackle wildcats. As a matter of fact, they frequently thought they *were* attacking wildcats. That mead will do it every time.)

It should be pointed out, in case it should lead to an investigation even at this late date, that the captain whose treatise on beagling is here under review, did whatever one does with beagles on his own and not on the Army's time. This he did notwithstanding the fact that many principles of war are also applicable to beagling, and presumably, vice versa. Or, as he said:

"...to follow the hounds with any degree of success demands the same qualities that are demanded of the present-day soldier."

> The private let moan in despair:
> "I wouldn't so very much care
> Being drilled like a hound
> If it weren't that I found
> That I'm really supposed to chase hare."

The captain went on to explain that lessons in camouflage, appreciation and description of terrain, and other subjects too numerous (I think the phrase goes) to mention, were to be learned from sniffing across the countryside with a pack of beagles.

"A few days with hounds will help develop in most followers who are prepared to take the trouble to learn," he said, "a useful eye for country and a healthy pair of lungs."

> *There's* a man with beagle training:
> Always tell it when you see
> How, although it isn't raining,
> He proceeds from treee to tree.
> — *Very old English countryman's verse*

Developing his theme, the captain said:

"The soldier who aspires to be an NCO (Nearly Collapsed Other-rank), or the NCO seeking a commission, can do no better in furtherance of this aim than spend his spare time following a pack of beagles at every opportunity available."

In other words, become an eager-beagle. Then:

Shed a tear for Private Smale,
There's a man who's going to fail,
Spends his time with army manuals,
And leans, in dogs, to cocker spanuals.

But, once more to our text: "Should he (the soldier) wish to make an even deeper study he would find several worthwhile examples of practical administration in the care, feeding and general maintenance of hounds."

(The nasty suspicion begins to raise its head here that what the captain is really trying to do is to unload that pack of beagles on somebody else.) However:

"Animal management is more closely related to man management than most people realize; the principles are almost identical, and failure to observe them is apparent for all the world to see."

Now *that* strikes a note.

The general care of dogs and men
Is more alike than many ken;
You will, I think, admit it's hard,
To tell some army food from Pard.

Y-o-o-o-o-o-o.
The voice of Bugle Ann?
No, the voice of Pte. Engleby. He just had breakfast. "Down, Engleby; down, dammit, down I say!" A can of sautéed Pard on fried bread in the morning and there's no holding him.

from I've Been Around and Around and Around and Around

Lord of the Fleas

Don Bell

With apologies to Stephen Leacock, whose story "My Financial Career" may have inspired the following. . . .

You've already read about the Anti-Serious Society, and how a Polish-born journalist named Stash Pruszynski marched during the McGill riot, holding up a sign announcing: "After the Riot, Eat at Joe's." For his bravado role in that story, I paid my friend Stash the sum of fifty dollars. And so began the financial careers of two most interesting individuals.

Stash was timid about accepting the fee. "You're the one who wrote the story," he said. "All I did was —"

"Since you insist," I said, withdrawing the cheque.

But Stash reached out and grabbed it from my hand. "On the other hand, I can use the money," he said. "I'm going to give you one share in Stash's Flea Market."

"That's wonderful," I said. "By the way, what the hell is Stash's Flea Market?"

Stash then explained his concept to me: What this country needed was an authentic flea market, in the style of Marché aux Puces in Paris, or Portobello Road in London, where a colourful atmosphere was provided for artisans to sell their wares. They would set up outdoor stalls and work and haggle out in the open. The public would love it.

We had many talks about the flea market. As a shareholder, I wanted to underline that there would be no decisions made without my approval. Even though Stash conceived the idea and owned the other ninety-nine shares, I felt it was my duty to help in the growth of the company. It was the first time I have ever been an important executive, and I wished to be right where the action was.

Realizing that our agreement wasn't down on paper, I invited Stash to dinner at the Club des Moustaches in back of the Bistro. After plying Stash with wine and boeuf bourguignon, I delicately brought up the subject of a contract. Stash agreed that it should be written, and scribbled his commitment on the paper tablecloth: "This is to certify that Don Bell has one share, or one per cent of the Marché au Trésor enterprise and is entitled to one per cent of the firm's profits as long as the Marché exists. Signed: Stash the Manager."

I folded the tablecloth, which had a few broccoli sauté stains on it, and carefully put it in my pocket. Later, I locked it in a metal strongbox that also contains my birth certificate, marriage contract, passport, vaccination certificate, and will.

In the spring, Stash found a site for the flea market on St. Paul Street opposite Bonsecours Market. Frankly, I had a few reservations about the site, but I finally gave my seal of approval — I wouldn't try to stand in Stash's way as long as my dividends were to come in regularly.

Stash set up about twenty-five stalls, and in the summer Stash's Flea Market was one of the most thriving enterprises in Old Montreal. Stash was interviewed by countless radio and TV stations. Hundreds of tourists visited the market; even the mayor and the Governor General dropped by.

With delight, I watched the value of my stock rise. By August, Stash estimated that it was worth $100 — twice its original value — but he advised me not to sell just yet. I would be a fool not to hold on to the stock, he said. No doubt, the profits alone would soon cover my capital outlay. I tried to bug Stash about the profits, but he said he wasn't in a position yet to pay off fat returns. For one thing, there was still the question of his rent, which was not the least of his debts; he convinced me that the wisest course just now was to sink all the profits back into the enterprise.

Every Sunday I visited the open-air market to make sure that all was running smoothly. I felt that my presence was needed. You can never tell when the charcoal portrait painter, for instance, would give vent to cubist impulses. Or the Pakistani trinket vendors would fight over stall privileges. A shareholder on the premises would have a cooling influence.

Stash introduced me to the resident artisans. They all looked at me with awe because they knew I was a bigshot, some Mafia wheel who had his fingers in the pie. I was called Sir and Mr. Big and other names. Stash introduced me to customers as "one of the shareholders." I smoked cigars and wore loud ties. Everyone was really impressed.

Stash may have had all the dynamism and energy, but I was the silent partner behind the scenes with the brains. One day, near the end of summer, Stash came up to me and said: "We're going to have to find another site."

"Why?" I asked.

"No lease. We're being kicked out."

"The dirty rats. We'll have to find another site," I announced.

The decision was made. Stash agreed we'd have to find another site.

Stash found a building with a large courtyard nearby on Notre Dame Street opposite City Hall. I gave him my blessings — luckily for the concern; this was no time for bickering at the top executive level. Stash signed the papers and we moved to our new premises, which is where the flea market is now located.

Stash did most of the physical work, painting signs, sweeping up, paying the rent and so on, but anyone who has a plug of intelligence can see that the flea market wouldn't be the same without my genius.

I must say, I was proud of the market. During lunch hour, I'd walk to Notre Dame Street and see how Stash was coming along in his chores. Sometimes, he would foist a paint brush or a broom upon me. After a while, I decided to go by car and admire the market from the outside instead as I didn't want to be in Stash's way. Often I would point out the market to friends.

"You see that building?"

"What?"

"That building on your right."

"Stash's Flea Market?"

"Yup."

"What about it?"

"I'm a part-owner. I have shares in it."

"Oh, — you've left journalism? Gone into business?"

"Not quite. It's one of my holdings on the side. The share is worth a fortune."

"*The* share? One?"

"Well, there are not too many shares. Outside of Stash and myself, I can't think of anyone else who has a share."

"How much is it worth?"

"I'd rather not divulge the figure," I said, sneaking a little smile. "Tax reasons."

In December, Stash had an Anti-Serious Society party at

the Flea Market. Admission at the door, 75 cents. I arrived with several out-of-town guests.

"That will be 75 cents," said the girl selling tickets.

"That's all right," I told her. "Let them pass."

"Let them pass nothing," she growled. "Admission 75 cents."

I took her to the side. My voice sounded threatening. "Do you realize who you're talking to?" I asked.

"I don't give a damn if you're the prime minister," she said.

"I'm one of the owners of this market. In a sense, I'm your employer."

She kind of jumped back and looked at me aghast. Her face turned a greenish shade. "Oh, I'm sorry," she gulped. "You should have explained."

"You were doing your duty," I told her. "I'll see that you get a bonus at the end of the year."

A group of people was just then coming out of the door. "Don't bother going in," said one collegiate type, with a girl strapped to his arm. "Great flea market but lousy party. Save your money."

"We have to go in," I said smiling. "I happen to be one of the owners."

"Then you're just the guy we want to see," said the girl. "What can you do about getting us our money back?"

"That's right," said the boyfriend, who looked like a bruiser on the college football team.

"Any complaints should be addressed to Stash," I said loudly. Then, quieter: "I'm only a small shareholder."

At that same party, Stash spoke to me for the first time about dividends.

"Dividends," he said.

"What?"

"You'll be getting a $10 dividend shortly," he said. "But can you hold on for a few weeks? I'm strapped for funds now."

"Yes, whenever you have it," I said, giving Stash a way out.

During the party, I did nothing but think of the dividend. How should I spend it? Should I just let all my dividends pile up in the bank? No, that was selfish. Besides, I'd have to claim them when making out my income tax. The tax question was something I hadn't thought of before; I didn't want government people hang-

ing around with a lot of queries. I decided that the only loophole
was to re-invest it in the flea market.

The next day I called Stash. "That dividend," I said, keeping my voice low. "I've made my decision: you can plow it back
into the company."

"I'm glad you made that decision," Stash said. "Here's what
we'll do for you. We'll regard it as a long term loan bearing you
8¾ % interest."

I looked at the phone, awed. It was such a simple expedient.
Why hadn't I thought of dividend re-investment months ago?
"'You're on," I told Stash, with genuine feeling.

The secret of most successful financiers is that they know
when to buy and sell. Choosing the ripe time is practically a question of intuition.

I realized that the time might be ripe to sell my share in
Stash's flea market. No one knows what the future augurs for
Stash or the fleas. But how could I break such news to my friend
Stash without hurting his feelings?

It so happened that it was Stash himself who made the first
move. Recently, the phone rang. Stash's voice at the other end.
Did I detect a note of urgency?

"Listen," Stash said. "This may be a surprise, but I know
someone who wants to buy your share."

"Me sell?" I said, playing difficult. "Never."

"A Polish friend of mine is willing to pay $200 for your
share," Stash went on. "That's four times your original investment."

I did some elementary arithmetic in my head. He was right.
It was four times my original investment. I'd make a killing.

"All right," I said. "I'll sell, but there's one condition." I
paused for effect. You could feel the tension over the phone. "I
would like to reserve the option," I said, choosing my words very
carefully, "of buying one of *your* shares at the market price at
my convenience."

There was a long silence at the other end. It was all or
nothing. I knew my strategy had to work, though, and I could
almost hear Stash's mental calculation. Finally, his voice, low but
firm: "You're on," he said. "It's a deal."

Through clever planning and careful manipulation of my
stocks, I'd become an overnight financial phenomenon. I heard that
Bay Street and St. James Street got wind of the deal and all money

was tight. The reverberations would be felt on Wall Street and as far away as the Bourse in Paris and the Taj Mahal in India.

However, there was a hitch. And there's a lesson to be gleaned from all this: Never — I repeat, never count your financial chickens until the transaction is down on paper, until the deal is signed and you've got the dough safely tucked into your pocket.

You see, at the last minute Stash phoned me with the news that the prospective buyer of my share got cold feet and decided to put the money in the bank instead, even though his returns would only be a fraction of what he'd get if he invested in Stash's Flea Market. Anyway, Stash said, I shouldn't be too disappointed because even had the share been bought it would have taken at least a year before I saw the money. Stash, who was acting as middleman in the deal, was planning to use the money to pay off some more of his back rent — but he intended to pay me $8\frac{3}{4}\%$ on the loan, which would have amounted to $17.50.

"By next year, your share may be worth double its present value," Stash hinted.

"Yes, I think I *will* hold on to it," I agreed. "With any luck, they'll be standing four deep by next year to get their hands on that share."

"I don't suppose," Stash said, "you know of anyone who would like to float a loan of $200 that will yield high interest?"

"How high?"

"Say fifteen per cent," Stash said.

"I can ask around," I told Stash. "I can't help you myself, but there may be dozens of others just dying to start a business career."

In a sense, I'm glad I didn't sell out, because beneath the hard façade of most businessmen is a tender spot. I'm a sentimental-ist at heart. It would have been sad to have passed by Stash's Flea Market and to have felt like a stranger.

Now, I drive by several times every week, and each time I get a kind of sinking feeling, and it's not without tears in my eyes that I've been known to boast: "This is mine — almost all mine."

With any luck, Stash will give me another share in the market once this gets printed. I don't call myself a pusher, but I figure if I play it right, gradually I can manoeuvre my friend Stash to a position where he has no choice but to cough up the whole flea market, fleas included.

from Saturday Night at the Bagel Factory

The Great Detective

Stephen Leacock

I

" 'Ha!' exclaimed the Great Detective, raising himself
from the resilient sod on which he had lain prone for half an hour,
'what have we here?'

"As he spoke, he held up a blade of grass he had plucked.

" 'I see nothing,' said the Poor Nut.

" 'No, I suppose not,' said the Great Detective; after which
he seated himself on a stone, took out his saxophone from its case,
and for the next half hour was lost in the intricacies of Gounod's
'Sonata in Six Flats and a Basement.' "

— *Any Detective Story.*

The publishers tell us that more than a thousand detective
stories are sold every day — or is it every hour? It does not matter.
The point is that a great many are sold all the time, and that there
is no slackening of the appetite of the reading public for stories
of mysterious crime.

It is not so much the crime itself that attracts as the unravel-
ing of the mystery by the super-brain of the Great Detective, as
silent as he is efficient. He speaks only about once a week. He
seldom eats. He crawls around in the grass picking up clews. He
sits upside down in his armchair forging his inexorable chain of
logic.

But when he's done with it, the insoluble mystery is solved,
justice is done, the stolen jewels are restored, and the criminal is
either hanged or pledges his word to go and settle on a ranch in
Saskatchewan; after which the Great Detective takes a night off at
the Grand Opera, the only thing that really reaches him.

The tempting point about a detective story — both for the
writer and the reader — is that it is so beautifully easy to begin.
All that is needed is to start off with a first-class murder.

"Mr. Blankety Blank sat in his office in the drowsy hour of

a Saturday afternoon. He was alone. Work was done for the day. The clerks were gone. The building, save for the janitor, who lived in the basement, was empty.

"As he sat thus, gazing in a sort of reverie at the papers on the desk in front of him, his chin resting on his hand, his eyes closed and slumber stole upon him."

Quite so. Let him feel just as drowsy as ever he likes. The experienced reader knows that now is the very moment when he is about to get a crack on the nut. This drowsy gentleman, on the first page of a detective story, is not really one of the characters at all. He is cast for the melancholy part that will presently be called The Body. Some writers prefer to begin with The Body itself right away — after this fashion:

"The Body was that of an elderly gentleman, upside down, but otherwise entirely dressed."

But it seems fairer to give the elderly gentleman a few minutes of life before knocking him on the head. As long as the reader knows that there is either a Body right away, or that there is going to be one, he is satisfied.

Sometimes a touch of terror is added by having the elderly gentleman killed in a country house at night. Most readers will agree that this is the better way to kill him.

"Sir Charles Althorpe sat alone in his library at Althorpe Chase. It was late at night. The fire had burned low in the grate. Through the heavily curtained windows no sound came from out-side. Save for the maids, who slept in a distant wing, and save for the butler, whose room was under the stairs, the Chase, at this time of the year, was empty. As Sir Charles sat thus in his arm-chair, his head gradually sank upon his chest and he dozed off into slumber."

Foolish man! Doesn't he know that to doze off into slumber in an isolated country house, with the maids in a distant wing, is little short of madness? Apparently he doesn't, and his fate, to the complete satisfaction of the reader, comes right at him.

Let it be noted that in thus setting the stage for a detective story, the Body selected is, in nine cases out of ten, that of an "elderly gentleman." It would be cowardly to kill a woman, and even our grimmest writers hesitate to kill a child. But an "elderly gentleman" is all right, especially when "fully dressed" and half asleep. Somehow they seem to invite a knock on the head.

After such a beginning, the story ripples brightly along with the finding of the Body, and with the Inquest, and with the arrest of the janitor, or the butler, and the usual details of that sort.

Any trained reader knows when he sees that trick phrase, *"save for the janitor, who lived in the basement,"* or *"save for the butler, whose room was under the stairs,"* that the janitor and the butler are to be arrested at once.

Not that they really did commit the murder. We don't believe they did. But they are suspected. And a good writer in the outset of a crime story throws suspicion around like pepper.

In fact, the janitor and the butler are not the only ones. There is also, in all the stories, a sort of Half Hero (he can't be a whole hero, because that would interfere with the Great Detective), who is partly suspected, and sometimes even arrested. He is the young man who is either heir to the money in the story, or who had a "violent quarrel" with the Body, or who was seen "leaving the premises at a late hour" and refuses to say why.

Some writers are even mean enough to throw a little suspicion on the Heroine — the niece or ward of the elderly gentleman — a needless young woman dragged in by convention into this kind of novel. She gets suspected merely because she bought half a gallon of arsenic at the local chemist shop. They won't believe her when she says, with tears in her eyes, that she wanted it to water the tulips with.

The Body being thus completely dead, Inspector Higginbottom of the local police having been called in, having questioned all the maids, and having announced himself "completely baffled," the crime story is well set and the Great Detective is brought into it.

Here, at once, the writer is confronted with the problem of how to tell the story, and whether to write it as if it were told by the Great Detective himself. But the Great Detective is above that. For one thing, he's too silent. And in any case, if he told the story himself, his modesty might hold him back from fully explaining how terribly clever he is, and how wonderful his deductions are.

So the nearly universal method has come to be that the story is told through the mouth of an Inferior Person, a friend and confidant of the Great Detective. This humble associate has the special function of being lost in admiration all the time.

In fact, this friend, taken at his own face value, must be regarded as a Poor Nut. Witness the way in which his brain breaks down utterly and is set going again by the Great Detective. The scene occurs when the Great Detective begins to observe all the things around the place that were overlooked by Inspector Higginbottom.

> " *'But how,' I exclaimed, 'how in the name of all that is incomprehensible, are you able to aver that the criminal wore rubbers?'*
>
> *"My friend smiled quietly.*
>
> " *'You observe,' he said, 'that patch of fresh mud about ten feet square in front of the door of the house. If you would look, you will see that it has been freshly walked over by a man with rubbers on.'*
>
> *"I looked. The marks of the rubbers were there plain enough — at least a dozen of them.*
>
> " *'What a fool I was!' I exclaimed. 'But at least tell me how you were able to know the length of the criminal's foot?'*
>
> *"My friend smiled again, his same inscrutable smile.*
>
> " *'By measuring the print of the rubber,' he answered quietly, 'and then subtracting from it the thickness of the material multiplied by two.'*
>
> " *'Multiplied by two!' I exclaimed. 'Why by two?'*
>
> " *'For the toe and the heel.'*
>
> " *'Idiot that I am,' I cried, 'it all seems so plain when you explain it.' "*

In other words, the Poor Nut makes an admirable narrator. However much fogged the reader may get, he has at least the comfort of knowing that the Nut is far more fogged than he is. Indeed, the Nut may be said, in a way, to personify the ideal reader, that is to say the stupidest — the reader who is most completely bamboozled with the mystery, and yet intensely interested.

Such a reader has the support of knowing that the police are entirely "baffled"— that's always the word for them; that the public are "mystified"; that the authorities are "alarmed"; the newspapers "in the dark"; and the Poor Nut, altogether up a tree. On those terms, the reader can enjoy his own ignorance to the full.

A first-class insoluble crime having thus been well started, and with the Poor Nut narrating it with his ingenuous interest, the next stage in the mechanism of the story is to bring out the personality of the Great Detective, and to show how terribly clever he is.

II

When a detective story gets well started — when the "body" has been duly found — and the "butler" or the "janitor" has been arrested — when the police have been completely "baffled"— then is the time when the Great Detective is brought in and gets to work.

But before he can work at all, or at least be made thoroughly satisfactory to the up-to-date reader, it is necessary to touch him up. He can be made extremely tall and extremely thin, or even "cadaverous." Why a cadaverous man can solve a mystery better than a fat man it is hard to say; presumably the thinner a man is, the more acute is his mind. At any rate, the old school of writers preferred to have their detectives lean. This incidentally gave the detective a face "like a hawk," the writer not realizing that a hawk is one of the stupidest of animals. A detective with a face like an orang-outang would beat it all to bits.

Indeed, the Great Detective's face becomes even more important than his body. Here there is absolute unanimity. His face has to be "inscrutable." Look at it though you will, you can never read it. Contrast it, for example, with the face of Inspector Higginbottom, of the local police force. Here is a face that can look "surprised," or "relieved," or, with great ease, "completely baffled."

But the face of the Great Detective knows of no such changes. No wonder the Poor Nut, as we may call the person who is supposed to narrate the story, is completely mystified. From the face of the great man you can't tell whether the cart in which they are driving jolts him or whether the food at the Inn gives him indigestion.

To the Great Detective's face there used to be added the old-time expedient of not allowing him either to eat or drink. And when it was added that during this same period of about eight days the sleuth never slept, the reader could realize in what fine shape his brain would be for working out his "inexorable chain of logic."

But nowadays this is changed. The Great Detective not

only eats, but he eats well. Often he is presented as a connoisseur in food. Thus:

> " 'Stop a bit,' *thus speaks the Great Detective to the Poor Nut and Inspector Higginbottom, whom he is dragging round with him as usual; 'we have half an hour before the train leaves Paddington. Let us have some dinner. I know an Italian restaurant near here where they serve frogs' legs à la Marengo better than anywhere else in London.'*
>
> "*A few minutes later we were seated at one of the tables of a dingy little eating-place whose signboard with the words 'Ristorante Italiano' led me to the deduction that it was an Italian restaurant. I was amazed to observe that my friend was evidently well known in the place, while his order for 'three glasses of Chianti with two drops of vermicelli in each,' called for an obsequious bow from the appreciative padrone. I realized that this amazing man knew as much of the finesse of Italian wines as he did of playing the saxophone.*"

We may go further. In many up-to-date cases the detective not only gets plenty to eat, but a liberal allowance of strong drink. One generous British author of to-day is never tired of handing out to the Great Detective and his friends what he calls a "stiff whiskey and soda." At all moments of crisis they get one.

For example, when they find the Body of Sir Charles Althorpe, late owner of Althorpe Chase, a terrible sight, lying on the floor of the library, what do they do? They reach at once to the sideboard and pour themselves out a "stiff whiskey and soda." Or when the heroine learns that her guardian Sir Charles is dead and that she is his heiress and when she is about to faint, what do they do? They immediately pour "a stiff whiskey and soda" into her. It is certainly a great method.

But in the main we may say that all this stuff about eating and drinking has lost its importance. The great detective has to be made exceptional by some other method.

And here is where his music comes in. It transpires — not at once but in the first pause in the story — that this great man not only can solve a crime, but has the most extraordinary aptitude for music, especially for dreamy music of the difficult kind. As soon as he is left in the Inn room with the Poor Nut out comes his saxophone and he tunes it up.

" 'What were you playing?' I asked, as my friend at last folded his beloved instrument into its case.
" 'Beethoven's Sonata in Q,' he answered modestly.
" 'Good Heavens!' I exclaimed."

Another popular method of making the Great Detective a striking character is to show him as possessing a strange and varied range of knowledge. For example, the Poor Nut is talking with a third person, the Great Detective being apparently sunk in reveries. In the course of the conversation the name of Constantinople is mentioned.

"I was hardly aware that my friend was hearing what was said.
"He looked up quietly.
" 'Constantinople?' he said. 'That was the capital of Turkey, was it not?'
"I could not help marveling again how this strange being could have acquired his minute and varied knowledge."

The Great Detective's personality having thus been arranged, he is brought along with the Poor Nut and Inspector Higginbottom to Althorpe Chase and it is now up to him to start to "solve" the mystery. Till a little while ago, the favourite way of having him do this was by means of tracks, footprints, and other traces. This method, which has now worn threadbare, had a tremendous vogue. According to it, the Great Detective never questioned anybody.

But his real work was done right at the scene of the crime, crawling round on the carpet of the library, and wriggling about on the grass outside. After he has got up after two days of crawling, with a broken blade of grass, he would sit down on a stone and play the saxophone and then announce that the mystery is solved and tell Inspector Higginbottom whom to arrest. That was all. He would not explain anything but what the Poor Nut, half crazy with mystification, begged him to do.

" 'The case,' he at last explained very airily, 'has been a simple one, but not without its features of interest.'
" 'Simple!' I exclaimed.
" 'Precisely,' said he; 'you see this blade of grass. You tell

*me that you see nothing. Look at it again under this lense. What
do you see? The letters ACK clearly stamped, but in reverse, on
the soft green of the grass. What do they mean?'*

" 'Nothing,' I groaned.

" 'You are wrong,' he said, 'they are the last three letters
of the word DACK, the name of a well-known shoemaker in
Market Croydon four miles west of the Chase.'

" 'Good Heavens,' I said.

" 'Now look at this soft piece of mud which I have baked
and which carries a similar stamp — ILTON.'

" 'Ilton, Ilton,' I repeated, 'I fear it means less than ever.'

" 'To you,' he said. 'Because you do not observe. Did you
never note that makers of trousers nowadays stamp their trouser
buttons with their names? These letters are the concluding part
of the name BILTON, one of the best-known tailors of Kings
Croft, four miles east of the Chase.'

" 'Good Heavens!' I cried, 'I begin to see.'

" 'Do you?' he said drily. 'Then no doubt you can piece
together the analysis. Our criminal is wearing a pair of trousers,
bought in Kings· Croft, and a shoe bought in Market Croydon.
What do you infer as to where he lives?'

" 'Good Heavens,' I said, 'I begin to see it.'

" 'Exactly,' said the Great Detective. 'He lives halfway between the two!'

" 'At the Chase itself!' I cried. 'What a fool I have been.'

" 'You have,' he answered quietly."

But unfortunately the public has begun to find this method
of traces and tracks a "bit thick." All these fond old literary fic-
tions are crumbling away.

The Method of Recondite Knowledge

In fact, they are being very largely replaced by the newer
and much more showy expedient that can be called the Method
of Recondite Knowledge. The Great Detective is equipped with
a sort of super-scientific knowledge of things, materials, sub-
stances, chemistry, actions, and reactions that would give him a
Ph.D. degree in any school of applied science.

Some of the best detectives of the higher fiction of today
even maintain a laboratory and a couple of assistants. When they

have all this, all they need is a little piece of dust or a couple of micrometre sections and the criminal is as good as caught.

Thus, let us suppose that in the present instance Sir Charles Althorpe has been done to death — as so many "elderly gentlemen" were in the fiction of twenty years ago — by the intrusion into his library of a sailor with a wooden leg newly landed from Java. Formerly the crime would have been traced by the top heaviness of his wooden leg — when the man drank beer at the Althorpe Arms, his elbow on the side away from his leg would have left an impression on the bar, similar to the one left where he climbed the window sill.

But in the newer type of story the few grains of dust found near the Body would turn out to be specks from the fibre of Java coconut, such as is seen only on the decks of ships newly arrived from Java, and on the clothes of the sailors.

But, by the one method or the other method, the "inexorable chain of logic" can be completed to the last link. The writer can't go on forever; sooner or later he must own up and say who did it. After two hundred pages, he finds himself up against the brutal necessity of selecting his actual murderer.

So, now then, who did it? Which brings us to the final phase of the Detective Story. Who really killed Sir Charles?

III

The Tramp Solution

According to one very simple expedient, the murder was not committed by any of the principal characters at all. It was committed *by a tramp.* It transpires that the tramp was passing the Chase late that night and was attracted by the light behind the curtain (as tramps are apt to be), and came and peered through the window (as tramps love to do), and when he saw Sir Charles asleep in his chair with the gold watch on the table beside him, he got one of those sudden impulses (such as tramps get when they see a gold watch), and, before he knew what he had done, he had lifted the window and slipped into the room.

Sir Charles woke — and there you are. All quite simple. Indeed, but for the telltale marks on the grass, or the telltale fibre on the carpet, or the telltale something, the murderer would never have been known.

And yet the solution seems paltry. It seems a shame to drag

in the poor tattered creature at the very end and introduce and hang him all in one page.

So we have to look round for some other plan.

The Murder Was Committed by Somebody Else Altogether Different

A solution, which is a prime favourite with at least one very distinguished contemporary author, is to have it turn out that the murder has been *committed by somebody else altogether different.* In other words, it was committed by some casual person who just came into the story for about one half second.

Let us make a simple example. At the Althorpe Arms Inn where the Great Detective and the Poor Nut are staying while they investigate the death of Sir Charles, we bring in, just for one minute, *"a burly-looking man in a check suit drinking a glass of ale in the bar."* We ask him quite casually, if he can tell us anything about the state of the road to Farringham. He answers in a surly way that he's a stranger to these parts and knows nothing of it. That's all. He doesn't come in any more till the very end.

But a really experienced reader ought to guess at once that he committed the murder. Look at it: he's burly; and he's surly; and he has a check suit; and he drinks ale; and he's a stranger; that's enough. Any good law court could hang him for that — in a detective story, anyway.

When at last the truth dawns on the Poor Nut.

" 'Great Heavens,' I exclaimed, 'the man in the check suit!'
"The Great Detective nodded.

" 'But how on earth!' I exclaimed, more mystified than ever, 'were you ever led to suspect it?'

" 'From the very first,' said my friend, turning to Inspector Higginbottom, who nodded in confirmation, 'we had a strong clew.'

" 'A clew!' I exclaimed.

" 'Yes, one of the checks on his coat had been cached.'

" 'Cashed,' I cried.

" 'You misunderstand me; not "cashed," CACHED. He had cut it out and hidden it. A man who cuts out a part of his coat and hides it on the day after a crime is probably concealing something.'

" 'Great Heavens!' I exclaimed, 'how obvious it sounds
when you put it that way. To think that I never thought of it!' "

The Solution of the Thoroughly Dangerous Woman

According to this method, the crime was committed by
a thoroughly bad, thoroughly dangerous woman, generally half
foreign — which is supposed to account for a lot. She has just come
into the story casually — as a nurse, or as an assistant bookkeeper,
or, more usual and much better, as a "discarded flame" of somebody or other.

These discarded flames flicker all through detective literature as a terrible warning to persons of a fickle disposition. In any
case, great reliance is placed on foreign blood as accounting for
her. For Anglo-Saxon readers, if you put a proper quantity of
foreign blood into a nurse and then discard her, that will do the
trick every time.

To show how thoroughly bad she is, the Dangerous
Woman used to be introduced by the writers of the Victorian age
as smoking a cigarette. She also wore "high-heeled shoes and a skirt
that reached barely to her ankles." In our time, she would have to
do a little better than that. In short, as the key to a murder, we
must pass her by. She would get acquitted every time.

Let us try something else.

The Solution that the Murder was Committed by
Blue Edward

According to this explanation of the mysterious crime, it
turns out, right at the end of the story, that the murder was not
done by any of the people suspected — neither by the Butler, nor
the Half Hero, nor the Tramp, nor the Dangerous Woman. Not
at all. It was the work of one of the most audacious criminals ever
heard of (except that the reader never heard of him till this second), the head and brain of a whole gang of criminals, ramifying
all over Hades.

This head criminal generally goes under some such terrible
name as Black Pete, or Yellow Charlie, or Blue Edward. As soon
as his name is mentioned, then at once not only the Great Detective but everybody else knows all about him — except only the
reader and the Nut, who is always used as a proxy for the reader

in matters of astonishment or simplicity of mind.

At the very height of the chase, a new murder, that of a deputy police inspector (they come cheap; it's not like killing one of the regular characters), is added to the main crime of killing Sir Charles. The manner of the murder — by means of dropping a bullet fired three miles away with its trajectory computed by algebra — has led to the arrest. The Great Detective, *calculating back the path of the bullet,* has ordered by telephone the arrest of a man three miles away. As the Detective, the Nut, and the police stand looking at the body of the murdered policeman, word comes from Scotland Yard that the arrest is made.

> *"The Great Detective stood looking about him, quietly shaking his head. His eye rested a moment on the prostrate body of Sub-Inspector Bradshaw, then turned to scrutinize the neat hole drilled in the glass of the window.*
> *" 'I see it all now,' he murmured. 'I should have guessed it sooner. There is no doubt whose work this is.'*
> *" 'Who is it?' I asked.*
> *" 'Blue Edward,' he announced quietly.*
> *" 'Blue Edward!' I exclaimed.*
> *" 'Blue Edward,' he repeated.*
> *" 'Blue Edward!' I reiterated, 'but who then is Blue Edward?' "*

This, of course, is the very question that the reader is wanting to ask. Who on earth is Blue Edward? The question is answered at once by the Great Detective himself.

> *" 'The fact that you have never heard of Blue Edward merely shows the world that you have lived in. As a matter of fact, Blue Edward is the terror of four continents. We have traced him to Shanghai, only to find him in Madagascar. It was he who organized the terrible robbery at Irkutsk in which ten mujiks were blown up with a bottle of Epsom salts.*
> *" 'It was Blue Edward who for years held the whole of Philadelphia in abject terror, and kept Oshkosh, Wisconsin, on the jump for even longer. At the head of a gang of criminals that ramifies all over the known globe, equipped with a scientific education that enables him to read and write and use a typewriter with the greatest ease, Blue Edward has practically held the police of*

the world at bay for years.

"*'I suspected his hand in this from the start. From the very outset, certain evidences pointed to the work of Blue Edward.'*"

After which all the police inspectors and spectators keep shaking their heads and murmuring, "Blue Edward, Blue Edward," until the reader is sufficiently impressed.

IV

The writing of a detective story, without a doubt, gets harder and harder towards the end. It is not merely the difficulty of finding a suitable criminal; there is added the difficulty of knowing what to do with him. It is a tradition of three centuries of novel writing that a story ought to end happily. But in this case, how end up happily?

For example, here we have Blue Edward, caught at last, with handcuffs on his wrists — Blue Edward, the most dangerous criminal that ever interwove the underworld into a solid mesh; Blue Edward, who — well, in fact, the whole aim of the writer only a little while before was to show what a heller Blue Edward was. True, we never heard of him until near the end of the book, but when he *did* get in we were told that his Gang had ramified all the way from Sicily to Oklahoma. Now, what are we to do?

If it is not Blue Edward, then we've got to hang the Tramp — the poor tattered creature who fried potatoes by the hedge. But we are called upon to notice that now he has "a singularly vacant eye." You can hardly hang a man with a vacant eye. It doesn't do.

What if we send him to prison for life? But that's pretty cold stuff, too — sitting looking at four stone walls with a vacant eye for forty years. In fact, the more we think of it, the less satisfied we are with hanging the Tramp. Personally I'd rather hang Meadows the Butler, as we first set out to do, or I'd hang the Nut or the Thoroughly Bad Woman, or any of them.

In the older fiction, they used to face this problem fairly and squarely. They hanged them, — and apparently they liked it. But nowadays we can't do it. We have lost the old-fashioned solid satisfaction in it, so we have to look round for another solution. Here is one, a very favourite one with our sensitive generation. If I had to give it a name, I would call it —

The Criminal with the Hacking Cough

The method of it is very simple. Blue Edward, or whoever is to be "it," is duly caught. There's no doubt of his guilt. But at the moment when the Great Detective and the Ignorant Police are examining him he develops a "hacking cough." Indeed, as he starts to make his confession, he can hardly talk for hacks.

> " 'Well,' says the criminal, looking round at the little group of police officers, 'the game is up — hack! hack! — and I may as well make a clean breast of it — hack, hack, hack.' "

Any trained reader when he hears these hacks knows exactly what they are to lead up to. The criminal, robust though he seemed only a chapter ago when he jumped through a three-story window after throttling Sub-Inspector Juggins half to death, is a dying man. He has got one of those terrible diseases known to fiction as a "mortal complaint." It wouldn't do to give it an exact name, or somebody might get busy and cure it. The symptoms are a hacking cough and a great mildness of manner, an absence of all profanity, and a tendency to call everybody "you gentlemen." Those things spell finis.

In fact, all that is needed now is for the Great Detective himself to say, "*Gentlemen*" (they are all gentlemen at this stage of the story), "*a higher conviction than any earthly law has, et cetera, et cetera.*" With that, the curtain is dropped, and it is understood that the criminal made his exit the same night.

That's better, decidedly better. And yet, lacking in cheerfulness, somehow.

It is just about as difficult to deal with the Thoroughly Bad Woman. The general procedure is to make her raise a terrible scene. When she is at last rounded up and caught, she doesn't "go quietly" like the criminal with the hacking cough or the repentant tramp. Not at all. She raises — in fact, she is made to raise so much that the reader will be content to waive any prejudice about the disposition of criminals, to get her out of the story.

> "*The woman's face as Inspector Higginbottom snapped the handcuffs on her wrists was livid with fury.*
> " '*Gur-r-r-r-r!*' she hissed."

(This is her favourite exclamation, and shows the high percentage of her foreign blood.)

" '*Gur-r-r-r! I hate you all. Do what you like with me. I would kill him again a thousand times, the old fool.*'

"*She turned furiously towards my friend (the Great Detective).*

" '*As for you,*' *she said, '*I hate you. Gur-r-r! See, I spit at you. Gur-r-r-r!*' "

In that way, the Great Detective gets his, though, of course, his impassive face never showed a sign. Spitting on him doesn't faze him. Then she turns to the Heroine and gives her what's coming to her.

" '*And you! Gur-r-r! I despise you, with your baby face! Gur-r-r! And now you think you will marry him! I laugh at you! Ha! Ha! Hahula!*' "

And after that she turns on the Nut and gives him some, and then some for Inspector Higginbottom, and thus with three "Gur-r-r's" for everybody and a "Ha! ha!" as a tiger, off she goes.

But, take it which way you will, the ending is never satisfactory. Not even the glad news that the Heroine sank into the Poor Nut's arms, never to leave them again, can relieve the situation. Not even the knowledge that they erected a handsome memorial to Sir Charles, or that the Great Detective played the saxophone for a week can quite compensate us.

from Laugh With Leacock

The Reluctant Specialist

Harry Symons

[A young business man who has been visiting a young doctor in a small Ontario city accepts his friend's invitation to sit in on his Saturday night office practice.]

As we took a proffered chair our position slowly dawned upon us. Here we were in a, yes, a doctor's private office. Undoubtedly some of those men and, yes, women would later be coming in. Then there would probably be discussions and — and diagnosis. Perhaps even — yes, perhaps even *examinations!* We shuddered and looked around. Sure enough there was a kind of operating table thing right beside us!

Doctor Pat was studying some notes as we timidly suggested that we needed some cigarettes. We told him that we'd just ramble out and get them around the corner, and then quietly wait for him in his car. Without looking up, the Doctor felt in one pocket, fished out a package and tossed them to us. "Sit right where you are, my boy. You won't be in the way at all. Nothing can happen in these things, y'know. It never does. So relax, and keep quiet. We'll be at home in an hour."

Nothing can happen? No? Well, we just wondered, that was all. A layman sitting in on medical interviews! The thing seemed to have possibilities to us. O well, we were young. We'd get over it, given time, no doubt.

Just then the prim nurse knocked and entered. She was precise and businesslike. The Doctor asked her some routine questions which she answered glibly. No, Doctor Philpots wasn't in yet. He was expected at any moment. But Miss Young, Miss Lee Young, was there. Yes, *she* was there. Had the Doctor seen her? Yes, thank you, he had. Well, she'd come long before everybody else. She hadn't had an appointment really. But she'd flounced and fussed so much that perhaps Doctor Spence would see her first. It probably wouldn't take very long. Her family was one of the — well, you know — the old pioneer strain, so to speak. And Miss

Young, Miss Lee Young, was the very *last* of that rare vintage, apparently! All of which the Doctor seemed to know.

Our heart fluttered as he looked at us. For one instant he paused and a questioning light gleamed in his eyes. "Ahem," he said "just show Miss Young in, will you please?"

We started to rise from our place. Doctor Spence, without a word, pointed to the chair we were leaving. At the same moment a rustle of skirts came from the doorway. We sank down, trembling. But the strange part of it was that the Doctor didn't introduce us to Miss Lee Young at all. No, sir! Both he and Miss Lee simply ignored us. Just as if we weren't in the same room. We were completely baffled by this intriguing form of medical etiquette. It was new to us. And it relieved our minds just to be expendable — like that.

Miss Young launched into her symptoms with unpleasant vehemence. To us they sounded dreadfully final. They all had to do with her stomach, evidently. And we wondered, after listening to her, that she lived even to tell the tale thus far. We wondered, too, if we sounded as gruesome and final to our own doctors when we discussed our illness details with them. Probably we did, only worse.

Doctor Pat sat quite solemnly throughout ten minutes of the steadiest discharge of lurid description we have ever had the misfortune of listening to in our time. He said no single word — and his face was as bland as that of any baby. Once or twice he nodded his head augustly, whilst he brought his separate fingertips together in that pontifical manner so abused by the clergy. In other words his bedside manner was perfect!

At the first break in the deluge, and just when Miss Young was winding up to break out in her second wind, the Doctor arose gently and raised one hand to command attention.

"Will you excuse me just for *one* moment, Miss Young? This is a most interesting case. I must have *all* the details, of course. Without them it would be useless to suggest treatment."

Miss Young was highly pleased by the Doctor's diplomatic interest, and nodded her head to his request that he interrupt for a moment. That was as it should be.

Somewhere we smelled a rat. We didn't know where — or how. And we didn't know what sort of a rat, either. But when Doctor Spence arose from his chair, and stepped calmly toward the door we had a dreadful feeling as of impending doom. There was a quiet, collected look about the Doctor's face which spoke volumes, if only we could have read it.

Just at the doorway, and with his hand already on the knob, Doctor Pat swung around casually. His face lighted up almost with ecstasy as he beamed upon us both.

"Miss Young, I have to be with my associate, Dr. Philpots, for just a moment or so, on *another* urgent matter. But before I go I would like to introduce to you an old colleague of mine from Boston. One of the world's great specialists in the complaint from which you seemingly suffer. My good friend, here, the brilliant Doctor Symons. It just so happens that he stayed over a train tonight on his way to Detroit, to have a friendly visit with me. I know he'll be happy to diagnose your case while I'm gone. You're *very* lucky, Miss Young. Doctor Symons is a very *real* expert in his own field!"

The next few minutes are still a trifle hazy in our mind. We remember we got up and bowed deeply the while Miss Young fluttered and nodded stiffly. We then sat down, with black murder in our hearts, coupled with the wish that the earth would open and enfold us. But it didn't, of course.

For a moment or so, while our heart-beat climbed slowly back to normal, we hemmed and hawed and cleared our throat, by which time our mind, such as it is, started to function once more. Our entire urge was to rush blindly from that room, fall upon Doctor Pat Spence and slowly choke him to death with our bare hands. Instead of which we gazed intently at Miss Young, cleared our throat again, and, in desperation, commenced asking of her the simplest rudimentary questions about this stomach of hers that, as a layman, we could conjure up.

"Did it work every day?"

Miss Lee Young fluttered indignantly, blushed, looked down — and shook her head. "Probably not quite. Did most people's?"

We looked at Miss Young in feigned amazement. "Why, Miss *Young*, of course they did! Hadn't she known?"

Miss Young lifted her gaze sadly from the floor.

"Did these pains occur in the upper or lower bowel, Miss Young? This was most important!"

In all the bowels, Miss Young thought. But which bowel was which?

"Well, when you were standing up then the upper was, of

course, the upper bowel. Whereas, when you were lying down, the lower was the — you understand?

"And there was discomfort in the lower right quadrant? Or was it the lower left? And, mostly, when?" (We remembered some doctor discussing stomachs that way. By quadrants. It had always had a rather nautical ring to it, we felt.)

Miss Lee Young fanned herself gently with her gloves, and her eyes took on a look of desperation, coupled with mild respect.

"I think," she murmured, "all quadrants, Doctor Symons. Each one in turn. Moving clockwise."

At those words from Miss Young, we relaxed completely. We felt we had reached safe ground. Miss Lee Young didn't even know what a quadrant was!

Ten minutes later Doctor Spence marched boldly in. His brown eyes twinkled mischievously.

"How have you two gotten along, Miss Young? And what does the Doctor, here, recommend?"

We rose gently but firmly and edged circumspectly toward the door. Doctor Pat paid no attention to us for the moment.

"Doctor Symons is *quite* certain it's epedidimus of the front, upper, left quadrant, Doctor. He feels you must operate at once. If not, infection will set in."

Miss Young, Miss Lee Young, paused, then with a gulp went on faintly. "I have faith in Doctor Symons' diagnosis, Doctor. My mind is *firmly* made up. Nothing will deter me. I will go straight to the hospital if you are *quite* ready, Doctor Spence!"

Silently we sped from the room without a by your leave.

Doctor Pat Spence set up practice in the States shortly afterward, and took to using these gauze masks behind which to do his laughing. He doesn't carry a little black bag any more. It's a brown one instead.

from   The Bored Meeting

Fischer Wins!

Ben Wicks

"Mr. Fischer does not take calls. You may leave your number."

I left my number. Five times. I was not the only person to leave a number.

In an effort to dissuade Bobby Fischer from withdrawing from his world title chess match against Boris Spassky, the White House had phoned to remind him of his patriotic duty. They might just as well have saved their dime.

"Mr. Fischer does not take calls. You may leave your number." Hardly elated at this news, Fischer's lawyer wailed, "This makes him harder to get on the phone than Chou En-lai."

I reminded Weekend Magazine of this fact.

"Maybe he doesn't like Nixon," said an editor helpfully.

I went after the story.

I stalked Robert James Fischer. I tracked him through the Catskills in upstate New York, furtively following his trail through the dense undergrowth of that wild, untamed region. Sometimes I lost sight of him, but always I was able to pick up his spoor again. Relentlessly I hunted Bobby Fischer and, like a man caught in a Knight fork at KB2, he never knew. I found him at Grossinger Hotel, having read in a newspaper that he was there.

I insinuated myself into the inner workings of this impenetrable hotel by renting a room. I developed contacts. I talked to the tennis pro, a lifeguard and a waiter. They said Bobby Fischer was a good tennis player, swimmer and eater. I struck it rich with the waiter when I said to him: "Boy, I'd sure like to meet the great Bobby Fischer." My cover, you see, was that of your ordinary star-struck hotel guest and this is the way you're supposed to talk when that's your cover.

So well did I play my part that the waiter agreed to seat me at Fischer's table that very night.

That very night I was sitting at a table that was supposed

to be the one at which Bobby Fischer would sit. Three elderly ladies were also sitting there. "And what do you do?" they asked me, in the manner they always ask that question in such dining rooms.

I was about to say that I was just an ordinary hotel guest but I realized that didn't sound right, so I said I was a travelling salesman. I sat there and played with my food and worried about whether Bobby Fischer would show. They talked to each other about their former husbands.

Halfway through dessert he arrived. Introductions were made. Before the ladies had a chance to ask Fischer what he did for a living, he had ordered fish, opened a book (Damen Gambit 1 by Rolf Schwarz) and sunk out of hearing. How could I open a conversation? I took a deep breath.

"Er, I have an advantage over you, Mr. Fischer. I, er, know who you are." He kept reading. "In fact, you're the reason I'm visiting Grossinger's." He turned a page.

"Hmm . . ."

At last. A breakthrough. I distinctly heard a sound. Throwing all caution to the wind, I let him have it between the eyes. "I'm a journalist!" I stuck the spoon in my dessert and began shovelling ice cream into a fluttering stomach. The conversation at the table came to an abrupt end as all eyes turned toward me. Slowly Damen Gambit was lowered to the table.

"You're a what?" whispered Fischer.

"A magazine writer . . . I'm here to do a story on you . . ."

As if to protect himself from some deadly snake, he whipped Damen Gambit up to his face.

The women began talking again. Having compared husbands they now spread their conversation to the merits of their various birthplaces.

"You were born in Chicago, weren't you Bobby?" I asked in my best one-big-happy-party voice.

"I'm not talking," he answered and retreated again behind the barricade of Mr. Schwarz.

The rest of the table excused themselves from our lively discussion and left.

"Do you play tennis?" I asked.

"Do you?" he asked back.

"Er, no . . . I play table tennis."

"Any good?"

"I can beat the hell out of you," I answered and smiled. He turned for the first time and looked at me.

"Who's the story for?"

I told him and asked if he'd like to play ping-pong.

"Just one game," he said. We left the dining room and found the ping-pong room.

"Your serve." He threw me the ball.

"Is your mother still living in England, Bob?"

"I won't answer that . . . 0-5, my serve."

"Ever play chess for fun?"

"Rarely . . . 8-2."

"Why do the Russians produce all the chess champions?"

"4-11 . . . your serve. Because they're subsidized."

"Any thoughts of marriage?"

"Won't answer that."

"Who's had the greatest chess influence on you?"

"Morphy . . . Paul . . . last century . . . 14-6 . . . my serve."

"How does the World Tournament work?"

"We play 24 games. One point for a win, half-point for a draw. As the challenger I have to make 12½ points. Get on with the game."

"Right, er, what's the score?"

"18-7."

"Are you at your peak?"

"Nowhere near."

"How do you compare yourself with Boris Spassky?"

Suddenly it was all there. A competitive animal waiting for the kill.

"Spassky!" he spat the word out. "I'm sick of being compared with him. What's Spassky like? How does he compare? I'll tell you how . . . he doesn't. He's not in my class and never will be." The ping-pong game ended. The interview ended. Only a chess match in Reykjavik still had to be played. But, in Bobby Fischer's mind, that too was already settled.

from Weekend Magazine

In the Malemute Saloon

Joan Walker

MY first Monday morning in Val d'Or dawned fine and bright. I talked myself out of getting up to breakfast with my office-bound husband quite easily. And in a perfectly logical manner. If anyone is looking for such an alibi for themselves they can have it for free. One bathroom — two people. Two into one won't go. This won't work out in the home, of course. One can potter around in a housecoat doing things to coffee percolators and toast while one's pride and joy shaves and showers, and take one's bath after he has left for work. But in an hotel room it works admirably.

Jim woke me up again when he left to tell me that he'd bring me up some coffee if I liked, or I could get breakfast in any of the umpteen cafés along the main drag when I finally got up. I said, "Ung," which he rightly interpreted as "Go away, darling, and don't bother me," and went back to sleep again.

Around ten I finally got up and bathed and dressed and hoisted myself onto a tall stool at the counter of a café a few doors up from the hotel, ordering orange juice, toast and coffee.

Faintly nourished by my breakfast, I went out into the street in search of my first project, a place to live. I called in a drug-store for a newspaper.

The man behind the counter wore a Stetson hat and an enormous cigar.

"The morning paper, please," I said, blinking slightly and wondering if a bad breakfast was giving me hallucinations.

"Which one?" the man asked as the cigar rolled and twitched.

I was delighted. I hadn't thought such a small town would have more than one.

"Which one carries the best apartment-vacant advertisements?" I asked.

There was a horrible silence. The drug-store man re-arranged a package of cough drops with meticulous care. He removed his hat and scratched a totally bald head. Then he said carefully, "The *Val d'Or Star* isn't out until Friday. We're sold out of last week's copy. I didn't know you meant a local paper. We have the Toronto and Montreal dailies. Only, of course, they're two days old."

I looked at him with horror. As a newspaperwoman I had breakfasted for years behind at least four morning papers, scanning the main items in each. I lunched behind the early editions of the evening papers, and read the final editions as and when they appeared.

"No daily paper," I said hollowly.

"No daily paper," he echoed. Then he added helpfully, "As a matter of fact, no apartments either."

This, I thought, had better turn out to be a joke. Anyway, I was used to people saying there were no apartments anywhere in the world since the war, but somehow I had always managed to find one. I said, "Where would I look for house agents, please? Are they on the main street?"

The drug-store man sighed. I could see I was rapidly becoming a bore.

"The house agent, singular," he told me, "is right across from here. But he won't have any apartments for rent. There hasn't been one vacant since 1941 when the apartment block was built and the tenants moved in before it was finished."

"*The* apartment block?" I asked weakly.

"The apartment block," he said. "There are a few apartments over the stores as well, but they are all owned and tenanted by the store owners. I guess you're new to the North country?"

I nodded, thanked him and crossed the street, looking the wrong way as usual and narrowly missing a truck. Having already been snatched from death a thousand times by passing pedestrians, I wondered once again what demented Englishman decided that our traffic should keep to the left while the traffic of the rest of the world kept to the right.

The house agent, who doubled as an insurance agent, stood an imposing four foot ten in his stockinged feet. He hastily shuffled his stockinged feet into a pair of slippers when I walked into his office and bid me a cheerful *"Bon jour."*

I said, "Good morning," out of sheer laziness. I speak, or thought I spoke until I came to Quebec, passable French, but in company with every Englishwoman worthy of the name I prefer to speak my own tongue if I possibly can. We are, lingually speaking, the laziest race under the sun without a doubt.

"Ha!" he said. "Eengleesh."

I thought this showed remarkable acumen on his part. After all, I had only spoken two words, and I didn't think my accent was showing. Later I discovered that in Canada, English means anyone who isn't French-Canadian.

I told him about my little project. I wished to rent an apartment for preference, but if that was impossible, a small house would do. I would even, if the worst came to the worst, take a furnished place for the time being.

It was of a difficulty unsurpassed, he said, but as it happened he had one, just one furnished apartment on his books. I was the lucky one, was I not?

He wrote the address down on a grimy scrap of paper and told me how to reach it — two blocks down and turn to the right, very simple. I shot out of the office like a bat from hell, not even bothering to ask the rent, and broke all records for the quarter-mile to get there.

The apartment was one flight up and I rapped on the door.

It was opened by an enormous woman in a flowered house-dress who entirely filled the hall. Only it wasn't the hall, it was the living-room. It was five feet wide by nine feet long and was furnished, apart from the proud owner, by a sofa and chair in a sort of nightmare Jacobean style with brightly varnished wood creeping in and out of red-and-green patterned plush, and about two thousand framed photographs of various people being married or taking first Communion.

The kitchen was roughly the size of Buckingham Palace and liberally sprinkled with rocking chairs, radios, washing machines, a dinette suite of chromium with bright-red leatherette trimming, and enough counter space to prepare a banquet for forty and still have room to lay out and embalm a few deceased relations if you were studying for a mortician's degree through the mail.

The bedroom consisted of a three-quarter double bed, a Habitant hooked rug and a statue of the Virgin Mary on a fret-wood bracket. There might have been room for a very thin child to undress in it, but that is open to doubt.

The owner, apparently taking my shocked silence for bemused joy, led me swiftly out of the front door and across the passage to a minute room in which was squashed a very small bath, a basin large enough to wash one hand at a time and the inevitable john.

"We share the bathroom with the apartment across the hall," she explained.

We went back into the living-room and I made rapid calculations. I could slip-cover the horrific suite and remove the photographs; maybe I could screen off half the kitchen to make a dining-room. It was horrible, but it was a roof over our heads, and although a shared bathroom made my flesh creep, the rent couldn't be very much.

I enquired.

"One hundred and fifty dollars a month," she said happily. "And you may have it for three months while we are away. Naturally, you will also have to buy the fuel for the furnace."

When I regained consciousness, I explained that the rent seemed a little — how should I put it? — high, no?

"High?" she asked. "High?" She patted the plush sofa. "With such beautiful and valuable furniture?"

I tottered, literally, back to the house agent.

"Do you know what they are asking for that — that boot-box?" I said. "One hundred and fifty, plus heating."

The house agent raised his eyebrows.

"It is possible they accept one hundred and twenty-five," he suggested.

"Not from me, they don't," I told him. "Why, the only room in the whole apartment in which you can turn around is the kitchen. Let us not take leave of our senses."

He circled his thumb and forefinger in the air.

"Ah!" he said. "The kitchen. The room dear to a woman's heart. In which she spends all her time. Such a beautiful kitchen."

"Not me," I said, losing my grammar in the excitement of the moment, "I couldn't care less about the kitchen. But do you mean to tell me you think one hundred and fifty is reasonable for that rat-hole?"

"In Val d'Or, yes," he said. "This town is booming. People make their fortunes here."

"Not at my expense," I said brutally. "It can do its booming without me. Now what else have you got?"

He gave a Gallic shrug.

"Nothing," he said. "Nothing at all. That is the first apartment I have had for rent since I have been here, since 1937.

People they come to Val d'Or, they buy a lot and they build. That is the way it goes. Now I have some nice lots for sale. Yes?"

"No."

"You have not been married long, yes?" He went on. "I am right, no?" I nodded absent-mindedly. "Then the life insurance your husband does not have? I call upon him."

"No," I said hastily. "No life insurance to-day, thank you." I backed out and went back to the hotel.

I sat on the edge of the bed, unmade, although it was a quarter to twelve, and stared at the sign on the door giving the price of the room as $3.00 single, $4.50 double. For this sum one had a bed with the aforementioned mattress stuffed with rocks, an uncarpeted floor, a dressing-chest with one leg missing, propped up on a Bible donated by the Gideon Society, a bare-topped, unstained table and two kitchen-type chairs and, the only joy, a private bathroom. Although the bath was so small that even I, height five foot three and a half, had to wear my knees under my chin when in it.

Suddenly the penny dropped and I multiplied $4.50 by the days in the month. Mathematics have never been my strong point, and after reaching totals of $1,350.00 and $13.50 respectively and discarding them hastily, the awful truth finally dawned upon me that to live here would cost us $135.00 per month, plus our food, which at Val d'Or prices, even eating at "greasy spoons" all the time, would total another six dollars a day at least for the two of us. Add on cigarettes, and we both smoke fairly heavily, the odd show and bottle of beer, and you have a grand total of four hundred bucks a month. Which wasn't even remotely funny. Especially as Jim didn't earn that much.

I lit a cigarette and thought how lucky it was I was a working woman. Next port of call was quite obviously the local weekly newspaper. In Fleet Street the lowest wage the journalists' union allowed for a cub reporter was £9. 9s. a week, and I was hardly a cub reporter. I should be worth a couple of hundred a month to booming Val d'Or and for that I was prepared to do everything; report, re-write, make up the pages, proof-read, and even rustle up the occasional advertisement and write the copy for the advertiser, too.

When Jim came back for lunch I was still scribbling on the back of envelopes.

"What you doing?" Jim asked.

"Facing the facts of life," I said. "Do you realise what it's costing us to live in this apology for an hotel?"

Jim picked up the envelope.

"Dear God!" he said. "What's this $1,350.00?"

"No, no," I told him. "That's a mistake."

"I hope!" he said quickly. "No luck with the apartment?"

I told him the whole sorry story.

"I thought as much," he said. "Matter of fact, I ran an advertisement in the local paper for a month before you came over, asking for an apartment. Not one single reply."

"It wouldn't be cheaper to take that horrible fox-hole at a hundred and twenty-five and eat at home, I suppose?"

Jim thought for a moment. He is the sort of genius who can do sums in his head, and what's more, sums that come out right. I am always lost in admiration.

"No," he said, "not with fuel on top, and electricity and telephone. Over a long period maybe, but not for three months. Besides, how do we know you can cook?"

He certainly had something there.

"Then a cheaper hotel?" I suggested, wincing slightly at the thought. This one seemed bad enough.

"Not unless you like bed bugs," Jim said.

"Well, what do people *do*?" I asked.

Jim shrugged.

"They run up a shack in their free time or live in a room in a private house. Most companies, C.I.L. and that sort, build houses for their managers and rent 'em cheaply."

"But not our company?"

"Not our company," Jim said. "Come on, let's eat."

After lunch — chicken noodle soup, purely a courtesy title; the nearest that soup ever got to a chicken may have been that someone dipped a bird in and out of lukewarm water and added aunty's knitting; an egg sandwich and cool coffee, price eighty-five cents — I toured the drug stores until I ran to earth a copy of the local weekly newspaper.

After all, I thought it advisable to take a cursory glance at the thing first rather than to burst into the edior's office saying, "Lafayette, I am here!"

Not having the advantage of built-in over-stuffed cushions on my rear end, I decided that the foyer of the hotel, with its comfortable leather armchairs, would be more to my taste than the kitchen variety in my bedroom, so I settled myself down with cigarettes and the newspaper.

The lounge was on the dreary side. Brown armchairs, a potted rubber plant, a malignant and moth-eaten moose head on the wall and a series of brass objects on the floor that looked almost exactly like chamber pots. I puzzled over these for a few moments and then decided that, since they clearly could not be what they appeared to be, they must be ash trays, so I hooked the nearest towards me with my foot and flicked ash into it from time to time.

Minutes later I discovered my mistake when the man in the next chair leaned slightly to starboard and sent a stream of spittle expertly over my lap into the "ash tray." It landed with a startling clang. I was utterly entranced. As a child, when an occasion called for a spit I had always aimed for distance, never for any degree of accuracy, and I was seized with an almost overwhelming desire to try my luck. Only the thought of the possible disgrace and con-demnation that would transpire should the wife of the manager of a finance corporation be found spitting in the public lounge of an hotel stopped me.

I brooded for a while on the deficiencies of my education. That one could reach years of discretion without recognising a cuspidor seemed incredible. Happily, I didn't realise then to just what extent my education had been lacking in various other respects.

I thumbed my way through the *Val d'Or Star* and giggled to myself. The journalistic style had to be seen to be believed. All fires were conflagrations. Local ladies did not pour tea, they "presided at the urns." And the culminating glory was a report of a child who had died of pneumonia the week before, which started: "Death stretched out his icy hand and laid a finger upon a tiny tot in this community Tuesday . . ."

It was too good to be true. I rolled my copy up and pasted paper around it and mailed it forthwith to my ex-editor in London, where, I am told, it was received with loud cries of joy and pursued a more and more tattered course around the pubs and clubs of Fleet Street, gathering fame as it went, until it finally disintegrated.

At any rate, there was plenty of scope for my talents here. I just couldn't miss. . . .

from Pardon My Parka

They Know when a Man Answers

Eric Nicol

I am learning to use the telephone. Although I am only forty-six years old, I have mastered the technique of telephone answering. Yes, sir, it's claphands time at our house.

Until only a few weeks ago, the way I answered the phone was to pick up the receiver — after the phone had rung, or at least after I had heard *some* kind of ringing in my ears — and say: "Hullo?" It has taken all these years for me to realize that "Hullo?" is not an intelligent noise to make into a telephone. Beyond the fact that something animate has picked up the receiver and whoofed into it, "Hullo?" does not convey much information. The operator or secretary on the other end has to follow up with:

"May I speak to Mr. Eric Nicol, please?"

"Yes," I say.

"Is that Mr. Nicol?"

"Speaking."

"One moment, please."

All this has taken time, especially my time. It loses man-hours, thousands of them over a lifetime, assuming you live to be a couple of hundred. "Hullo?" is not efficient. In this world, I told myself, the difference between success and failure can be measured in the seconds lost to empty hallooing. Look what happened to John Peel.

So, in a brilliant flash, I hit upon the idea of answering the phone with: "Nicol here." Identification. Affirmation. Decisiveness. The Scotland Yard image. Chief Inspector Nicol, pipe in hand, responding with the succinctness typical of his splendidly organized brain.

Aside from one or two callers who misheard my "Nicol here" as the operator's asking them to deposit another coin — I have lowered my voice an octave to forestall this confusion — the new system has worked well. I am receiving a new deference from secretaries. Some callers, rather than engage further with what is clearly a steel trap of a mind, hang up without uttering another word. As I said with some satisfaction to my wife:

"They know when a *man* answers."

My wife nodded appreciatively.

The only flaw in my new telephone-answering gambit is that people call me at the wrong times. When you have run to the phone from the bottom of the garden, or have your mouth full of banana bread, much of the crispness is lost. All of my three children can, and do, beat me to the phone unless I am actually sitting on it. And it is difficult to sound like the Chief Inspector after one of your little ones has informed the caller: "Daddy's gone to the bathroom." I might as well revert to "Hullo?"

I have tried to persuade my wife and children to answer the phone with: "This is the Nicol residence." This would pave the way nicely for my brisk, executive "Nicol here." But it is hopeless to expect a woman, be she maid or matron, to reply to a phone call with other than "Hullo?" How else can she encourage the wrong number? My wife has longer chats with wrong numbers than I do with people I've known all my life.

But as a man's man, I am sticking with "Nicol here" and the heck with any dark brown voices who were expecting maybe Clancy. I feel encouraged to move on to the next phase: learning how to *place* phone calls efficiently. This will take a sight more figuring, I know, and I should live so long.

from Still A Nicol

from The Luck of Ginger Coffey

Brian Moore

. . . Coffey was hungry. He ate his sausages and helped himself to more gravy and potatoes. Fork halfway to his mouth, he noticed her standing in the door, her face pale, her eyes bright. Still in a rage. He put the forkful in his mouth and winked at her.

"How much *do* we have left?" she said.

He smiled, gesturing that his mouth was full.

"Answer me. The truth, mind."

Eighty and fourteen — well, make it an even — "About a hundred dollars," he said.

"Oh my God!" She went away.

He finished the spuds and wiped his plate with a bit of bread. What did Vera know about money anyway? An only child, brought up by a doting mother, pretty, with plenty of beaux, until she met and married him. And, even so, in all those years of marriage, the Army years, the years at Kylemore and in Cork, had she ever bloody starved? Had she? Give him credit for something. And remember, Vera, you married me for better or for worse. This is the worse. Ah, but supposing she won't put up with the worse?

Now that was nonsense. She loved him in her way and despite her temper. And she had Paulie. He could hear the two of them talking now in the living room. Paulie, home from her dance practice, had gone straight in to see Vera. And, as usual, not even hello for Daddy. They were like sisters, those two, always gossiping away about womany wee things he knew nothing about.

There was the phone. He got up to answer, because Vera hated the phone.

"Ginger?" It was Gerry Grosvenor. "Listen, how would you react to a hundred and ten a week?"

"Get away with you!"

"No, seriously, there's a job going as deskman on the *Trib-*

une. And the Managing Editor happens to be a friend of mine."

"Deskman?" Coffey said. "But Gerry lad, what's that? What does a deskman do? Make desks?"

"Copy editor," Grosvenor said. "Easy. This is on the international desk, all wire copy, very clean. It's just writing heads and putting in punctuation. Nothing to it."

"But I have no experience on a newspaper. I never wrote a headline in my life."

"Never mind that. Would you take the job?"

"Would a duck swim!"

"Okay. Wait. I'll call you back."

Coffey replaced the receiver and looked down the long railroad corridor hallway. Total silence from the living room, which meant she and Paulie had been listening. So he went in. "Hello, Apple," he said to Paulie. "Had a good day in school?"

"Was that Gerry?" Veronica asked in an angry voice.

"Yes, dear. He says he can get me a job. Hundred and ten dollars a week to start."

"What job?"

"On the *Tribune.* It's an editing job. I pointed out that I'd no experience, but he said not to worry."

"I'd worry," Veronica said, "if I were you. This isn't acting the glorified office boy, or playing poker and drinking pints in barracks."

He gave her a look intended to turn her into Lot's wife there on the sofa. Imagine saying that in front of Paulie!

"Go and have your supper, Apple," he told Paulie. He waited as, unwillingly, Paulie trailed out of the room. "Now, why did you say that in front of the child, Vera?"

"She might as well know."

"Know what?"

"What sort of a selfish brute she has for a father."

Suffering J! No sense talking, was there? He went out and, while he was in the bathroom, the phone rang again. He hurried up the corridor.

"Yes," she said to the phone. "Yes — wait, I want to explain something. I mean apropos of this afternoon. Ginger doesn't *have* our passage money home. He spent it.... Yes.... So that leaves me no choice, does it? ... Yes ... yes, here's Ginger. I'll let you tell him yourself."

"Ginger?" Gerry's voice said. "It's all set. I've given you

a good build-up and old MacGregor wants to see you in his office at three tomorrow afternoon."

"Thanks a million, Gerry. But what did you tell him?"

"I told him you'd worked on a Dublin newspaper for two years and said, after that, you'd been a press officer in the Army, and then that you were a good public relations man for Irish whiskey out here. It sounded good, believe me."

"But, Holy God!" Coffey said. "It's not true. I never worked on a newspaper."

At the other end of the line there was a Remembrance Day hush. Then Grosvenor said: "Ginger, the point is, do you want this job or don't you?"

"Of course I do, but —"

"But nothing. Everybody bullshits out here. Every employer expects it. The point is to get in. After that, doing the job is up to you."

"But maybe I can't do it," Coffey said.

"Beggars can't be choosers," said Vera's voice. She reached out, took the receiver from him and said: "Thanks, Gerry, you're an angel. Thanks very much. . . . Yes. . . . Yes, I know. . . . Good night." She replaced the receiver, turned away, walked down the hall and went into their bedroom. He followed her but she shut the door. When he tried the door, it was locked.

"Vera? I want to talk to you?". . .

On the fourth floor of the *Tribune*, the night's business was just beginning. Under fluorescent lights, lit all year round, a few reporters studied the afternoon papers. A police radio blared routine calls in a corner and in the nearby teletype room a jammed machine tintinnabulated incessantly, calling for attention. In the centre slot of a large horseshoe desk a fat man in a woollen cardigan sliced open the afternoon's crop of wire-service photographs. He looked up as Coffey approached. "Yes?"

"May I speak to Mr. MacGregor, please?"

"Boy! Take this man to Mr. Mac."

An indolent adolescent shoved a rubber cylinder down a communications tube, then hooked a beckoning finger. Across the City Room he led and down a corridor to a partitioned-off office on the opened door of which a small brass plaque announced MANAGING EDITOR. The boy pointed to the plaque, then went away, wordless. Inside, Coffey saw three young men in shirt sleeves looking over the shoulders of an old man who was seated at a large, scarred desk. He was a thin old man with a pale, bony face, a pumping blue vein in his forehead and eyebrows thick and crumbling as cigar ash. His voice, a Low Church Scottish rumble, could be heard clearly in the corridor. For once, Coffey was not comforted by the fact that he faced an older man.

"Dorrothy Dix? Where's Dorrothy Dix?"

"Here, Mr. Mac."

"O.K. Now, where's the funnies?"

"Here, Mr. Mac."

"Make sure that Blondie is up top and then Mutt and Jeff and *then* Moon Mullins. *Not* Rex Morrgan, M.D. Some bleddy rascal in the composing room changed the order in the Early last night."

"Right, Mr. Mac."

"O.K. Now, away with ye."

The three young men clutched up page proofs and galleys and rushed out, jostling Coffey in the doorway. For the love of J, how was he going to tell this sulphur-breathing Scottish Beelzebub that he was an experienced sub-editor? Grosvenor must be daft.

The old man spiked a scrap of paper, like Calvin downing sin. His eye picked out Coffey in the doorway.

"Come in. State your business."

"My — my name is Coffey. I believe Gerry Grosvenor spoke to you about me?"

"Grrosvenor? Och, aye, the cartoonist. Come in, come in, sit you down. Where's my notes? Aye, here we are. Deskman, aren't you?"

"Yes, sir."

"What paper did you work for in the Old Country?"

Confidence, Grosvenor had said. The time and tide that leads on to fortune. One good lie and — But as Coffey opened his mouth he was taken with a sort of aphasia. The old man waited, becoming suspicious. "I — ah — I worked on the *Irish Times*, sir."

"*Times*, eh? Good paper."

"Yes. Yes, isn't it?"

"Grrosvenor said you were in the Army?"

"Yes, sir."

"Officer, weren't you? Serve overseas?"

"I — I was in the Irish Army, sir. We were neutral during the war."

"Indeed?"

"I — I was press officer in the Irish Army," Coffey added, trying to correct the hostility in that "Indeed?"

"Press officer," the old man said. "Trying to keep the facts from the public, that is the services' job. However, I need a man who has some knowledge of wurrld events. Most Canadians have none. How about you?"

"I — ah — I try to keep up, sir."

"Grrosvenor tells me you were a publicity man for a whussky company?"

"Yes, sir."

"Scotch whussky?"

"No, sir. Irish."

"No wonder you're out of a job, then. Did you wurrk on the foreign desk at the *Times*?"

"Yes, sir. Ah — part-time."

"What do you mean, part-time?"

"Well, ah — summer holidays and so on. Filling in."

The old man nodded and consulted his notes again. Coffey fingered his moustache. A good touch that summer holidays. He was pleased with himself for thinking of it.

"When was it you wurrked for the *Times*?"

"Oh — after I got out of the Army. About — ah — six years ago."

"How long did you wurrk there?"

"About" — what had Grosvenor said? — "about eighteen months."

"I see." The old man picked up one of the phones on his desk. "Give me Fanshaw," he said. "Ted? When you were in Dublin, did you ever hear of a subbie on the *Times* by the name of Coffey? ... Aye, about five years ago. ... Hold on." He covered the mouthpiece and turned to Coffey. "What was the name of the foreign editor?"

Coffey sat, his eyes on his little green hat.

"Well?"

He raised his eyes and read a title on the bookshelf behind MacGregor. *Holy Bible.*

"Right, Ted," the old man told the telephone. "Disna'

matter." He put the phone down and glowered at Coffey under the crumbling ash of his eyebrows. "If you'd been a Scot," he said. "You'd have come in here wi' references in your hand. But you carry nothing besides your hat and a lot of cheek. Och, aye. You may fool the likes of Gerry Grrosvenor, but there isn't an Irishman born that I'd trust to pull the wuul o'er *my* eyes!"

Coffey, his face hot, stood up and put his hat on.

"Where are you going?" MacGregor said.

"I'm sorry I took up your ti—"

"Sit down! Are you hard up for a job? Tell me the truth."

"Yes, sir."

"O.K. Can you spell? Spell me parallel."

Coffey spelled.

"Correct. Are you married?"

"Yes, sir."

"Children?"

"One daughter, sir."

"*Hmm.* . . . Have you a vice?"

"Advice, sir?"

"Are you deaf? I mean, have you a weakness? Booze or horses or wimmin? Own up now, for I'll find out, anyway."

"No, sir."

"O.K. You say ye've been a P.R. That may be. But what a P.R. knows about the wurrkings of a newspaper could be written twice over on the back of a tomtit's arse and still leave room for the Lorrd's Prayer. So you'd best start at the bottom. Do you agree?"

Coffey took a deep breath. He was too old to start at the bottom.

"Well? Don't stand there gawking."

"Well, sir, it depends. I'm not a boy of twenty."

"I'm proposing to start you off in the proofroom," the old man said. "So that you can acquaint yourself with the rudiments of our style. That's the best training there is."

"A — a p-p-proofreader, did you say, sir?"

"I did. My readers are not unionized, thank the Lord. And I happen to be shorthanded there at the moment. If you wurrk well, I might try you out on the floor as a reporter. You might even wind up as a deskman if you play your cards right. What do you say?"

"Well I — I'd have to think about that, sir. How much — how much would that pay?"

"Fifty dollars a week, which is more than you're wurrth. Start at six tonight. Go and think it over now, but let me know no later than half-past four, if you want the job."

"Thank you — "

"Clarence?" Mr. MacGregor shouted. "Where's Clarence?"

A fat man rushed in, notebook at the ready.

"What's the last two paras of Norrman Vincent Peale doing in the overset, Clarence?"

"Don't know, Mr. Mac."

"Bleddy well find out, then."

The fat man rushed out. Mr. MacGregor spiked another galley. "All right, Coffey. Good day to you."

Coffey went away. Fifty dollars a week, reading galleys. A galley slave . . . He passed along a corridor lined with rolls of newsprint, wandered across the wide desert of the city room and out past the brass plaque to the elevator. The red light flashed above the elevator door. Going down. Down, down, all his high hopes failed; with Veronica waiting below, Veronica who wanted to know that the bad days were over, that they could move to a better place . . .

"Ground floor," the elevator man said. "Ground floor. Out."

There she was under the big clock, the nervous beginnings of a smile on her face. Poor Kitten, it was not fair to her, not fair at all, she'd be in such a state —

Maybe, through Gerry Grosvenor, maybe he might just manage? Maybe. And so, he went towards her, his mind made up. Don't tell her now. Smile instead, be the jolly Ginger she used to love. He kissed her, squeezed her and said: "Steady as she goes."

"Did you get it, Ginger?"

"I did, indeed."

"Oh, thank God."

"Now, now," he said. "What's that? Sniffles? Come on, come on, it's laughing you should be. Listen — let's — let's go and have a cup of tea. How would you like to sail into the Ritz, just like the old days?"

"Oh, Ginger, I'm so glad for you."

"Glad for *me?* And aren't you glad for yourself, Kitten?

Ah, it's going to be super. Just super. Come on now. We'll take a taxi."

"But we can't afford it, Ginger."

"Come on, come on," he said, out in the street now, signaling a cab. "Let me be the judge of that. In with you. Driver? The Ritz-Carlton Hotel, on the double!"

from Nursery Rhymes to Be Read Aloud by Young Parents with Old Children

George Bain

The Beaver's teeth grow constantly to compensate for wear and tear. If a Beaver stopped chewing trees for a couple of weeks and its teeth kept growing, it could be in real trouble. That may explain the Beaver's having got a reputation for being busy. It's not that the Beaver is so industrious but that it has to stay ahead of its teeth.

The Beaver's nose and ears are protected by watertight valves. The lips are so loose that the Beaver can hold a branch in its mouth and have enough lip left over to form a watertight seal around it. This presents rather an unappetizing picture, but there you have it.

The second toe of the Beaver's hind foot is cleft and it uses this to comb its pelt. If the child wants to know which foot, tell him it depends on whether it's a left-footed or a right-footed Beaver.

Beavers were very much in vogue at the time when all gentlemen wore beaver hats. The Beaver was glad when *that* craze died out.

The Beaver is Canada's National Animal. It was chosen

because it keeps busy and because it remains true to one mate, traits which also characterize Canadians.

The Beaver isn't as smart as it is sometimes made out to be. When the Beaver chews through a tree, the tree sometimes falls on the Beaver, mashing it into the ground. Not much is said about this in Canada.

Beavers breed in midwinter when life isn't just one damn tree after another.

> The Beaver lives in ponds and streams
> And hews to quite ambitious schemes,
> He picks his trees and chews them through
> And drops them where he wants to do
> And when the pile's the proper height
> He makes the structure watertight
> By filling it with mud and sand
> And sticks and stones and what's to hand
> And there he lives, preserved from harm,
> His lodge is padded, snug and warm,
> And what is more, one ought to note,
> He lives there in a beaver coat.

The only Fox that climbs trees is the Gray Fox.

Foxes are just about as clever as they're supposed to be, especially the Arctic Fox.

An eighteenth-century Danish naturalist shipwrecked in the Arctic said about Arctic Foxes, "They knew in such an unbelievably cunning way how to roll off a weight of several poods from our provision caches and to steal the meat from thence that at first we could hardly ascribe it to them."

As an anecdote that admittedly leaves something to be desired, but if it doesn't help the nippers to go shutty-byes, there's nothing left but Nembutal.

If they ask, "Daddy, what is a pood?" reply smartly, "A pood is 36.113 pounds." This sort of answer is guaranteed to enhance your standing no end. If you really want to score one up, the thing to do is to say, "Do you mean the pood avoirdupois or the Russian pood?" The Russian pood is 40 pounds.

The Red Fox is a very good father. It hunts for the family, guards the den, uses various stratagems to divert predators whenever they appear, and in general is an all-round Dad.

Vulpes vulgaris (Common Fox)
Endures a life of frequent shocks;
If, pointy-nosed, he dares to snoop
Around some farmer's chicken coop
He makes, he knows, his bushy tail
The target for a leaden hail
And in the fields where he was born
He walks alert to hear the horn
Foretelling huntsmen, horses, hounds,
On hearing which, he mutters, "Zounds!
Here come the so-and-so's again
— I'd like *their* place just now and then."

The Common Man

Joseph Schull

Lyon's Corner House, Piccadilly.
The restaurant of the Common Man. The stranger with the moustache and the flat Canadian voice grinned at me across the table as the waitress set down his aromatic order. "Kippers. These people over here don't appreciate their blessings."

"They haven't many of them at the moment."

"Maybe not. But take herrings, for instance. You have to live fifteen hundred miles from the sea to really appreciate them."

"Indeed?"

"When I was a boy I lived out in Saskatchewan. With my grandfather. He had a grocery store."

"Did he keep herrings?"

"Never without 'em. First week of every month a big barrel of pickled herrings came from Nova Scotia. Stood five feet high, three feet across. Herrings in brine. We used to lift 'em out with a big steel hook.

"The barrel was sort of a focal point in the store. Customers would draw up boxes and chairs around it to sit and chat. Nights when Grampa was down at the pool hall or a lodge meeting I used to get some of the kids in and we'd use the barrel for a stage — put a board across it and stand on our heads; pretend we were pirates walking the plank. It had a lot of uses. First thoughts I ever had on politics came out of that herring barrel."

The big man clawed expertly at his kipper; looked up, grinning reminiscently; returned his attention to his plate.

"Used to be a little no-good Peter Binney around the town. Divided his time between the pool hall, the jail and a little shack he lived in down by the creek. Bit of a campaigner for the rights of man when he was drunk. Had a beard and eyes like a prophet just out of the wilderness. Might have been anywhere between fifty and a hundred, and maybe took a bath every birthday. Anyway, Peter was mighty fond of herrings and never had any money to buy 'em.

"Gramp was a tough old conservative and he had no particular use for Peter. But the two of 'em — along with the loafers who were always hanging round the store — sort of worked out an arrangement. Toward the last of the month Peter would come in and go over to the herring barrel. There wouldn't be anything in it by then but a lot of brine and a couple of herrings at the bottom. And somehow the herring hook could never be found. I think Peter always suspected Grampa of hiding it, but he never said anything.

"He'd just look in the barrel, look over at Grampa, and Grampa would nod. Everybody in the store would grin and edge over toward the barrel; Peter would take off his cap and coat and roll up what was left of his shirt sleeves. Then he'd climb up on the edge of the barrel and dive down into the brine. He'd come up with his hair in his eyes, his beard streaming salt water and fish flakes, and the last two or three herrings in his hand. Everybody thought it was a great show. Grampa'd give him a paper bag for the herrings; Peter would grin around the circle of us and walk out dripping like a mermaid and smelling to heaven.

"Even as a kid I remember thinking Grampa demanded too much entertainment for a couple of herrings.

"Peter came in one day when I disapproved of Grampa more than usual. The day before had been my birthday and I'd wanted a rifle. Grampa had given me an old silver watch of his father's; which was my idea of no present at all. I'd sulked all day and when Grampa went out at night some of my pals and I had staged a bigger circus than usual, complete with headstands, handstands and fights. In the morning, not only was the store a shambles, but I'd lost the watch; and I got a first class whopping. By the time Grampa and the customers saw Peter Binney coming and hid the herring hook I was in a very radical mood.

"Peter and Grampa went through their usual performance. Peter could have the herrings that were left, but nobody knew where the hook was. I figured I'd get back at Grampa for the licking; and I made signs to Peter behind his back, pointing to the place under the counter where the hook was hidden. Peter got the idea, gave me a grateful smirk and started to go for it. Then he looked round the circle watching him and stopped. I guess he figured that if he didn't put on his usual show there might come a time when Grampa'd have no herrings for him.

"He turned back to the barrel, stripped off his surplus clothes and dived in. Came up with three herrings the first time and dropped 'em into his paper bag. Then he made another dive; fumbled around for a long while and came up wetter and dirtier than usual. He shook his head; no more fish. Everybody in the store except me was laughing at him as he worked into his coat, picked up his paper bag and walked out, leaving a trail of brine. Gramp was rumbling and shaking with chuckles. It was then I realized that he was a tight-fisted capitalist, callous and indifferent to the needs of the common man. You might call it the moment of my conversion.

"I don't know how Peter guessed it, though. I was surprised next day when he sneaked up to me on the street and dragged me down an alley with him. 'Hey, Johnny,' he said, 'Got something for you.'

"He stuck his hand in his pocket and pulled out a crumpled-up five dollar bill. 'Found a watch in the bottom of that barrel. Walked over to Millville and sold it for five dollars. Here's the money. Want you to have it because you ain't like the rest of 'em. Don't tell your grampa.'"

The big man looked up from the last of his kipper and smiled dreamily. I smiled back. "It shows the quality of the common man, all right."

"Yeah," he sighed contentedly. "So did the rest of it. I was over in Millville a month later and found out he'd got ten dollars for that watch. Always felt more comfortable with old Peter after that. Fifty-fifty. That's the Common Man."

from Saturday Night

from And Now . . . Here's Max

Max Ferguson

. . . Doug Trowell was funny, alright . . . there was no denying that. I could enjoy more laughs in one minute from Doug Trowell than I could in a lifetime of Bob Hope, Red Skelton, and Danny Kaye combined. The only problem was that around CFPL that summer there was no legally authorized outlet for Doug's brilliant impromptu flights of comic invention. Consequently, when the mood was upon him, he had the habit of heading lemming-like for the nearest studio and, regardless of what program was in progress, he would burst in upon the poor devils trying to do their job and utterly devastate them and the program.

One of his characterizations was an old salt whom he called Scott C. Mulsion. He got the idea from the label of those codliver oil bottles whose labels always carried the picture of a grizzled old chap in oilskins and a sou'wester, bent double under the weight of a huge codfish which he had slung over his back. I can well remember standing around the microphone with three other actors in Studio B, partway through a dramatic sketch, when the door of the studio flew open and in came Doug Trowell, a battered fedora on his head with the brim pulled down all the way 'round to suggest a sou'wester. His hands gripped an imaginary fishline, and he was bent double under the weight of a huge, non-existent cod slung over his back. To make matters worse, whenever he was Scott C. Mulsion, Doug always spoke in that crazy, sub-human voice which I later blatantly stole and used for the loud-mouthed character on my Rawhide program. He fixed us with a wild stare for several agonizing seconds, while we desperately tried to ignore him and carry on in the character roles we were portraying.

Then came that awful voice. "I'se Scott C. Mulsion. Man and boy, dere, I'se carried dis here codfish on me back for over forty years, and I'se worth ten of any of youse, dere. What are yez all doin' dere sayin' all dem crazy things into dat microphone? What are yez talkin' in dem crazy voices for? What's wrong wid your real voices? I know all of yez, and I'm sick of your tom-foollery. Yes, I mean you, Roy Kervin and Max Ferguson, and Keith Chase!"

At this point, while we tried vainly to hold onto our character voices in the play, good old Scott C. Mulsion named every one of us by our real names, the ones by which we were pretty well known around London. For actors even of our humble status, this was something akin to being stripped naked at the corner of Bloor and Yonge. He then staggered to the studio door, turned to emit three raucous but incredibly realistic seagull cries, and vanished, leaving us in the ruins of our play, hopelessly trying to win back the listeners' "willing suspension of disbelief."

CFPL's most prestigious program that summer was a nine o'clock morning newscast sponsored by the London branch of one of Canada's foremost department store chains. This dandy little money earner was held in such high esteem by management that it was never entrusted to just one announcer. It was always a two-man job. CFPL's chief announcer, John Trethewey (now with the CBC's Montreal outlet) handled the principal duties, and my first "big-time" break came when I was appointed second announcer. In this role, sharp on the dot of nine each morning, I would shout into the microphone in an embryo Marvin Mellobell voice, "Headlines of Your World Today ! ! !"

Then, seated next to me at his microphone, John Trethewey, in a much more mature and authoritative voice, would read out three dramatic world headlines.

While he rested from the effort, I leaped in again with, "In a moment, the details of these stories, but first —" At this juncture, London matrons enjoying their second cup of coffee by their radios would learn what delights awaited them that morning at our sponsor's store in the way of panties, half slips, or nursing brassieres. After one minute the ladies and I would return from our jaunt to Nirvana, and Trethewey would continue on prosaically with the main body of the news. From all this you can certainly see that the Huntley-Brinkley idea is not a new one.

One morning in mid-August, the above-outlined format had rolled on with all the smoothness of a Rolls engine, and Trethewey was just nearing the end of his news. With less than two minutes to go he launched into a news item that recalled that this very morning was the anniversary of the death of Jumbo, the gargantuan Barnum and Bailey elephant who had been killed many years before while crossing the railway tracks at St. Thomas, Ontario, about eighteen miles from London. John had just reached the line, ". . . and was carried off by an untimely death as he lumbered across the tracks at St. Thomas into the path of a through train in the year . . . ." There was a momentary pause, a hesitance over the date.

I had been sitting rather inattentively up to this point, probably planning how much candy I'd be able to buy with my twenty-five dollars that week, when I suddenly realized that John's voice had ground to a halt. Shooting a quick glance across at the news copy that was lying on the table in front of him, I soon spotted the reason the cat had his tongue. In place of the date of Jumbo's death on the yellow news copy were two asterisks, a comma, and a capital N. Teletype machines have a habit of doing this whenever, due to atmospheric conditions, their clever little metal fingers became all thumbs. Since Trethewey was in the habit of visiting the teletype machines at about two minutes to air time and ripping off huge fistfuls of news, he hadn't been able to read it over carefully and foresee this trap he'd now fallen into. However, to his credit, he was nonplussed for only a second or two. Even back in those days he'd been in the business long enough to have learned the announcers' credo, "Fake it and forge on!" Completely at random, he pulled the date, 1900, out of the air, and confident that no-one had noticed his momentary dilemma continued smoothly on.

To this day I don't know how Doug Trowell reacted so quickly. Of course, he was always lurking outside studio doors, waiting hopefully. I think he must have had an anticipatory sixth sense that could spot moments of on-air distress even before they occurred. Whenever he felt that tiny telepathic tug on the finely spun silk of his maliciously inventive mind, he never failed to pounce. At any rate, there he was within three seconds of Trethewey's hesitation over the date of Jumbo's death, lumbering through the studio door. He had removed his suitcoat and thrown it over his head, so that one empty sleeve hung down in front and was swinging to and fro like an elephant's trunk. He stopped a foot or two inside the studio and emitted one or two muffled stentorian grunts from underneath the coat. Fortunately Trethewey hadn't seen or heard him yet, and I was far enough to one side that my convulsive heavings of desperately stifled laughter weren't visible to the golden voice of our biggest commercial account. I clung to the hope that Trowell, satisfied with the reaction he was getting from me, would now abandon his little charade and withdraw. Trowell, however, was just warming up.

He began to lumber slowly around the studio, the empty sleeve swinging back and forth in front of him, until he came up immediately behind Trethewey, who was still rolling on with all the confidence in the world, telling listeners how big a void had been left in the hearts of all who had seen and loved old Jumbo. Trethewey never really had a chance. His first intimation of impending disaster was when Jumbo's clumsily reincarnated trunk slithered obscenely over his face from behind. When the open end of the empty sleeve was directly in front of the microphone, a hollow, booming voice rolled out with the indignant correction, "I was killed in 1885!"

I have never since seen a break-up in radio to equal that one. The operator behind the control-room glass was too dumbfounded to even cut the mikes and fill with recorded music. Trethewey and I made no attempt to stifle our explosion of laughter. To have done so would have meant a double hernia for both of us. We simply folded our arms on the table in front of us, and resting our heads on our arms so that our respective mouths each faced an open mike, we laughed, hysterically and uncontrollably, for the remaining ninety seconds of sponsored time. For all the rest of that day, CFPL management conferred behind closed doors with outraged executives of the big department store. Rumours flew that our nine o'clock gold mine was finished, but eventually the dark clouds blew over and there was peace in our time.

When it came to nurturing the spiritual growth of its listeners, CFPL was certainly no slouch. I'm sure one of the most unique, if not bizarre, religious programs to be aired over any station in Canada was a once-a-week evening spectacular called *The Gospel Ship*. A small knot of five or six men and women whom nobody seemed to know and who, I always felt, simply wandered in off Richmond Street to escape either rain or noisy traffic used to take their places in Studio B. When the on-air light flashed, one of their number, a meek little man, stepped up to the microphone with a hot-water bottle and began sloshing the contents back and forth for about twenty seconds. Then in a most plaintive, almost whining voice (I'm still using it as one of my radio character voices) he would ask, "Won't you come aboard the Gospel Ship, where you're never a stranger twice?"

From the program's inception, Doug Trowell and I would never miss one of these openings. Somehow our hearts went out to this poignant little fellow we stood watching that strange opening each week with our faces pressed against the studio window. To us he was a symbol of courage against odds, a synthesis of all the world's lost causes, turning up week after week with his hot-water bottle, gamely attempting, through the magic of radio, to evoke in the listeners' minds that wonderful world of make-believe — striving to make them see and feel the sting of salt spray as white-foamed breakers hurled themselves against the shuddering hull of the Gospel Ship. And all the while there wasn't a hope in hell of the listeners' seeing anything in their mind's eye except someone standing in front of a microphone, sloshing water back and forth in a hot-water bottle.

Of quite a different order was CFPL's weekday morning religious program, *In the Chapel*. This calm, tranquil program was to be the vehicle through which Doug Trowell earned for himself a special niche in the Radio Hall of Infamy and in the process put me through the most petrifying experience of my radio career to date. *In the Chapel* opened each morning at 8:30 with the playing of sacred choral music on record. At the end of the first verse, the operator in the control room would fade down the recording and open my microphone. Then in my most sanctimonious voice I would read from a prepared script, "As the doors of the chapel open and the swelling voices of the choir are heard, won't you join us for a few quiet moments . . . (dramatic pause) . . . In the Chapel?" At this point I would introduce the morning's guest minister, who would fill the rest of the fifteen minutes with a prepared sermon and a final blessing. Then over a soft background of sacred music I would sign the program off with the mellifluous invitation to, "Join us again tomorrow for a few quiet moments . . . In the Chapel."

On the Doomsday morning in question, the control room operator informed me at about two minutes to air time that we would have no guest minister that morning. He hadn't shown up. After a hurried consultation, it was agreed that I would make an apology announcement and the operator would fill the time with sacred recordings. We got the program underway and I was in the middle of explaining, with divinely inspired ad-lib, that our guest minister was unable to be with us In the Chapel on this occasion. Suddenly my words were interrupted by the noisy opening of the studio door. I glanced up briefly and saw what I thought was our missing minister — black vestment all across the front with a flash of white collar just showing above. The figure had his hand extended toward me in what seemed at the moment to be a natural and characteristic gesture of Christian fellowship and goodwill. I was halfway out of my chair to accept the extended hand when suddenly it dawned on me — it was Doug Trowell! He had removed his tie and was wearing his suitcoat back to front. The face was wreathed from ear to ear in a warm Christian smile.

Determined not to give him the slightest encouragement, I sank back in my chair and continued on with my interrupted apology announcement. I could feel the saliva begin to dry in my mouth as I watched him noisily settling himself into the empty minister's chair beside me, obviously getting ready to say something. I shot an anguished glance at the on-air light on the studio wall, desperately hoping to find it off. But there it was, burning brightly, and indicating that the operator had not killed the studio microphones. I couldn't even give a "cut" signal, because there wasn't a sign of the operator through the control-room window.

"Well, Mr. Ferguson," Trowell began with a hearty slap on my shoulder, "this is certainly one hell of a way to arrive for a broadcast. Believe me, I ran like a son of a bitch all the way from my church, but you know what that bloody traffic's like on Richmond Street. I sure as hell hope I haven't ruined the damn program."

At this point he had not only ruined the program, the series, and both our jobs, but had partially destroyed, I was certain, about four square feet of my acid-corroded stomach lining.

I longed to be able to tell him all this, but with the mikes open I could do no more than fix him with a look of panic-stricken appeal, which he blithely ignored. Before the fifteen-minute ordeal had ended, he managed to fit in an off-colour sermon and two or three smutty parables, all delivered in a very prim and proper ministerial voice.

I seemed to sound horribly implicated in the whole disaster when I signed off in thin, quavering tones, "Won't you join us again tomorrow for a few quiet moments . . . In the Chapel." I don't really know why I bothered. It was a pretty safe bet that nobody would be joining me tomorrow, next week, next year, or ever again in the shattered ruins of that little chapel. Trowell let me languish in a blue funk all that day before divulging that the whole thing had been rigged for my benefit. With the operator's electronic connivance, the on-air light was kept burning, even though the studio mikes had been safely cut (a trick I've never seen done since), and while the listening audience were fed a program of recorded sacred music from the control room, my ears and my ears alone were assailed by Trowell's nightmarish performance. . . .

One of the first program duties I can recall performing after my arrival at CBC Halifax was inserting the all important surf and seagull cries into the body of the Sunday morning program, *Harmony Harbour*. While the organist, Marjorie Payne, the Acadian Male Quartet, and the narrator, Syd Kennedy, all gave of their best in the ballroom of the Nova Scotian Hotel, I sat a couple of miles away in the main CBC studios on Sackville Street with a sound-effects record of surf and gulls poised on the turntable beside me. With a copy of the script in front of me I was able to follow the narration and also listen to it by means of earphones. Whenever I came across the bracketed cue, SURF AND GULLS, my job was to let the record go and regulate the volume so that the surf and gull sounds would enhance the narrator's prose without being intrusive.

It was pointed out to me by the other announcers at the very outset that the monotony of this task could be relieved by making a little game of it. The object of the game was to see how thoroughly each time one could drown out the narrator's voice with the surf and gulls. The narrator was Syd Kennedy. He'd been the voice of this popular Sunday morning network program for years, and even though he was at that time manager of the Halifax station, he jealously guarded this prestige assignment from the regular announcers and made sure that each Sunday his was the Lorelei voice which tugged at the hearts of exiled Maritimers all across Canada with that familiar opening siren call:

> And inland, where the dark hills rise
> Between you and the salt-thick foam
> You hear the surf — the seagulls' cries
> And Eastward, turn your hearts toward home.

It would have been difficult, of course, for a narrator to have missed with the magnificent and moving prose which Frank W. Doyle, a Halifax newspaper editor, wrote for those *Harmony Harbour* broadcasts. It had the Joseph Conrad touch and read like a musical score. The subject material, drawn from the Maritimes' historical past, did, however, have a slightly lugubrious quality. It dealt mostly with the shipwrecks and the incursions made against early Maritime settlements by marauding Indians, French, and New England privateers. It seemed that almost every anecdote ended with such lines as, ". . . and with a mournful shudder the Brenda Marie went to the bottom, taking with her 108 souls who were never to see their home port again," or, ". . . putting the entire village to the torch, slaughtering 112 of its inhabitants, and then making off overland with 140 wretched survivors who were never again to see their native land." This proclivity of *Harmony Harbour* for disaster prompted one unfeeling Toronto radio critic to write in his column, "Having listened to *Harmony Harbour* since it began, I've now been able to compute that an average of 420 poor souls have been either drowned, massacred, or carried off every Sunday morning for the past fifteen years. How in hell can there be anyone left down there?"

For a period of nearly a month, Syd Kennedy almost succeeded in undermining our little diversion of drowning out his voice with surf and gulls every Sunday morning. As he read his script to the network from the CBC's Nova Scotian Hotel studios, he hit upon the counterstrategy of anticipating our inserted sound effects from the main studios a mile away. Consequently, whenever he approached to within a sentence or two of the underlined cue, SURF AND GULLS, he would start "building" — increasing his voice in volume and intensity — so that try as we would, with our surf and gull effects going at full blast over his voice, there was always a tiny but audible vestige of a thin, shrieking human voice cutting through.

His triumph was short-lived. Some unsung Leonardo of the Halifax announce staff whose name I've forgotten suggested that on such occasions when Kennedy anticipated, we would refrain completely from putting in any surf and gulls whatever. The resulting effect was most rewarding — ten times more hilarious than our former attempts to drown him out. I'm quite sure that thousands of unwitting listeners, in the privacy of their living rooms across Canada, must have been stunned by that screaming Hitler-like voice shouting its message of doom and disaster and must have felt that Kennedy was holding them all personally responsible for those poor devils who were in the process of being "carried off, never to see their native land again." I can still see the Grand Old Man of Radio, as we used to call him, bursting into Studio B every Sunday morning about four minutes after *Harmony Harbour* had gone off the air. This was the approximate time it took him to race from the ballroom of the Nova Scotian Hotel, leap into the CBC staff car, and come screaming up to our main Sackville Street studios to confront me with a wild outburst of profanity just as I was sheepishly putting away my surf and gulls record for another week. . . .

Almost any employee in any region of the CBC's far-flung empire will understand immediately my shocked disbelief at learning that I had exceeded Allan McFee in inefficiency of service rendered to the Corporation — such is his legendary ill-fame. To impart to a non-member of the CBC family, however, the extreme unlikelihood of anyone's ever achieving such a distinction, the bizarre chronicle of McFee's eccentric interpretation of his duties to the CBC would have to be set forth. This would entail several volumes and someday, if I'm still around when McFee has gone to that Great Studio in the Sky, I might write them. Certainly such a literary effort could never be decently undertaken in McFee's lifetime. There are too many McFee anecdotes which, if divulged openly, even at this late date, would likely result in his immediate dismissal from the CBC.

His favourite line of self-pity used to be, "When I consider how my days are spent, squatting like a toad in this fetid little cell, waiting for that challenging moment every half hour to say 'CBL, Toronto,' I'm engulfed in black clouds of depression."

I know for a fact, though, that McFee during his hours of duty in CBL studio did much more than merely squat like a toad. Quite early in his CBC career he discovered that, by simply opening his microphone in that "fetid little cell," he could send his voice out over whatever program the CBC was airing at the time.

It would not be an exaggeration to say that McFee's voice has turned up at one time or another, completely unauthorized, on just about every program on the CBC schedule. The incongruously masculine and terribly vulgar throat clearing that Ma Perkins gave after a sweet word to Willie and Shuffle, the stentorian nose blowing which would accompany a celestial French horn passage in a symphonic performance . . . all came from the toad in his fetid cell. His specialty was a sound so obnoxious and startling that I've literally jumped at hearing it issuing forth from my radio in the privacy of my living room. He usually reserved it for the caesural pause in poetry readings or as a followup to such inviting dramatic dialogue as, "John, darling, this will come as a shock, but I've felt for a long time now that you must hear it!" Strangely enough, McFee was able to lay all these rude little eggs like a malicious cuckoo-bird in the nests of unsuspecting producers and they were never traced to him. They were always faithfully and erroneously entered into the CBC daily log as "unidentified noise on the line." That is, with the exception of one nightmarish occasion when his diversionary pastime backfired.

The story was told to me by J. Frank Willis who, like a latter-day venerable Bede, seems to have mentally chronicled everything that ever happened in the CBC. The incident occurred some years before I arrived on the Toronto scene back in the days when the CBC, as part of its late afternoon radio fare for kiddies, used to receive by direct line from New York and transmit over its Toronto station a dramatized version of the comic strip, *Terry and the Pirates.* The program always opened with a noisy Chinese street scene — a cacophonous melange of rickshaw wheels, gongs, and shrill Chinese voices which lasted for about fifteen seconds before the U.S. announcer came in. During this period, McFee would open his mike and in a sing-song Chinese voice send out all his repressions toward the CBC and its executives in some rather salacious and defamatory language. The listeners at home, of course, were never able to distinguish McFee's libellous catharsis from the general noise of the Chinese street scene which camou-flaged it. However, the routine had a rather effective shock value from the studio end. Anyone who happened to tiptoe into the studio while it was in progress would hear only McFee and not the U.S. origination, since the studio speakers always cut off when a microphone is opened. There would be McFee sitting in front of an open microphone sending out over 50,000 watts of power some pretty awful things about the CBC and the men who ran it. Frank Willis, having seen the stunt pulled on several occasions by McFee, knew that it was quite harmless, but the fun lay in watching the face of anyone not in the know who might slip into the studio while McFee was in the middle of it.

One day as McFee was in the middle of his act, chanting, "O yang quong kee . . . stupid old CBC . . . soo yung . . . crazy knuckle-head (censored name of CBC executive) . . . him velly dumb, velly useless . . . sit on big fat bum all day . . . do nothing . . . o yang soo . . ." and so on, Willis noticed that the operator in the control room seemed to be in a bit of a frenzy as he gesticulated through the glass trying to get McFee's attention. Willis hastily alerted McFee with a dig in the ribs; McFee then cut his microphone to restore the speaker feed of *Terry and the Pirates*, and they both listened. There was stony silence. Where normally there would have been a noisy Chinese crowd scene, there was absolutely nothing, due to a failure in the transmission of the program from New York. McFee's virtuoso performance had been going out over 50,000 watts with not a sound to disguise it.

For anyone else such a traumatic experience would have served as an object lesson, but when I came to Toronto some years later, the only noticeable disciplinary effect the incident had produced on McFee was that he had abandoned recognizable spoken words and was now relying solely on throat clearings, nose blowings, and that previously mentioned loathsome sound to herald his uninvited appearance on just about every program that went out over the CBC Toronto transmitters.

It is only fair to mention that, on the credit side, there has been during the last three or four years a noticeable change for the better in Allan McFee. He's still far from what you'd call a "company man," but a great deal of the former perverseness and destructive drive has gone. I won't attempt to offer any psychological reasons, but I'm convinced the personality change has something to do with getting rid of his dreadful old car, which for years must have been the most uncared for, mistreated, and shockingly dilapidated wreck on the streets of Toronto. One of my earliest recollections of McFee was seeing him in the back parking lot behind the Jarvis Street studios one morning, slowly walking around his car and methodically kicking dents in all four fenders. When I asked him what the trouble was, that suave, well-modulated, rich, warm, sincere voice that I'd heard so often on network radio explained very rationally, without a trace of malice, that the car had been reluctant to start that morning. As punishment he had driven it down at top speed without changing out of low gear and now was administering the final discipline so that such a thing wouldn't happen again. The frightening part of it was that he made it all sound so plausible and reasonable . . . a perfectly natural thing to do to a mass of disobedient steel.

Canada as She Is Misunderstood

Peter McArthur

Dear Mr. Punch, – Reverting to your recent article under the title "The Great Misunderstood," let me say that I am *so* glad that I did not publish my great work on "Canada, Her History, Customs and Resources" before visiting England. As planned, it would have been very unsatisfactory to people with settled opinions, of whom I have met several since landing on your hospitable and interesting shores.

As you are doubtless aware, the old contention that "What is, is" is rapidly giving way to the doctrine that "What is believed to be is is." (It is just possible that there is an "is" too many in that sentence, but as that only increases its metaphysical subtlety I hope the proofreader will let it stand.) Having this in mind, I have recast the materials of my book along new lines and added much that will be received here with placid approval, and in Canada with joyous wonder. By publishing the following prospectus you will confer a great favour on a fellow British subject.

"CANADA, HER HISTORY, CUSTOMS AND RESOURCES"

Chapter I. — The discovery of Canada by the French and its recovery by the British — the original inheritors of the earth.

Chapter II. — The invention of the tuque and snowshoe costume, with a study of their subsequent effect on "The Ballet of all Nations" as it is still presented in all the capitals of Europe with the original cast.

Chapter III. — The geographical position of Canada, with map and historical footnote showing the value of disputed territory when Downing Street wishes to establish friendly relations with Washington.

Chapter IV. — A digression in which the author proves conclusively that when the North Pole is finally discovered it will be found to be somewhere near the centre of Canada.

Chapter V. — An appreciation of the Roast Beef of Old England and Wiltshire bacon as met with on the hoof in Ontario and the Canadian Northwest.

Chapter VI. — An exhaustive paper on Canadian fruits, in which it will be shown to the confusion of the scientific world that apples, grapes, peaches, pears, and plums ripen within the Arctic Circle.

Chapter VII. — Interviews (properly expurgated) with prominent Canadians regarding Mr. Kipling's "Lady of the Snows," and Sir Gilbert Parker's Hudson Bay Stories as an advertisement of Canada.

Chapter VIII. — The exports of Canada, dealing fully with Sir Wilfrid Laurier, philanthropic millionaires, and several plausible brands of red whisky.

Chapter IX. — The imports of Canada, with special reference to younger sons who need a change of venue. Instances will be cited of black sheep pasturing for a few years on the plains of Canada, and then returning to their happy homes with only slight Southdown markings.

Chapter X.— Conclusion — Canada's place among the younger nations that can ride and shoot. Assurances of continued loyalty and selections from the best "O-My-Country" poetry of "Canada's lyric choir."

It may interest you to know that I intend to remain in London for some time. To tell the truth, I am a trifle afraid that, when my book is published, popular enthusiasm will run so high that each of my fellow Canadians will want a fragment of me as a souvenir.

Yours warmly,

C. A. NUCK.

from   To Be Taken With Salt

Let Me Call You, Sweetheart

Richard J. Needham

It's been said for a good many years that if you get your university degree, you're certain of obtaining a good job immediately upon your graduation. Such was in fact the experience of a young lady named Priscilla Prism, who obtained her Master of Social Work degree from the University of Toronto, and in less time than it takes to tell found herself selling plates, cups and saucers at $1.90 an hour in the Woolco store which dominates Gangster's Mall.

Like all young women, Priscilla daydreamed about some interesting young man who would suddenly come into her life. He would be, she hoped, something of a romantic who would write poems about her and sing love songs to her. He might even serenade her from the sidewalk while she smiled at him through the window of her furnished room, occasionally dropping him a scented note or a flower or a bran muffin baked with her own little hands.

One day there was a terrible rainstorm outside the store, and a young man came dashing in to escape it. He stood by her counter, looked at her, looked over the merchandise, and then bought a cup. He walked around the store with it, came back, looked at her again, and bought a saucer. On the next go-round, he bought a plate, which made Priscilla say, "You don't have to keep buying things just to take shelter. Besides, the rain has stopped, it looks nice outside." The young man gazed into her eyes, saying, "It looks even nicer inside," and Priscilla felt herself go goose-pimples all over.

The young man kept buying cups and saucers and plates until he was loaded down with them, and people started getting curious and gathering around, and Priscilla began getting embarrassed. The young man then drifted away but not before he had asked her name and had given her his — Romeo Raskolnikov — and sang a little ditty to her, "You were selling china, but when I saw your eyes, I kept buying china until the crowd got wise."

The next day, Romeo phoned Priscilla at the store, saying, "You do something to me. Jeepers creepers, where'd you get those peepers? I'm flying high but I've got a feeling I'm falling, falling for nobody else but you. If I had a talking picture of yoo-hoo, I would play it every time I felt bloo-hoo. You must have been a beautiful baby, 'cos, baby, look at you now. I took one look at you, and then my heart stood still. Good night, sweetheart, till we meet tomorrow."

Priscilla thought this was very romantic, the more so when he took her out to lunch the next day and all the way through the meal sang to her thus and as follows: "You're the tops, you're the Easter Bunny, you're the tops, you're Mel Lastman's money, you're the girl I really want to understand; you're a Davis plane, love's old refrain, you're Disneyland. You're the tops, you're a Rembrandt picture, you're the tops, you're Buckley's Mixture, you're the one from whom I get that certain thrill, you're Rinso White, the Edge of Night, you're Bowmanville. You're the tops, you're the Book of Knowledge, you're the tops, you're Rochdale College; just knowing you exist makes me feel great; you're

Secretariat, you're Ben Hur's chariot, you're Watergate."

Romeo kept coming to see Priscilla at Woolco's, or else telephoning her with such messages as, "You were meant for me. I'll be loving you always. You ought to be in pictures, oh what a hit you would make. I love to spend this hour with you. Take good care of yourself, you belong to me. Just one look at you, my heart goes tipsy in me; you and you alone bring out the gypsy in me."

Romeo telephoned Priscilla so much and came to see her so much during his supposed working hours that he finally lost his job at the Dominion supermarket across the way. When he told Priscilla of this, she said, "Oh, that's terrible." He replied, "No, it's wonderful. Now I can spend all my time telephoning you and coming to see you." Priscilla replied, "No, Romeo, you mustn't. The management here at Woolco's is complaining about it and threatening to fire me."

The young man looked stricken with grief, then sang, "What'll I do when you are far away, and I am blue, what'll I do? With the parting of the ways, you took all my happy days, and left me lonely nights. My heart sighs for you, cries for you, dies for you. I'll be loving you always, with a love that's true always. I'll never smile again till I smile at you. I don't want to walk without you, baby," and he continued calling and coming into the store until the management gave Priscilla a final warning.

When Romeo came to her counter the next day, he had a guitar with him and sang as he strummed. "I get no kick from John White; putting the bite on some poor widow's mite ain't the right or the bright thing to do, but I get a kick out of you." Priscilla replied, "You're going to get a kick out of me, alright," and with the aid of her section manager, she booted him clean out of the store.

Priscilla gave up the idea of romance, and is now going out with a cold-blooded newspaperman who tells her, "You're the grease in my coffee, you're the tooth in my stew, you will always be my catastrophe, I'd be blest without you." When his friends ask how he met her, he likes to reply, "I found a five-and-ten cent baby in a million-dollar store."

from The Globe and Mail

Mice in the Beer

Norman Ward

One of the most thought-provoking spectacles to be seen in this country is that of a mouse in a beer bottle. The one I saw was in repose on his back, his hands all but clasped across his chest. His face was wreathed in smiles, and his ears were at a rakish angle. He was dead, but he had died happy.

Now these are days when anything that can be found out to the discredit of animals should be widely publicized, so as to make man seem a little better by comparison. Too much nonsense is written about the wisdom and industry of the lower creatures, and not enough about man's. As a result of the discovery of this sodden mouse, it can be reported with confidence that mice in Canada appear to be heavy drinkers.

The disclosure was made by a bottle-counter in a keg-and-bottle exchange to which I had assisted a friend to convey a few empties. On the way to the exchange we had noticed a peculiar odour hanging about, but we had taken it for granted as my friend has several children, all of them capable of fastening a dead cat under a car. The trained nose of the bottle-counter, however, quickly acquitted the children. "Mouse," he said tersely, expertly holding each empty up to the light as he counted it.

The man's assurance, and the fact that he was obviously accustomed to meeting mice, naturally led to interested investigation. It transpired that in addition to being an outstanding bottle-counter our man was also a well-informed mouse-finder with an inquiring mind.

Mice often crawl into empty beer bottles, he said, no doubt attracted by the malty smell. A mouse in a bottle, having lapped up the few remaining drops of liquid, commonly finds himself unable to negotiate the return journey to the outside world. A few drops for a mouse, our informant ventured to say, was roughly the equivalent of a pailful for an average-sized man.

This was not all our bottle-counter had to offer. His employment had given him a splendid opportunity to assess the drinking habits of mice over a vast area of the Canadian West, and it was clear to him that country mice are worse topers than their city cousins. Either the rural dwellers drink more heavily, he said, or the city ones are shrewder at knowing when to hit the road. Far more mice show up in shipments of bottles from scattered prairie oases than in those brought in by urban people. My friend and I received the impression that we had acquired around the keg-and-bottle exchange a notoriety that would not soon leave us.

By a coincidence, that day's paper had carried a story about a speech made by one of the province's leading temperance advocates. Using one of those striking figures of speech that seem to fascinate the teetotal world, this citizen had allegedly asserted that enough beer had been sold in our province during the past year to keep everybody over the age of fourteen drunk for three weeks. My friend had during the day made a number of unfriendly references to those who had got his share, but he was somehow cheered to think that it may have been the mice.

from Mice in the Beer

from Jupiter Eight

Francis Pollock

. . . Derrock resigned himself. He hadn't really meant to go to Wellington London's studio, but he would have to go now; and once inside, Lloyd would have to stop talking.

They went up in the elevator. London's studio was a vast place on the top floor of the highest business building in Toronto. He said he liked the air and light. He also liked the elevation, which was somehow symbolic. This was his headquarters. He lived here with his sister, but he had branch establishments in Montreal and Winnipeg.

Derrock tapped gently with the little brass knocker. The

door opened gently, and the pleasant elderly face of Miss London appeared, peering out with an infinite precaution of silence. She gazed at them near-sightedly, and Derrock doubted whether she recognized either of them; but she gave them the pleased professional smile that she gave to every well-dressed person who came to her brother's place of business.

"Come in. So glad you came!" she said under her breath. "Wellington's still working, but the light is beginning to fail, and he'll be through in a few minutes."

They tip-toed in like people who have come late to church, but Derrock caught the painter's quick irritated glance at the disturbance. Dead silence was in the vast studio, though there were more than a dozen people there, seated about on chairs as if at a spectacle. Dead silence was the condition of being admitted to see the great Anglo-Canadian painter at work. London liked to paint before an admiring audience. It stimulated him, and he said laughingly that if he could paint on the stage of a filled theatre he would produce a masterpiece. But without that he produced masterpieces all the time.

Enormously tall, bony and bald-headed, London stood at the easel at the far end of the room, under the dead glare of the top-light. He almost faced his audience, who could see only the back of the canvas. His right sleeve was rolled over his bony forearm. His left arm hung at his side. His left hand was crippled with an old injury, so that he could not carry a palette, and he used a porcelain-topped painting table for his colours. He stepped quickly to and fro, forward and back, dabbing at the canvas. His little black eyes darted from the canvas to the figure on the model stand opposite him. Here sat a gorgeous figure against a purplish-dark curtain, in the full dress uniform of an officer of the North Ontario Highlanders, scarlet tunic, black and green kilt, hairy sporran, straps and belts, brass swordhilt and sallow bare knees. Above the gold-embroidered collar rose a round red face with small cunning eyes. This was Major McMack, an honorary officer of the Great War, and one of the leading crockery manufacturers of Toronto.

He posed with an air of bored, modest pride, and in breathless silence the audience watched him, and watched the greater painter. It was going to be one of London's greatest successes. He was going to get five thousand for it – no, ten thousand – but that was nothing! Though now close to sixty,

Wellington London seemed to be at the height of his powers. He was the greatest painter in Toronto, in Ontario, in the whole of Canada. He was said to be the greatest Toronto painter in the world.

He had been christened John Wesley Loudon in Manchester where he was born. Emigrating to Canada, his parents had brought him with them at the age of six. In Toronto he developed his aptitude for painting, and had exhibited at all the provincial galleries before he was twenty. Realizing that he had a future, he dropped the "John" from his name, and changed the "Wesley," with its nonconformist suggestion, to "Wellesley." Much later, this became "Wellington," by natural historical transition; and by the simple inversion of a single letter "Loudon" became the much more impressive "London."

At the age of twenty-five he went back to England to play the role of a colonial genius. But he made no headway in London. The international pace was too fast for him; he was hopelessly outclassed. He made a plucky fight, but in eight years he had to give up. He had not the money to hold out longer, and at that crisis in his affairs, he had his hand crushed in a motor-bus accident.

But this did not quell his spirit. He obtained £100 from the bus company in compensation, and luckily it was his left hand. It did not interfere with his painting, except that he had to use a painting-table instead of a palette. He returned to Toronto, spent most of his indemnity in giving an exhibition, and, with the prestige of his eight years in London, he was an almost immediate success. He perceived that he should have come home sooner.

He presently developed a mission. It was to be an Imperial painter, a Kipling of the canvas, an artistic interpreter between Canada and the Mother Land. All the Anglophile circles encouraged him, took him up, all the English, all the would-be English, the official, the rich. He painted a number of lieutenant-governors and men in uniforms. He could paint cloth and gold lace excellently, but he painted everything, men, women and horses, still lifes and landscapes, and every year he was able to raise his prices. When the Great War broke out, he was one of the first to offer himself for enlistment, indifferent to his crippled hand. He was not accepted, but he was highly praised for his patriotism. Even the post-war slump did not check his progress. He opened studios in Winnipeg and Montreal, kept up permanent exhibitions there, and spent some months in each city, working hard to fill his numerous orders. He did not belong to the Royal Canadian Academy, nor to any of the provincial Associations, though they had invited him, and though he was always a welcome guest exhibitor; but he said that he did not wish to identify himself with any local group, but with the Empire as a whole. There was no nonsense about modernism in London's work, no Continental impressionism. "The style of old Sir Joshua is good enough for me," he was accustomed to say; and he painted every button, every finger and hair with true British pluck and thoroughness. Several times he had gone back to London to hold an exhibition there, but lately these visits had grown infrequent; and he had even been heard to say that painting in England had gone crazy, and that the future of art must be looked for in the Dominions.

In silence and in almost religious reverence his audience watched him paint. Most of the people in the studio were women, and Derrock knew many of them. Some had been clients of his own. They were women with artistic leanings, expensive women from up-town, from the wealthy, the official, the imperialist, the Daughters of the Empire Circles where London chiefly traded. Among the few men he saw Carlton Maitland, the book reviewer of the *Week*, dark and accursed-looking as usual, and he noticed Mr. Charlemagne Roncesvalles, the eminent art critic of the same paper, portly and puissant, leaning on his cane and smiling secretly and indulgently as he watched the painter. And sitting rather by herself Derrock saw a striking figure in black and old-gold, with a hat like a helmet of bronze and iron, bronze shoes, bronzy stockings, and also a great deal of real gold and black fur. She sat quite impassive, but women's faces were continually turned toward her in secret glances of hostility and cold disapproval and burning curiosity.

"I'll bet there's the secret of the Black Belt decision," Lloyd whispered. "Lola Matanzas," he added.

Derrock looked with great interest at the Spanish-Cuban actress, whom he had previously seen only on the stage. She was playing minor roles in a local stock company, but she had been in Toronto all winter, and was already a celebrity, or a notoriety. On a salary of perhaps thirty dollars a week, she lived at the Imperial Royal Hotel and dressed like a millionaire's daughter or a gambler's mistress. Wallie Weatherford looked after her, and neither of them made any secret of it.

"I'll bet Wallie has told her something about the decision, if he's heard anything," Lloyd said. "I'll bet she has a good notion how it's going to go."

"But what's she doing in this gallery — in the arty crowd?"

Lloyd, who knew everything, explained that Wellington London had been painting her portrait. It was Lola's latest freak to have herself exhibited at the spring show of the National Academy. It might cost a few thousands, but she didn't care what it would cost; and neither did Wallie, who had been in the rise in Motors from the start, and must have cleaned up a quarter of a million from that alone.

Miss London had been sitting beside her, to keep her in countenance — as if she needed it! But Lloyd, who knew everybody, knew Miss Matanzas, and he went over and whispered to her, and then beckoned to Derrock. He mentioned Derrock's name under his breath, and Lola turned her full, blank stare upon him, the famous stare that she cultivated, without any more expression than an empty dinner-plate. She had a face that always looked made up even when it was not, a large face, heavy and square, with a creamy, powdery, darkly-perfect skin almost destitute of any colour. Her mouth was too full, too wide, too crimson, her eyelashes too heavy, her eyes too large, like great brown-black pools with nothing in them, not even any bottom. Her rather large head looked larger with the heavy coils of her famous hair, thick and black and coarse, which no barber had ever scissored, wound in masses under her bronze helmet. She sat quite still, almost stupidly inert, but all around her was a compelling and exciting and irritating aura or aroma.

"I saw you last night in your new role, Lola," Lloyd said. "You were absolutely perfect. You were so perfect that you killed the scene. Nobody could look at anything but you."

Lloyd, who hated women, always addressed them in that tone of derisive compliment, which women hated. Lola looked at him blankly without saying anything, and then turned her full, powerfully-vacant stare upon Derrock again.

"I've heard of you. You're a house decorator, ain't you?" she said. She had a rather husky, middle-western voice, for her real name was Lulu Riggs, and she came from Matanzas, Iowa.

"Not at all. I'm a novelist."

"Novelist nothing! I've heard of you, lots of times. Solly Leviticus told me he was going to get you to do over his house.

Say, what do you think of this?" with a jerk of her finger toward London. "Do you think he's any good? He's painting me, you know," she added, without at all lowering her natural voice.

Faces had been turned angrily toward them. There was now a shocked "s-sh!" London gave a furious start, coughed fiercely, and then, seeing the Weatherford commission, he coughed again apologetically, and went on painting. Lola continued to stare at Derrock, without any appearance of interest, but as if her gaze were too heavy to be easily removed.

"Why don't you come to see me?" she said. "You know where I live. There's always tea at five, except days when I've got a matinee."

"Thanks," said Derrock. "But you're forgetting that I've just now got to know you. How could I have come before."

"You could have known me any time, if you'd wanted to."

"And me — can't I come to tea, too?" asked Lloyd.

"Oh, I don't want you," returned Lola, without even looking at him. She looked at Derrock powerfully, blankly, and suddenly smiled, ever so little, just a curving of the corners of her mouth, but it turned her blank beauty into something so sensually seductive, so suggestive, that he felt as if he had been suddenly sprayed with a potent aphrodisiac. He choked and stammered with the shock of it.

"Thanks . . . yes! Yes . . . thanks! I'll certainly come."

"That's all right then," Lola's face returned to its heavy vacuity. "Did you know that London's painting my portrait? Have you seen it? Come along and I'll show it to you. I know where it is — right over there against the wall."

She got up and moved toward the other side of the studio. At this outrageous disturbance there was another startled "s-s-sh." Miss London, hovering benevolently about, looked shocked as at a sacrilege. Derrock was horribly embarrassed, but he had to follow Miss Matanzas, while she went almost to the edge of the model stand and took out her canvas, that was faced against the wall.

"Here it is. Do you think it's any good?" she said loudly.

This was too much. Wellington London coughed explosively, ferociously, and laid down his brushes.

"Ha!" he barked. "Time's up. All done for to-day. Ha! Ha!"

The studio rose into life, stirred into sound. The major

arose stiffly; he stepped ponderously down, in pomp of scarlet and gold.

"Got it nearly done, London? Let's have a look at it. Come on, I want to see it. I can't give you more than a couple more sittings anyhow."

"Oh yes, do let us see it. Show it to us, Mr. London, please!" the women chattered.

London was reluctant. He hated to show his pictures half finished, but there were many thousands of dollars of possible business in that room, and he could not risk giving offence. So he took down the wet canvas unwillingly, and stood it against the easel-leg to face the room.

"Well, what do you think of it? It it any good?" Miss Matanzas insisted, still presenting her own portrait, and quite ignoring the major's.

"I think it's going to be bully," Derrock said.

He perceived at once that London and Lola had been created for one another. The portrait was nowhere near completion, but its essential qualities were already there. It represented the famous Spanish-Cuban actress in full face, with her famous stare, blank as a dinner-plate, and her large eyes like empty inkwells. London would get this effect to admiration. Her immense blankness was exactly the quality of his genius, and the picture was going to be as good as a photograph.

"It's certainly going to be one of London's greatest successes."

Lola looked at him without any gratitude, studied the portrait critically herself, and then faced it back against the wall.

"I've had about all I can stand of this joint," she said loudly. "I've got Wallie's car here, and I promised to bring it back early. Are you going anywhere? I'll drive you if you like."

"But aren't you going to stay for some tea. They always have tea at this stage."

Everybody was crowding up to look at the major's portrait, with cries and chirps of admiration. What glory of colour! What flesh tones! What cast shadows! Sargent, Picasso — Rembrandt! The phrases were all ready and overflowing, having been bottled up for the last hour.

"Wouldn't those red tones remind you exactly of Cezanne, my dear? Or perhaps, of Augustus John?"

London took this as no compliment, for these painters were

his horror. But from long experience he knew what was coming to him, and he set his teeth and held his tongue.

Mr. Charlemagne Roncesvalles arose, limping slightly on his cane, and made his way up to the picture. Everybody stood respectfully back while he considered it in silence for some minutes. Then he turned without saying a word, and limped back to his seat again, portly and puissant, smiling secretively in his beard, as if he had a vast number of opinions which he was not at present prepared to impart to anybody.

"Good likeness — what?" said London.

"You've got the uniform right — that's all I know about it," the major wheezed. . . .

This Here Ballet

Eric Nicol

"**Y**ou got to hand it to these ballet dancers," said the big man at the next table. "They got to be on their toes." He signalled for two more beers.

"You seen it?" said the small man.

"Last night. The wife's sister got us tickets. She thinks I'm a slob."

The small man nodded understandingly.

"Last night we seen 'Swan Lake.' Very interesting."

"Who's in it?" the small man asked politely.

"Nobody you'd know," said the big man, lipping his beer. "All ballet dancers."

The small man nodded again and waited while his friend's whistle was wetted. Then the big man went on:

"This 'Swan Lake,' it's a sort of fairy story. You got to buy a program to figure it."

"Like Lansdowne," said the small man.

"Yeah," said the big man. "Except after two hours and a half you still don't know who paid off."

The small man eyebrowed surprise.

"But, as the wife said, you can see it's beautiful, what they're doing. This dame who's a swan is terrific."

"The dame's a swan?"

"Yeah. You got this bunch of happy peasants running around the stage, see, beside this lake. They're celebratin' something, Christmas, maybe. After them comes this band of hunters, bouncing onto the stage. They're waving bows and firing arrows that are strictly imaginary, since the season ain't open yet."

"Ducks?" said the small man.

"Swans," said the big man. "You ever eat swan?"

The small man shook his head.

"Me neither. Anyhow, these hunters are led by a rummy the program says is the Prince, his pants being even tighter than the other guys', if possible. This Prince leaps in with a grand jet, the wife says, which I believe since he can take off straight up. Right here is where the flock of swans come barreling down the runway. The hunters make like they're going to pot the works, but the Prince gives 'em an as-you-were, having noticed that the swans ain't swans at all but dames in short, fluffy skirts."

"You got to be careful hunting," nodded the small man. "I shot me a Guernsey once."

"So this Prince, his eye is caught by the Queen of the swans, a kid with a naturally long neck and very well stacked. Right here is where I wish the wife's sister had bought us seats somewhere nearer than the last row of the balcony, the cheapskate. All I can see good is the program, which says the Queen and the Prince are alone so they can do a *pas de deux*, in French."

The small man blinked and said, "I never heard of a guy doing it with no swan."

"This Prince does it, him grabbing her around the middle and her revolving on her axis, being very graceful about not givin' him the knee. That was the end of the first period."

"Still no score, huh?" said the small man.

"It gets sad from there on," said the big man. "The Queen of the swans cashes her chips, and they bring her back as a ghost. The other swans go nuts over her, but I couldn't see her so good as when the lights were on and I guess I sort of dozed off. The wife said the ending was terrific, though."

The small man drained his glass and said:

"I like a good tap dancer. You don't see them no more."

"With this ballet," said the big man, "you got to develop a taste, like olives. You got time for another beer?"

from Still a Nicol

from Sex and Security

Dave Broadfoot

As a man deeply involved in and committed to the political life of this country, I found myself some years ago becoming frustrated with the Canadian political process. I asked myself why. Why was I frustrated with our political parties? The answer was obvious: there were only four to choose from. It saddened me that the members of the four political parties in existence could never look at issues logically, the way I saw them. Apparently Canada needed a fifth party.

And so, necessity became the mother of our convention, and the New Apathetic Party was born. The party adopted the name "Apathetic" in order to appeal to the average Canadian. And now, finally, after years of determined effort, we are beginning to see the light at the end of our long tunnel. *Apathy is on the march!*

I have been asked on occasion by some nonbelievers in our cause, what qualifies me to be the leader of a political party. I humbly refer these doubters to the historical and unfailing good judgement, and, if I may say, wisdom of my constituents.

When I received the leadership nomination at the founding convention of our party in Kicking Horse Pass, it was a landslide. I was their national dream come true. The conventioneers were perceptive enough to see that I was Mackenzie King, Louis Riel, and Bobby Hull all rolled into one... with a dash of Genghis Khan thrown in.

What, you may ask, is my background? My grandfather was the first French-speaking Jehovah's Witness. In the Second World War, my father was presumed missing in Camp Borden. He was the first Canadian soldier to have a drink named after him: the Zombie. My mother, a self-taught trucker, was the first woman to be recognized by the Teamsters. However, she eventually gave all that up to become a celibate nun and to work with a lay priest among the Westmount Rhodesians. My cousin was the first Canadian actor to win the Order of Canada medal for best supporting actor in an American film. And because my family owned a distillery, we held a position of moral leadership that made the Eaton family look like the Beverly Hillbillies.

Still, I could not take my acceptance for granted. I did everything expected of a one-hundred-percent Canadian. I sold my company to an American. I bought a Toyota. I bought Indian paintings and Eskimo carvings. I even did a bit of chiselling on my own. I experienced the great silence of Sunday in Edmonton, and the greater silence of Dominion Day in Trois Rivières.

I knew that to reach Ottawa as a representative of my party would mean relentless campaigning throughout the riding, and I did just that — day in, and day out, astride my Shetland pony, spreading my charisma behind me.

My first priority was to heal the ethnic wounds of the past. Doing that took considerable ingenuity. I gave a dinner for the Orange Order, the Knights of Columbus, the Sons of Freedom Doukhobors, and the Canadian Legion. Chief Dan George was the guest of honour, Rabbi Feinberg came out there to hand out the funny hats, and W. A. C. Bennett flew in to cook the sukiyaki.

During my after-dinner speech, I spoke about my vision of a Just Society, and saw toughened old veterans of two world wars break down and cry. When I spoke about participatory democracy, an old white-haired woman wearing a rosary swore she saw a halo forming around my head. I tried to deny it, but it was too late. I had the Catholic vote wrapped up.

I spoke briefly in Italian, Ukrainian, and Chinese, and held the Jewish members of the audience spellbound while I praised the reforestation of Israel in Hebrew. Then with a couple of references to "Occupied Arab Lands," I was able to win over all the anti-Zionists in the crowd.

After the speech came the dancing, with music provided by the Oscar Peterson Trio. By midnight, the people of Kicking

Horse Pass were ready to lynch anyone who stood against me. And so I went to Ottawa. . . .

We constantly hear politicians at the highest levels of government complaining about "leaks" to the press. We even have an "Official Secrets Act" in Ottawa. The New Apathetic Party would abolish this legislation. We admit that it could have been embarrassing for Canada if blueprints of such projects as the Montreal-Toronto Turbo Train, or the Glace Bay Heavy Water Plant, or the Canadian Forces' Hydrofoil had fallen into the wrong hands. It was embarrassing enough when they fell into the hands of the Auditor General. He never did get over it. But just imagine the embarrassment if a Russian spy had gotten hold of those designs. Can't you see the headlines? TRAIN SERVICE BETWEEN LENINGRAD AND MOSCOW PERMANENTLY CRIPPLED, AS U.S.S.R. INTRODUCES REVOLUTIONARY CANADIAN-TYPE TURBO ENGINE . . .; SOVIET NUCLEAR GENERATORS SIT IDLE AWAITING SUPPLIES FROM CANADIAN-DESIGNED HEAVY-WATER PLANT IN THE UKRAINE . . . ; NEW SOVIET HYDROFOIL SETS RUSSIAN NAVY BACK TEN YEARS AS ENTIRE DEFENCE BUDGET IS EXPENDED. . . .

For the great majority of Canadians, any examination of the national economy would have as its first priority the careful scrutiny of the salary of their Members of Parliament. There are still people who think their Member is underworked and overpaid. It is the people's privilege to think what they like, for this is a free country. On the other hand, if they say what they think out loud, just before an election, I want to know who the hell they are and what dirt I can dig up to use against *them*.

To seek to deny a man a decent living is, to say the least, unpatriotic. We Members of Parliament have no union and no right to strike. The last work to rule effort went completely unnoticed. We have to arrive at a raise in pay by gaining a consensus in Parliament. To those who are opposed to this system of escalation by consensus, I would ask: what are the alternative sources of revenue open to an M.P. if his salary is less than his expenses and he has no private means?

Every Member wants to earn his money honestly. If he accepts a cash gratuity to do someone a favour, he is going to do it. Not to follow through would be dishonest. After all, a man has to live with himself. Who would trust him if he let his friends down?

It is a tribute to the calibre of the men we have in government that, if an arrangement is made to do a friend a favour, it is never put in writing. A simple handshake with a sealed envelope in it is enough.

But there is another and wiser way of alleviating the burden on the poor in the House of Commons. No longer need a Member bring his lunch pail to work. By living at the Y.M.C.A. and darning his own socks, he can now afford to patronize the subsidized meal program in the Parliamentary Cafeteria, where a good hot meal can be had at about one-third of the normal price.

If only the people who are knocking our Parliamentary Welfare Program could see the difference a few dollars makes in our way of life, they would know their money was being well spent. To put the taxpayers' dollar to the best possible use was uppermost in our minds when we finally voted to increase our salaries. It was as simple as that. Nonetheless, it took great courage on the part of the Members to see the vote through. It makes one wonder how many of the lay critics out there would be capable of such bravery under fire.

Many Members were disturbed and uneasy in their seats when they first got the idea of increasing their own salaries with funds out of the pockets of the taxpayers they were elected to protect. We all searched ourselves deep into the dark reaches of the night. I know I did. In fact, I got up at one point, in a cold sweat, turned on the light, looked at myself in the mirror and asked myself: "Am I really worth it?" I don't mind confessing that most men in political life feel very insecure. For instance, one hears rumours of René Lévesque buying Canada Savings Bonds.

Many members felt that there was a conflict of interest in voting money into their own pockets. We asked ourselves, when we talked it over in the bar, "Should we abstain?" "If we do abstain, will there be enough Members voting *for* the measure to carry it?" These were the soul-searching questions to which we who are high in the temple of democracy — the House of Commons — had to address ourselves.

Today, that is all history. The Division bells rang, and they rang for us. I was obliged to bow to the will of the majority, for that is the great principle upon which our parliamentary system is based. We got our raise, and then were faced with the need to go home and face our ridings, if we wanted to hang on to our seats.

To my constituents in the Pass I spoke straight from the

shoulder: "If you disapprove of my raise in pay, you can vote me out of office . . . providing, of course, that you can find some rich scab who will do a second-class job for nothing. . . . This salary of mine is now the law of the land! I know that neither my friends in the labour movement, nor those who work for a living, will support a fink wage-cutter." Needless to say, I received a standing ovation.

    Now, I say to you as I said to them, I have nothing to hide and even less to expose. Anyone is free to examine my books at any time. Here is a list of my expenses covering the past two months:

Shoe laces	.39
Hospital Insurance	350.00
Hairdresser	18.00
Max Factor	21.00
Expenses incurred in good-will mission to Hull, Que.	78.93
Secretarial services re: above trip (Greta)	50.00
Bodyguard at Women's Lib Rally	100.00
Purchase of research materials: War Cry	
Christian Science Monitor	
R.C.M.P. Quarterly	
Canadian Tribune	
Watch Tower	
Midnight	
Cattle Breeders' Manual	
Total	23.80
Settlement with Dr. Pacard covering medical expense incurred by secretary (Greta)	350.00
Jelly beans for children of constituents	30.00
Laxative	3.95
Installation of microphone in ashtray	130.00
Dissemination of published speeches	N/C
Presentation of bugle (second-hand) to Kicking Horse Pass Boys Band	12.95
New saddle for Filibuster (Campaign Horse)	325.87
Preparation H	4.89
Contributions to Knights of Columbus and Orange Order	.41
Entertainment of New Apathetic Party bag-man and wife	1137.00
Premium for re-election insurance	852.00
Visit to federal prison for interview with bag-man	28.73
Refreshments for Ladies Auxiliary of the Committee to Re-elect the Member for K.H.P. (6 cases)	94.00

Luncheon Date with Elwood Glover	2.50
15% Tip	.37
Total	4.98
Gold Cross Award to Mother of the Year	1.59
Boarding of Filibuster	12.32
To Dr. Gusthaf Milthoven Vet. (Spanish Fly for Filibuster's wedding)	38.00
Testimonial Dinner given in my honour	2000.00
To Dr. Gusthaf Milthoven Vet. (Treatment of Filibuster's irritation)	10.00
Parliamentary Delegation trip to Peking	N/C
Purchase of *Thoughts of Mao*	2.00
Chopsticks for Greta	.39
Ping-Pong bats	N/C
Total cost of trip	2.39
Toy for Justin	200.00
Salaries to Partisan Claque at Welcome Home Rally	235.00
Dr. Pacard (treatment of burning sensation)	15.00
Farewell Office Party for Greta	175.00

If you are concerned about the future of Canadian culture, if you want to be better informed in this regard, to gain a deeper insight and awareness of your cultural heritage, I commend to you the wealth of knowledge in the following literary works:

Hockey Heroes	*George Edward Sullivan*
Hockey Heroes	*Ron McAllister*
Hockey Showdown	*Harry Sinden*
Hockey Is My Life	*Phil Esposito with Gerald Eskenazi*
Hockey in My Blood	*Johnny Bucyk with Russ Conway*
Hockey, the Fastest Game on Earth	*Mervyn Dulton*
Hockey's Greatest All-Stars	*Howard Liss*
Hockey	*Richard F. Vaughan*
Hockey	*Lev Filatov*
Hockey	*Zander Hollander and Hal Bock*
Hockey!	*Richard Beddoes*
Hockey Scrapbook	*Frank Orr*
Hockey Is My Game	*Bobby Hull*
Hockey Night in Canada	*Foster Hewitt*

Hockey Night in Moscow	*Jack Ludwig*
Hockey – Here's Howe	*Gordie Howe*
Hockey, The Right Start	*Georges Lariviere*
Hockey, Special Photography	*Ken Regan*
Hockey Photos	*Harold Barkley and Trent Frayne*
Hockey Stars of '74	*Stan Fischler*
Beginning Hockey	*Information Canada*
How to Play Better Hockey	*Information Canada*
Coach's Manual, Hockey	*Information Canada*
Ice Hockey Rules	*Robert Scharff*
A Thinking Man's Guide to Pro Hockey	*Gerald Eskenazi*
The Secrets of Winning Hockey	*Emile Francis*
Andy Bathgate's Hockey Secrets	*Andy Bathgate and Bob Wolff*
Russian Hockey Secrets	*Anatoli Tarasov*
Tarasov's Hockey Technique	*Brian McFarlane*
Howie Meeker's Hockey Basics	*Howie Meeker*
How to Play Hockey	*Tom Watt*
Let's Play Hockey	*Lynn Patrick and D. Leo Monahan*
Let's Play Hockey	*Gordie Howe*
Let's Play Better Hockey	*Ken Dryden*
Pro Hockey	*Jim Proudfoot*
Ice Hockey	*Mark Mulvoy*
Ice Hockey	*Edward John Jeremiah*
Ice Hockey	*Thomas Knight Fisher*
The Fundamentals of Ice Hockey	*Caswell D. Bingham*
The Encyclopedia of Hockey	*Robert A. Styer*
The Pocket Hockey Encyclopedia	*Modern Canadian Library*
Great Moments in Pro Hockey	*Allen Camelli*
Everything You've Always Wanted to Know About Hockey	*Brian McFarlane*
Playing Hockey the Professional Way	*Rod Gilbert*
The Hockey Handbook	*Lloyd Percival*
Ice Hockey, How to Play It and Enjoy It	*Frank Mahovlich*
Ice Hockey in Pictures	*Robert Scharff*
Ice Hockey	*Jack Riley*
The Hockey Handbook	*W. V. Roche*

Official Professional Hockey Guide and Who's Who in Hockey	*James C. Hendy*
National Hockey League Guide	*James C. Hendy*
Footloose in Hockey	*Ed Fitkin*
Coaching Hockey	*John W. Meagher*
The Men in the Nets	*Jim R. Hunt*
More Hockey Stories	*R. M. McAllister*
Young Hockey Champions	*Andy O'Brien*
Play the Man	*Brad Park*
Inside Hockey	*Stan Mikita with George Vass*
Headline Hockey	*Andy O'Brien*
Goal Tending	*Jacques Plante*
Great Goalies of Pro Hockey	*Bobby Orr*
Down the Ice	*Foster Hewitt*
Face-Off, A Guide to Modern Ice Hockey	*George Sullivan*
Face-Off at the Summit	*Ken Dryden with Mark Mulvoy*
Face-Off '73-'74	*Martin Lader*
Face-Off of the Century	*Gilles Terroux*
The Stanley Cup	*Brian McFarlane*
The Stanley Cup Story	*Henry H. Roxborough*
The Trail of the Stanley Cup	*Charles Coleman*
On the Hockey Beat	*Ed Fitkin*
High Stick	*Ted Green and Al Hirshberg*
It's Easy, All You Have To Do Is Win	*Trent Frayne*
The Ice Men	*Gary Ronberg*
The Gashouse Gang of Hockey	*Ed Fitkin*
Hello Canada and Hockey Fans in the United States	*Foster Hewitt*
Les Canadiens	*Andy O'Brien*
The Leafs I Knew	*Scott Young*
Detroit's Big Three	*Ed Fitkin*
The Blazing North Stars	*Stan Fischler*
The Champion Bruins	*Stan Fischler*
Chicago Black Hawks	*Stan Fischler*
The Fast-Flying Wings	*Stan Fischler*
Saga of the St. Louis Blues	*Stan Fischler*

The Flying Frenchmen	*Maurice Richard and Stan Fischler*
The Conquering Canadiens	*Stan Fischler*
The Brothers Esposito	*Phil and Tony Esposito with Tim Moriarty*
Behind The Cheering	*Frank J. Selke with H. Gordon Green*
The Blue Shirt	*Stan Saplin*
Clancy, the King's Story	*Brian McFarlane*
Goal! My Life on Ice	*Rod Gilbert*
I Play to Win	*Stan Mikita*
Orr on Ice	*Bobby Orr with Dick Grace*
Rocket Richard	*Andy O'Brien*
Maurice Richard, Hockey's Rocket	*Ed Fitkin*
A Year on Ice	*Gerald Eskenazi*
Come on Teeder	*Ed Fitkin*
Gordie Howe	*Stan Fischler*
The Bobby Orr Story	*John Devaney*
Bobby Orr and the Big, Bad Bruins	*Stan Fischler*
Red Kelly	*Stanley Obodiac*
The Jacques Plante Story	*Andy O'Brien*
Max Bentley, Hockey's Dipsy Doodle Dandy	*Ed Fitkin*
Turk Broda of the Leafs	*Ed Fitkin*
Goaltender, Cheevers of the Bruins	*Gerry Cheevers with Trent Frayne*
The Famous Bentleys	*Walter H. Thurn*
Road to Olympus	*Anatoli Tarasov*
The Fans Go Wild	*John Gault*
Superstars	*Andy O'Brien*
Power Skating	*John Wild*
Skating	*J. M. Heathcote*
Hockey Bibliography	*Dave Broadfoot*

from The Grass Is Never Greener

Robert Thomas Allen

Travel is supposed to be a wonderful thing not only for children (it's so educational) but for writers, who, according to the popular notion, have to get around and see all sorts of things to have something to write about.

This worked in reverse for me. When I lived in Toronto, I wrote stories about mountain climbing in the Alps and big-game hunting in Africa, most of which ended with storms and didn't sell any better than the ones that ended with fires. Now that I was living in the middle of the desert, surrounded by mountains, rattlesnakes, prospectors, Navajos, cowboys and white-faced Herefords, I wrote a story about a man in my home town who stuffed birds and I sold it. I also wrote an article recommending that people stay at home and sold that too. This was the peak of my career. I made $450 in nine months, or slightly more than a good sitter, then folded up.

Anyway, I got so busy writing letters that I hardly had time to write anything else. This is a problem of going to the Perfect Place to Live: you have to write thousands of words back home to the people who didn't go there. A mathematical law works against the one away from home. If you want to keep in touch with, say fourteen friends, each of whom writes once a week, you have to write two letters a day. This doesn't sound much until you miss a few days.

My wife and I were sometimes as busy with our correspondence out there among the sidewinders as two debutantes at the opening of the social season. We often worked so late that we began sending out those laboured efforts that go, "Things are about the same at my end and hoping you are the same at your end." We grew bleary-eyed staring at little words like "took," "tooke," "tuk," which we wrote out on separate pieces of paper to find out what suddenly made them look queer, like husbands.

But more than offsetting the effort was the pleasure of hearing from our friends, which was one of the best things about living away from home. Many of them wrote a lot better stuff than I was writing for editors, and it was sometimes intriguing to study the various approaches to letter writing. I used to like particularly to read the letters my wife got from an English girl friend, who larruped right in with low shoes, a lot of feeling and a conviction that the things that were happening inside her were far more interesting than the things that were happening outside her. She'd write:

> My Dear: Please don't think me too beastly for not writing sooner, but life is such a bore at times that one finds that one simply can't face writing one's friends, then one finds oneself suddenly walking in the country and thinking of something simply heavenly with red sideburns and a little moustache. . . .

And I used to love to hear from a niece of mine in Sarnia, who would write:

> Dear Uncle Bob: I fell in the river yesterday. I like being wet. Sally had four more kittens. I saw a skunk. Joan won't let me play with her doll. I hope she dies. I hope you are well. Love . . .

I also got letters from a man who wrote about something I'd said in my story about stuffing birds and with whom I struck up a gruff but friendly correspondence. I used to picture him sitting amid books and old dinosaur bones with a pipe clamped between his teeth, surrounded by the smell of good tobacco and ideas. He would grumble:

> Dear Allen: Darwin said that the horse, ass, zebra, quagga and haemonius were all evolved from an equine animal striped like the zebra but differently constructed and that the ancestors of all domestic animals. . . .

And through my one article, I had my first contact with one of those people who write mysterious, cranky letters to editors, frequently quoting Chaucer or someone who sounds like Chaucer.

> Dear Allen: I've just finished your garbage about travel.
> Obviously you want to be a movie star. Why don't they?
> As if you didn't know. Oh well —
>> "I'll fit sonne gonyan day,
>> Thou saydest eek, that there
>> Been thinges thre. . . ."
>> In disgust . . .

But getting letters from our friends had become one of the most vital things in our lives, as Christmas was only a few weeks away, and we were getting properly homesick. To make matters worse, we went to hear a children's choir in one of the stores. We listened to "O Holy Night" and "Hark! the Herald Angels Sing," standing in the washtub department, with the desert sand whispering against the windows and the tears pouring down our faces. Lean ranch hands in blue jeans walked around us buying blowtorches and things, and a fierce-looking Navajo family watched us, obviously thinking if the white man got any softer, the Indians would have the country back in no time.

But Christmas was livened up by the kids, who didn't care where they spent it as long as they got some toys, and by an expedition to a near-by mountain for a Christmas tree. I went with my Texas friend, who ended up in a dire scene with the owner of some ranch land, both of them making veiled threats about who could shoot the other faster, something that got my mind off the fact that I was homesick.

We stayed in the desert until the temperature went up to 117° in the shade, and our front doorknob, which was in the sun, was so hot that I began letting myself into the house by putting my hand in my pocket, standing on tiptoes and wrapping the knob in a handful of my pants.

We decided that it was time to go home, take stock of all we'd seen and decide where we were going to live.

"After all," we told each other, our eyes glowing at the thought of moving again, "that was the original idea."

But first we wanted to see the coast. We were all packed and ready, and on our last day in the desert I went down to the bank building to see my Texas friend, who looked after the machinery in the basement. As I approached the building, I noticed a lot of activity outside. Workmen were busy tearing up a big strip of roadway, and there was a lot of water around. I went into the bank and was told I could find my friend at the lunch counter across the street. I found him having a cup of coffee. He looked very sad.

"Remember all those valves I showed you?" he said, without expression. "Turned the wrong one last night. Let a hundred and eighty-five pounds pressure into the wrong line. Blew up fifteen feet of sidewalk."

I haven't seen him since. I hope he is happy and working at something that doesn't have valves.

Next day we drove across the remaining desert that separated us from the coast. Very little of the North American desert has those sand dunes they use in movies about sheiks and German spies. A great portion of the desert is about like a sandy city lot on which a brick building has been torn down, with coarse shrubs rooted in the rubble at distances of twenty or thirty feet, causing the desert to look green from a low angle. Multiply that picture a few million times, add barren mountains, sprinkle with cactus, stir well until everything is cracked and fissured and warm considerably before serving, and you have a rough idea of some of the terrain we drove through that day.

Late that afternoon we reached the coast. We rented a snug little ranch house in Pasadena, owned by a man who had gone in for taxidermy, and settled down for a month amid china cabinets full of stuffed owls to discover how we liked the California that most people think of as California — the land of palms, red-tile roofs, swimming pools, blondes, muscles and flowers. When my wife saw it she began to wonder whether we should go home after all, even for a visit. Here was a sunny, snowless civilization, with cool nights, razzle-dazzle shopping districts and supermarkets like the foyer to heaven. Maybe this was The Place.

My wife was more enthusiastic than I was. I found it hard to see past those formal gardens and shrubs shaped like wieners. I've never liked cultivated flowers; to get me into a flower show has always been like trying to give a dog a bath. And here I was in the biggest flower show on earth, with green wieners added and the whole thing accompanied by the tinkling, unreal music of the

Good Humour Man, which used to float faintly through my window to me at night like something coming from under a distant toadstool.

My wife and I often stood peering out windows, one looking east and the other west, and my wife frequently got a look in her eye as if weighing me against Pasadena and trying to keep from laughing. But the children needed a father. Or did they?

Now we not only weren't sure where we wanted to live but whom we wanted to live with. The kids, in the meantime, oblivious of everything, including California, quietly played with the snails they found under the green wiener trees.

When I wasn't looking at the stuffed owls, I sat with my fingers poised over my typewriter, looking out onto a deceptively quiet street, the lone spectator of a nether world of mayhem, treachery and propaganda, as the preschool-age children were turned outdoors, one by one, their little faces wiped clean of toast crumbs and their souls full of diabolical plans. They passed my window all day long, in thin-column formation, in a perpetual state of spine-chilling, dead-pan, passionless war. They wore hunting caps, long pink nightgowns, their mothers' shoes and lace curtains. Sometimes they moved by on wheels, sometimes on foot, but they all had one objective: to frame one another.

By lunchtime each day things had become so snarled that it was impossible to tell who was telling the truth. Right and wrong got so balled up in one gumbo mixture of bubble gum and tricycles that none of the mothers could sort them out, even if they'd wanted to. They just didn't worry about it.

One day I watched two little boys with shaved heads ride around a tree on their tricycles, slowly and aimlessly, from eight in the morning till suppertime, telling each other in agitated voices that they'd break each other's tricycles, that they'd climb up onto lamp posts and drop rocks on each other's heads, that they'd put each other in jail. Around eleven o'clock, one of them got off his trike, went over and hit the other in the mouth, then went home hollering, "Mummy! Pete hit me."

His mother came out, looked at him sharply, said, "Pull your pants up," and went back in.

Two strange little boys meeting for the first time would stand looking into each other's faces for a moment, then start conscientiously kicking each other until one started howling and went home.

Little tots with legs like noodles toddled off each morning in pigtails, bows and pocket-size dresses, on their way to play a day-long game, the object of which was to try to get somebody else spanked. When they scored, they all stood around sucking Popsicles, watching. They didn't laugh or gloat or show any excitement. Their faces would be completely expressionless.

Every other minute they'd go and tell their mothers. If they didn't have anything to tell them, they made something up. Sometimes they told their own mothers, sometimes they told the other kid's mother. If they couldn't find either mother, they told the breadman. It was a peculiar world, where the idea seemed to be that if you could stay with it until everyone was grown up, it would all sort itself out.

One day a little girl with a head of white curls let out a nerve-shattering scream that brought six mothers racing from their doors, three of them in curlers.

"Doris! What *is* it!" gasped one of them.

Doris put her hand on her flat little chest, looked across a geranium hedge at another little girl and said in a hoarse stage whisper, "Gail looked at me!"

"It's time you came in for lunch, anyway," her mother said.

One afternoon three little girls were playing. Suddenly two of them pushed the third off the verandah, then picked up her doll, threw it at her and kicked over a house she'd made out of old cartons. I was almost ready to leap up from my typewriter and cross the road to lecture them on the rudiments of justice, sportsmanship and the Geneva Conference. The little girl who had been shoved off the verandah screamed. The other two screamed back at her. The woman of the house came out.

"They broke my house," the little girl wailed.

"Why did you break Susan's house?" the woman asked, mechanically retying a bow.

"We were through playing with it," one of them said.

"Pull up your socks," the woman said, "and don't get dirty."

One time I listened to one youngster ask in a flat monotone, at intervals all morning, if another would let her play with her doll carriage.

"Can I have your carriage?" she'd say.

"No."

At noon the mother of the kid with the carriage put her

head out the door and called her daughter in for lunch. The youngster put the top of the carriage up, started home and fell down the verandah steps. She lay on her back, reaching for a sound proportionate to the fall. I could hear the scream coming like water working its way up to the nozzle of a garden hose. Just before it arrived, the other kid, who stood looking down at her like a little gangster in pigtails, evidently figuring that she was going to die, said, "Can I have your carriage now?"

Evidently mercy is something that begins to show itself around voting age. Jane, who although going to school was still young enough to retain the preschool spirit, would chatter away at lunch, telling about the things that had happened at school.

"There's a boy in our class named Johnny," she said one day, industriously spooning chicken-noodle soup into herself. "He talks all the time."

"M-hm," I said.

"This morning the teacher said, 'Well, I'm going to put you in the middle of four good little girls, Martha, Joan, Dianne and Jane.'"

"So?"

"'And if you talk,' she said, 'I'm going to ask Martha, Joan, Dianne and Jane to tell me, and I'm going to send you to the office.' We had great fun."

"How do you mean?"

"We tried to get him to talk so we could tell the teacher."

"You what!" I brought her into focus, as it dawned on me what she'd said.

"We tried to see how we could get him to talk," she said, getting up to get some more soup.

My wife said, "Oh, Jane. You shouldn't!"

"Shouldn't what?" Jane said in surprise.

"Shouldn't take more soup," my wife said.

I discovered that in the world of women and children, promises and systems of ethics are held together lightly by a thin coating of orange juice and hair fix and an occasional safety pin. It often left me wishing that I were back amid the jolly cutthroat atmosphere of big business. There people did one another in according to firm principles. At home nobody would have recognized a principle if she'd found it in her shredded wheat. It amounts to the same thing, probably, but it's easier on the nerves when it doesn't take place on a quiet, sunny street.

In fact, if I'd been downtown instead of sitting like an old possum at my typewriter, watching everything that was going on, some of the things that happened wouldn't have occurred. I decided that I'd straighten out some of the little adventures in misunderstanding around my own house with a few Solomon-like decrees. It was something like someone who has been smoking a flat fifty cigarettes a day for twenty years giving it up in favour of contemplating cosmic truths. It's a wonderful idea, but if he tries it too suddenly, he'll end up being chased around by a man with a net.

At this time Mary, who was toddling around with a face as guileless as a carving off a harp, started using what the psychologists call naughty words. I can't tell you the word Mary favoured, but it was one used usually on dead car batteries.

But I ignored it, on the principle that if we paid no attention, she'd forget it, and she went on using it regularly – on her dolls, building blocks and the little windmills she made out of her Tinker Toys. It was like watching a Little Golden Book version of *The Picture of Dorian Gray*.

She also started lying at the same time, so that she'd swear, then look me straight in the eye and say it was Mummy who said it.

I had already decided that neither of my kids was learning any sense of responsibility and that they were fighting too much and eating too many candies, and in a rash of parenthood I decided to cure everything at once. I made a rule that both children were to have candy only on Monday and Friday; that each night they were to tidy up their own rooms and hang up all their clothes before seven-thirty or I would take a dime off their allowances. In an effort to forestall future fights, which I decided arose from the fact that they had no way of getting away from each other, I pronounced what I thought was my master stroke.

"If either one of you wants to play in a room by herself," I said, "all she needs to do is come and tell me."

I'm not quite sure yet why I added, "The one who *doesn't* come to me has the first choice of rooms."

The next night, hard upon a series of shrieks and crashes and the sound of dolls' heads against little girls' heads, Jane confronted me with: "Mary wants to play by herself in the bedroom, so she's going to keep kicking me until I ask you if I can play by myself, then she's going to say she wants the bedroom."

I'd already forgotten what the rule was, but I didn't want

to admit my confusion, so I asked Jane how *she* would solve this little problem, pretending that I could. Her solution was that the one who came to me should have the choice of rooms. It seemed all right to me. Jane chose the living room. Then, minutes later, Mary came out and announced sweetly that she had picked up all her toys and cleaned up her room. She pointed to the clock and reminded me that Jane had just lost a dime from her allowance.

To go back on the rule was going to put me in the position of a father who showed indecision and lack of character. In a panic I said I wouldn't dock Jane, but Mary could have a candy. My wife called to me that it wasn't candy day, and Mary, in the bedroom, let go with a clearly audible, "Oh — !"

I got out of the whole thing by promising to let them both play with my typewriter the next night. It turned out to be a wonderful idea. Mary used her word on it a few times when the keys got jammed, but the psychologists were right. She finally did stop. They began to ruin my typewriter, but I figured letting them play with it would work out only to an extra expense of about twenty dollars a year in depreciation, and it gave me a chance to get my mind off the problems of being a parent and concentrate on our unsettled future and what we were going to do when we arrived back north.

Our visit to Pasadena, although out of our way, had been planned as part of our return trip to Canada; we had made our arrangements, written to our friends and family, even forwarded a deposit on an apartment in East Toronto. Even my wife, who still thought Pasadena was getting close to paradise, didn't make any serious proposal to stay. Anyway, neither of us was quite sure of what we should do. It was just that each wanted to make sure not to miss the Perfect Place to Live just for the sake of a bit of salesmanship.

from The Great Fur Opera

Kildare Dobbs

Mister Gooseberry and his brother-in-law were impressed with the greatness of England.

Every year there was something great.

First the Great Plague of 1665. Then the Great Fire of London in 1666. And in 1667, the Great Boost to shipbuilding when the Dutch sailed up the Medway and set fire to the Royal Navy.

The court was in Oxford when they arrived. They were introduced by a royal favourite who had found them in Boston, where he had been trying to explain Restoration Comedy to the Puritans.

The two renegades from New France had an Idea.

Between themselves, the Idea was to dodge tax. But they told the English Gentlemen it was a way to found colonies, make fortunes in fur, and outsmart Louis XIV, the Fun King.

Mr. Radisson did most of the talking. Everyone liked his stories.

Radisson laid it on pretty thick about the savages, as he called them.

"I love these people well!" he said, describing how they had pulled out his finger nails, chewed on his knuckles, broiled his feet. He didn't want Englishmen horning in on his territory. Not yet. He just wanted their money.

The Hon. Robert Boyle, Fellow of the Royal Society, listened attentively.

None other than the author of Boyle's Law, it was he who had demonstrated that the volume of an elastic fluid, such as air, varies inversely with the pressure. Posterity was to know him as the founder of pneumatical philosophy — and the brother of the Earl of Cork.

The Frenchmen were impressed. Especially when Boyle turned out to be a friend of the King's.

No one realized they were being asked to set up a chain of department stores.

London, early in 1670.

"How are we to describe this company," the attorney asked Hayes.

"You're the solicitor."

"How about: The Governor and Mystery of . . . ."

"It's not a mystery."

"That's what the Muskovy Company calls itself."

"Pox take the Muskovy Company. And anyway, our Committee is mysterious enough."

"As you please, Sir James. What about: The Governor and Company of Merchant Adventurers of . . . ."

"No, no. Not *Merchant* Adventurers . . . ."

"But the Muskovy Company . . . ."

"Damn the Muskovites, I say!"

"We're paying good money for a copy of their charter."

"Throw it out. The Prince is *hardly* a merchant."

"Then: The Governor and Company of Gentlemen Adventurers of Eng . . . ."

"Strike out 'Gentlemen'."

The attorney slipped off his high stool. He pulled off his wig and dashed it to the floor. Then he jumped on it, three times.

"Sir, I am at a loss." He was panting. "Am I to understand, then, that the Prince is not a gentleman? That his grace of Albemarle is not a gentleman? That m'lord of Arlington is not a . . . ."

"Govern your temper, sir." Sir James took a pinch of snuff. "This is a delicate matter. . . . Gentlemen do not engage in trade."

The attorney bent, groaning, to retrieve his wig.

He clapped it on his head, saying nothing. He climbed to his stool and began writing with a goose quill.

"Here!"

He handed Sir James the paper. Sir James read:

The Governor and Company of Adventures of England tradeing into Hudson's Bay —

"Hudson apostrophe ess?" he observed. "But let it stand. 'Tis brave. It has a singularity."

Somewhat mollified, the attorney gave a grunt.

"Now as to the territories His Majesty is conveying . . ."

"Sir, I leave that to you. I am your obedient."

Hayes bowed and left.

The territories. What was the attorney to make of the territories? Master Norwood's map was vague, to say the least. The problem was to convey land not yet discovered.

There was no question about the type of tenure.

The lands were to be held in free and common socage.

How did one pronounce that? The attorney's rage had left him confused.

In free and common sockage? Together with bootage, pantage, trouserage, and other nether garbage. Possibly with footage, leggage, hippage, waistage. Also wastage, luggage, portage, and Northwest Passage.

Or was it in free and common sausage? With porridge, spillage, spoilage, and beverage. Certainly with beaverage.

Annual rent to the Crown of two elks and two black beaver whenever the King, his heirs and successors, should set foot in the territories.

To be known as Rupert's Land.

The Adventurers to be true and absolute lords and proprietors.

Now the attorney was thoroughly confused.

"I'll begin again," he muttered.

He stared at the map.

Ridiculous names these islands had. Briggs His Mathematicks. What kind of a name was that?

Then he remembered the story. Briggs, yes. The thrice learned mathematician who had calculated from tidal drifts that there was an opening here to the west. Captain Luke Foxe had used his chart in 1631. Sighting islands where Briggs had predicted a channel, Foxe had named them for the armchair navigator.

"River beds!" the attorney suddenly exclaimed.

He had hit on the secret of Canada.

He began to scribble a draft:

Sole Trade and Commerce of all those Seas Streightes Bayes Rivers Lakes Creeks and Soundes in whatsoever Latitude they shall bee that lye within the entrance of the Streightes commonly called Hudsons Streightes together with all the Landes and Territoryes upon the Countryes Coastes . . .

When in doubt, he decided, warming to his work, give them everything.

"Odds Fish!" the King said. "I'll swear I heard a seal bark!"

Nell Gwynne made a face. It was not true that he never said a foolish thing. It was his own fault for rising so early.

Beyond the door, the Lord Privy Seal cleared his throat a second time.

"And no quips about privies!" Nell warned.

"This morning," the King said, yawning, "we are to seal the charter for the Hudson's Bay adventurers. Cousin Rupert will be waiting."

He swept the dogs off the bed with a regal gesture and began pulling on his silk stockings.

"Another day in the life of Charles the Second," he said.

"Charles the Third," Nell corrected him. Her first king, he was her third Charles.

It was May the second, 1670.

The long life of the Hudson's Bay Company was about to begin.

Pay Attention, Now

Doug Fetherling

What with all the interest in astrology these days, some horoscope columnists and the like have all but become folk heroes, as popular as American baseball players or matadors in Spain. Although I don't want to enter into the arguments as to whether these star-gazers can actually foresee the future and offer fruitful advice, I do want to reserve a tentative seat on the bandwagon. So I've been doing a little reading of the zodiacal charts of our listeners and have come up with the following for today.

Aries: Financial reverses are likely today if you make unwise deals involving money. Beware of Greeks bearing coups d'etats. A stitch in time saves nine. Your sister-in-law may visit from Winnipeg.

Taurus: Watch out for falling rocks. Soft shoulders may prove a problem, especially in the forenoon. Keep your eyes to the ground and your nose in the air. Should be a good day for going barefoot.

Gemini: Don't be afraid to exercise your intuition when buying muskmelons. Discretion today will prove improprietous. Remember, a map is not a journey. Take all precautions against toothaches.

Cancer: Your right shoelace may break between 1:26 and 2:07 p.m. unless you are careful. Attend a favourite operetta but watch crossing one-way streets.

Leo: Certain differences between your husband and yourself will today become apparent: your husband is a man. Overexertion may bring on exhaustion. Ask a stranger for a ride.

Virgo: You could become overdrawn at the bank if you aren't already. Be kind to stray dogs and cats but don't let them walk all over you. Your love life may improve if you don't wind up in hospital. On second thought, forget the dogs and cats.

Libra: Skip lunch, leave the phone off the hook and be thankful. The Dow Jones average will reach its highest peak since yesterday. Rain is likely in some part of the country.

Scorpio: Nervousness could prove an asset. The war in Asia will continue. Do a chimney sweep a favour and see what happens. An excellent day to purchase that xylophone.

Sagittarius: An unexpected turn of fate will greatly surprise you. Nothing's too good for your neighbours, within certain limits. Hasn't your sister-in-law shown up yet?

Capricorn: That bridge hand you dreamed of will be thwarted. Don't spread mendacities you know to be untrue. A wise man once said, "He who follows me is no leader of men." Ponder that, and worry.

Aquarius: Go out of your way to be nasty with some pastry cook; the rewards will be great but not immediate. Shun all attempts to become a sex symbol. Quitters never win but who cares?

Pisces: Logical, well-thought-out actions taken in haste will bring on nothing but regret. Air pollution can be employed to great advantage. Avoid rides in Zeppelins today and above all disregard your horoscope completely.

from a CBC Radio Broadcast

from Tempest-Tost

Robertson Davies

Eight days before the first night of *The Tempest* the following advertisement appeared in the Salterton evening paper for the last of five successive publications:

AUCTION

The complete Household Effects of the late Dr. Adam Savage will be sold at auction at his former residence, 33 King Street, on Friday, June 8, beginning at 10 o'clock a.m.

All furnishings, ornaments, china and glass, carpets, bed linen, etc. will positively be sold to the highest bidder under the conditions posted on the door. No catalogue. View day Thursday, June 7.

Do not miss this sale which is the most Important to be held in Salterton so far this year.

And for this fifth appearance the following note was appended to the advertisement:

We are directed by Miss Valentine Rich, executor of the late Dr. Savage, to announce that his splendid library, comprising more than 4300 volumes of Philosophy, Theology, Travel, Superior Fiction and Miscellaneous will be open to the clergy of all denominations from 10 o'clock Wednesday, June 6, and they may have gratis any volumes they choose. This is done in accordance with the wish of the late Dr. Savage. Clergy must remove books personally.

ELLIOT & MAYBEE
Auctioneers and Valuers

This addition to the auction notice was printed in no larger type than the rest of the advertisement, but it caught a surprising number of eyes on the Tuesday when it appeared. Anything which concerns a subject dear to us seems to leap from a large page of print. Freddy Webster, who was no careful reader of newspapers, saw it, and snorted like a young warhorse.

"Giving away books!" said she. "But only to preachers! Damn!"

Later that evening she met Solly, who was in the garden wondering, as all directors of outdoor performances of *The Tempest* must, whether the arrangements for the storm-tossed ship in the first scene of the play would provoke the audience to such derisive laughter that they would rise in a body and demand the return of their money at the gate.

"Yes, I saw it," he said in answer to her question. "Pretty rotten, confining it to the clergy. Not that I care about Philosophy, or Theology, or even Superior Fiction. But there might just be something tucked away in Miscellaneous which would be lost on the gentlemen of the cloth."

"Whatever made Valentine do it?"

"Apparently, two or three years ago, the old chap said something, just in passing, about wanting his books dealt with that way. And they're quite unsaleable, you know. A bookseller wouldn't give five cents apiece for the lot."

"Have you seen them, Solly?"

"No; but you know how hard it is to get rid of books. Especially Theology. Nothing changes fashion so quickly as Theology."

"But there might just be a treasure or two among them."

"I know."

"Still, I don't suppose a preacher would know a really valuable book if he saw one. They'll go for the concordances and commentaries on the Gospels. Do you suppose Val would let us look through what's left?"

"Freddy, my innocent poppet, there won't be anything left. They'll strip the shelves. Anything free has an irresistible fascination. Free books to preachers will be like free booze to politicians; they'll scoop the lot, without regard for quality. You mark my words."

Freddy recognized the truth of what he said. She herself was a victim of that lust for books which rages in the breast like a demon, and which cannot be stilled save by the frequent and plentiful acquisition of books. This passion is more common, and more powerful, than most people suppose. Book lovers are thought by unbookish people to be gentle and unworldly, and perhaps a few of them are so. But there are others who will lie and scheme and steal to get books as wildly and unconscionably as the dope-taker in pursuit of his drug. They may not want the books to read immediately, or at all; they want them to possess, to range on their shelves, to have at command. They want books as a Turk is thought to want concubines — not to be hastily deflowered, but to be kept at their master's call, and enjoyed more often in thought than in reality. Solly was in a measure a victim of this unscrupulous passion, but Freddy was wholly in the grip of it.

Still, she had her pride. She would not beg Valentine to regard her as a member of the clergy for a day; she would not even hang about the house in a hinting manner. She would just drop in, and if the conversation happened to turn upon books, as some scholarly rural dean fingered a rare volume, she would let it be known, subtly, that she was deeply interested in them, and then — well, and then she would see what happened.

With this plan in view she was at the residence of the late Dr. Adam Savage at five minutes to ten on the following morning, dismayed to find that an astounding total of two hundred and seventeen clergymen were there before her, waiting impatiently on the lawn. They ranged from canons of the cathedral, in shovel hats and the grey flannels which the more worldly Anglicans affect in summer, through Presbyterians and ministers of the United Church in black coats and Roman collars, to the popes and miracle workers of backstreet sects, dressed in everything under the sun. There was a young priest, a little aloof from the others, who had been instructed by his bishop to bespeak a copy of *The Catholic Encyclopaedia* which was known to be in the house, for a school library. There were two rabbis, one with a beard and one without, chatting with the uneasy geniality of men who expect shortly to compete in a race for a shelf of books on the Pentateuch. There were High Anglicans with crosses on their watch chains, and low Anglicans with moustaches. There were sixteen Divinity students, not yet ordained, but trying to look sanctified in dark suits. There was a stout man in a hot brown suit, wearing a clerical stock with a wing collar; upon his head sat a jaunty grey hat, in the band of which was fixed a small metal aeroplane; it was impossible to say what he was, but he wore a look of confidence which bespoke an

early training in salesmanship. There was a mild man with a pince-
nez, who was whispered to be a Christian Science practitioner.
There was no representative of the Greek Orthodox, the Syrian or
Coptic Churches; otherwise Christianity in its utmost variety was
assembled on that lawn.

It was never discovered how clergymen for a radius of fifty
miles around Salterton got wind of Dr. Savage's posthumous
bounty. The local newspaper took the great assembly of holy men
as a tribute to the power of its advertising columns; indeed, as
Freddy approached, a press photographer was climbing into a tree
to take a picture of the extraordinary sight. However, the orgulous
pride of newspapers is widely understood. The gossips of Salterton
decided, after several weeks of discussion, that the matter was
beyond any rational explanation, but that the Christian Church
must be better organized, and more at one on certain matters, than
they had thought.

At five minutes past ten, when the clergy were beginning
to buzz like bees, a car stopped in front of the lawn and young
Mr. Maybee and Valentine climbed out of it. They were a good
deal surprised and discomposed to find a crowd waiting for them,
and hurried to open the front door. It had been their intention to
sit quietly in the library at a table, arranging some final details of
the sale and welcoming the occasional clergyman who might drop
in for a book. Instead they were closely followed up the steps, not
rudely, but as cattle follow a farmer with a pail of hot mash. When
the door was opened the clergy increased their pace, still without
rudeness, but with a kind of hungry fervour, and Valentine and
young Mr. Maybee found that they were entering the library at
a brisk trot. It was a room of moderate size, and might perhaps
have held fifty people when full. Seventy rushed into it in sixty
seconds, and the remainder crowded as close to the entry as they
could.

One does not describe the activity of clergymen in a library
as looting. They were, in the main, quiet and well-bred men, and
it was in a quiet and well-bred manner that they went to work.
The pushing was of a moderate order, and the phrase "Excuse me"
was often heard. Natural advantages, such as long arms, superior
height, and good eyesight were given rein, but there was no
actual snatching nor were the old intentionally trodden upon. No
very wide choice, no thoughtful ranging of the shelves, was possible in such a crush, and with good-humoured philosophy the

visitors seized whatever was nearest. There were a few friendly
disagreements; a shovel hat and the brown suit had each got hold
of five volumes of a nicely bound ten-volume set of the works of
a Scottish metaphysician, and neither could see why the other
should not yield his portion. The rabbis, pushed into a corner
where there was little but New Testament material, struggled
feebly to reach their Promised Land, without knowing precisely
where it was to be found. The young priest found his encyclopaedia, but it was too bulky to be moved at one time, and he knew
that it would be fatal to leave any part of it behind him, in the
hope of making a second trip. An elderly Presbyterian fainted, and
young Mr. Maybee had to appeal in a loud voice for help to lift
him through the window into the open air; Valentine took her
chance to crawl out to the lawn, in the wake of the invalid.

"What shall we do?" she asked the auctioneer, who was a
nice young man, and supposedly accustomed to dominating crowds.

"God knows," said Mr. Maybee. "I've never seen anything
like it."

"You must cope," said Valentine, firmly.

Mr. Maybee climbed back upon the windowsill. "Gentlemen," he called in a loud voice, "will those who have chosen their
books please leave as quickly as possible and allow the others to
come in? There is no need to crowd; the library will be open all
day."

This was no more effective than a bus-driver's request to
"Step right down to the rear, please." The clergy at the door
would not budge, and the clergy in the library would not attempt
to leave until they had filled their pockets and heaped their arms
impossibly high. Young Mr. Maybee at last climbed down from
the windowsill, and confessed defeat to Valentine.

There are times when every woman is disgusted by the
bonelessness of men. Valentine had, in her time, directed outdoor
pageants with as many as five hundred supernumeraries in the
crowd scenes. She quickly climbed upon the windowledge herself.

"This won't do," she cried in a loud, fierce voice. "You
must follow my directions to the letter, or I shall have to call the
police. Or perhaps the Fire Department," she added, noticing that
the magical word "police" had done its work upon these ministers
of peace. "All those in the hall go down to the lawn at once."
With some muttering, the brethren in the hall did as they were bid.
"Now," she cried, to the crowd in the library, "you must take

the books you have chosen and leave by the back door." In three minutes the library was empty.

By half past eleven two hundred and thirty-six clergymen had passed through the library, some of them three and four times, and the shelves were bare. Dr. Savage's bequest had been somewhat liberally interpreted, for an inkwell, a pen tray, two letter files, two paperweights, a small bust of Homer, a packet of blotters and an air-cushion which had been in the swivel chair were gone, as well. The widest interpretation had been placed on the word "library" in the advertisement, for some of the visitors had invaded the upstairs regions and made off with two or three hundred detective novels which had been in the old scholar's bedroom. Even a heap of magazines in the cellarway had been removed.

"I don't think there is a scrap of printed matter left in the house," said young Mr. Maybee.

The Instruction

Harry J. Boyle

It happened after dinner on Sunday, where the odd bits of gossip and information picked up at church were digested along with roast chicken.

"Ellie told me she is now a grandmother," said my mother, adding a discreet cough which was usually an indication that the information was not to be discussed in general.

Father spearing a drumstick didn't appear to notice the cough.

"Janie with an eight-pound son. Doesn't seem possible."

I said without thinking, "They were only married at Christmas time."

A terrible silence settled over the room. Mother started passing plates. That was her usual tactic to cover up a blunder. The meat, potatoes, vegetables and gravy plates whirled around like dodge-'em cars at the midway. The tension eased off and the conversation took a safe track once again. I had crossed the invisible line by mentioning a taboo subject. Janey and Bert had left high school suddenly at Christmastime. They were married, had a shower and got settled in a small house, while Bert acquired a job in the grist mill operated by Janey's father in a little short of a week. Now four months later they had a family. It was amazing, but I shouldn't have mentioned it.

There was a pleasant myth in our community, comforting to parents and bewildering to children, that boys and girls on the farm acquired knowledge about biology and reproduction by some mysterious process. Knowledge just came. Most of us did learn a little by observation, gleaned some more information from older boys who were probably as ignorant as ourselves and listened carefully to the talk of the threshing gang, all lusty men.

While this process of learning the facts of life wasn't satisfactory, it was at least better than the dreaded "man-to-man" talk with Father. The thought of it reduced us to complete embarrassment. It obviously did the same for parents. The result was that we tried to avoid asking questions or starting conversations which might lead to an instructional talk. I had opened the door to it by blurting out that rather indelicate statement at the dinner table. My innocence was showing, and, since I was at that gawky, gangling stage and wearing trousers and would be leaving the next year for continuation school, I feared the worst.

After dinner I vanished to the swamp, and, when it grew too close and hot in there, I sneaked along the creek and came to the spring. It was cool by the spring, and after a great draught of cold water I slumped back to watch the white clouds scudding through the sky. I must have fallen asleep. When I came out of the dream, where I had been pursued by a vengeful Janey, I found my father sitting beside me chewing a straw.

"Have a good sleep?"

"Just dozed off."

The first of many awkward pauses settled in. Finally he spoke.

"Been meaning to have a talk with you."

"Oh."

We both welcomed Snap's taking after a groundhog, but, unfortunately, he came back to loll in the grass and Father had to go on. "Anything you want to — is there — well — I mean — do you have anything on your mind?"

I wasn't helpful, but I didn't know what to say.

"Not especially."

He groaned.

"Well, you're getting to be a big boy now. Wearing long pants and all that and going to town next year and you'll be — be —"

Something seemed to be stuck in his throat. It finally exploded.

"Meeting girls."

I felt like saying that I had been meeting girls since I was in rompers, but all I mustered was a feeble, "Yes, I guess so."

By this time we were both reduced to heel pounding. That was a favourite habit in the country. When we were stumped for talk we pounded our heels in the soft turf. I sneaked a glance at my father and saw that his tanned face was wrinkled up into a grimace that suggested pain.

"Now," he said, clearing his throat, "there's a few things you got to remember."

He seemed to have forgotten them himself, because he stopped there. I wasn't too anxious to start the conversation again, so the silence hung between us.

"That was too bad about Bert and Janey," he said finally. "Those things happen and they don't do anybody any good. Of course they got married. Now you got to watch out for that sort of thing."

Then he stood up in obvious relief and said, "Well, I'm going back to see if the cattle have enough salt. I'm mighty glad we had this talk. It pays to clear the air about such things."

He walked away leaving me completely confused but at least relieved. Then I met Grandfather on the way up the lane. He motioned to me to sit down under a choke-cherry tree.

"You know all there is to know about this whole business?" he asked waving his hand.

I made my second mistake of the day.

"Well," I replied with hesitation.

He sighed and puffed on his pipe.

"It's this way."

Then he puffed like a steam engine until the smoke wreathed around his head.

"There's a man and a woman — or a boy and girl —"

He puffed again.

"Let's say they want to get married."

I nodded emphatically.

"Well, they have to be — well — there are a lot of things about getting married — that, well — they should go to somebody and find out —"

This time I nodded in complete mystification. Grandfather took my nod as agreement.

"You see what I mean," he said, "Bert's father and Janey's mother should have had a good talk like this with them and then this — well — they would have known — and what happened — wouldn't have happened."

He poked with a stick at the grass.

"Do you follow me?"

I wanted to tease him, but I didn't have the heart, so I said, "Yes, Gramp."

"Good," he said with the air of a man who had accomplished a great task.

Then he got up and walked away, and I sat on in bewilderment. At supper time Father and Grandfather were in very good humour. I went up to bed, and, just before I went to sleep, my mother came in and stood with her arms folded and looked at me. She had obviously been talking to Father.

"I'm so glad," she said, leaning over to kiss me, "that you have had a chance to talk to your father. Now I know you'll be a good boy."

She went off to bed obviously pleased that the difficult task of instruction for manhood had been accomplished.

from   Homebrew and Patches

Not Just Any Damp Candidate Accepted by State Department

George Bain

It now looks as if occasional bed-wetting isn't going to keep anyone from getting a job as a code-clerk in the United States Department of State.

This unfortunate failing reigned as an undeniable hazard to employment until David A. Belisle, a security officer in the department, quietly withdrew a psychological test which had been in use for less than a month.

But it was too much to hope that withdrawal could keep quiet a test which asked applicants if they sometimes wet the bed, or had problems of any kind with their sex-life — an invitation, God wot, to all sorts of lurid reminiscences — or if they perspired for no good reason. What, surely, would give anyone good reason for perspiring, copiously, was the test itself. It ran to thirteen pages. Applicants were told it might take one to five hours to complete. And they were warned not to seek advice in answering ("Do I wet the bed, dear?" "Yes, I'm afraid you do.")

Not every single Secretary's brightly intellectual;
Assistants often serve for years though wholly ineffectual,
And many men have done their terms in posts ambassadorial
Who wouldn't know an aide mémoire from leading editorial.
Diplomacy does not disbar the nastily acidulous,
And men have often served abroad though frankly rather
  bibulous;
To all of these positions those with failings may aspire
— But you cannot be a code-clerk if you needlessly perspire.

Mr. Belisle said the tests were for medical information and had nothing to do with security, an assurance that was oddly welcome. The thought that the State Department might be worried about the security aspects of fingernail-biting, or laughing while asleep, leads to some wild fantasies. For instance:

A pale shaken little man sits under a spotlight, five agents of a Foreign Power in a circle around him. One of them speaks: "Hokay, Fotheringill, the code. We-want-the-code. We're through being easy with you. Either we get it or tomorrow the world knows you for what you are – a fingernail-biter."
[Terrified cries of, "No, no; not that!"]
Or, perhaps: "The jig's up, Fotheringill. We're prepared to unmask you for the bed-wetter that you are."
[Fotheringill faints dead away.]

The quiz also asked prospective code-clerks how they got along with their wives, and, "Explain any sources of conflict in your marital life. (If none, what factors contribute to promoting harmony?)" There was in this, of course, the clear implication that if the candidate could not produce some substantial evidence of conflict, he had better be prepared to clear himself of the suspicion of being mealy-mouthed and untrustworthy.

The quiz also asked applicants if they were ever tired or run down, and if they depended on medicines, sedatives, or laxatives.

Officials aren't required to swear to lives of sweet tranquility,
Nor owning nerves possessing less than normal frangibility,
And if their dreams are filled with things all vilely fanged and
   hideous,
They're not required to make this known for use perhaps
   invidious;
Diplomacy is thus revealed as not unduly quizzical
To find its topmost people's faults, the mental and the
   physical,
But still the lowly code-clerk must establish it's a fact
That he's not the one for purges of his alimentary tract.

Applicants were asked how often and to what extent they felt tense or keyed up; whether they ever had difficulty falling asleep or staying asleep; if they were restless, jumpy, jittery and couldn't seem to sit still; and if things sometimes appeared strange, peculiar, unnatural, or unreal. (Candidates who thought the test appeared strange, peculiar, unnatural and unreal presumably were prudent not to say so.)

They were asked if their hands trembled, or if they feared crowds, heights, water, places, or needles. Goodness knows why needles.

A strange dislike of needles very seldom would be critical
In saying who would get the post of French Affairs
    (Political);
A tendency, if kept in bounds, to bouts of saturnalia,
Would rarely bar a man's being sent as envoy to Australia;
And furthermore the very thought is laughably erroneous
That married life of diplomats is never inharmonious;
There's that tolerance of weakness when it touches those ahead
— But you cannot be a code-clerk if you sometimes wet
    the bed.

It gives one to think.

from I've Been Around and Around and Around and Around

from The Clockmaker; or, the Sayings and Doings of Sam Slick, of Slickville

Thomas Chandler Haliburton

Slick, who overshadows his companion, enunciates his famous theory of "soft sawder" and "human natur'."

I had heard of Yankee clock peddlers, tin peddlers, and Bible peddlers, especially of him who sold polyglot Bibles — all in English — to the amount of sixteen thousand pounds. The house of every substantial farmer has three substantial ornaments: a wooden clock, a tin reflector, and a polyglot Bible.

How is it that an American can sell his wares at whatever price he pleases where a Bluenose would fail to make a sale at all? I will inquire of the Clockmaker the secret of his success.

"What a pity it is, Mr. Slick" — for such was his name — "what a pity it is," said I, "that you, who are so successful in teaching these people the value of clocks, could not also teach them the value of time."

"I guess," said he, "they have got that ring to grow on their horns yet which every four-year-old has in our country. . . ."

"But how is it," said I, "that you manage to sell such an immense number of clocks, which certainly cannot be called necessary articles, among people with whom there seems to be so great a scarcity of money?"

Mr. Slick paused as if considering the propriety of answering the question and, looking me in the face, said, in a confidential tone, "Why, I don't care if I do tell you; for the market is glutted, and I shall quit this circuit. It is done by a knowledge of soft sawder and human natur'. But here is Deacon Flint's," said he. "I have but one clock left, and I guess I will sell it to him."

At the gate of a most comfortable looking farm house stood Deacon Flint, a respectable old man who had understood the value of time better than most of his neighbours. . . . After the usual salutation, an invitation to "alight" was accepted by Mr. Slick, who said he wished to take leave of Mrs. Flint before he left Colchester.

We had hardly entered the house before the Clockmaker, pointing to the view from the window, and addressing himself to me, said, "If I was to tell them in Connecticut that there was such a farm as this away Down East here in Nova Scotia, they wouldn't believe me. Why, there ain't such a location in all New England. The Deacon has a hundred acres of dyke —"

"Seventy," said the Deacon, "only seventy."

"Well, seventy; but then there is your fine deep bottom. Why, I could run a ramrod into it —"

"*Interval* we call it," said the Deacon, who, though evidently pleased at this eulogium, seemed to wish the experiment of the ramrod to be tried in the right place.

"Well, interval if you please — though Professor Eleazer Cumstick, in his work on Ohio, calls them bottoms — is jist as good as dyke. Then there is that water privilege, worth three or four thousand dollars, twice as good as what Governor Cass paid fifteen thousand dollars for. I wonder, Deacon, you don't put up a cardin' mill on it; the same works would carry a turnin' lathe, a shingle machine, a circular saw, grind bark, and —"

"Too old," said the Deacon, "too old for all these speculations —"

"Old!" repeated the Clockmaker. "Not you. Why, you are worth half a dozen of the young men we see now-a-days. You are young enough to have —" Here he said something in a lower tone of voice which I did not distinctly hear; but, whatever it was, the Deacon was pleased: he smiled and said he did not think of such things now.

"But your beasts, dear me, your beasts must be put in and have a feed. . . . "

As the old gentleman closed the door after him, Mr. Slick drew near to me and said in an undertone, "That is what I call *soft sawder*. . . ."

"Now I find —"

Here his lecture on soft sawder was cut short by the entrance of Mrs. Flint.

"Jist come to say good-bye, Mrs. Flint."

"What, have you sold all your clocks?"

"Yes, and very low too; for money is scarce, and I wished to close the concarn. I am wrong in sayin' all; for I have jist one left. Neighbour Steel's wife asked to have the refusal of it, but I guess I won't sell it. I had but two of 'em, this one and the feller of it that I sold Governor Lincoln. Gineral Green, the Secretary of State for Maine, said he'd give me fifty dollars for this here one — it has composition wheels and patent axles; it is a beautiful article, a rael first chop, no mistake, genu*ine* superfine — but I guess I'll take it back. And, besides, Squire Hawk might think kinder hard that I did not give him the offer."

"Dear me," said Mrs. Flint, "I should like to see it. Where is it?"

"It is in a chest of mine over the way, at Tom Tape's store. I guess he can ship it on to Eastport."

"That's a good man," said Mrs. Flint, "jist let's look at it."

Mr. Slick, willing to oblige, yielded to these entreaties and soon produced the clock, a gaudy, highly varnished, trumpery-looking affair. He placed it on the chimney piece, where its beauties were pointed out and duly appreciated by Mrs. Flint, whose admiration was about ending in a proposal when Mr. Flint returned from giving his directions about the care of the horses.

The Deacon praised the clock. He too thought it a handsome one; but the Deacon was a prudent man — he had a watch — he was sorry — but he had no occasion for a clock.

"I guess you're in the wrong furrow this time, Deacon. It ain't for sale," said Mr. Slick. "And if it was, I reckon Neighbour Steel's wife would have it; for she gives me no peace about it."

Mrs. Flint said Mr. Steel had enough to do, poor man, to pay his interest without buying clocks for his wife.

"It's no concarn of mine," said Mr. Slick, "as long as he pays me, what he has to do; but I guess I don't want to sell it. And, besides, it comes too high; that clock can't be made at Rhode Island under forty dollars.

"Why, it ain't possible," said the Clockmaker, in apparent surprise, looking at his watch, "why, as I'm alive, it is four o'clock, and if I ha'n't been two hours here. How on airth shall I reach River Philip to-night? I'll tell you what, Mrs. Flint. I'll leave the clock in your care until I return on my way to the States. I'll set it a-goin' and put it to the right time."

As soon as this operation was performed, he delivered the key to the Deacon with a sort of serio-comic injunction to wind up the clock every Saturday night. . . .

"That," said the Clockmaker, as soon as we were mounted, "that I call *human natur'*. Now, that clock is sold for forty dollars. It cost me jist six dollars and fifty cents. Mrs. Flint will never let Mrs. Steel have the refusal; nor will the Deacon larn until I call for the clock . . . how hard it is to give it up. We can do without any article of luxury we have never had, but . . . it is not in human natur' to surrender it voluntarily. Of fifteen thousand sold by myself and my partners in this Province, twelve thousand were left in this manner; and only ten clocks were ever returned. . . . We trust to soft sawder to get them into the house, and to human natur' that they never come out of it."

How the theory of soft sawder operates to advantage appears at the next halt.

As we approached the Inn at Amherst, the Clockmaker grew uneasy. "It's pretty well on in the evenin', I guess," said he, "and Marm Pugwash is as onsartain in her temper as a mornin' in April. . . . I wonder what on airth Pugwash was a-thinkin' on when he signed articles of partnership with that are woman. . . . She reminds me of our old minister Joshua Hopewell's apple trees. . . .

"Now, Marm Pugwash is like the minister's apples, very temptin' fruit to look at but desperate sour. If Pugwash had a watery mouth when he married, I guess it's pretty puckery by this time. However, if she goes to act ugly, I'll give her a dose of soft sawder that will take the frown out of her front-piece and make her dial plate as smooth as a lick of copal varnish. It's a pity she's such a kickin' devil too; for she has good p'ints: good eye, good foot, neat pastern, fine chest, a clean set of limbs, and carries a good — But here we are. Now you'll see what soft sawder will do."

When we entered the house, the traveller's room was all in darkness; and on opening the opposite door into the sitting room, we found the female part of the family extinguishing the fire for the night. Mrs. Pugwash had a broom in her hand and was in the act . . . of sweeping the hearth. The strong flickering light of the fire, as it fell upon her fine tall figure and beautiful face, revealed a creature worthy of the Clockmaker's comments.

"Good evenin', Marm," said Mr. Slick. "How do you do; and how's Mr. Pugwash?"

"He!" said she. "Why, he's been a-bed this hour. You don't expect to disturb him this time of night, I hope."

"Oh, no," said Mr. Slick, "sartainly not; and I am sorry to have disturbed you, but we got detained longer than we expected. I am sorry that — "

"So am I," said she, "but if Mr. Pugwash will keep an inn when he has no occasion to, his family can't expect no rest."

Here the Clockmaker, seeing the storm gathering, stooped down suddenly and, staring intently, held out his hand and exclaimed, "Well, if that ain't a beautiful child! Come here, my little man, and shake hands along with me. Well, I declare if that are little feller ain't the finest child I ever seed. What, not a-bed yet? Ah, you rogue, where did you get them are pretty rosy cheeks; stole them from your mamma, eh? Well, I wish my old mother could see that are child; it is such a treat."

"In our country," said he, turning to me, "the children are all as pale as chalk or as yaller as an orange. Lord, that are little feller would be a show in our country. Come to me, my man."

Here the soft sawder began to operate. Mrs. Pugwash said in a milder tone than we had yet heard, "Go, my dear, to the gentleman; go, dear."

Mr. Slick kissed him, asked him if he would go to the "States" along with him, and told him all the little girls there would fall in love with him; for they didn't see such a beautiful face once in a month of Sundays. "Black eyes. Let me see; ah, mamma's eyes too, and black hair also. As I am alive, why, you are mamma's own boy, the very image of mamma."

"Do be seated, gentlemen," said Mrs. Pugwash. "Sally, make the fire in the next room."

"She ought to be proud of you," he continued. "Well, if I live to return here, I must paint your face and have it put on my clocks."

"Did you ever see," said he, again addressing me, "such a likeness atween one human an' another as atween this beautiful little boy and his mother?"

"I am sure you have had no supper," said Mrs. Pugwash to me. "You must be hungry and weary too; I will get you a cup of tea."

"I am sorry to give you so much trouble," said I.

"Not the least trouble in the world," she replied. "On the contrary, a pleasure."

We were then shown into the next room, where the fire was now blazing up. But Mr. Slick protested he could not proceed without the little boy, and lingered behind me to ascertain his age; and concluded by asking the child if he had any aunts that looked like mamma.

As the door closed, Mr. Slick said, "It's a pity she don't go well in gear. The difficulty with those critters is to get 'em to start. Arter that there is no trouble with 'em if you don't check 'em too short. . . . Pugwash, I guess, don't understand the natur' of the critter; she'll never go kind in harness for him.

"When I see a child," said the Clockmaker, "I always feel safe with these women folk; for I have always found that the road to a woman's heart lies through her child."

Accepting the oysters, the Squire listens to the Clock-maker's flings at the Nova Scotians, who "must recede afore our

free and enlightened citizens. Already," adds Slick, "I hear the bugle
of destiny a-soundin' of their retreat.

"Now, if you want to know all about us and the Bluenoses
— a pretty considerable share of Yankee blood in them too, I tell
you; the old stock comes from New England, and the breed is
tolerable pure yet, near about one-half apple sarce and t'other half
molasses, all except to the easterd, where there is a cross of the
Scotch — jist ax me, and I'll tell you candidly. I'm not one of them
that can't see no good p'ints in my neighbour's critter and no bad
ones in my own; I've seed too much of the world for that, I guess.
Indeed, in a gineral way, I praise other folks' beasts and keep dark
about my own. Sais I, when I meet a Bluenose mounted, 'That's a
rael smart horse of your'n; put him out, I guess he'll trot like mad.'
Well, he lets him have the spur, and the critter does his best; and
then I pass him like a streak of lightnin' with mine. The feller
looks all taken back at that.

" 'Why,' sais he, 'that's a rael clipper of your'n, I vow.'

" 'Middlin',' sais I, quite cool as if I had heerd that are same
thing a thousand times; 'he's good enough for me, jist a fair trotter
and nothin' to brag of.' That goes near about as far ag'in in a
gineral way as a-crackin' and a-boastin' does. Never tell folks you
can go ahead on 'em, but do it; it spares a great deal of talk and
helps to save their breath to cool their broth."

Inspired by these observations, Slick grows poetical.

"Jist look out of the door," said the Clockmaker, "and see
what a beautiful night it is, how calm, how still, how clear it is.
Bean't it lovely? I like to look up at them are stars when I am away
from home; they put me in mind of our national flag, and it is
ginerally allowed to be the fust flag in the univarse now. . . ."

The next morning was warmer than several that had
preceded it. It was one of those uncommonly fine days that
distinguish an American autumn. "I guess," said Mr. Slick, "the
heat today is like a glass of mint julip with a lump of ice in it;
it tastes cool and feels warm. It's rael good, I tell *you.* I love such
a day as this dearly. It's ginerally allowed the finest weather in the
world is in America; there ain't the beat of it to be found anywhere." He then lighted a cigar and, throwing himself back on
his chair, put both feet out of the window and sat with his arms
folded, a perfect picture of happiness.

"You appear," said I, "to have travelled over the whole of

this Province and to have observed the country and the people with much attention. Pray, what is your opinion of the present state and future prospects of Halifax?"

His opinion, it is unnecessary to add, is not flattering. The politicians, he says, have "a smile for all the world as sweet as a cat makes at a pan of new milk. Then they get as full of compliments as a dog is full of fleas, inquirin' how the old lady is to home and the little boy that made such a wonderful smart answer they never can forget it till next time; a-praisin' a man's farm to the nines and a-tellin' him how scandalous the road that leads to his location has been neglected, and how much he wants to find a rael complete hand that can build a bridge over his brook and axin' him if he ever built one." And the people deserve to be duped. "You've seed a flock of partridges of a frosty mornin' in the fall a-crowdin' out of the shade to a sunny spot and huddlin' up there in the warmth? Well, the Bluenoses have nothin' else to do half the time but sun themselves."

from Bartleby

Chris Scott

CHAPTER SIXTEEN: "This won't do!" said Damon Gottesgabe.

CHAPTER SEVENTEEN "I don't suppose it will," said I, "but the chapters are running straight at last — if I could find them, that is."

"And you have established the identity of Bartleby's jesting friend," said he. "That was no mean feat."

"True," said I, "and if the reader has any doubt on the matter, he should know I intend to pursue it, but cannot because of the immediate intelligence I expect of Bartleby's Aunt and Guardian, the high-born and royal-blooded Alice."

"That *is* candid of you," said Damon.

CHAPTER EIGHTEEN Beginning the Adventures of Alice, Wherein Is Sung the Sorrowful Saga of Sybil, Sepulchral Sister of Our Saviour.

"What will you think of next," Gottesgabe expressed his admiration for my tactic, "filling in the missing chapters?"

"Ah, but our discussion was meant to carry the reader over the impasse," said I.

"There is nothing like a friendly exchange of views," Damon smiled, "to clear the air."

Henceforward, reader, the narrative will proceed in a spirit of scientific objectivity, as a narrative should.

Speaking of Alice as I am, I think the reader must by now be anxious for information concerning her character, habits, and demeanour, such information indeed that you will have *in the next paragraph but one!*

"Oh wretched me, oh painful blow! Woe and misery, alas! Oh dolorous heart, lamentable fate! Oh melancholy and piteous grief! Oh aching void and expectant morn! Oh rue, rue! Alack the day and night! Oh tumult without end! Oh who will extinguish this raging fire and still the tempest within my breast? Oh volcanic furor; agonizing allure! Oh tumult without end! (Again!) Oh who will free me from this evil charm! Unsurpassable craving! Oh unquenchable thirst! Insatiable appetite! Oh hunger beyond compare! Oh dismal decree and blackest fortune! Oh priceless agony! Oh despairing desperate self! Oh! . . . *Ichabod!*"

" 'M 'fraid," said the creaking serving man, "that the situation his b'yond hall 'ope, Mum."

Thus the scene, reader, in the oak-panelled dining room of Bartleby's former home in the country as Aunt Alice pined away the breakfast hour, regarded her toast, and saw that her marmalade jar was empty — !

"If I may make so bold, Mum," said this Ichabod, a faithful

servant, retained — it appears — solely for the purpose of this —

"*Ichabod*! I'm surprised. At your age too, when there's not a drop of marmalade to be found in the house!"

— solely for the purpose of this chapter, for I can find no mention of him elsewhere; not, at least, as far as I have read, which leads me to remark on the impropriety of introducing super-numaries, unless —

"But thank you, Ichabod, thank you for offering to put your-self out," said Alice.

"Seventy next Christmas, Mum."

"There's been nothing like it since the War," Auntie con-tinued, "but I made sacrifices then and there were compensations: the refugees were here — do you remember? — how many of the little dears became fond of country life and wouldn't leave at the end of it all. Then there were the Americans, and *they* always had marmalade, especially the flying officers."

"They dropped it all over Europe, Mum," Ichabod's eyes shone with the memory.

"Indeed they did, Ichabod. How we waited for it!"

"They gave it to the Russians, Mum," Ichabod advanced, "and I read in the papers that they give it to the Japanese now, begging your pardon Mum."

"God forbid that we should harbour grudges against our enemies, Ichabod; there *ought* to be enough marmalade to go round. I can't understand what will become of the world. Even in the Depression" — Ichabod coughed — "it could be had at a price" — and Ichabod creaked, reminding Auntie of his proposition — "but it would have been a great strain, too great a strain, Ichabod, at your age: the more so because he's been gone for such a time. Ichabod! Keep your hands off" — aha! a vital function, even for a spear carrier, so to speak — "off the *marmalade jar*!"

"Beg pardon, Mum, but there's a bit at the bottom that might be scraped out."

"I do not mean to speak unkindly, Ichabod. You may have what is left, though it's very little. Dear, kind Ichabod, I am not myself; I am on edge. The situation demands my personal atten-tion, and you know what that will entail."

"Indeed, Mum."

"Then when you've eaten the marmalade, see to it, Ichabod; saddle him up, Ichabod!"

"But, Mum, he won't go without. . . . "

— "Who *else*," I said to Damon, "would have *saddled the horse?*"

— "You never cease to amaze me," he shook his head, "knowing, as you do, the significance of marmalade."

The Night the Thing Got In

Jan Hilliard

. . . One of the highlights of our Salt-box days was an incident that we always referred to afterwards as "The Night the Thing Got In." It was a dark night in late August. A storm was coming up and the wind, getting ready for a good three-day blow, was undecided which way to go. It prowled around the corners of the house, and shook the windows, making sudden assaults on the honeysuckle, so that the loose vines tapped and whispered against the shingles. A spooky sort of night to begin with. Uncle Harry was out. Aunt Belle said the Thing would never have got in if Uncle Harry had been home minding his own business instead of gallivanting about the country.

Aunt Liza had been visiting us all evening. That was just after she took the spell of imagining that a family of Greeks who kept a restaurant in town were out to get her with poison gas. They were all set, she believed, with a long rubber tube like a garden hose, which they intended to insert through a hole bored in the wall of the house, and a bicycle pump. Aunt Liza had seen them, or thought that she had seen them, busily working away at their devilish scheme.

"They're up there now," she told us.

Aunt Belle assured her that the Greeks were all busy in their restaurant downtown.

"They're hiding," Aunt Liza insisted.

At about half past nine we were all sitting around the big kitchen table eating scones and drinking tea by the dim light of the kerosene lamp when the back door blew open suddenly and a gust of wind almost extinguished the flame. With the wind, a large dark shapeless Thing catapulted silently into the kitchen, streaked across the floor and disappeared under the kitchen table, the end nearest the door, where nobody was sitting.

"What's that?" Emily jumped up on her chair and pulled up her skirts.

Frightened out of our wits, we all followed her example. "It's the Greeks," Aunt Liza quavered weakly, holding her full skirts up past her knees. She wore stockings with the stripes going around her legs, which looked like toothpicks wound with coloured thread.

Another gust of wind whipped through the open door. It sent a shiver through all of us. "Oh, what is it?" Aunt Belle cried. We looked at each other, trembling. There was no sound from beneath the table. But the Thing was there. Although its flight across the kitchen had been so swift that nobody had been able to tell its shape or give it a name, we knew it was there. It seemed to be about the size of a large cat, though Emily swore later that it was as big as a wolf. Of course she didn't know much about wolves.

Emily raised her voice. "Help! Somebody! Help!" hoping to attract the attention of Mr. O'Brien whom we had seen earlier taking the air in his garden.

Lance cautiously lifted the tablecloth and peered underneath. "I can't *see* anything," he cried, throwing us into a fresh frenzy of fear.

"Get the gun, Lance," Aunt Belle ordered, trembling. "No, don't. You might shoot one of us. Get the kettle." Her idea was to throw boiling water on the Thing.

Lance nervously measured the distance between his chair and the stove, where the kettle was boiling noisily.

He was saved by Emily. "Don't put your feet down," she warned. "It might bite." She shouted for Mr. O'Brien again then picked up a cup and hurled it through the window, hoping the crash might attract his attention.

Louise shrieked that it was going up her leg. She shook with terror. She could take the ghost in the attic, which she almost believed in herself now; not this real but still unknown and terrifying Thing. Vicky whimpered and climbed on the table, knocking over a jug and a glass of milk.

"It's not going up your leg, you idiot," Lance tried to excuse his cowardice with bluster. "It's too big."

"Oh, what is it?" Aunt Belle asked distractedly. The Thing was so *silent*. That was what frightened us more than anything. It seemed supernatural, the way it had swept silently across the floor and now, under the table, made no sound. "Lance, see what it is," she begged. "Chase it out."

Lance lifted a corner of the tablecloth again. "Get along, you!" he shouted. "Scat!"

"Mr. O'Brien!" Emily bellowed.

"It touched me!" Louise scrambled frantically to the table beside Vicky, knocking cups and spoons to the floor with a deafening clatter. At that, the Thing glided swiftly and silently across the kitchen floor and out into the night.

"There it goes!" Emily exclaimed. She hurled the teapot in the general direction of the retreating Thing. It hit the doorpost.

Cautiously we climbed down from our chairs and removed Vicky, who was sobbing hysterically, from the table top. Louise refused to leave her lofty perch. "I didn't see it go out," she declared.

Footsteps sounded on the porch. "There they are again!" Aunt Liza warned. But it was only Mr. O'Brien.

"I hear somebody calling?" he asked. "You want me?"

"It was a Thing!" Emily gasped in explanation. "It went out again."

"Thing?" Mr. O'Brien looked skeptical. "What kind a thing?"

"We don't *know*," Emily wailed. "We didn't see it."

Mr. O'Brien looked even more skeptical. "*I* didn't see nothing," he said. "What's she doing on the table?"

"I didn't see it go out," Louise blubbered.

"See *what* go out?"

"The Greeks," Aunt Liza explained.

"Well," Mr. O'Brien started to back out, cautiously, like a man who has opened a door by mistake. "I guess you're all right now."

Aunt Belle was regaining her composure. "Thank you, we're perfectly all right now, Mr. O'Brien," she said stiffly, beginning to feel a little foolish.

"Sure?" Mr. O'Brien glanced at the broken teapot and the dishes on the floor.

"Yes, thank you," Aunt Belle remembered suddenly that she was still holding up her skirts. She let them fall. "Good night," she said, dismissing Mr. O'Brien.

He left, with another puzzled glance at the broken dishes.

Louise stayed on the table for half an hour, until Aunt Belle threatened to whip her if she didn't behave herself. Aunt Liza was so worked up that we persuaded her to sleep in one of our beds. "They'll never think to look for me here," she agreed, pleased.

Uncle Harry scoffed when we told him what had happened. "Women!" he snorted. "Got more imagination! And where were you all this time?" he demanded of Lance.

"It would never have happened if you'd been home minding your own business instead of gallivanting about the country," Aunt Belle retorted, defending Lance.

from The Salt-Box

A James Bond Story

(Not by Ian Fleming)

Walter O'Hearn

Bond was in his flat, idly peeling a tomato, when the telephone rang. It was the direct line from M.

Bond hastened to answer, dropping the tomato. She picked herself up gracefully and left the room.

"Bond," the voice on the blower was chipped and terse.

"Yes."

"Prepare to go to Nassau, I have had a tip. Mac the Knife is going to be butchered."

"What cover shall I use?"

"I'll tell you when we're under cover. Get over here immediately."

It was a matter of minutes until Bond was sliding out of his sleek, graceful 1924 Maxwell and striding into M.'s headquarters, which were disguised as a used-furniture emporium in the Tottenham Court Road. M. wasted no time coming to the point.

"About your cover. You cannot go to Nassau as yourself. You are a marked man. Indeed I might describe you as a criss-crossed man. You must adopt the only disguise available."

"The Prime Minister's valet?"

M. was contemptuous.

"In view of Macmillan's waistcoats, nobody would believe he had a valet. Besides, the PM mustn't know. We represent a higher authority than mere parliaments."

"A journalist, then."

"No, that's out. We have information that Dr. No, Auric Goldfinger, and the head of SMERSH are in Nassau now, all disguised as journalists. The head of the U.S. CIA is disguised as a photographer. An agent of the John Birch Society is there disguised as Pierre Salinger.

"No, there is only one recourse. It will be hard on you, Bond. Who is the one person who can wander into Anglo-American meetings, whether invited or not?"

"The Canadian Prime Minister."

"Exactly. You will be the Canadian Prime Minister. Don't worry about the real Prime Minister. We'll deal with him. Now hop to it."

The next twenty hours were spent by Bond in a projection room in a Wardour Street basement. M.'s collection of Diefenbaker clips was fabulous. Time after time Bond watched Diefenbaker triumphant, Diefenbaker sorrowing, Diefenbaker in pain. Diefenbaker speaking English in Toronto, Diefenbaker speaking French in the City of Quebec. Diefenbaker catching trout in Saskatchewan. Diefenbaker catching goldeye in Manitoba. Diefenbaker catching hell in Ottawa. Diefenbaker shooting down the Common Market in London.

At last Bond was ready. The oratorical style was going to be difficult, but he had anticipated this. Stuffed in his pocket was a volume of nineteenth-century sermons. So equipped he presented himself to Max Anodyne, the wig-maker of Panton Street, whose innocent shop front concealed the most skilful plastic surgeon and the most cunning rogue in Europe.

By noon the following day, with a muffler concealing his

face, Bond had presented himself at M.'s desk. There he stood to attention while the master spy looked him up and down.

"Hmm. Almost perfect. An excellent job. Hair right, profile right. Full face (Open your mouth, Bond) very good. Clothes a little too . . . well, never mind. You'll do."

"This will present difficulties," Bond told his chief. "You know my habits. This fellow doesn't smoke."

"No."

"Doesn't drink."

"No."

"Avoids the gaming tables."

"Yes."

M. eyed his subordinate shrewdly. Then he added:

"Your other hobby is out, too."

Bond sighed and shrugged his shoulders.

"Stop those continental gestures," M. snapped. "Anybody caught shrugging his shoulders in Prince Albert would find himself at the foot of the poll. And be sure your Canadian accent is on straight. Now off you go and good luck to you."

It was late at night when Bond, disguised as Prime Minister Diefenbaker, descended by parachute near Uplands Airport. An agent, blinking his torch, gave the agreed signal and guided Bond to the rendezvous. The real Prime Minister lay there, trussed and chloroformed. In an instant the exchange was effected.

At the take-off Bond was letter perfect. He delivered his farewells in the ringing tones of the Canadian statesman. Once airborne, he settled in his chair for a well-earned nap, to prepare him for the ordeal ahead.

The Caribbean sun was bright as Bond-Diefenbaker walked down the gangway. In the distinguished crowd gathered to greet him, the agent's experienced eye noted the Governor's second footman, the junior secretary of the Board of Trade, a bandmaster of the footguards, a pipe-major of the Seaforths, and a p.r. from the Tourist Bureau. Off in the distance, clutching notebooks, were Dr. No, Auric Goldfinger, and the head of SMERSH.

A dark, rotund man clutching a steel guitar was the cynosure of all eyes. Advancing down the strip he boomed in his great voice:

Welcome, Mr. Diefenbaker
Welcome to Nassau.
Six years ago you here,
Then you came for the fishin'
Now you here on a very different mission!

It augured well for his enterprise, Bond thought. Now let the Americans try to slice up Mac. He would be at the victim's side.

Some seventy-two hours later a dejected Bond was on the carpet before M. Anodyne had already begun to restore his original face, but curling grey locks still hung in dispirited fashion over his eyebrows.

"So you failed," M. snapped.

"Yes, I failed. They butchered Mac the Knife."

"You know the rules of the service, Bond. No explanation for failures. No defence admitted. Nevertheless, I am curious. How could an agent of your experience, with the cover provided, fail so abjectly?"

"The cover was the whole trouble."

"The cover? You were letter perfect."

Bond squared his shoulders.

"Too perfect."

M.'s face was a note of interrogation.

"Yes, too perfect. I was the Canadian Prime Minister. I thought him, I talked him, I lived him night and day. Then I made an amazing discovery.

"Nobody at these conferences takes a Canadian Prime Minister seriously. They don't talk to him, except small talk. They open every door to him except the important ones."

M. pursed his lips.

"I might have thought of that. Let us begin planning for next time. There will be a next time and the knives will be out. Can you suggest a cover?"

"I have the perfect cover," Bond assured him smugly.

"The perfect cover?"

"Yes, I shall go as Peter Sellers. This would gain me entrée everywhere."

from Lady Chatterley, Latterly

The Day Jake Made Her Rain

W. O. Mitchell

I could feel both of my legs getting kind of numb the way they do when you are sitting on the edge of something a long time. But Jake and Old Man Gatenby didn't let on they were getting numb. They were too mad.

Jake was sitting beside me on our horse trough and he had his long legs kinked up at the knees just like a grasshopper ready to spring. "You take Hatfield," he said.

"You take him," Old Man Gatenby said real snappy. Old Man Gatenby and Jake are both old, but Old Gate's face has taken it worse than Jake's — enough wrinkles to hold a three-day rain.

Even under the grey stubble you could tell from Jake's face that he was mad. It was red and had knotty sort of bulges at the corners of his jaw. His Adam's apple was jumping too. Like he was trying to get a hold of himself he kept quiet a minute whilst he stared at a Wine-dot pecking in the dust; his eyes that are that faded sort of blue, stared at Old Man Gatenby's dog lying with his long tongue spilled out and panting.

There hadn't been any rain the last three weeks of July and even the hen looked thirsty.

"He brung rain to Medicine Hat," Jake said. "Then there was that other fella — come through Crocus districk with alla his machinery set up on a c.p.r. flatcar. He — "

"Jist a sprinkly little shower didn't even lay the dust," said Old Man Gatenby.

Jake shifted to get himself easier on the edge of the trough. He squinted up at some fat popcorn clouds over top of us; he kept right on looking at that hot blue sky that had forgot how to rain. "He contracted to git paid fer any rain he brung over an' above the average rainfall."

"Didn't do so good out Yalla Grass way," said Old Gate. "Ner at Brokenshell — ner Union Jack — they run him outa Broomhead."

"Nothin' to do with him rainin'," interrupted Jake.

"It shore as—"

"That was accounta the power game over the China-man's—"

"Was not!"

"She was!" Jake looked right into Gate's eyes the way they were like cloves stuck into a little round apple — one you let lay around a long time till it got all puckered and shrively.

Old Man Gatenby pulled out a plug and squeezed off a corner with his knife. Then he lifted her to his mouth. "No rain maker," he said with his voice stubborn and slow and like it hurt him to keep it down the way he was doing, "with no rain machine never brought no rain to nobody!" Then he spit.

"Don't!" Jake yelled and Gate nearly fell into the trough.

"Huh!"

"Don't spit!"

Old Man Gatenby gawped at Jake.

"It's sinful," Jake said.

"Sinful!"

"Wastin' yer moisture that way."

Old Gate looked at Jake like he was a fork going into a thrashing machine. "Tryin' to change the subjeck when yer sooperstishus—"

" 'Tain't sooperstishus," Jake said. "If they got the right kinda machine, then they kin do it."

"They kin do it in a pig's ear," said Gate.

"A heck of an awkward place to raise wheat."

"They kin not—"

"They kin so! I seen it done!" yelled Jake.

"You ain't." I was thinking it's funny how when old folk get to arguing they do it a lot like the kids do at recess at Rabbit Hill.

"I done it myself!" Jake was bellering.

"You did n—!" Old Man Gatenby's mouth snapped shut. His little eyes sparkled at Jake. "You whut!"

Jake swallowed quick. "Why — I — afore I come to Crocus districk."

"You bet it was afore you come here," agreed Gate. "Where the heck did you do any rainin'?"

"In o' four — Manyberries way."

"Is that so?" Old Gate's voice was real polite.

"Yep," said Jake. "Use to call me Sheet-lightnin' Trumper."

"Did they now? You have much of a success of this here rain makin'?"

"In a way I did," Jake said. "Then in a way I didn't."

"Either you brung her down er you didn't bring 'er down," said Old Gate.

"I brung her down all right," said Jake. "Trouble was I didn't have no control when I rained. Lotsa power — no control — none a them light misty rains — them skimpy quick little summer showers — when I rained I really rained."

"That's nice," said Old Man Gatenby and the way he said it you knew he didn't think it was nice at all.

"Take Dominion Day in o' five — got her turned on an' couldn't git her turned off all through August an' September. Har'ly nobody got thrashed at all so she had to stan' in the stook right through till spring — then they didn't git no crop."

"Why not?"

"Mice," said Jake. "Stooks was fulla mice. Go by a field an' see alla them spikers an' field pitchers working without no pants — "

"Without any pants, Jake!" I said.

"Yep. Stick a fork into a stook an' out run the mice an' up a fella's pant leg. Had to thrash without no pants. Mice et alla the wheat — jist straw left. Can't thrash straw."

"To git back to this here rain makin'," Old Gate said nasty. "How did — "

"Never got away from her," said Jake. "Jist explainin' how come folks wasn't so fussy about me rainin'! Too much moisture. Then, too, she was sort of a onhealthy rain — onnatural — folks got all kindsa stuff outa it — colds — flu — that's when my rheumatism started up the first time."

"I'd settle fer double pneumonia to git some moisture on that flax a mine," said Gate. Old Man Gatenby had two hundred acres of flax — flax is just as thirsty as wheat or rye or oats. "An' the way this here droughty weather has bin, makes a fella real disgusted to hear you blowin' about how you kin rain an' what all rain makers kin do with their machines — 'nough to give a gopher the heartburn." He went to spit, then changed his mind. "Sacerlidge."

"You don't believe me," said Jake.

"You bet I don't! Er else you'd rig up yer rain machine an' rain."

"I told you why I quit."

"You ain't told noth' cept a whoppin' jag a lies — Sheet-lightnin' Trumper."

Jake's Adam's apple was going up and down like a bucket in a well. "Ef I wanted to rain," he said, "why I could do her right now."

"I'm callin' you," Old Gate said and his little eyes looked at Jake real cold. "Bring on yer rain machine."

"I ain't got her made."

"Well, make her."

"I ain't — the — 'tain't all that easy to —"

"See what I mean — just like I said — a whoppin' jag a —"

"Don't say it," Jake warned him, "er you won't never see rain again!" He got off of the horse trough. "I'll rain," he said.

"When?" said Gate.

"Soon as I git my machine put together."

"When'll that be?"

"When I'm ready." Jake spit.

"Don't!" Old Man Gatenby yelled and Jake just looked at him.

"Come on, Kid," he said, "we got chores to do."

Jake was quiet all through supper and Ma looked at him like she wondered what was the matter. She said: "I guess this dry weather is getting on everyone's nerves."

Jake went right on with his saskatoon pie, eating it real careful with his knife and fork. Jake is a neat eater.

"Jake's going to make a rain machine," I said.

There was a clatter and Jake was looking up from a purple stain over the oilcloth. Ma's eyes were wide and dark on Jake.

"If a person would keep his mouth shut," Jake said, "he wouldn't get him into so much trouble." He got up jerky from the table and he started for the door. He turned back. "Not that he won't have him a crop a trouble anyways, but maybe she won't go so many bushels to the acre. An' maybe, if he keeps his mouth shut, she won't grade so high when he gits her. Number one hard." He turned to the door, then back again. "Don't fergit that, Kid." As he went out he said, "Like I done this afternoon."

I didn't dare ask Jake what he was going to work on when he got out paper and a stubby pencil that night before bedtime. He bent over the table with his shadow all sprawly over the kitchen wall and flickering from the lamp light. I pretended like I was reading *The Prairie Farm Review* and all about folks with critters that are sick with something and how to can vegetables. You could hear the cream separator purring out in the back shed where Ma was and the moths ticking against the lamp chimney.

Jake grunted and threw down the pencil. "Yer bedtime, ain't it, Kid?"

All the next day, whilst we were haying, Jake was quiet and he would say yes or he would say no or he would grunt at you. That was all. I was kind of glad to leave him and the rack and go down to the road for the mail. When I got a look at the *Crocus Breeze* that Mr. Cardwell had left in our box, I ran for Jake. He was really in trouble.

When Jake saw it, he just stood there with his fork in his hand and he looked kind of sick. "It's Gate," he said. "He done it."

"What are you going to do, Jake!"

Jake shook his head slow and his eyes were looking off over our crop turning brown along the edges for want of moisture. He rubbed his chin and it made a scrapy sound. He looked up at the sky, then off to the horizon. Way off there you could see a speck.

"Only one thing to do, Kid," he said.

"What?"

"Make me a machine."

"But — "

"This here," Jake slapped at the paper, "this here about me bein' a rain maker an' about me makin' a machine — it — Kid, I guess there's worse things than havin' folks laff at you, but I don't know what they are."

The speck off in the sky wasn't a hawk; you could hear it now. Jimmy Shoelack. Jimmy was in the Air Force and he farms for Mrs. Christiansen who went back to the Old Country. He has a little yellow plane he uses for crop dusting and taking fellows out hunting antelope and folks up for rides at fairs around our district. That's the only thing Jake and Old Man Gatenby agree about — hating Jimmy Shoelack's airplane the way it buzzes all over like an angry wasp, scaring teams and stock.

But Jake wasn't paying any attention when Jimmy's plane came over us low. He said:

"I'm knocking off for the rest of the afternoon, Kid. Gotta git busy with some inventin'."

Three days later Old Man Gatenby showed up at our place to borrow our post-hole auger — at least that was what he said.

Jake was real polite to him, just like he didn't get them to print that story about Jake in the *Crocus Breeze*. After Jake had got him the auger, he said:

"'Bout that there machine. Lotta folks been askin' me when she'll be ready. August Petersen figgers his crop's only good fer another week, an' — "

"I'm workin' on her," Jake said. "I'm workin' on her."

"Well," said Old Gate, "it would be kinda nice to see somethin'."

Without saying anything Jake turned away and started walking toward the chophouse, me and Old Man Gatenby following after. Jake threw open the door and he stepped aside.

Old Man Gatenby's face, with his chin nearly touching his nose, poked out like a rooster getting ready to fight. He peered into the chophouse. "What's that!"

"A rain machine," said Jake.

I looked in. I saw sort of a cross between a wind electric and a gas motor and two lightning rods. I looked again. There were two blue bulbs.

"Call that a rain machine!" said Old Gate.

"She shore is," said Jake. "Ain't got her perfected yet."

"Turn her on," said Gate. "Let's see her run."

"Can't."

"Why not?"

"She's set for hail."

"Well then — onset her."

"That's what ain't perfected," Jake said. "She's all ready to go except fer that one little bug in her. I ain't bringin' no hail down on — "

"Say," said Old Man Gatenby, "ain't them blue bulbs sort of familiar?"

Jake almost caught Gate's nose in the door when he slammed it shut. "That there's the machine I used bufore. She worked then. She'll work agin. She was shore dry them days — had this skinned a mile. Dry! Not a slough in the districk, jist dust. Seen the frogs settin' up to their eyes in dust, jist their two bump eyes showin'."

"Them blue bulbs — " started Gate.

"All over the prairie where the sloughs use to be, little puffs a dust where the frogs was jumpin'. You'd see a frog jump, there'd be a plop a dust, then you'd see him swimmin' the way a frog does — underdust swimmin' — not quite so clear as underwater swimmin'. Hearin' 'em croakin' in their dust spring nights was kinda nice, made a fella remember she was spring at first — "

"At first, Jake, what — "

"After a couple of dry years, them winds lickin' up the top soil an' pilin' it against the fences an' houses an' granaries, wasn't no dust left in them sloughs no more." Jake stared at the ground and he said real sad, "Come the next spring not a frog in a slough, kinda tragical the way they died, lacka dust."

Old Man Gatenby had his face screwed up sour. "When," he said, "do you intend on rainin'?"

Jake cocked his head and he pursed his mouth. "End a this week, the beginnin' a the next."

"That's all I wanted to know," said Gate.

"More likely beginnin' a the next," said Jake, and I heard him muttering something about change of the moon.

Now Jake didn't seem so happy about his rain machine; he didn't act so perky about it as he had when he was showing it to Old Man Gatenby. He tinkered with it a bit, but most of the time whilst we finished up the haying, he was looking up into the sky. When you felt that wind oven-hot against your cheek, and when you tasted the dust dry in your throat, it was kind of hard to believe what Jake said about rain machines.

Wednesday our well went dry.

Thursday the *Crocus Breeze* announced Reverend Cameron was going to have a praying-for-rain Sunday. There was a little piece saying that Jake Trumper was going to rain on Tuesday next at Tincher's back forty where the ground rose between the correction line and Government Road. "He picks my day an' he picks my place," was all Jake said.

Friday Queen and Duke bolted so Jake fell off a load of hay and lit on his head. Here was how it happened.

We had a big load on and I had a hold of the lines and Jake was crawling to me when Jimmy Shoelack's plane came low and fast as a scalded coyote over the rise of the draw. He headed straight for the team. Duke reared up in his harness, then Queen; then they both began to run. It took me the whole field and the load of hay to get them stopped. I turned to Jake, only he wasn't on the load any more.

I tied them to the fence, then I ran back to where we'd been loading.

With his feet straight out in front of him, Jake was sitting on the bald-headed prairie right where he'd landed.

He wasn't cussing. He was just sitting there and looking off into the distance.

"You all right, Jake?"

He just went right on sitting there and looking kind of stupid.

"You all right, Jake!"

He was getting up slow and creaky, breathing hard the way you do after you've run a long ways. He started off walking.

"This way, Jake," I said.

He didn't even hear me. Just like he was dreaming he kept on walking in the opposite direction from our house. I ran to catch up. "You better come home, Jake. Take a lay-down till you feel bett — "

He shook me off.

"That's the wrong way, Jake."

"Wanta use Tincher's phone."

"I'll go phone Dr. Fotheringham," I said.

"Wanta use Tincher's phone. Wanta git Jimmy Shoelack bad."

"Jake," I said, "just report him. They'll fix him for what he did — "

"Wanta use Tincher's phone. Wanta thank him."

"Thank — Jake!" I yelled, "you come on home with me on the rack!"

Jake kept right on walking.

He got back late, whilst Ma was cleaning up the supper dishes. He went out to milking, singing "The Letter Edged In Black"; he came back with the milk pails, singing "The Baggage Coach Ahead."

He didn't go to church with Ma and me on Sunday, said he had to go over and see Jimmy Shoelack. The Reverend Cameron prayed for rain; he said for everybody to go right on praying next week and he'd take another try at her the following Sunday.

Monday a big parcel came for Jake in the mail.

"Is that for the rain machine?" I asked him.

"You might say she was, Kid."

"You worried, Jake — about tomorrow?"

He looked up at the sky.

"Do you really think she'll make rain?"

" 'Tain't a rain *makin'* machine," Jake said sharp.

"But you told Old Gate — "

"She's a rain machine. Ain't no machine kin *make* rain — that's plumb silly — jist bring her down if she's up there."

"I see," I said. "Jake."

"Yeah?"

"Those there blue bulbs Old Man Gatenby said — "

"Don't pay no attention to what he says."

"But, they look a lot like your — "

"Kid," Jake said, "when you say yer 'Now I Lay Me Down' tonight, after that there part about blessin' folks, stick in about sendin' a bunch of grey cloud tomorrah."

I promised I would.

The Lord must of heard. The next day, whilst Jake put up his rain machine on a platform in Tincher's corner, the grey clouds built up. By afternoon she was dark clear to the horizon, but that didn't mean anything; she'd done that lots of times without raining.

Everybody from our district came. They brought their lunches; they sat in the shade of their cars or their rigs and ate and drank coffee out of Thermos jugs. Mr. Tincher organized some kids' races just like a Sunday-school picnic at Ashton's grove. Stevie Kiziw and me came first in the potato sack race; Axel Rasmussen was first in the egg and spoon race. Jimmy Shoelack was taking folks up for a cent a pound.

About four o'clock Jake got up on his platform. He looked down at the folks all gathered around and some kids playing tag at one end of the platform. He looked up at the sky thick with soft grey like a goose.

"Now look," he said, "this here is a rain machine. I made it." He stopped like he was looking for words. "I aim to rain with it. I — ain't gonna explain the principle she works on — rain makin's a lot like other things, she takes faith. I'd say rain makin' was about one per cent machine an' ninety-nine per cent faith."

"Fergit the hot air an' git on to the rain!" yelled Mr. Botton.

" 'Tain't more wind we want!" That was Old Man Gatenby.

"All right," Jake said back at them. "But she won't work without faith, no more'n what she'll work without gas. I gotta have yer faith — all the faith in this here districk. It's gotta grow outa you folks wantin' the rain I'm gonna bring. You gotta wanta smell her cool on the air, an' wanta hear her slappin' loud on the roof, fillin' up them thirsty cracks in yer land, sloppin' outa yer stock troughs, fillin' an' risin' in yer sloughs an' wells!

"I gotta have faith from the women folk, too. You gotta want me to rain as bad as you want pansies lookin' up at you from yer flower beds, as bad as sweet peas an' hollyhocks is thirsty fer something besides soapy throw-out water, as bad as you wanta write down stuff outa the Hudson's Bay catalogue fer yer kids!"

Jake's grey hair was standing right up on end, kind of misty. He seemed to be looking through the crowd for something. I turned around and I saw Jimmy Shoelack slipping away.

Jake said, "You gotta have faith she's gonna happen! You gotta know it in yer gizzard an' yer heart an' yer soul! You gotta know her — if I was you I'd take an' put something over my head, Mrs. Totcoal!" Mrs. Johnny Totcoal reached back and came up with a quilt from the democrat for her head and shoulders. "You gotta know her!" Jake was yelling, "clear as spring water!

"Any of you folks has snuffy teams get a good holt on them lines!" I saw Mr. Sawyer reaching forward for the reins. "I want yer faith — an' I'm a gonna git it!"

He had it. You could tell. I'm only a kid, but I could smell faith all over the place. You could see it in folks' eyes. They knew Jake was going to rain; they knew it because it was ten times easier to know he would than it was to know he wouldn't.

"Stan' well back, folks!" Jake was yelling, "an' gimme room! Git a holt of yer kids fer I aim tuh rain!"

He gave the flywheel of the rain machine a spin; she coughed, she missed, she coughed again. Then she was going full blast. Jake struck a match on the seat of his overalls. *Whoooshshshs*, like a long breath between your teeth — and another and another and another — four rockets were trailing their fire tails into the sky.

Long and lean and angly Jake was facing the crowd again. You could hear his voice high and thin above the machine and something else. Then I realized it was the sound of Jimmy Shoelack's plane taking off. You could smell gas sharp on the air and you could see sparks wriggling and twisting between the two blue bulbs on the rain machine. Looking at those lightning rods pointing straight up to the sky and that motor chugging along, you could almost feel the machine hauling and drawing and pulling at that moisture up in those grey clouds – just like sucking pop through a straw and out of a bottle.

Something was wrong. The machine had stopped, and Jake was looking off to where the sound of Jimmy Shoelack's plane was fading away. He said real quiet:

"That's her, folks."

You could hear them breathing loud all around you. Old Man Gatenby coughed. The Botton kid let a holler out of him. There was the tinkle of halter shanks, the creak of harness. A car horn honked loud from somebody moving quick and hitting it with their elbow. Mrs. Totcoal took the quilt off of her head. Everybody was turning their eyes away like they were embarrassed.

I looked up to the platform where Jake was still standing. Just a dead machine – a gas motor, two lightning rods, the blue bulbs off of a rheumatism machine and our hired man.

There was no faith in the faces of folks hooking up their traces and turning to their cars and taking a hold of their kids by the hands and not saying anything.

She sort of burst; she didn't take a few minutes for you to realize what was happening; she didn't start off with a few drops spanking you on the head or the cheek or the back of your hand; she up and let go all of a sudden. Folks quit whatever they were doing and they stood with their lower lips over their upper ones like it was something to taste and eat; the hides on all the horses were all of a sudden dark and gleamy; the shoulders on Jake's coat were soaked in no time and the drops running crooked white tracks down through the dust over his face; the women's dresses were plastered to them like your cotton bathing suit after a swim. She was sure rainin'!

Johnny Totcoal let a whoop and he off with his coat and he ripped open his shirt without doing the buttons and stood with the rain streaming through the hair on his chest. Up went the Reverend Cameron's long arms and he shouted, "The Lord be praised!"

Old Man Gatenby's mouth came shut like a gopher trap. "The Lord nothin'!" he yelled. "Sheet-lightnin' Trumper!"

Jake just stood there in his rain.

It was after we got home I said:

"Jake, why did Jimmy Shoelack – "

"Like everythin' else," Jake said, "there's bin a lotta

advancement in rain makin'! That day Jimmy's plane sent me kitin'
off of the hay, kinda reminded me of a article I read in the *Prairie
Farm Review*." He looked down at me for a minute. "Ever hear
tell a dry ice, Kid?"

I looked right back at him. "Sure," I said, "it was all over
the prairies the year of the blue snow. That was when the dust
all froze into solid cakes."

Jake looked at me kind of funny. He started to say something, but he changed his mind.

He knows better than to try fooling me.

from Jake and the Kid

Finding a Coffin for a Dead
Snake Is No Easy Matter

Alexander Ross

Two weeks ago, when I was lying flat on my back in a
hospital bed, recovering from an appendicitis operation and bored
out of my mind, I made a resolution: I will not write a column
about getting my appendix out. Even when Kildare Dobbs
reminisced about his appendix, I stuck to my vow. Last week, when
George Bryant devoted most of his column to how he almost got
his appendix out in Nepal, I was sorely tempted, but finally
resisted the impulse to inform you about the state of my
peritoneum.

And so I won't. Instead, I give you the actual transcript of
an actual telephone conversation with an actual animal clinic right
here in an actual Canadian city. It is amazing what can happen
when you're lying there, with a telephone beside your bed. I
dialled a number, and a nice lady with a brisk Scottish accent
answered the phone:

"Uh, this is Mr. Ross. Do you have a pet cemetery?"

"Yes we do."

"Oh. Uh, I've got this snake that, ah, seems to have died, and he's been with me a long time and I'd like to, you know, enquire about your service."

"What kind of a snake is it?"

"Well, it's an Eastern Fox Snake. That's what they told me at the museum. He's five, five and a half feet long."

"Well, I'd think the snake would possibly be the same as what a cat grave would be, and that would be $50."

"Fifty dollars, eh . . . Well, the trouble is, I mean, he's nearly six feet long."

"What's that got to do with it?"

"Well, he wouldn't fit in a cat grave, would he?"

"Well, you don't have him stretched out six feet long. Even a dog isn't stretched out like that."

"Well, he's sort of stretched out like that right now, I mean. I've got him at home."

"Yes, I mean, a snake is just turned around. I mean, he doesn't have to lie straight out."

"Well, I'd want him to lie straight out."

"Well then, we couldn't do that."

"You couldn't. Um . . . well then what about a coffin? Do you supply those?"

"No. They go into a wooden box, and it goes to the size that we give them. But if you want your snake in a box six feet long we cannot give that, we cannot accommodate you."

"So my snake would have to be curled up?"

"That's right."

"How big is the box?"

"He would go in a box the size for a cat would be."

"I see. And how big is that?"

"I haven't measured it, sir. Maybe 14 inches by 20, something like that."

"Well, do you think he'd fit in?"

"I would think so. I can't see why not."

"My snake is. . . ."

". . . A snake doesn't sleep all stretched out, does he? You'd put him into a natural sleeping position, the same way as you would with a dog or a cat. When a dog goes into a box his legs aren't straight out. He's in a sleeping position. I mean, let's just face it, you'll have quite a difference in cost and everything else together. We just cannot give you a bigger crate."

"Well, I'd be willing to pay extra."

"Well, we can't do it. I'm sorry."

"All right then: my snake would have to be curled up."

"I think so. In a natural position."

"Well the trouble is, he's sort of pretty straight right now, and he's pretty stiff . . . Ah, what should I do — just bring him to you? Or do you. . . ."

"Yes, he would have to be brought to us, yes. Now how would you bring him?"

"Well, I guess in my car. I have a station wagon. But . . . how would you curl him up? I mean. I'm concerned about this, because. . . ."

"Well, I don't know, I think I would have to face it once I see it. I've never come across this problem before. But as far as I know, there isn't anything very particular in a snake. I mean, there's no bone structure or anything. There's no reason — I can't see why we couldn't curl him up."

"Even with rigor mortis?"

"Well, how long is he dead?"

"Well, I don't know. For a long time there, I thought he might be asleep. I mean, for about four days. You know, he didn't move and I thought, you know, it's spring or something. But then, you know, I've been looking at him, examining him, and there's no sign of life. I'm pretty sure he's dead. I'm sure he's dead. Anyway, you say it would cost $50. Does that include a marker?"

"Yes, it does."

"What will the marker say?"

"It will just have your name on it, and the snake's name. . . ."

"His name is Albert. . . ."

". . . and how old he was and when he died."

"And $50 would be the only cost, eh?"

"I would think so. You make it sound as if this was something that's almost impossible — because he's a snake, being so big, and you can't turn him around, and everything else together. If I find out there is no way of him curling up into a small box, then it will cost you much more. But we would tell you before we would get involved. Now, the only thing that you can do is bring your snake here, so we can see what is involved. Okay?"

"Thank you, ma'am."

I hereby apologize to that nice lady from the pet hospital. But it's amazing what you're driven to when you're laid up with appendicitis and have taken a vow not to write about it.

from The Toronto Star

A Reservation

In which the proprietor stands by his pledged word
— to the best of his ability

Merrill Denison

A motor boat approached me one afternoon while I was out swimming in the lake. It was a perfect afternoon in August. The water was warm, my wilderness retreat was filled, there was a heat wave in the Middle States, and no new guests were expected to arrive that day. I had seized upon this conjunction of happy events to rid the resort of my executive presence, and had chosen the lake as the spot where I could most likely accomplish this restful purpose.

Lulled by a false security, I did not think the boat could have anything to do with me until it had run me down. When I came up I saw that Bill, the clerk, was in the boat. It was a small craft, so that we were able to converse easily over its side.

Bill looked startled and anxious.

"Can't I even take a swim without you dogging my breast strokes?" I said.

"Get in here, quick," said Bill. "A couple of new guests are waiting for you at the end of the dock."

"Why the dock?"

"They couldn't get any closer walking."

"No new guests were expected."

"I know," said Bill. "That's the trouble."

"Who are they?"

"A man and his wife."

"Are they both on the dock?"

"No. He sent his wife back. She couldn't stand bloodshed."

"What bloodshed?" I demanded.

"Yours," said Bill.

"Say, what's the matter with this bird?" I asked. "Didn't you tell him we had no rooms."

"He didn't want a room."

"Then what's eating him?"

"He wanted one of the cottage tents."

"Did he see them?"

"Yes, but he still wanted one. His heart was set on a cottage tent."

"We haven't got a cottage tent. They're all taken."

"That's what I told him," said Bill. "Don't you think you'd better get in the boat?"

"Not yet," I said. "What did he say when you told him there were no cottage tents?"

"Nothing. That was when he tore his collar off and told his wife to go back to the verandah. She was a nice looking woman. Reserved, but nice."

"What kind of a man is this?" I asked, working my way down the boat.

"Don't swamp us. We've got to get back in this boat," cautioned Bill. "He's about your weight and build. You might have a little reach on him, but it ought to be an evenly matched fight, although he has moral purpose on his side. If he doesn't take a wallop at you when you're getting out of the boat, I'd say that it'd be an even money affair."

"We might land some other place."

"His wife has us covered with a pair of binoculars."

"These people must be cuckoo," I said. "Doesn't he know he can't barge into a popular resort in August without making a reservation?"

"That is the main bone of contention. He says he made a reservation, last April."

"Last April! What's his name?"

"Jones."

"I've heard the name somewhere."

"He says he has a letter from you saying you reserved a cottage tent commanding unexcelled views of the lake and mountains and that you expressed the hope that you would have the pleasure of welcoming him personally, and conducting him to his cottage tent. He seems to remember the part about your pleasure of welcoming him, best of all."

"That sounds like something I might have said in April," I admitted. "But I recall no Jones. Did you see the letter?"

"Ah, no," murmured Bill. "That is another of the unhappy sidelights on the case. The letter is on the top of his suitcase."

"Where is his suitcase? Did he forget it?"

"In part," said Bill. "He got it as far as the station and put it on the train, but he forgot to take it off the train. I was talking to the station agent about it and he thinks he can get it back in a couple of days. I told Mr. Jones."

"How did he take the news?"

"Badly. That was when he ripped his shirt off trying to get the neckband undone. The collar button is in eight feet of water off the end of the dock."

"What was wrong with his neckband?"

"He didn't say, but I gathered it was choking him."

"Hasn't he got a shirt on?"

"Only an undershirt and he might gnaw that to pieces any moment."

"I hope there were no ladies on the dock."

"Not at first, but a large gallery was collecting when I left. You ought to have a good house when you pull off your fight."

"I'm not going to fight a man because he's lost a suitcase. When I fight, I want a cause célèbre."

"Mr. Jones thinks he has one. His trunk, and his wife's dressing case are with the suitcase. He checked them but the baggage man must have thought he was fooling."

"What of it?" I said. "Lots of people have lost their clothes for a few days before this. Besides, there's a heat wave coming."

"It would have been easier at any other time."

"What's wrong with this time?"

"Nothing, nothing," repeated Bill tenderly. "Nothing. Only they were just married. He's a bridegroom. The lady is a bride. They are on their honeymoon."

"How do you know?"

"He told me."

"That's no guarantee. People often pull that stuff off at hotels. They do it to attract attention."

"Not this man. He made me promise to keep it a secret. He was very sensitive. When I offered to put up a couple of cots for him in the loft of the boat-house, he didn't say a word but kept looking at a knot hole in the floor."

"Which one?"

"The one we take the oars up through in the fall."

"That isn't a knot hole. That's a trap door."

"It's hard to tell them apart," said Bill.

"You offered to fix it, I hope."

"No, but I told him we could put a rug over it."

"Have we got a rug?"

"No, but I made the offer."

"How did he respond?"

"Poorly."

"Was this before or after he had the trouble with his neckband?"

"After."

"Then there was nothing left for him to take off?"

"Nothing but his shoes and stockings."

"Surely to God he had his trousers."

"I wasn't counting them. A man doesn't take off his trousers when he's angry."

"He doesn't take off his shoes and stockings either."

"He might," said Bill. "You haven't seen Mr. Jones."

"Why should I see him? There is nothing I can do."

"I told him that, but he still said he wanted to see you," said Bill. "You'd better get in the boat."

"I might tip it."

"We'll have to take a chance."

"Why can't you tow me in?"

"Your position," said Bill. "You got to impress this man with your dignity. You wouldn't look dignified being towed to shore."

"I won't look dignified anyway in a wet bathing suit and that boat."

"You'll look better than being towed like something that had been washed up on the beach."

"You might be right," I said.

I let Bill help me into the boat. He is a strong fellow.

"Is there any place we can put Mr. Jones and his bride?" I said after Bill had me in the boat and was baling it out.

"Nowhere they would go."

Bill started to work over the engine. It took him some time to get it going. It started twice but each time it died.

"Did you see if you could find a copy of that letter?" I asked when it died the second time. Bill was getting angry at the engine.

"What sense would there be in that?" said Bill. "You know your filing system."

"What's wrong with our filing system?" I demanded.

"Nothing," said Bill. "Only it takes time to use it."

I thought it better to leave Bill to the engine. It started unexpectedly in the frantic manner of outboard motors. With the engine running speech was impossible and thought difficult, but I couldn't help thinking of Mr. Jones standing at the end of the dock waiting for me. I could see that he would be expecting a great deal of me once he found me. I tried to imagine what I would feel like if I were in Mr. Jones' place and I decided that I would feel very much as Mr. Jones did, except that I hoped I'd be more careful with my clothes.

"We must try to do something for Mr. Jones," I called to Bill, above the angry drone of the motor.

"What," said Bill.

"I say, we must try and do something for Mr. Jones."

Bill stopped the engine.

"Did you say something?" he said.

"I said, we've got to do something for Mr. Jones."

"What in hell do you think he is waiting on the end of the dock for?" said Bill.

He started the engine again.

I went on thinking about Mr. Jones.

I saw him a long way off. He was thinking, too. He was walking up and down the dock and every few feet, he stopped to shake his fists at someone in an airplane. There wasn't any airplane, of course, but Mr. Jones acted as though there were. I looked for all the people Bill had said were gathering but I could see no one but Mr. Jones. When we were nearing the dock,

Mr. Jones stopped marching and looked at us. I signalled Bill to stop the engine.

"We'd better row in slowly," I said to Bill. "We don't want to take an unfair advantage by rushing up on him."

Bill rowed the boat in toward the dock. When we got closer I saw that Mr. Jones had put on his coat and had the collar turned up to hide his neck. He was a small man with a red face and fat hands. He didn't seem to be able to keep his face or hands still. He seemed to be anxious to do something with them.

"I don't think he's much of a swimmer," I said to Bill. "Just pull up there in deep water, a few feet off the end of the dock."

Mr. Jones didn't recognize us at first. Bill's back was to him, and it was the first time he'd seen me. One long look seemed to satisfy him. He turned and crunched his way up the dock.

"Tell him now," I said to Bill when he was near the end.

"Tell him what?" said Bill.

"Tell him I'm here."

Bill turned around.

"Well, Mr. Jones," he said. "I found him."

Mr. Jones turned around and looked at us. First at Bill, and then at me.

"Where is he?" he said.

"Did you want to see me?" I asked.

"I want to see the man who runs this dump. Are you the manager?" said Mr. Jones. He said a lot more, but that gives the gist of his speech.

"No, I am only the proprietor," I answered pleasantly. He didn't seem to believe me. "I may not look like much in this bathing suit but I am the proprietor, nevertheless. Was there something I could do for you?"

He wasn't convinced then but he came down to the end of the dock.

"You can tell me what you mean by writing me that you'd reserved a cottage tent, and then get me in here twenty miles from the railroad and no way of getting out, and then have some clerk tell me there isn't a bed in the place."

"Did Bill tell you that?" I said. "There are lots of beds."

"I've seen some of them," said Mr. Jones, "and I want the cottage tent I was promised. I came here expecting a cottage tent and I'm going to get a cottage tent."

"They're all full," I said.

"I don't give a damn what they are. I was promised one and I'm going to have one."

"But how can you have one when there aren't any?" I asked.

"That's your worry, not mine. I've got your letter and I'm going to hold you to it."

"Could you show me the letter?"

"Get out of that boat and I'll show you a lot more than the letter," said Mr. Jones.

"I can hear you all right from here," I said. "But if you could show me the letter we might get things straightened out. I don't need to read it. Just wave it to me. I can tell one of my letters quite a distance away."

"I haven't got the damn letter," snarled Mr. Jones. "It's in my suitcase."

"Well, then," I said, "let's get your suitcase and look at it. Perhaps you didn't read it over carefully. People can jump to conclusions about letters. I do, often. Where is your suitcase?"

Mr. Jones just looked at me.

"Surely you brought your suitcase, Mr. Jones," I said.

Mr. Jones felt for the neckband of his shirt, but it was gone, as Bill had told me.

"It's on the blasted train, together with my trunk and wife's dressing case," he said, when he found his shirt was missing.

"That's hard luck," I said, "but it should get here in a week, at the outside."

I waited to see if Mr. Jones wanted to say anything, but he didn't.

"Now, tell me about this letter," I said. "What kind of a letter was it? Was it a white letter, or a brown letter?"

"It was a letter, damn it. A letter."

"Ah!" I said, "if you can't remember what colour it was, even, I can't tell whether it was my letter or not. How was it signed? With initials or a full name?"

"How in hell should I know?" said Mr. Jones.

"It's important to know," I said. "Some months I sign my full name and some months initials."

"Well, I don't know what you signed. All I know is I got this letter in April and it promised me a cottage tent. If I had that suitcase, I'd damn soon show you."

"Mr. Jones," I said. "I, too, wish you had the suitcase, the dressing case and the trunk, but particularly the letter, because I can't remember ever promising anyone named Jones a cottage tent in April. Could you have written under another name perhaps? Your wife's maiden name?"

I saw that he was beginning to get angry.

"What would I want to write under another name for?" he said.

"I don't know," I said, "but strange things do happen."

"The strangest thing is anyone coming to this hole."

"Oh, don't feel that way about it, Mr. Jones," I said. "You'll grow quite attached to the place after you've been here a few days. Bill, let's go ashore and see if we can't fix Mr. Jones up."

"I showed him everything there was," said Bill. "I don't see where we've got any cause to worry if he can't show us his letter."

"I know, Bill," I said. "But courtesy costs nothing."

Bill rowed ashore and I got out. Mr. Jones was waiting for me.

"Now, look here," he said. "I'm going to have a cottage tent. I was promised one and I'm going to have it, letter or no letter."

When I stood up beside him, I saw that Bill had been wrong. Mr. Jones was much lighter than I was, and hadn't as much reach. He seemed out of condition, too. I looked at him.

"Mr. Jones," I said. "We're going to do the best we can for you, but before we discuss the matter any further, do you mind if I point out to you that you're making a great mistake to argue so heatedly on the end of the dock with a heavier man, if you can't swim?"

"My God, man!" he said, "Don't you realize that I was just married this morning?"

"I know it," I said. "If you were yourself, you'd not attempt such unreasonable demands. Now. Why didn't you like the boat-house? Most of the boats are in by midnight, and you wouldn't be disturbed after then."

"I'll not sleep in any boat-house," said Mr. Jones. "There were knot holes you could lower a horse through."

"I know," I said. "We take the boats up through them in the fall, but how about the Inn? Bill, did you show Mr. Jones a room in the Inn. We might get a couple of guests who know each other to move around for a couple of days."

"Where's the Inn?" said Mr. Jones.

"That is where you washed your hands," said Bill.

"I'll not go in the Inn," said Mr. Jones.

"Oh, I'll fix you up with a shirt and collar," I said.

"It was because of the location, not myself," said Mr. Jones. "I'm going to have a cottage tent."

"You'd like to have a cottage tent," I corrected, "but there are none. There might be one tomorrow."

"I want one now. Tonight," said Mr. Jones.

"Then, we'd better go and have dinner," I said. "You'll feel grateful for some food before the night's out. I'll lend you a shirt."

"I don't eat till I find where I'm going."

"Then you don't eat," I said, "but how about your wife? You've no right to starve her."

"Well, if we do eat, what guarantee have I that you'll fix me up after dinner?" Mr. Jones demanded.

"None at all," I said. "All you can do is hope. All I can do is to talk to some of my guests and see if they won't help you."

By this time, Mr. Jones was pretty well played out and he let Bill lead him away and put a shirt on him. I went up and took a look at Mrs. Jones and was pleased to see that she had a sympathetic audience clustered around her. It spoke well for the Jones's chances of getting a place to sleep.

During dinner we had a conference of those guests with whom the management was on friendly terms and Bill talked to the guests who liked him personally, while I talked to a couple of guests who'd known me before I was a summer resort keeper. Everybody was friendly and helpful and took a warm interest in the plight of the bewildered Mr. Jones. By rearranging the entire place, we took care of them.

A kindly old lady moved in with her daughter and we put the grandchild on a cot, half in the cupboard and half in the room. Two of Bill's friends in a big corner room moved into the grandmother's room and two people from one of the cottages moved up to the corner room. This left a cottage free and we were just debating whom we would ask to move out of a cottage tent into the cottage, when Mr. Jones appeared and said he would take the cottage. It would do, for one night, he said, because he was leaving in the morning anyway. Then we borrowed clothes and toothbrushes for them and by midnight everything was peaceful.

In the morning Mr. Jones was a new man. He said that he

was sorry for all the trouble he had caused the night before and asked if he could keep the cottage.

"Certainly, you may, Mr. Jones," I said, "and please don't apologize. I appreciate how it looked to you."

"I'll be glad when the suitcase comes so that I can show you that letter," he said. "You don't think yet we really had a cottage tent engaged."

"It's possible, Mr. Jones," I said. "Possible but not probable."

His suitcase turned up in about three days. I was glad because Mr. Jones could wear my clothes almost as well as I could. I waited for him to bring me the letter. I waited all that evening and all the next morning. Mr. Jones seemed to be avoiding me. I joined him at lunch. He said nothing about it. Days went by and still no sight of the letter.

He came to me the morning he was leaving to return a few articles of clothing he had found when packing, and to tell me how much he and Mrs. Jones had enjoyed themselves.

"What ever happened to that letter?" I asked.

"What letter?" he said.

"That letter you got in April."

"Oh, that letter," said Mr. Jones with a strange laugh. "It's a funny thing about that letter. I had a lot of letters, you see, and I thought there was a letter from this place among them. I could have sworn I had written here too, but when the suitcase came I looked through all the reservations I'd made, and I couldn't find it any place. I honestly thought I had a reservation here when I arrived but I was mistaken. You know how it is when you're married for the first time."

"Don't apologize," I said. "We all have to get married once. I hope you'll come back again next year."

"Possibly not next year," said Mr. Jones. "Things might not work out so we could come back next year, but the year after that, most certainly."

I saw the Joneses off on the bus and went in to see Bill.

"Bill," I said, "where did you put the copy of Mr. Jones' letter?"

"In the safe," said Bill.

"I don't see why it couldn't go back in the files," I said. "They've gone."

from Boobs in the Woods

from The Mayor of Upper Upsalquitch

John Crosbie

Thursday March 6

Dropped in to see Bill Huggins at the drug store this morning. Accepted his kind offer of a milkshake. Real purpose was to see how my books were selling. Bill and I have a little deal going. I see to it that the drug store stays the only place in town where the kids can buy their schoolbooks. Bill, in turn, keeps an eye on the kids who drop in on their way home from school. If he sees one of them carrying a book that looks a little ragged, he gives the kid a new one and puts it on the parents' account. Over the school year this racks up a surprising number of extra sales. And since I get ten per cent on all books sold, I'm really proud of how well-equipped our students are.

Easter Sunday
Sunday April 6

Saw people at church today I haven't seen for a year. Had trouble recognizing some of the women, though. The hats they wear these days!

The Reverend Angus was in fine style. Put it right on the line: he's not a rabbit lover. Down on coloured eggs, as well. I think he'd have gone on to putting down women for their Easter finery too, but his wife, Nellie, was sitting right under his nose in the front pew wearing a big purple hat topped with a yellow bird squatting on red and green daisies.

The choir was in its usual form, mis-handling "The Messiah."

The concept of resurrection has always appealed to me. I always make a point of paying off promptly on life insurance claims, but I'm religious enough to wait four days — just in case.

Saturday May 31

Annie stopped by for a while this afternoon. Did a washing for me. Then asked me to do her a favour: please stop talking about fiddleheads.

Had to admit that when I get an idea I hate to let go. Also admitted that all the pots with green water she found in the kitchen this morning were from secret late-night experiments.

We cleaned them up together and that will be the end of it. Once I get the stains out of the sink.

Sunday June 1

After church I rolled up my sleeves and went at it. A couple of hours later the sink was its old self again.

It was kind of sad, pouring those good gallons of fiddlehead consommé down the drain. But I have to be honest with myself: if someone had served it to me at a dinner I would have wondered what it was. Without meaning to, I think what I really invented was a swamp.

Thursday August 21

The advance agent for the circus showed up today. Came right to see me. (I had promised full cooperation on the phone.) Took him to Sim Jack's for coffee. But he was restless and wanted to get going. As we came out, he said, "Well, let's go downtown and slap up some posters." I said, "This *is* downtown!" and he turned sort of green. However, he finally went off to do what he could and I called Milky Becker and told him to give the agent a day and then arrest him for defamation of property.

Tuesday August 26

The circus put on two shows yesterday and two today. I showed up again for today's evening performance. It was kind of sad. The mosquitoes didn't have enough people to go around. The owner buttonholed me afterwards, looking pretty worried. "Where is everybody?" he asked.

"That *is* everybody," I replied. "And I must compliment you. They've all enjoyed it."

"Enjoyed it, hell," he cried. "We're losing our shirts!"

"Oh now," I reassured him, "I'm sure everything will come

out right. After you've paid the property rent you'll still have a nice profit."

"Property rent!" he screamed. "What property rent?"

I explained that the town always charged for the use of its land. "But don't worry," I says, "it's only a thousand dollars for the whole week." He went into a sort of fit but I had to leave before I could see the end of it.

Wednesday August 27

The Councillors were right on my tail going into the meeting tonight. Casey Irving asked the question I was expecting. Before I could get a grip on my gavel he demanded, "What happened?" We all knew what he meant.

During the night the circus had disappeared. Gone. Tents, wagons, calliope and all. Well, not quite all. The advance agent was still handcuffed to Milky Becker's furnace and Milky, who had been waiting with our special deputy Dusty Miller, had stopped the exodus at the farm gate long enough to take their animals into custody as security against the rent.

Since it didn't seem likely the circus would be playing many dates with neither advance advertising nor animals, I said I felt our chances of collecting were pretty poor.

"Well, then," demanded Casey, "what are we going to do with those animals?"

"Do?" I replied. "Why, we're going to have a zoo, that's what. A *real* tourist attraction!"

Golf Lesson

Jack Scott

One of the most interesting cases to be heard at the Winter Assizes will be the attempted murder charge against Henry Pludge.

Since I am in a position to know the background of the story, I've no doubt the jury will acquit him. Unless, of course, there happens to be a woman on the panel.

Emily, herself, I'm happy to say, has almost completely recovered. She has forgiven him, putting it down to a simple matter of temporary insanity. She has given up golf and . . . but perhaps I'd better review the whole case from the beginning.

Emily Pludge complained so much about being a golf widow that last Christmas Henry presented her with a set of clubs.

"I realize I've been selfish about this," he said, "always going off with the fellows and all that. There's no reason in the world why we can't play the grand old game together."

"Oh, Henry," said Emily. "You are a husband in a million."

As it turned out there were several reasons why they couldn't play the game together, the most obvious being that Emily was completely hopeless on the links. Henry was patient with her. He did his best to teach her the little he knew about the fundamentals of the swing. Even when she missed the ball completely and burst out giggling, as she frequently did, Henry was somehow able to keep himself under control.

Fortunately, it took no more than a half-dozen games to thoroughly discourage Emily. The clubs were put away in the hall closet. Henry went back to playing with his regular pals. And there, it seemed, the matter might have ended amicably.

Might have, in fact, if it hadn't been for my wife. This is how I happen to know about the whole thing. My wife, you see, decided to take some golf lessons from a professional named Mel White and she invited Emily to go along with her.

This was about three months ago. They were taking a lesson every Tuesday and each Tuesday night I was given a blow-by-blow description of Emily's progress. She was obviously a remarkable student under any tutelage but that of her husband.

"Emily got her first birdie today," my wife would report, or, "Emily broke a hundred today," or "Emily had six par holes today."

Whenever I saw Mel himself, he made a point of talking about his star pupil.

"She's amazing," he confided. "It's going to be interesting when her husband takes her on."

Henry has given me a full description of that fateful day.

At the first tee, it seems, Emily stepped up and whacked one 185 yards straight down the middle. It shook Henry. He put everything he had into his drive. It was slicing five feet off the tee. The ball cleared a row of maples, crossed over a four-lane highway and vanished into bushland.

"You're bringing your left shoulder back," Emily said, pleasantly enough. "Mel says that's bad."

Henry dribbled his second shot a scant fifty feet into the rough at the right of the fairway.

"You're not bringing the clubhead in-to-out," Emily said. "You've got to keep that left arm straight on the backswing."

Henry had a twelve on the hole or eight over par. It was this way all around. On the third, where he hooked into a school playground, Emily showed him what was wrong with his grip. On the easy par-three fifth where he shanked a nine-iron into that pretty little stream, Emily demonstrated the correct relationship of the ball to the feet.

"You're not keeping your head down," she told him on the seventh, at which point he was twenty-three blows over par. "Mel says you just can't hit a ball if you lift your head."

She then pitched to within four feet of the cup and sank her putt for a bird.

He'd have killed her, I guess, if some of the members hadn't been sitting out on the porch that overlooks the ninth green, where it happened.

As soon as they saw him swinging at her with his driver they were running. He could not have hit her more than five or six times before they had him pinned down.

They say he was pretty hysterical. "Mel says, Mel says," he kept babbling. He was still muttering it when they came to take him away.

So that's how it all happened and I guess it will all be bared at the trial. Out at the club, of course, we've rehashed it a thousand times and there isn't a male member there who isn't critical of Henry.

Imagine using a driver when a No. 5 would have done the trick!

from From Our Town

Fifi and Her First-Class Man

Richard J. Needham

Once upon a time, and in — of all places — Toronto, there was a girl named Fifi Fahrenheit. She had come here from Lunenburg, N.S., for precisely the same reason that other girls come here from Lindsay, Leamington, Lethbridge, London, and Luebeck — that is, to find an interesting, intelligent, polite, and (what is most important) unattached man.

She quickly obtained a job with the Irrational Trust Company, where she spent all day typing lengthy memoranda in Swahili addressed to junior executives who tore them up without reading them. She also made the acquaintance of the Bay Street belles, to whom she confided her real purpose in coming to Toronto. They laughed so loudly that they could be heard in the farthest Babbitt-warrens of Tormented Township.

"Foolish Fifi!" said one of them. "You will shortly learn that there are no interesting, intelligent, polite, unattached men in Toronto. There are no interesting, intelligent, polite men in Toronto. There are no interesting, intelligent men in Toronto. There are no interesting men in Toronto. There are no men in Toronto. There are no men, and that is why I have taken up triple brandies as a way of life."

Another one said, "I was told you have to go out with

creeps in order to meet real men, but all I have ever met by going out with creeps is or are more creeps. That is why I have taken up skiing, hat-making, and eating garlic sausage as a way of life."

Another one said, "Miracles do happen, and I deem it possible that you will find a man in Toronto who is interesting, intelligent, polite, and unattached. You will also find, however, that he has a severe drinking problem. Or else you will find that he is deeply attached to his mother, whom he calls Lover, Mumsy, or Sweetie-pie, and whom he telephones every half-hour when he is out with you. That is why I have taken up bowling, chain-smoking, and Kahlil Gibran as a way of life, if you can call it life, which I very much doubt."

Like all Nova Scotia girls, Fifi was strong and brave. She refused to believe what the Bay Street belles told her, but insisted on finding things out for herself. As she did. For her first three months in Toronto, she didn't have a single date. Then she began meeting men and going out with them. But they certainly fell far below the standards she had set for herself when she boarded the MacKenzie bus at Lunenburg.

She went out with men who wore hats, men who wore rimless spectacles, and men who wore sharply pointed shoes with paper-thin soles. She went out with men who read Zane Grey, men who believed in British Israel, and men who were secretly in love with Juliette. She went out with men who carefully studied and added up the restaurant bill. She went out with men who furtively leafed through the photography magazines on the newstands.

She went out with men who didn't drink or smoke, but got their jollies by looking down the front of the waitress's dress. She went out with men who smoked cigars in automobiles. She went out with men who asked her humbly first, and thanked her profusely afterwards. She went out with men who tipped an exact ten per cent, down to the last penny. She went out with men who took her to Fort York, the Royal Ontario Museum, and HMCS *Haida*.

She went out with men who didn't call her the morning after. She went out with men who told her at length and with many tears that their wives didn't understand them, but they couldn't get a divorce on account of the kids. She went out with men who, on sitting down at the restaurant table, took the napkin and breathed upon and polished every piece of cutlery. She went out with men who combed their hair up over their bald spots. She went out with men who sucked Clorets just before they kissed her.

She went out with men who put unlit cigarettes behind their ears, and with men who held lighted cigarettes between their bent fingers with the glowing end toward the palm. She went out with men who got drunk and quarrelled with her; with men who got drunk and threw up; with men who got drunk and telephoned newspaper offices demanding to know who won the Kentucky Derby in 1897. She went out with men who put their correct names and addresses on LCBO purchase slips.

Fifi finally broke down. She started crying and drinking and wearing needle-heeled shoes and stockings with seams and sack dresses and dark fuchsia lipstick. She started reading newspaper editorials and voting in elections and listening to Johnnie Ray records. She stopped using eye make-up and joined the YWCA and enrolled for an evening course in conversational Australian.

In short, she was thoroughly mixed up and just about ready for a series of $75-an-hour sessions with Dr. Rorschach Blotz. As a desperate last measure, she sat down to her IBM electric, and wrote a single-word letter — "Help!" — which she sent to Rudolph J. Needleberry, a venerable newspaper columnist who appeared to have some scant knowledge of the Toronto scene.

The kindly old philosopher naturally invited her to lunch at the Venetian Room of the Royal York. "You can easily identify me," he said, "because I am eight feet tall, totally bald, and have a dark-green complexion. In view of our surroundings, I will of course be wearing my gondolier's outfit. I do not doubt that you and I will be the only mixed couple in the place, except for a husband and wife who after twenty-five years of marital bliss haven't a word to say to each other."

After Fifi had finished her first manhattan, and he had downed his fourteenth, she described the nature of her problem to him. He beamed like a Cheshire cat and replied: "My dear young lady, you are not alone. Hundreds and indeed thousands of Toronto women are in precisely the same situation. There are roughly 600,000 grown men in this vast metropolis; most of them are happily married and should therefore be written off, though I am led to believe that they are by no means averse to a nice furtive little week-end in some such handy place as Niagara Foibles or St. Calamity."

He ordered a fifteenth manhattan, and continued: "Now, as for the unattached men, you will find that a rather large number of them are madly gay, so they must be written off, too, at least so far as young ladies like you are concerned. The remainder are available, one might say, and some of them meet your specifications; but these are hard to find, and when you do find them are surrounded by a bevy of other women who got there first and defend their claim with razor-honed letter-openers. The rest are largely or totally unsuitable, and should not be allowed out with a female orangutan, let alone a nice girl from Lunenburg, N.S."

Lighting his eighty-seventh cigarette of the day, he concluded: "The men of Toronto puzzle and amuse me. What they all have in common whether they are married or not, and perhaps especially if they are married, is that they don't really like women. To this situation I have devoted years of thought, oceans of Gilbey's gin, millions of Rothmans, and hundreds of dollars' worth of noisy heterosexual dinners at Hold Handgelo's, but have yet to come up with the reason for it, let alone the remedy. For my own part, I would say of women what Churchill said of brandy; they are God's greatest gift to suffering humanity; but I know only one other man who agrees with me, and he has been deported to Hamilton."

Fifi started to cry, and he patted her hand. "Dry your tears," he said. "There may be hope for you yet. I recently met a woman who in every sense is an absolute witch, and thus pleases me greatly. She is here in Toronto, being witchy hither and yon, and also witching at me through many a long and liquid lunch at The Hunters. I will ask her to perform a miracle of witchiness and produce, for you alone, what I like to describe as a first-class man."

Fifi thanked Mr. Needleberry, but didn't really believe anything could come of it. "He was just trying to cheer me up," she thought that evening as she stumbled through a typical Toronto May blizzard to her apartment in the Village Grim. "Poor old fellow, he means well, but it would take a whole battalion of witches to produce a truly first-class man in this creepy city." It was then that she saw a man's feet sticking out of a snowbank, the rest of him being totally buried.

Fifi quickly cleared away the snow, pulled the unfortunate fellow to his feet, and gave him a nip from the bottle of Paul Masson brandy she kept in her purse. "Thank you very much," he said, "and permit me to introduce myself. My name is Yves Ladifférence, I recently arrived here from Montreal; and, being somewhat lonely, dipped too deeply into the Dewar's. It is true, as William Blake says, that you never know what is enough until you know what is more than enough. Had it not been for you, I would likely have perished, which means that the very least thing I owe you is dinner at La Scala with barrels of Bardolino and an immense bunch of flowers from Gallagher's."

He saw her home, took her telephone number, kissed her lightly on the hand, advised her she was the most attractive woman he had ever met, and added, "Mais vos yeux! Ma petite, que vous avez souffert!" As he departed, humming a pleasant allegro strain from Handel's *Water Music*, Fifi knew she had at last found a first-class man — one who weighed in, as sporting parlance might have it, with Marcello Mastroianni, Herbert von Karajan, and Peter O'Toole.

Yves was all the things a man ought to be with a woman, but rarely is. He took Fifi out to lunch every day; he was always on time with a bouquet of flowers under his arm; and, if she was late, insisted that the clock must be wrong. Every morning, she got a love letter from him at the office, and every evening she got two love letters from him at home. He wrote poems about her beauty and charm, and had them privately printed, and stuck them up all over downtown Toronto. He never criticized her in any way, for, as he pointed out to her (and especially in front of other women), there was nothing in her to criticize; she was perfection itself.

Fifi told him the story of her life, to which he listened attentively; and he told her quite a bit about his own. "I must tell you, Fifi," he said, "that I have travelled in many parts of the world, and that there were other women before you — Dresden dolls, Worcester saucies, unorthodox Greeks, Tasmanian devils, Scotch friskies, Devonshire creamies, Icelandic volcanoes, Welsh minors, Chinese puzzles, Strasbourg geese, Persian lambs, Dover soulfuls, French undressings, San Francisco earthquakes, and a Bengal tigress named, as I recall, Jacqueline. But they were only the playthings of an idle moment; you are the first one whom I feel I can really love and trust."

When the Bay Street belles saw the way in which Yves Ladifférence held doors open for Fifi, and helped her with her coat, and kissed her right in the middle of Simpsons and knelt down to put on and take off her high black suede boots — when they saw all this, their rage and jealousy knew no bounds. One would mutter, "Only flits have manners like that." Another would say, "I wouldn't be surprised if he turned out to be a secret drinker," and still another, "You mark my words; the Montreal police will be along to pick him up for embezzlement, or for running dope, or for some awful offence involving small boys."

But Fifi smiled; she knew what she knew — that he was absolutely first-class. They went happily along for many weeks until one day he showed up for lunch without any flowers. Fifi was a little bit upset, and asked rather coolly, "Where are they? What's gone wrong?" He explained that a truckers' strike had prevented deliveries. She accepted his explanation, and their lunch was as pleasant — well, almost as pleasant — as the ones they had had before.

Then came the time when he was a bit low on funds; so instead of taking her to dinner at Le Provençal, he took her to Diana Sweets. Fifi made a little joke out of it, and said he must be spending his money on some other woman; but Yves didn't laugh, he just looked pensive and lit another cigarette. "Tell me honestly now, Yves," she said. "How many packs a day do you smoke?" He said three, maybe four. "That's an awful lot," said Fifi. "It seems to me you are asking for trouble. I think you should smoke a pipe instead and it just so happens that I have bought you one and have it with me."

Yves smoked a pipe from there on. At Fifi's suggestion, he gave up rolling his shirtsleeves, and started keeping a budget, and wore striped shirts instead of white ones, and moved from his pad on Spadina Avenue to a much nicer one in Rosedale. One day, Fifi said to him: "You frequently mention a woman in your past named Véronique, and I suspect you had quite a thing about her, and I want to know exactly who she is, and if she is in Toronto right now, and if you ever see her, and exactly what relationship you have with her. Am I the only woman in your life, or are there others whom you keep hidden away from me?"

He assured her she was the only one, and then she cried a bit, and said she didn't mind about there being other women, so long as she was the No. 1 girl. Some weeks later, she demanded:

"Who was the last woman you made love to before you met me, and what was it like, and how long was the interval between her and me?" The end came when, on reaching her office one morning, Fifi found Yves had written her only a three-page love letter instead of the usual five-pager. Telephoning him immediately, she said: "I know now that you have deceived me, and are carrying on with one or more other women. Tonight, Yves, you and I are going to have a long and serious talk about us."

At which point, Yves Ladifférence disappeared from Fifi's life and indeed from Toronto. Some people said he had fled to Madrid by CPA; and others that he had gone to Australia by BOAC; and still others that he had vanished into Finnair. Fifi is still here, of course. She is at present going out with a man who believes that the earth is flat, that poverty and war can be abolished, that the Senate plays a useful role in Canadian life, and that there really is such a person as Douglas Fisher.

from Needham's Inferno

Turvey Attends a Court-Martial

Earle Birney

The sun was a colourless wafer in a steely sky, and the January cold, invisible but bitter, filtered efficiently through the cracks in the little wooden nests of Number Two Security Regiment. In the feeble afternoon sunlight four soldiers stood shivering and stamping their feet on the bare porch of a square hut known somewhat grandiosely as the YMCA Hostel. A casual observer would have been puzzled to know why a sergeant, a corporal, and two privates continued to linger in such a cold spot for no apparent military purpose, and without the benefit of greatcoats. They made an oddly chummy and idle foursome; one of the privates was even smoking, in full view of the mid-day camp and of possible prowling officers.

Turvey would have enjoyed the cigarette more if the sergeant, in permitting it, had not added, "It's the last you'll smoke for a month of Sundays, my boy. Nothing like that where you're going. They got a real brassballs from Ottawa running the courts this week. Colonel Sloggin, Old Fishface, they call him. You won't pull your panties over *his* eyes."

The frost-rimmed door behind them abruptly screeched and opened. A little bald soldier peered out, winked heavily at the sergeant and jerked his thumb inwards. "O.K."

"Chuck cigarettes," the sergeant hissed quickly, then instantly transformed himself into a stiffbacked loudspeaker. "Escort-n-prisner ten-HOWN," he bellowed and, suddenly *sotto voce* again, "allri, allri, corp'ral in front, prisner, then you, Davis." Then the loudspeaker blared. "RrriiiiTUN, weeeeeek MATCH." The little procession clomped briskly into the blessed warmth of a square room, past stacks of upturned chairs and tables, and a handful of officers and men standing at attention beside benches. Turvey heard the sergeant behind hissing something about "head-dress" and somebody neatly whipped his melton skull cap from his head. Clump, clomp, clump, clomp they went toward a ruddy Winnipeg heater and a low platform against the far wall, on which three officers were perched behind a table spread with papers.

" 'Scortnprisner, HALLT!! . . . Riii TUN . . . 'Scort two-pacestep-back MATCH." Turvey felt his companions vanish from beside him, and began absorbing the stare of the three sets of officer eyes on the dais. The middle ones were especially formidable; they were steel blue and glittered beneath an impressive redbanded officer's hat, and above two red neck-tabs and the brassy shoulder adornments of a Full Colonel.

Turvey reached his hand up to smooth his hair, and stopped, his arm paralyzed by the Full Colonel's eyes. They seemed to be saying that, however solidly the officers of the court might squat on their chairs, he, Turvey, the prisoner, was to stand at attention.

The sergeant was right, Turvey thought; the colonel's eyes, behind thick rimless spectacles, looked remarkable like those of a trout, and Turvey unaccountably remembered what Calvin Busby had said about the army being a fish hatchery. This colonel looked about the room with the calm unwinking orb of the fish that knows itself several sizes bigger than any other in his tank. A big plump Dolly Varden swimming in a pool of documents, Turvey thought, with a Sam Browne belt and a bright row of buttons for belly stripes; the two redtabs were his gills. The way his cheeks sloped into a tiny chinless mouth was fish-like too.

The Big Trout stared down at a paper one of his two flanking troutlings slid in front of him, stared up at Turvey, opened his puckery mouth as if about to gulp air, and, miraculously, spoke:

"Are you B-08654732 Private Turvey, Thomas Lead-beater?" The voice was cold and clear and utterly colourless.

"B-086547 TWO 2, Private Turvey, sir, yessir," said Turvey brightly.

There was a small stir in the papery pool above him until it was discovered that the mistake was the colonel's, not the documents. The colonel sucked air again: "Take your place beside your Defending Officer, Turvey. The court will now be sworn in."

"I swear by Almighty God," the Great Trout said ex-pressionlessly and paused; all the minnows throughout the stuffy little room opened their mouths in unison and echoed the words and the tonelessness: "swearbymightygad . . . To tell the truth . . . "

He was glad to feel that he was still within warming distance of the stove. His toes and fingers throbbed slowly into life. Then the Orderly Sergeant sat Turvey on a bench on the left of the court and for the first time he was able to look around. Opposite him sat a solemn private with a long nose like a badger's and a lap full of files; next to him was a captain, a newcomer to the unit, remarkable for a large fierce moustache, RAF pattern, set in the middle of a small baby-face. Behind them he identified his old Hut Corporal and Platoon Sergeant, and the provost who had brought him back from the border. He stole a glance behind him and spotted the R.A.P. Sergeant, the M.O., and the Nut Doctor who had visited him in the guard house this morning.

And, beside him, breathing a most exciting odour of whiskey into his right ear, was Lieutenant Sanderson, the pay-master, a devil-may-care character with a literary turn of mind who had been sent back from England officially as overage; he was popularly rumoured to have been returned because he paid off the same regiment twice in one week in a burst of alcoholic benevolence; he was also said to be the author of some plain-

spoken ballads of army life circulating in the camp. It was this
gentleman who, Turvey had been surprised to learn yesterday, was
defending him.

He had received the news from that old terror of the Short-
Arm Inspection, the R.A.P. Sergeant, who had breezed into the
Camp Brig, redfaced and wild-eyed as usual, slapped Turvey
jovially on the back, asked him if he'd been getting lots, and rasped
out with bewildering speed an elaborate set of plans for Turvey's
defence. There were so many courts martial this week, the R.A.P.
Sergeant had told him, that there was no use Turvey standing on
his rights and choosing his own defending officer. The paymaster
was the only one available and even he was still busy in a Court
of Enquiry regarding six rifles that a guard post had unitedly
dumped in the canal last week, so he wouldn't be able to see
Turvey personally before the trial. The sergeant had assured him,
however, that Pay had a masterly plan for Turvey's defence. The
R.A.P. Sergeant himself was going to be Turvey's chief witness.
At the most he would only get C.B. and loss of pay to equal the
number of days he had been on the loose. Or they might even get
him off.

That was, of course, the sergeant had rattled on, if Turvey
himself said as little as possible and they could get the Nut Doctor
on their side. O sure as hell, yes, said the sergeant, shifting a wad
of snoose to his other cheek, Pay had discovered in Turvey's
documents that he was due to see a Nut Doctor again any time
now. And the M.O. was getting the Area's Travelling Psychiatrist
to come over and see Turvey that very day. The sergeant had
slammed Turvey over the kidneys again, expressed a hope that the
Buffalo girls had appreciated his battle scars, spat brownly on the
doorstep, and clattered off in a burst of tremendous bronchial
laughter.

And now the swearing was over and the president had
swivelled his eyes to the opposite side of the room from Turvey,
bringing them to rest on the equally expressionless face of the
long-nosed private that Turvey had noticed sitting with a thick
file of papers. "The Clerk of the Court will now read the charge
against the accused."

The clerk rose instantly, released by some secret spring,
holding the wad of papers in front of him like a choir soloist.
He began to recite the charge in a shrill nasal monotone, running
the clichés together.

"The accused, B-08654722, Private-Turvey-Thomas-Lead-beater, on-a-strength-of Number-Two-Skewerty-Regiment, Cam-Byng-tario, soldier — Canain-Active-Army-s-charged-with-w'en'n-Active-Service," here he took his first breath and his voice rose another notch, gaining speed, "SENTING-SELF-THOUT-FICIAL-LEAVE in-that-he . . . did-sent-self-from twenty-two-hunrd-hours Friday cember-twenyfour-nin'n-hunrd-forytwo . . . un'l apprehen'd-an-return-barracks steen-hunr-sen-hours Saday-Janwy-fteen-nin-hun-for-three . . ." The clerk's voice shifted into an even higher gear and raced dizzily through a computation of the exact number of hours and minutes Private Turvey had deprived the Canadian Active Army of his activity, and the precise clauses and provisions of the Army Act which had anticipated such conduct and laid down the appropriate punishments.

"Do you plead guilty or not guilty?" It was the Big Trout again, the clerk having subsided as abruptly as he had arisen.

Turvey suddenly couldn't remember how the R.A.P. Sergeant had told him to plead. But he could see they had everything down exactly and no argument, and he was about to acknowledge his guilt, a little surprised that the president should think it debatable, when the paymaster came to life and stood up. His leathery, whiskey-veined face dimpled in a great mock-hearty smile, rakish with a gold molar. He annnounced to the colonel, as if it were the most natural thing in the world:

"He pleads not guilty, sir."

The glassy vision of the President of the Court-Martial rested briefly on the paymaster.

"You have been appointed, Lieutenant uh-er-"

"Sanderson," whispered the Righthand Troutling.

"Lieutenant Sanson," the president went on majestically, "to defend the prisoner, not to plead for him. Private Turvey, are you guilty or not guilty of the charge as read?"

Turvey shifted the weight on his feet; he was really stumped. Had the president given a peculiar emphasis to the last two words? Perhaps there was a loophole somewhere. And yet, come to think of it, nothing the president had said really had any emphasis to it at all. The paymaster was now elbowing him in the ribs most energetically, and had screwed his mouth up into an elaborate almost-silent "Not Guilty," shaking his head, and winking all at the same time.

"Whatever you gentlemen like." He paused. There was

silence, except for a smothered whisper from the paymaster. The president's face for the first time betrayed impatience and even some anxiety. Turvey groped in his mind for something that might please everybody and suddenly thought of what Ballard had said about a nice compromise in Scottish law. "Not Proven," he said, louder than he intended.

"Write down Not Guilty," said the president crisply. "You have not sufficiently instructed the defendant, Mr.-uh-Sansom," he added: even the president's voice was beginning to betray emphasis; there was a sharkish edge to it which did not bode well either for defendant or his counsel. After some general remarks on court-martial procedure, he held a whispered consultation with his two supporting judges, and announced that in view of the inclemency of the weather, witnesses would remain in the court-room until their testimony had been given. "The prosecution will commence."

Up stood the captain with the moustaches. He had been nervously twirling the ends; now one was curled jauntily up and the other hooked villainously down; but the rest of his face looked as childlike as ever. His voice was a jittery imitation of the president's; that is, it would have sounded impartial if it had not quavered slightly. While Turvey listened with interest, the prosecution proceeded to establish the undisputed fact that Turvey had been absent on the dates set down. Turvey's Hut Corporal gave the greasy Bible a gingerly peck and swore, with the clerk's prodding, "by mighty-Gad-tell-trut-whole-trut-nottin-buta-trut." He testified that Turvey was not in his hut at bed-check 2300 hours Christmas Eve. Then Turvey's Platoon Sergeant plodded through the same ceremony to assert that Turvey had not responded to rollcalls since 1400 hrs December 24th, and produced his roll-books in proof. They were duly accepted as exhibits for the evidence of the court.

As the trial droned on, Turvey got the feeling they were talking about someone else; the facts fitted him, but they had all ceased paying him any attention. All, that is, except the paymaster, who kept up a succession of sighs and soothing murmurs beside Turvey's right ear, a kind of punctuating rebuttal to each damning sentence of evidence. Turvey would have been quite comforted if the lieutenant's aromatic gusts had not blown into him a growing longing for a good stiff drink.

Then came a beefy provost corporal, circumstantial and

bored. He testified to having received into his care the body of one Turvey, Thomas Leadbeater (whom he also identified as the prisoner) from the custody of a United States Police Officer at the International Border, Niagara Falls, N.Y. He produced signed documents to prove it, and to prove also that he had delivered the same body later the same day to the corporal in charge of the guard house, Number Two Security Regiment.

A slight hitch developed here when the president's lefthand Troutling discovered that the guard house corporal had signed for Turvey on the wrong line. The president reproved both the corporal and the provost for this carelessness, and offered the paymaster an opportunity to enter an objection. But the latter cheerfully waived his rights, as he had waived all suggestions up to now that he cross-examine or in any other way enter the proceedings except by quiet wheezes and grunts to Turvey. The president thereupon decided that the document could be entered as evidence, together with a special emendatory form which the clerk had been rapidly making out in quadruplicate.

Then the clerk, who continued throughout the proceedings to be by far the busiest man in the room, released the secret spring in his knees and bounced up to intone a long series of reports which had been delivered up to the provost along with Turvey's sinful body. Although, from the point of view of an intimate chronicler, these documents revealed disappointing gaps, they nevertheless proved to be the most interesting of the day.

They informed all who might be concerned that the said person, giving his name as Thomas Leadbeater Turvey and admitting to being a Canadian citizen and a soldier in the Canadian Army, had been taken into custody in the bedroom of number nine Paradise Apartments, Raintree St., in the City of Buffalo, N.Y. The apartment, the report went on to specify, was legally and jointly tenanted by a Miss Ruby O'Reilly and a Miss Helga Bolinski, employees of the Earthquake Aircraft Corporation. The soldier had been apprehended in the course of a routine investigation arising out of a complaint by a tenant in the next apartment — who objected to the noise of night parties emanating from the windows of number nine. The soldier had been unable to produce evidence that he had legally entered the United States or that he was on official leave from his unit, and he had therefore been taken into custody as a potential deserter.

This somewhat tantalizing report was duly passed to the

clerk, and then passed to the paymaster at the latter's request. Turvey was somewhat startled to gather from Lieutenant Sanderson's chuckles and admiring wheezes that his Defending Officer had not previously examined this document at any leisure, if indeed at all. The lieutenant's tsst-chah's finally became so audible that the president sent a freezing ray from his eye over Turvey's right shoulder, the chuckles ceased, and the document was returned to the clerk.

The Prosecuting Officer, both horns of his moustache now sagging piratically, indicated that his case had been presented. The paymaster again airily declined to cross-examine, and the president called upon him to begin the defence.

With a great odorous wheeze Lieutenant Sanderson arose beside Turvey and beamed at the president. "Well, Your Honour —"

"The President of a Court-Martial is addressed as 'sir'," said the Great Trout coldly.

Lieutenant Sanderson's cheeks purpled a little more but otherwise he seemed unperturbed. "Sir," he said, "our first witness is Sergeant Sawyer here."

The R.A.P. Sergeant, his face a somewhat rosier reflection of the lieutenant's, stumped noisily from a side bench and was sworn in. Turvey thought his expression looked a little unnatural and then realized that for the first time he was seeing the sergeant when he was not chewing snuff.

"Tell His Hon — tell the court, sarge, about the pitiful condition of the prisoner when he was brought into camp."

"At sixtin-fittin hours on January fiftint," the sergeant rattled on at once, obviously well-rehearsed. "I 'as called from the regimentl aid post to guard hut t'attend a prisner here, Priv' Turvey, wh'ad jus been brought in. I foun him na highly nervous nweakened condition. Hands tremblin. Pulse slow. Eyes bloodshot. Very, uh-tired." He paused, his green eyes darting over the impassive faces of the judges as if to measure his effect.

"Was he drunk?" asked the president casually.

"Nassir. Very sober. Well, had a hangover, mebbe. Walked kinda splay-legged, but," the sergeant chuckled bronchially, "I'll bet tha was jus a case a lover's n—"

"Kahumph," the paymaster intervened with a breezy cough. "Tell us what you did for the prisoner."

"Objection," said the moustachioed captain suddenly. "All this is irrelevant to the charge."

"What are you seeking to prove by this testimony, lieutenant?" asked the president.

"Ah, sir, many things, many things." The paymaster made a large vague gesture with one arm. "This lad here, he's a good lad, sir, but nervous, very nervous. We shall present expert testimony to prove this. Impulsive, you know. And penitent, penitent too. Like the Ancient Mariner, sir. 'This man hath penance done and—' uh. Coleridge, sir. The, uh, the sergeant here is giving you first-hand evidence of this, this really pitiable nervousness."

The president looked skeptically at his watch. "The witness may proceed. But make it short."

The sergeant began rasping away at once. "He ast me fer a drink, a drink a — water." He pronounced the last word with a long twist of his great mouth as if the word itself proved Turvey's strange and heart-rending condition. "When he took the glass, sir, his hand shook so much he spilled it." The sergeant paused for the full effect of this to penetrate his hearers. "Had to give him a bit a brandy to pull him to."

"Is that all your testimony?" asked the president with some bewilderment, as the sergeant stood silent.

The paymaster and the sergeant beamed common assent. The president shifted his glittering eyepieces to the Prosecuting Officer. "Do you wish to cross-examine?"

"One question, sir. Sergeant Sawyer, you handed a glass of brandy to the accused after his ah — poor trembling hands had spilled the water?"

"Yassir."

"Did he spill the brandy, too?"

"Nassir."

"That's all, sir," said the captain, his moustache tips quivering triumphantly. The sergeant stood down.

"My next witness," said the paymaster, seemingly as confident as ever, "is not available. He is Private Horatio Ballard who was reported absent without leave at the same time as the prisoner and who has not yet returned. I hope to show that it was Private Ballard who planned this unfortunate uh-expedition and prevailed upon this poor lad to accompany him. He was the brains, gentlemen, the Mephistopheles, and young Turvey here was the uh – was the victim. I now ask for an adjournment of these proceedings until such time as Private Ballard is available as a witness."

Even the president's equanimity was upset by this barefaced bid to derail his trial. He stared glassily, sucked air, wriggled in his seat almost as if he were flicking a great tail-fin, and denied the lieutenant the support of Private Ballard.

The paymaster looked, for the first time, really put out. He licked his lips abstractedly. Then he nodded to himself, bent over and whispered to Turvey: "It's all right, old boy, we'll finagle a little break." He put on his most winning gold-toothed smile:

"With the court's permission, sir, the prisoner asks for a five-minute recess. He has to attend to the duties of nature."

Turvey was startled, since he had made no such request, but the interruption was welcome.

The president agreeing, none too graciously, Turvey was duly marched out and around to the latrine on the side of the Hostel. While his guards were standing shivering outside its partly open door, Turvey was surprised to see the paymaster brush between them into his privacy. Without a word the lieutenant closed the door, reached over Turvey's dutifully seated figure to a dark recess between the roof braces, and drew forth a half-empty bottle of Haig & Haig.

"After you, my boy. And make it snappy. We've just time to finish it. 'Freedom and whiskey go together.' Robbie Burns. The Immortal Memory. Hope you don't mind drinking out of the crock." Turvey didn't mind at all.

When the court had reassembled, the paymaster called briefly on the M.O. to corroborate Sergeant Sawyer's impression that Turvey was of a nervous temperament. The M.O. seemed to have little of any consequence to say, however, and that little was immediately objected to by opposing counsel. He was stood down, to give place to another officer.

Captain Norton Montague, Temporary-Acting-Neuro-psychiatric-Consultant, was a tall, elegant young man – surprisingly young, Turvey had thought when the captain interviewed him in the camp brig last night. Following a fashion popular among officers in combatant arms he had extracted the wire framework from his peaked cap and wore the shapeless residue at a rakish yachtsman's angle. His buttons shone more brightly even than the president's and he was adorned with the neatest black pencil-line of a moustache Turvey had ever seen. After the clerk had droned the oath Captain Montague took the Bible in a gloved hand and casually kissed the air in front of it.

Under the breezy promptings of the paymaster, who had recovered marvellously his normal magenta hue and his confidence, the captain testified that he had indeed examined the prisoner on the previous evening.

"Just give us your report, doctor." Lieutenant Sanderson beamed expansively around the room as if there could be no doubt what the good young doctor would say.

Captain Montague drew a neat sheaf of papers from a shining briefcase, and flaired horn-rims from a leather pouch in his pocket. He seemed to be in no hurry and he managed to smile in a way that suggested he thought the proceedings, however necessary, a trifle quaint. But the Great Fish wasn't intimidated:

"We haven't time for you to read all that, you know," he remarked testily. "This case is taking far too long anyway." He glittered briefly in the paymaster's direction.

The young doctor bowed slightly but charmingly to the president. "I will endeavour to be brief, sir. But I must claim the privileges of what this court calls, I believe, an Expert Witness." He began to read in a most professional voice, skimming his papers. "Umm, yes, Turvey, Thomas Leadbeater. Private. Let me see. No admitted history of venereal disease, mental illness, fits. No present symptoms . . . No apparent addiction to drugs or alcohol." He raised his eyes. "For purposes of this court, addiction may be taken to mean a habit marked enough to interfere with, ah, ordinary duties." He flipped another page. "Memory and concentration normal. No certain mental deficiency. No vertigo, tinnitus, parasthesiae, incontinence, nystagmus, diplopia or rombergism. Normal stereognosis and two-part discrimination. Orientation for the time and place probably ah- normal. Examination of glands, joints — "

"For God's sake, captain, was this an autopsy? This man is accused of being absent without leave! What's all this gibberish got to do with it?" The president had, for the first time, quite lost his temper. His little mouth puckered in and out and he bounced up and down on his seat.

The paymaster hastily interposed. "What we most want to know, doctor, is about this lad's nerves, you know. Now don't you think he's pretty high-strung, eh?"

"Objection!" shrieked the Prosecuting Captain, twirling his moustaches, and dropping a paper.

"Sustained!" boomed the president. "This is your last warning, Lieutenant, uh, Samson. If you ask another leading question, the witness will be stood down."

"No signs of organic nervous or mental disease," Captain Montague went on blandly, as if no interruption had taken place. "I rather think, however," and here he paused professorially, "that the subject's personality *tends* towards that of the, ah, constitutional psychopath."

"Constitutional what?" barked the president.

"Constitutional psychopath, sir. Probably of the inadequate type."

"What's that?" the president asked grudgingly.

"Ah, this is a classification sometimes used in psychiatry" — Captain Montague's manner had gradually become that of a somewhat sophisticated professor speaking to an unusually callow freshman class — "to denote a personality which, though apparently not suffering from any of the psychoses which might respond to treatment, nor classifiable legally as insane, ah, nevertheless presents a settled pattern of marked instability. This type — and of course I am venturing only the most tentative of diagnoses, and suggesting in the case of the prisoner merely an approximation to a type — this type is, for example, likely to be reckless with himself and with others, to come into conflict with the law and the, ah, social mores —"

"Come, come, captain. Cut it short! You mean the fellow's immoral?"

"Let us say," the captain permitted himself a worldly smile and an arch of the eyebrows, "the type (to which he *may* belong) is often in trouble over women, ah, is fond of liquor (without necessarily being an addict) and gambling, the usual things. A large percentage of our civilian jail population is made up of such psychopaths. Unfortunately there is still considerable disagreement as to whether the pattern is acquired or congenital. In either case," he finished brightly, "they are generally considered incurable." He was about to sit down when the president made a sound as if he were strangling and then found breath:

"What *has* all this to do with it? What *are* you trying to tell us? That this man is crazy? Or, or what?"

"O dear no, sir. It is my opinion that he is and has been, for all legal purposes, civil or military, in his, ah, right mind."

"But — ," the paymaster jumped up. He had been winking agonizingly without effect at Captain Norton Montague and looking very much like a boy whose pet hamster had suddenly taken to gnawing the leg of a valued visitor, "but you wouldn't say, now would you, that—" he stopped and looked apprehensively at the president. "Well, would you say that he was fully aware of the nature of his act when he — when he went on the loose?"

"Perfectly aware," said Captain Montague calmly. Then, as if to assure the paymaster he hadn't entirely deserted him, he added, "though to what extent he has a normal understanding of whether it is right or wrong to do such a thing, I couldn't really say. *Or* to what extent —" here the young doctor cast a professional eye on Turvey who happened at the moment to be wearing his fatal nervous grin — "to what extent he actually experiences such common feelings as guilt, penitence, pity or even, ah, fear."

"Have you *quite* finished, captain?" the president enquired with savage politeness.

"Unless there are any more questions?" The captain looked about him with elegant disinterest. The Prosecuting Captain stood up and opened the little pink mouth under his great moustaches, but before he could speak Captain Montague added: "I understand, of course, that the report of an Expert Witness is not subject to cross-examination." The prosecutor sat down, his mouth still ajar. Captain Montague bowed once more to the president.

"Quite, sir," he said and sat down.

The president sucked his thin lips in until they disappeared.

"And have *you* quite finished?" He flashed his spectacles at the paymaster. But the latter, though punch drunk, was not yet on the canvas.

"I claim the time-honoured right, sir, to introduce this poor boy, the — the prisoner, into the stand in his own defence."

The president glared, gulped air, and seemed to be counting to ten. But there was no explosion. The paymaster had him.

Turvey was alarmed. The R.A.P. Sergeant had been so confident Turvey would get off easily he hadn't coached him for rising to his own defence. But there was no time to brood. The paymaster, with one of his large easy gestures, was already wafting Turvey to the stand. The clerk bobbed up in the same instant.

"Ye-swear-a-might-gad-tell-tru-nothin-but-a-trut?"

"Sure," said Turvey, "yes, sir," taking care to implant an

especially firm smack between two grease spots on the black Book.

"Say 'I do'," said the clerk unappeased.

"I do."

"Now, Turvey," said the paymaster affably, "suppose you just tell us your story, the one you told Sergeant Sawyer yesterday, you know. How you lost out on your leave, and then didn't like being shot at by McKelvie; and how Ballard, your, uh, evil genius so to speak, how he talked you into going —"

"Objection," yelped the Prosecuting Captain. "The witness is being led!!"

"Objection sustained," said the president effortlessly. "Just tell your story, Private Turvey, without further promptings. And," he looked at his wrist watch again, "you are warned that you must be brief."

Turvey obliged. He gave some account of McKelvie's shooting prowess, his own disappointment at loss of Christmas leave, his conversations with Ballard, and their faring-forth on Christmas Eve. They had been lucky enough to get a lift with an American trucker on his way back from a Buffalo-Toronto run. The trucker, it appeared, had somewhat anticipated the Christmas festivities and had been in the proper mood to smuggle them, under a pile of sacks and empty crates, across the border. Once over, they found that their uniforms and the season together created a passport to free food and a surprising number of drinks all the way to Buffalo. The trucker had by this time grown so enthusiastic about Canada's role in the war that he brought them to his home for the night and for most of Christmas Day. They had then proceeded to an address known to Ballard, the address at which Turvey was later discovered.

"May we presume you had settled down there for the duration?" the president asked, with acidity.

"O, no, sir," said Turvey, round-eyed and earnest. "We were goin to come back next, uh, that night, but the girls wanted, well, that is, it was Christmas and we got hoistin a few and we thought we might just as well hang around another day."

"Tomorrow and tomorrow and tomorrow, creeps in this petty pace from day to day." It was the paymaster, suddenly, beaming with pride at his own literary wit. "He just put it off, sir, a human — "

"Has the defendant anything more to say?" the president cut in grimly.

"Well, sir, only this, sir," said Turvey, stumbling desperately. "I woulda come back right away except I was, I was waitin for Ballard. The day after Christmas he started off to hitchhike to Cleveland. Said he had a nant there he was going to hit up for a loan and I wasn't to go back till he come. He said it'd be better for me if we come back together on our own steam; then he could explain I was, I just went along with him for the ride."

The president sniffed faintly. "How long did you intend to wait for Ballard?"

"O, of course, I was goin to nip back anyhow before my twenty-eight days was up. Ballard told me we hadda do that, or else we'd be charged with desertion and not just bein AW Loose."

"Do you realize," the president retorted implacably, "that the charge against you may still be altered to one of desertion? No evidence has been presented in this court that you were still in uniform when apprehended. *Were* you in uniform, by the way? Remember you are under oath." There was an ominous smile about the president's lips, a thin, icicled smile.

"No, sir," said Turvey, faltering and hanging his head.

"Hah," said the president shortly, "so you admit to being apprehended in civilian clothes."

There was a pause. Turvey ran his finger under the collar of his battleblouse.

"No, sir," he said bashfully.

"Come, come" — the president was irritated — "you must have been in one or the other, you know, unless — " He paused, struck apparently by an interesting new idea.

"I was in the bed, sir," said Turvey blushing now. "I didn't think to take my pajamas when we went over the line."

There was a snicker, which quickly died under the president's revolving stare. "*The* bed?" the president could not quite conceal a note of salacious curiosity. "Was there only *one* in the apartment?"

"Yes, sir." Turvey's voice had faded to a shy whisper.

"Do you mean to say you were sleeping with both these women?"

"Well, not exactly," said Turvey, as one who didn't wish to boast. "You see, sir, one of them was on day-shift at the airplane plant, and the other was on nights." Turvey paused, and added in a burst of honesty, "They did change shifts the second week I was there. Ruby went on nights and took over shoppin and keepin up the uh – liquor supply – I didn't go out, a course, cause I mighta got picked up by a Namerican M.P. or somebody. I always kept my uniform hung over a chair, though, O, gosh, no, I wouldn't put on my civvies" – Turvey seized on the thought with horror.

This time the president allowed the court-room reaction to go unreproved. For a long space he peered at Turvey, as if seeing him for the first time. Then he trained his little glassy headlamps on the empurpled paymaster.

"Lieutenant," he asked with his most precise and military accents, "do you consider yourself a nervous type?"

"Me, sir?" The paymaster was definitely caught off base. "O, dear no, sir. Average, uh – sta-stability, I should say, sir. Hic! At least average."

"Hah! And do you suppose, lieutenant, that if you had spent the previous fortnight taking alternate shifts with two ladies in the same bed, and indulging in apparently alcoholic parties of sufficient, umm, exuberance to prompt complaints to the police from a neighbouring apartment house – do you suppose, lieutenant, that your hand would not have trembled when you were suddenly transported to one of His Majesty's guard rooms and handed a glass of water?"

It was the president's moment; the paymaster had no reply. The Great Trout, having clearly established his greatness, stilled the little commotion his coup had wrought with a finny flick of his hand, and looked left and right to his silent admiring Troutlings. "Does either of my colleagues wish to question the defendant?" But they shook their heads quickly; any question from them would be an anticlimax, if not actually a piece of insubordination, at this moment. Turvey was stood down, and his somewhat deflated counsel began the hopeless task of summing up for the defence. When that was over, the bristled captain had merely to ask tartly for a conviction on the evidence given, and the court-room was cleared, leaving the three large fish to decide on the fate of Turvey the minnow. Fortunately (it seemed colder than ever outside, and there was no shelter) the judges took almost no time to confer. The court was reassembled and Turvey informed that the findings would be promulgated.

"It means you're guilty," whispered the paymaster cheerfully, behind his ear again, "but don't worry, you won't get much."

Turvey wondered how much was much to the paymaster. The length of the sentence had something to do, he knew, with the state of his "crime-sheet", his M.F.M.6. This the Clerk of the Court now proceeded to chant, much like a minister with a reading from the Scriptures. It wasn't too bad, Turvey thought with relief. "Three days' C.B. for being improperly dressed, in that he did appear without anklets in the streets of . . . . Two days' C.B. and one day's Field Punishment for . . . ." His little catalogue of sins having been read without comment, Turvey was informed that they would be weighed in considering his present sentence. His Majesty's Court-Martial was over.

"ULLLef . . . . ry . . . . lef . . . eye . . ."

Next day Turvey had to disrupt some newly formed friendships in the camp brig and betake himself to the much larger and grimmer District Detention Barracks, there to consider, for the next forty-five days, the wickedness of his life.

from Turvey: A Military Picaresque

Hair Does Nothing for People

Ted Schrader

To put it baldly, I have no hair. There's a monk's halo that grows a milligram or two, but the part has less coating than most people's tongues. I regard my condition as a triumph for evolution. Charles Darwin would say I had arrived.

As I understand it, nature provided animals with hair to protect them against the elements, but human animals can protect themselves. Hair is a nuisance. It gets in your eyes when you swim and wind makes it quiver and dance. The advanced members of the species need no hair.

My reason for bragging this way is that most people blush and squirm when they permit their eyes to dwell on my happy state.

The other evening, a lavender-type lady, who takes my night-school course, observed: "Pierre Berton would look much better on television if he wore a hair-piece." Then she broke into gaggling sounds and waxed a delicate pink. Within seconds she felt the social need to assure me that I had a handsome head, baldness suited me, and I was indeed a good-looking guy. (I wouldn't repeat her statements, except I am under oath to speak the truth.)

One day I was dallying with my coffee cup in a restaurant, when a pre-school child sauntered to my table, fixed his gaze on my dome, and squealed: "Look ma! He has no hair." The mother scrambled down the aisle, seized her social delinquent by the wrist, and wrenched him to his chair. I assured the young matron that her child had done nothing more than make an accurate scientific observation and he did not deserve the opprobrium of the entire cafe. She blustered that she would smite her offspring when she got home. What a pity.

Even my barber blushes. I know I need a haircut when my neck itches. Nothing is more unkempt than an uncut neck. I now keep track of this need by going on paydays: the ninth and the twenty-fourth. My barber snips for three or four minutes, massages my neck (my concept of sheer luxury), but refuses to accept payment. "I couldn't," he says, blushing. "I didn't do anything."

One of my journalism students observed: "If you would wear a wig, you'd look twenty-five." Who wants to look twenty-five? Except twenty-one-year-olds.

When I emerged from the swimming pool at the university, other members of the graduate club search for combs. (One man said: "If you don't mind communicating bacteria, you can have mine," which sounded erudite, I thought.) Not me. I don't even smooth my hair with my hands.

The only place I regretted being bald was in Southern California. I had been basking in the sun for seven weeks, and my head acquired the lustre of teak. The night before my departure, the apex of my head began to itch. In satisfying the itch, six square inches of suntan peeled off and I returned to Canada a blushing pink.

Hair does nothing for people and is a nuisance. I pity men who are on the lower scale of evolution.

from Dateline: Gloucester Pool

from Why Rock the Boat

William Weintraub

When you thought of the City Room you thought of men working at night, of one downtown building astir while all others were asleep. At noon it was an unfamiliar place, bright with sun, empty, dead. There was rarely anyone there except the Day City Editor, a white-haired old man who wore carpet slippers. He sat alone, ready to answer the phone. But it seldom rang, and the typewriters were silent, so he often pulled down his green eyeshade and dozed off.

Today the sun was brighter than ever and it took Harry Barnes a moment to focus his eyes. Then he noticed the desks. Every one was occupied. Some of the reporters were reading; some were staring into space; none were working.

Something cataclysmic was happening, but what? Had they all been summoned to watch him being drummed out of the regiment? Was Butcher going to rip off his epaulets publicly?

Thoroughly puzzled, he went straight to Butcher's office, without taking his overcoat off. Wearing the coat while being fired would give the impression that he was terribly busy and had just dropped in for a minute to get this tiresome formality over with.

"Did Mr. Butcher want to see me?" he said to the secretary.

"Yes, I'll tell you when it's your turn," said Miss Shields.

"My turn?"

"Yes, Mr. Butcher wants everyone to remain at their desk until it's their turn." Miss Shields, a tall, angular girl, strode out into the silent City Room, her heels saying "Flick-clack, flick-clack," as she went across to the Suburbs Editor's desk. Suburbs stood up, adjusted his tie, and followed her back to Butcher's office.

Harry tiptoed over to Al Sullivan's desk.

"What's going on, Mr. Sullivan?" he whispered.

"It's the Holy Inquisition," said Sullivan. "He's got the bonfire ready, but first he has to find out who did it."

"Did what?"

"You mean you haven't read the Final?"

"No."

Sullivan pushed that morning's Final Edition of the *Witness* across the desk. "There," he said, pointing to a one-paragraph story at the bottom of the front page:

DRUNK SENTENCED

"This man was corned, loaded and pissed to the very gills," Judge Elphège Boisvert said in Criminal Court yesterday as he sentenced Philip L. Butcher, local newspaper executive, to two years' hard labour. Butcher, charged with drunk and disorderly conduct, was arrested Tuesday in the lobby of the Imperial George Hotel, where he had climbed up the big Christmas tree and, with obscene cries, was throwing ornaments down on passing citizens.

As he read, Harry became aware of all the organs in his chest and stomach; they were melting together in a crescendo of nausea. The story was exactly as he had written it seven days earlier. Not a comma had been changed. At the time he had thought it one of the most successful of all his courtroom practice stories. He had managed to get Who, What, When and Where — plus a little colour — into only seventy-one words. The journalism textbook considered that quite good.

"Quite a little yarn, isn't it?" said Sullivan.

"Remarkable," Harry said, and he went to his own desk, his knees wobbling. Slowly, he read the story again. There was no doubt that this was his. For inexplicable reasons, some maniac had got hold of it and had smuggled it past the City Desk, past the printers, past the proofreaders and into the paper. As a feat, this was just about as simple as introducing five hundred crazed gorillas into a tea party at Buckingham Palace without anybody noticing.

Butcher's door opened and the Suburbs Editor came out. He went back to his desk. Miss Shields's heels went "Flick-clack, flick-clack" again. It was the Labour and Anti-Communist Editor's turn. As he followed Miss Shields one of his shoes squeaked loudly, proclaiming its newness and inexpensiveness. Every eye in the City Room followed the bargain brogues as they squealed and faltered into Butcher's office.

Thankful for the diversion, Harry eased open the desk drawer where he kept his practice stories. There were some old publicity handouts, three dusty back issues of the paper, a pair of scissors, a button, several forms to be filled out when applying for bus tickets and a small book entitled *Planned Parenthood for Beginners*. But there were no practice stories. There must have been about thirty of them, but every last one was gone.

He shuddered as he recalled them. Because of the fanciful incidents they described, the casual reader might find them frivolous, but actually they were serious exercises in journalistic style and form.

He had attempted everything — not only news stories but also the ponderous humour of the editorial page, the poetry of the sports columns, the grim realism of the society section. In some stories he had sought after brevity and conciseness, in others he had aimed at obfuscation through prolixity. And some of it had undoubtedly been good. He felt, for instance, that his account of the trial of Philip L. Butcher on an unspeakable morals charge had been a real accomplishment in the field of euphemism. And any City Hall reporter would admire the total incomprehensibility he had achieved in describing a deal in which the City of Montreal had expropriated some property belonging to Alderman Philip L. Butcher, paying him $870,000 for one small brick outhouse.

Oh you clod, he thought. You lavishly dumb clod . . . *Coming out strongly in favour of the Communist candidate, Philip L. Butcher yesterday said that . . . Denouncing motherhood, Philip L. Butcher yesterday told the Royal Canadian Society for White Slavery . . . In ordering a mental examination for Philip L. . . .* Oh clod of clods, clod supreme! Why did you have to be so damn funny? Why, why? . . .

Miss Shields's shoes clacked and the Labour and Anti-Communist Editor's squealed. It was now the Financial Editor's turn. He followed her meekly into the torture chamber.

Only one thing was certain, Harry realized. Butcher did not yet know who had written the story. So there was hope. The lunatic who had smuggled the thing into the paper had protected Harry, but now held Harry's fate in his hands. Who was it? Who, who, who?

He peered around the City Room, looking for a clue in the impassive faces. It couldn't have been Al Sullivan — he was too mature. The Suburbs Editor had a certain streak of frivolity, but he wasn't clever enough. The Military Editor had much better ways of occupying his time. In fact Military's phone had just rung and his voice, although low, could be heard as he answered it.

"Yes, Major," he was saying, "this is going to be a public relations demonstration. . . . Yes, for Miss Germaine Proulx of *Montréal-Soir*, a very important writer. . . . No, we don't want a full crew in the tank. Just the driver, down below. Miss Proulx and I are going to pretend *we're* the crew. That's angle on the story. She wants to be able to write, 'I'm the first girl ever to navigate a tank.' And I wonder if we could borrow some cushions from the Mess. . . . No, not over the assault course. Just some gently rolling countryside. . . . All right, we'll be on deck at three o'clock. . . . Right. Roger and out." He hung up.

The Financial Editor emerged from Butcher's office and Miss Shields followed. Well, this was it. She was heading straight for Harry's desk.

"It's your turn," she said, with obvious relish.

Harry walked with great care. His legs were in a peculiar condition; if he kicked his feet out too jauntily the knee hinges might work the wrong way and he would fall forward.

Butcher was busy examining some papers and he didn't look up as Harry entered. Harry stood in front of the big desk, balancing precariously on his patellar joints.

He had been in this office only once before, the day he had been hired. He remembered admiring its bareness and simplicity. Just a desk, a table with some newspapers on it, a padlocked filing cabinet, a bookcase, a chair for visitors.

The few pictures on the walls were gifts from the railroads and dealt with simple, standard Canadian themes. Most prominent was one entitled *Western Wheat Champion 1926*, a gloomy sepia photograph seven feet long and three feet high, framed in massive walnut. It showed a wheatfield stretching to the horizon. Standing in the foreground was the Champion, an angry-looking farmer; the wheat was so high that only his head protruded and his eyes, glaring at the camera, seemed to be saying, "What have *you* done for your country today?"

Harry averted his eyes from the Champion's and forced himself to look at Butcher. The man was pale and looked as though he was fighting a tremendous battle for self-control.

"Sit down, Barnes," Butcher finally said. "Make yourself comfortable."

Harry sat down.

"What's new, Barnes? How are you getting along?"

"Oh fine, sir, thank you."

"How are we treating you? Any complaints?"

"No, sir, no complaints."

"Just speak your mind, Barnes, if there's anything wrong. If you feel we're not running the paper properly, or anything like that."

"No, sir, nothing wrong."

"Then why did you do it, Barnes?" Butcher said very quietly.

"Do what, sir?"

"Why did you put this into the paper? You did put it in, didn't you?"

"No, sir, I didn't," Harry said truthfully.

Butcher took off his glasses and started polishing them. Harry couldn't bear to look at the little raisin eyes, now naked in the narrow face. He shifted his gaze to the bookcase, and the horsewhip that hung over it. It was a large horsewhip, varnished and mounted on a plaque like a swordfish. Long ago a dissenting reader had brought it to the office to use on a now-forgotten editor. In the scuffle, the editor had disarmed the reader; he had had the whip mounted, as a memento, and now it was a curious relic of the days when newspapers had been stimulating.

"So you didn't put this in the paper, eh Barnes?"

"No, sir."

The Wheat Champion glowered skeptically out of the photo on the wall.

Butcher got to his feet, paced the room twice, and then took a large black book from a drawer. "Do you believe in the Holy Bible, Barnes?" he said.

"Yes, sir." His heart jolted up against his rib-cage. Could he get out of this by throwing a fit or something? From the wall, the Wheat Champion was leaning forward to watch; now they were going to separate the men from the boys.

Butcher put the Bible in front of Harry. "I like to think of this Book as a great piece of journalism, Barnes," he said. "I hope you realize that the Great Reporter is covering this meeting."

"Y — yes, sir."

"Just glance at this, Barnes," Butcher said, handing him a sheet of paper. "If you agree with it, please put your hand on the Book and read it aloud."

Harry glanced at the paper, put his hand on the Bible and

read: "I hereby swear that I did not put the story in question into the paper. I also swear that I do not know who did."

The Wheat Champion frowned. Harry felt sure he was going to step out of the picture and ask who wrote the story, not who put it into the paper.

Butcher sat back in his swivel chair and stared at Harry for a long time. Harry, staring back, was starting to feel ashamed of himself. Butcher really wasn't such a bad egg, was he? He was simply a highly professional journalist, doing a job. It wasn't his fault if a managing editor's work, like certain abattoir jobs, called for unpleasant duties. But he was a man to be respected, a true managing editor, a man who understood dollars and cents, a virtuoso of the adding machine. . . . Why had Harry used his name in all those cloddish practice stories? What a crazy, childish, unprofessional thing to do. . . .

"One thing I'd like to make quite plain to you, Barnes," Butcher said. "There is not the slightest possibility that the person who did this will escape detection. It may take a long time, but it is inevitable. Is that clear?"

"Yes, sir."

"Then you may leave."

"Thank you, sir."

Harry got up and went to the door. As he passed the picture he noticed that the Wheat Champion was tearing his hair and stamping on his valuable crop.

The Fire

Gregory Clark

Ned's News Stande & Smoke Shoppe is just a hole in the wall amid the topless towers of the downtown. But it is a pleasant hole to go into, out of the hurly-burly, cozy with its stacks of newspapers and magazines, fruitful like a library with its walls tiered to the ceiling with the merchandise of tobacco in all its shapes.

Ned is a philosopher, though quite a small one.

"Dismal weather, isn't it, Ned?" say I.

"It could be worse," says Ned.

A philosopher is one who has the same point of view as you, but is not upset by it.

I bought my weekend paper and my Sunday's supply of cigarettes, and then leaned my elbow on the only available space on the counter to exchange a few generalities with Ned.

The cigarette I was smoking was down to the butt. I turned to flip it out the doorway on to the pavement outside, and awaited a gap in the passing parade of legs.

I flipped.

"Good heavens!" I exclaimed.

"What is it?" asked Ned.

"I flipped my cigarette butt," I cried, "right into the cuff of that fellow's trousers!"

"What fellow?" inquired Ned.

"The one who stepped past the door," I gasped, "just as I let her fly."

"Don't worry," said Ned. "It couldn't go in."

"But it DID go in!" I protested. "I saw it."

"Pant cuffs," soothed Ned, "don't gape."

"But this one did," I said with urgency. "I saw it. The butt just went flip, right in it!"

"Then," said Ned, "what are you standing there for?"

"Of course!" I shouted. "What am I thinking of? Here, watch these. Don't let anybody . . ."

And I shoved my paper and packs of cigarettes to one side and bounded out the door.

As I manoeuvred up the street amidst the two-way throngs of pedestrians, it seemed to me the man with the cigarette butt in his trouser cuff had been wearing a dirty old trench coat. I couldn't be sure. But that was my hasty impression. I angled over to the curb side of the pavement to make time, and by craning as high as I could, I saw a man in a dirty trench coat standing at the intersection fifty yards ahead, waiting for the lights to turn.

I made haste.

But the lights turned and my man was lost in the bevy of pedestrians crossing.

I scuttled across the intersection.

Half way across, a strong hand seized me by the shoulder.

"Greg!" said the strong man.

"Joe!" I cried. "Joe Morgan! Look, Joe . . ."

"I haven't seen you in a dog's age," said Joe, holding to my lapel and fastening me there in the middle of the intersection with everybody passing hurriedly both ways.

"Joe, look, I flipped a cigarette butt into a guy's pant cuff . . ." I sputtered.

"Hold on, hold on," soothed Joe, trying to turn me and lead me back to the corner I had just left. "I haven't laid eyes on you for . . ."

"Joe, look, I . . ." I whimpered, wrenching myself free just as the lights changed.

I dashed for the far side.

Which way had the man in the dirty trench coat gone? Straight on up? Or to the right or to the left? The home-going crowds were boiling this way and that at the intersection. It was impossible to see ahead in any direction.

This called for psychic powers. I decided on straight ahead. And again taking the outer curb, so that I could drop down on to the edge of the road to make time, I soon detected, quite far ahead, a figure in a dirty trench coat.

I was happy to note, as far as I could see, that no smoke was coming from his pant leg.

"Hey! Mr. Clark!" came a voice from a store doorway.

It was the optician, an old friend.

"I'll be back in a . . ." I called over my shoulder.

"Hold on," hallooed the optician. "That story the week before . . ."

But I held desperately to my course, though by taking my eyes off my quarry for only that instant, I had lost him. I dropped out on to the roadway and trotted.

He had vanished.

I stepped back up to the pavement and relaxed my pace to match that of the crowd.

"What a stupid thing!" I muttered.

A lady with whom I was in step gave me a sharp look and dropped back a pace.

It was at that instant I saw my man in the dirty trench coat standing in a shoe-store doorway, bent over and beating the cuff of his trousers with a folded-up newspaper.

I dashed to his rescue.

"It was a cigarette butt," I explained, when he glanced up at me.

"A what?" he asked.

Smoke was certainly coming from the smouldering cuff.

"I'm guilty," I informed him firmly. "I flipped a cigarette butt out a doorway down the other block, and I saw it go right into your pant cuff."

Between us, we squeezed and smothered and squashed the smudge out. There was a hole in the back of the pant leg about the size of an orange.

"I've been chasing you," I puffed.

He stood up, smiled broadly at me and held out his hand.

"I've been trying," he said, "for two winters now to get rid of this damn' suit. But my wife says it's still good."

"But . . . but . . ." I expostulated. "It's my . . . I'm . . ."

"Do you know," demanded the man in the dirty trench coat, "how much she spends on one permanent?"

I shook my head.

"Fifteen bucks!" shouted my man.

"I'm responsible," I insisted. "I'll pay for the new pants."

"Not on your life," said he. "I've been trying to get rid of this."

So we shook hands again and parted. On the way back down to Ned's, the optician had gone. Joe Morgan wasn't to be seen on any of the four corners of the intersection.

"Well," asked Ned, "did you catch him?"

"Yes," I said. "But you'd never believe what happened."

"Not from you I wouldn't," agreed Ned, handing me my paper and my cigarettes.

from   A Bar'l of Apples

Why Culloden Was Lost

Hector Charlesworth

A man designed by providence to add to the gaiety of nations was Charles Langdon Clarke, the cable editor. . . .

Clarke was for a time lured away to the staff of the publishing unit of which *Saturday Night* is the senior publication, and which embraces half a score or more of periodicals. Thus we were once more in daily association, and one summer Clarke wrote, and I helped to promulgate, a famous hoax relating to the Clan Maclean, which enlivened some of us for many weeks. We had on the staff at that time an elderly man named Maclean. He was not very diligent and seemed to be living in the eighteenth century so far as his intellectual interests were concerned. He was a typical Maclean with the stocky frame and antenna-like eyebrows of that clan from the Western Isles. His chief subject of conversation was the prowess of the Clan Maclean and its superiority to all other Scottish strains. Several of us, including Clarke and myself, claimed descent from other clans and the epic of the Macleans began to pall on us. One day Clarke wrote out an imaginary account of the Battle of Culloden, which was the last rally of the Highland clans supporting Bonnie Prince Charlie. The Highland warriors, inadequately armed and divided among themselves, were utterly overthrown by the Duke of Cumberland, whose subsequent conduct was brutal in the extreme, and his victory made the Campbells, who had sided with the Hanoverian cause for a long period, dominant in Scotland and hated by their fellow Scots. The battle occurred in April, 1756, but in certain districts of Canada it is still discussed from the standpoint of family tradition, as though it had been an engagement of the Great War.

In his account of the battle Clarke quoted a passage from an imaginary work, Stranways' *History of the Scottish Clans*, which recited how the Macleans, because of their boasting, had been placed in the centre of the battle line. But he went on to state that when faced with the steady advance of the forces under Cumberland, the Macleans had been seized with panic, flung down their claymores and fled "screaming like women." Victorious in the centre, it was an easy task for Cumberland to demolish either flank. So the sad story ran and wound up with the sentence: "Thus by the cowardice of a single clan was the cause of Scotland lost forever."

To make this hoax effective we drew up the story in this wise:

GREAT CAUSES LOST BY COWARDICE
(continued from page 3)

Several lines alluding to an episode in Spain followed, and these words, "Better known perhaps is the tragic outcome of the battle of Culloden, of which the following account is given in Stranways' *History of the Scottish Clans*." The story outlined above was then given in detail.

It is a simple matter to so fabricate what is apparently a newspaper clipping that it can only be refuted by a demand for the production of the entire newspaper, from which it is supposed to be taken. In this case I took the manuscript to an old friend who was foreman of a daily newspaper and had it set up in their usual style. Proofs were then pulled on the back of which was other news matter, so that no one could tell it from an actual clipping of a "continued" article such as frequently appears in the inner pages of newspapers. One day, when the stage was properly set with several members of the staff about, we showed the clipping to the scion of the Clan Maclean remarking that here was a historian who seemed to disagree with him about the prowess of his ancestors. When Maclean read it, his ruddy face actually became white and we thought he was going to be ill: —

"It was a Cawmbell wrot that, damn them!" he exclaimed.

"No, no. You see the name," said I, recovering the clipping before he could destroy it, "it is by the famous historian Stranways."

"Well his mither was a Cawmbell. I ken the hand of the lying breed," he retorted.

Finally (having several other copies) I presented him with the clipping on his promise not to destroy it, and we heard no more about the Macleans from him so long as he remained on the staff.

The hoax had worked so well in the office that we decided that it demanded a wider publicity. John Ross Robertson was still alive and in control of *The Evening Telegram*. He had no love for W. F. Maclean, a lineal descendant of the great chieftain, Maclean of Lochbury, or Maclean of the Bloody Hand, as he was known to legend. The veteran newspaper-owner was descended from the Robertson and Sinclair clans which in earlier times had been at odds with the Macleans. We therefore wrote a little note to *The Telegram* enclosing the clipping and asking if any of the newspaper's readers could verify Stranways' statements. The inquisitive correspondent stated that he had heard a somewhat similar story from his grandfather and signed himself "Archibald Ian Campbell." For weeks *The Telegram* contained letters from Scotsmen dealing with the pros and cons of the question. Whenever it showed signs of flagging my father-in-law, Peter Ryan, or myself would stir up the flames of controversy again. The end came after some weeks when a letter appeared from a book-collector in Cincinnati stating that he possessed the largest collection in America of works relating to the Highland rising of 1745 and the campaign of Bonnie Prince Charlie. He said he had never heard of Stranways and if such a volume as his *History of the Scottish Clans* existed he would gladly pay a very large price for a copy. We decided that it was time newspaper discussion should cease.

Personally I had a great deal of fun showing the bogus clipping to Scotsmen and noting their reactions. Few had the temerity to deny acquaintance with the works of the great Stranways. One old and rather religious newspaperman had a special grudge against W. F. Maclean, M.P., because the latter had once, in a platform controversy over Sunday street cars, called him a "crofter" and a "thick-tongued rooster." "True every word of it" he said when I showed him the clipping. "The Macleans have always ratted. It's all they are good for."

"But is this man Stranways a reliable historian?" I asked.

"The most reliable of them all," he said, "and the most impartial. I know his works well. He had access to papers that were unknown to other historians, and you may rely on it that what he says is the exact truth. He was above all things just, but his kindly feeling toward Prince Charlie is apparent, and he did not hesitate to expose those who betrayed him."

This I think was the most sincere tribute ever paid to an imaginary historian.

from More Candid Chronicles

If Seymour Can Dump the Rags, Benny Will Order the Pants

Tom Alderman

It is still not clear who outfinagled who in the Benny versus Seymour versus the Romanians affair. All that is known is that Benny Mintz and Seymour Frank, those well-known international tycoons from Montreal, are just back from Romania — and each claims victory for himself. Meanwhile, back in Bucharest, the Romanians also claim victory — even though they couldn't unload a single can of tomato juice on either Benny or Seymour.

Someone, obviously, is fibbing. You simply cannot put Seymour, Canada's foremost international rag pedlar, next to Benny, our leading purveyor of cheap clothing, and sit them across the bargaining table from a brace of Romanians without a little blood flowing. It is a fact of international tycoonery that someone has got to get hurt.

"Not me!" Seymour insists. "I got rid of all my rags and got paid in money. Benny's money."

"Not *my* money!" Benny counters. "I'd never give Seymour *my* money. But I have all these Romanian pants and shirts I didn't have before. Seymour got clobbered."

And the Romanians say: "We got the money, and we got the rags, and we got the order for the pants and shirts. We also, unfortunately, still got all this tomato juice."

Of course it's confusing. International finance always confuses us mere mortals. But because trade with Iron Curtain countries is becoming more important to our economy, it is essential that we at least try to make some sense out of this whole messy business.

To recapitulate: Seymour is a tall, dapper, prosperous-looking forty-seven-year-old who rose to his present eminent position as buyer and seller of rags and clippings through thrift, hard work and marrying the boss's daughter.

As a partner in Liberty Wool Stock Co. Ltd. of Montreal, he combs the world for textile leftovers and old, discarded clothes — which he then sorts into grades, depending on colour, quality, fibre and origin. Origin especially. The best rags are North American. In Canada, rags from Toronto and Montreal are better than rags from the Prairies, which are better than rags from the Maritimes, and West coast rags are best of all.

With his larder replete, Seymour sets off to peddle his goodies to lower-living-standard countries such as Poland, Hungary, Bulgaria, Romania and Czechoslovakia. His line is ordinarily snapped up, because these Communist bloc countries — with a cheap labour supply — can grind up and re-weave Seymour's rags into cheap clothes, which they then sell back to North America for solid capitalist dollars.

Before a country buys Seymour's lines, however, they make sure they'll have a market for the reincarnated goods. Enter Benny. If you've ever bought a garment labelled Made in China, or Japan, or Bulgaria, or some such exotic locale, Benny has doubtless had his finger in it. Chances are Benny *designed* it.

"I am the poor man's Pierre Cardin," says Benny, a balding, pipe-sucking ex-laundryman, also in his late forties, who rose to his position of influence with Montreal's Transcontinental Sales Inc. through thrift, hard work and — "Unlike Seymour," he sniffs, "I did *not* marry my boss's daughter.

"I married his sister."

The cheap clothes business being what it is, haute couture by Monsieur Benny is not an overly-aesthetic production. Benny fancies a $14.95 ladies' blouse in a specialty store, for example, and takes one on his next trip to Red China. "Make it for me for 67 cents," he tells the commissars, "and you got a deal for 3,000 dozen." Or perhaps a $6.98 pair of boy's corduroy pants catches Benny's discerning eye. Off he whisks to Romania to see if they'll make it for $1.23 — with zippers. Benny *insists* on zippers. It was Benny, in fact, who introduced the zipper to Romania.

"What's wrong with buttons?" said the Romanians. "We make pants with buttons for the Russians, and they don't complain."

But Benny will not compromise, aesthete that he is, and instantly sensitive to design trends, he always holds out for zippers. And it is through such negotiations that he lugs home for the discriminating Canadian market such born-again textiles as Chinese diapers (a dozen for $2.95), 10-cent Hungarian hankies, finely-tailored men's Polish suits for $29, 69-cent Bulgarian towels and original Hawaiian shirts made in Hong Kong, 49 cents apiece.

And much of the stuff is coaxed into such shapes from Seymour's rag collection which, in turn, is descended from textile clippings and those scruffy clothes we threw away a few years ago.

With such prices and materials, you'd think quality control might be a problem. Benny rejects such nonsense out-of-hand. "O.K., so sometimes there's a shirt button an inch or so out," he admits reluctantly. "Or, very rarely, the left suit jacket lapel is a few inches narrower than the right lapel. That's no reason to get excited."

Naturally, Benny *has* had his disasters. No one wanted his $29 Polish suits, for example, till they were knocked down to $8 and snapped up by an undertaker. And then there was that batch of 49-cent men's boxer shorts from Taiwan that arrived with no slits in front, but a nice wide horizontal slit behind.

But the resourceful Benny is often able to snatch a victory from the jaws of defeat. When a load of Japanese brassieres proved unsatisfactory for Canadian needs, Benny was able to unload them — they were snipped in half by a converter and sold as religious skull caps.

All of which is not to say Benny's customers don't get their money's worth. They've made him the largest soft goods importer in the Commonwealth, gobbling up his wares in retail stores across Canada (stores which prefer, perhaps understandably, to remain unidentified).

"My goods raise Canada's living standards," Benny argues with subtle reasoning. "People got so much money left over after buying them that they can then buy stuff they couldn't ordinarily afford."

"I also improve our living standards," says Seymour patriotically. "I turn old rags into new money which is pumped into our economy. We all benefit."

You're thinking that two such public-spirited citizens, being more or less in the same line, would be close confederates in their drive to improve our economy. Wrong. Benny didn't even know Seymour till eight years ago when Benny's wife drove their Chrysler into Seymour's used Cadillac. "So used," Benny swears, "it wasn't worth more'n $50. But that rat Seymour holds us up for $400 damages."

The two gentlemen of commerce became friendly and not friendly, a way of saying that they knew they needed each other but didn't want to admit it. Besides, the better break Benny gets on his finished garments, the worse break Seymour gets on the raw materials. They need each other, but they are deathly enemies.

To take one example, the Romanians need Seymour's rags in order to make the goods to sell to Benny so he can improve our economy.

That means Benny *also* needs Seymour's rags — though he can, in a pinch, go to other rag-pickers who can't touch Seymour's line. But Seymour also needs Benny at hand if he hopes to get real money for his rags.

For if Benny is not around, neither is there cash on the table, and the Romanians — with no firm order for re-processing Seymour's rags — just might try paying Seymour off in something like tomato juice. Such are the dangers of the commodity market. Seymour, being a man of the world, prefers money — the better to upgrade our living standards.

So it was that Benny and Seymour found themselves in Romania, friendly but not friendly, Seymour with his rags and clippings, Benny with his letter of credit, each anxious to take a bite out of the other, with the Romanians in the middle looking for a pants order, and prepared to pay off in tomato juice because they also covet Benny's letter of credit. And Benny is still stewing about those $400 damages. Of course, he won't admit this to

Seymour — it might put Seymour on his guard. But Seymour knows, anyway, and Benny knows Seymour knows, and both are wondering what the other's up to, and the Romanians know nothing except their warehouses are overflowing with tomato juice. It's not easy being an international businessman.

Seymour is sweating already because there's a razor blade salesman just left town, after peddling $100,000 worth of blades, who got paid off in sugar. Not that Benny is safe either. He once got stuck with 2,500 cases of mandarin oranges. "Couldn't unload a one," he recalls. "Had to give the stuff away. For six months, anyone walked into our warehouse got loaded up with oranges. Of course, we took it off the income tax."

For some unaccountable reason, it's occasionally a good idea for tax reasons to get paid off in some exotic commodity. (Benny is still gloating over how he got ruined on Japanese tuna, though not by design, and thereby saved a bundle.)

"Good morning, Benny. I trust you slept well. What are you up to today?"

"Well, I thought, after a leisurely breakfast, I'd take in the sights around town. And you, Seymour?"

"Well, perhaps a tour of the art galleries."

A half hour later, both are hard at it with the Romanian textile commissars.

"Make me this pant for $1.16," says Benny, "and you've got an order for 10,000 dozen."

"With zippers?" The Romanians still can't get used to zippers.

"With zippers."

The Romanians huddle, then take the offer to Seymour, who sits looking at his thumb in the next room, intensely interested.

"We're sorry about this, Mr. Seymour, but we'll have to go a little lower in our quote for your rags."

"Never. I won't budge."

The Romanians return to Benny.

"How about $1.23, Mr. Benny?"

"Give me my sample back. I'm taking it to Czechoslovakia."

This is a red flag to a commissar. There is great jealousy among Communist textile commissars. Any one who loses too many orders to another Red country is soon a commissar no longer.

Back to Seymour. "O.K., Mr. Seymour, we'll pay your

price, but we'll pay off in nice, wholesome Romanian tomato juice."

"One moment," says Seymour. He phones Benny in the next room. "It occurred to me while I was here at the art gallery, Benny," says Seymour, "that I don't think they can do it for $1.16."

"Sorry, Seymour," says Benny, delightful visions of car accidents dancing before his eyes. "It's $1.16 for me and tomato juice for you."

"If it's tomato juice for me, it's no rags for the Romanians. And no pants for you."

"O.K. $1.17. Not a leu more."

"If it's $1.17," says one of the Romanians, "we want a work-shirt order, too."

"O.K., O.K., break me," Benny cries. "Make me 7,000 dozen work shirts."

Seymour is swiftly calculating how much of his rag supply this uses up. "Ah, Benny, harrumph, could you make that *10,400* dozen pants?"

"O.K., but I want the shirts for two cents lower."

The Romanians are swiftly calculating how many more pants and shirts this is over last year. Because it's not the profit they're interested in (profit is for capitalists), it's the quantity.

"If they make less profit but more pants and shirts," says Benny, "they're the hit of the next Party Congress."

It's a 1,000-piece increase. "Sold!" say the Romanians.

Benny passes over his letter of credit to them. After extracting their percentage, they take it to Seymour in the next room. Seymour gives them a receipt for his rags. Already the stuff is being ground up, soon to once more cover the backs and gird the loins of Canadians everywhere. Benny and Seymour leave by separate entrances.

The money, so to speak, remains in Canada. The rags, so to speak, are soon to return. Benny didn't give his money to Seymour, so to speak. So he considers the car accident debt cancelled. And he also gets a marvelous deal on the shirts.

Seymour didn't get paid off in tomato juice — that's for the next British businessmen who arrive — and the Romanians are selling ever more clothes to the capitalists. Soon, after duty, taxes, freight, Benny's modest profit and the retailer's usual markup, we'll all have pants at $3.98 (compare to $6.98) and work shirts at $2.69 (compare to $4.95), thereby strengthening our buying power and subsequently our economy in the world market.

So everybody wins. And Benny and Seymour are off to Bulgaria, there to play tycoons once more — this time with terrycloth towels.

from The Canadian Magazine

God Help the Young Fishman

Ethel Wilson

The old fishman stepped out for a bit of lunch.

The elderly lady said to the young fishman, "I'd like a nice bit of cod."

The young fishman went to the window, took up a fillet of cod and balanced it tentatively on waxed paper on his hand. "How's this?" he said.

"I don't like it filleted. I like it in the piece."

"Then how's this. A nice small fish. Tail end. A matter of two pound or maybe a pound and three quarters."

Another customer came in, and stood waiting.

"Did you say a pound and *three* quarters?"

"I'll weigh it . . . there it is . . . all but two pounds."

"I'd like it with the skin off, and I'd like you to fillet it."

The young man looked at the latter half of the fish and said, "Well lady, that's filleted fish I showed you first in the window. You said you'd rather have the piece . . ."

Another customer came in.

"What I mean is, it's not so tasty when the fillet runs *that* way. Anyone'll tell you it's not so tasty."

"It's off of the same fish, lady."

"Well, it's not so tasty."

"Did you say you wanted it skinned?"

"Skinned? No, I don't want it skinned."

"You *do* know, lady" (knife hung in air), "it'll cost you more filleting this piece?"

"How much more?"

"Okay okay I'll fillet it . . . seventy-nine cents. Is there anything else?"

"No, nothing else."

Another customer came in.

"Oh just a minute just a minute," said the elderly lady, "'have you got a crab?"

"Say lady . . . I . . . there's a customer here . . ."

"All right then. You attend to that other party and I'll . . ."

The customer said, "I'd like a nice piece of salmon in the piece for boiling. Centre cut, about two and a half pounds, well not less than two and a half pounds and certainly not more than three . . . haven't you any white salmon, we like it much better than the red. . . ."

"No lady, only the red."

"Haven't you any of the pink?"

"No lady, only the red."

"I don't know whether I can wait," said the elderly lady, "but I *would* like to have a crab . . ."

"Let me see that middle piece," said the customer. "Oh . . . that's near the head end. That wouldn't do. My husband . . . Well, *that* piece. All right. Not more than three pounds."

"How's this?" asked the young fishman, laying his knife along the silver skin.

"I can't see. You're standing in the way."

"Did you say it was okay?"

"No. I say you're standing in the *way*. I can't see."

"Oh . . . well, *now* can you see?"

Another customer came in.

"Yes, now I can see. Oh that's not enough . . . just a leetle . . . no, that's too much. Oh I forgot to ask you how much is it?"

"Eighty-five."

"Well, move the knife a bit to the right then . . . there . . . that should do."

The fishman cut the fine thick silver red-fleshed fish. He weighed it. "Three and a quarter."

"Three and a *quarter*! I said not more than three! Couldn't you cut a steak off? Yes, just about . . ."

"Okay . . . that will be two fifty-five."

"Oh stop stop, I *am* sorry to ask you to undo it but couldn't you slip in a bit of that nice parsley for sauce . . . thank you *so* much. *Good-bye* . . . oh I forgot . . . *do* excuse me" (smiling winningly at the next customer), "my cousin asked me to get her two salmon steaks one for tonight and one for tomorrow night but I think she must have made a mistake. Better give me one salmon steak and one large fillet of sole. Or two small . . . oh, here she comes! She'd better choose! Hello Lucile how are you. There's some nice sole. And before you wrap that up again, just a teeny bit of shrimp meat, enough for sandwiches . . . no, that's too much. Oh thank you! Forty-five cents? Good-bye."

"Two salmon steaks or let me see," murmured the cousin.

"How much did you say the crabs were?" asked the elderly lady.

"Forty cents and fifty cents."

"They used to be twenty-five cents."

"They're forty cents and fifty cents."

"Which are the forty-cent ones?"

Another customer came in.

"That's forty cents."

"And is the other one fifty cents?"

"Yes ma'am."

"It doesn't look any bigger to me."

"Well it's bigger all right."

"It looks the same to me."

"Well it's bigger all right. Which one would you like, lady?"

"I'd like to feel the claws. I always like to feel the claws. No, turn it over."

"Say lady. . . ."

"I'll take the forty-cent one but I don't feel satisfied."

The fishman wrapped up the crab and said nothing but "Forty cents."

"Do *you* think, I mean as a fish person do *you* think it *really* makes a difference if there's an R in the month," asked the next customer. "Oysters I mean."

"We wouldn't keep them lady if they wasn't fresh."

"But what is your *own* opinion?"

The young fishman looked sideways and said nothing.

"Well then, I'll take a pint . . . I suppose you couldn't give me three quarters of a pint?"

"Pints and half pints is the way they come."

"Oh I do think it was nicer when they used to come in bulk!" The fishman did not express an opinion.

"Seventy-five cents," he said and looked about him at the customers. "Next?" he said.

"Two herrings," said a bad-tempered looking woman with a dark moustache.

"Did you say two herrings?" said the young fishman with light in his eyes.

"You heard me," snapped the customer.

What a lovely lady, thought the young fishman, what a lovely lady. He looked tenderly, earnestly at the bad-tempered-looking woman in whom all the sins of woman were forgiven on account of two herrings.

Still the young man gazed. Something was held suspended. The fish shop seemed to dream.

What's wrong with him, the bad-tempered-woman thought uneasily. God, what's he looking at; and instinctively she covered her moustache with her hand.

The young fishman gave her the small parcel and unwillingly withdrew his eyes from her. "Next," he said, and resumed.

Another customer came in.

Sometime he will take the fish knife to the whole lot of them.

from Mrs. Golightly and other stories

A Night in the Opera House

Max Braithwaite

. . . Harry King became pretty enthusiastic about that Athletic Club. It fit nicely into his philosophy of a healthy mind in a healthy body. Besides, he saw in it a way to advertise the school and indirectly himself. So he suggested that on the evening of Parents' Night, instead of the usual recitations and songs by students, we'd go all out and stage an athletic demonstration in the town hall.

"What kind of a demonstration?" I asked.

"Well, you know — club swinging, tumbling, pyramid building, maybe even boxing. I think it would go over big."

"It would take a lot of practice. The farm kids can't stay after school. Have to get home and do the chores."

"Take school time. Recess . . . noon hours. We might even manage some time off from classes."

"But . . ."

"Go ahead and arrange it. You've got a whole month to work on it. I'm leaving the whole thing up to you. I'm sure you'll do a good job."

Of all the phrases in the world, the most insidious is that one about being sure somebody will do a good job. What he really meant, of course, was that I'd damned well better do a good job or else.

So we began getting ready for the big Athletic Night. Art classes were put to work making posters of kids floating through the air like men on the flying trapeze. Music classes whomped up some songs for the occasion. Mothers were put to work designing special costumes. It became the talk of the town.

Everybody was tremendously enthusiastic about the project except for about twenty people — the twenty boys who made up my athletic club — and me. They didn't like it at all. I didn't like it at all.

But we practised as best we could. The program would consist of some club swinging, some tumbling, some boxing, and as a grand finale the pyramid building. Some of the kids were already pretty good at turning cartwheels, and Pete Walensky who was wiry and tough was learning to do handsprings. He'd got so he could do them by placing only one hand on the mat and was working at doing them without the use of hands at all — a sort of front flip.

The pyramids were simple enough. Tom Barker, the lightest kid in the club, was heaved up onto the shoulders of Johnny Gar. And then two other kids put one foot on each of Johnny's knees and stretched the other leg away out while holding his hands, and two more did handstands beside them. The boys looked very good doing this in their navy blue shorts with the white stripe and their white shirts.

The clincher was the big pyramid that included every member of the club. It was simple, really, but spectacular. The six biggest boys got down on their hands and knees in a row. The next five kneeled on top of them. Then four, three, two and one to make a pyramid of kneeling boys. It was all done very smartly, the boys dashing out and standing at attention to little blasts of my whistle, and then climbing up and taking their places. At the end they all smiled at the audience and stretched out stiff and the pyramid collapsed. It worked just great so long as no kid kept his knees bent and jabbed them into the kidneys of the boy below.

I was nervous about that last pyramid. There were inherent in its structure too many possibilities for trouble.

So we practised in the halls at noon hour and recess and as the day drew near we took time off from school. The boys got pretty good at snapping around at my whistled signals.

The dress rehearsal was in the Opera House.

The Wannego Opera House was really the upstairs of the municipal offices and the jail. This made it handy for the Mounties as they never had far to take an obstreperous drunk arrested at a dance. Since Wannego had once been a prosperous town, the town hall was a little better than most. Instead of a big pot-bellied stove near the door, there was a furnace in the basement and a furnace room. The stairs from the basement came up beside the stage and the open part of the basement was used by the cast as a dressing room.

"Tell them kids to keep the hell outa the furnace room," Looie Shanks warned when he heard of the arrangements. "Don't want none of them fooling around in there." To make sure of this he screwed a hasp on the door and put a huge padlock in it.

When Looie let us into the Opera House on Thursday afternoon, the place had that faint sour smell of a room that is accustomed to housing hundreds of sweaty bodies. There was another smell, too, that I couldn't quite place but Looie opened the windows and it went away.

Then I discovered something about my performers that I'd overlooked. As soon as they got on the stage they were petrified with fright.

Back in the school in familiar surroundings they had been fine. Going through their routines with good spirits and laughter. Kidding each other and playing little tricks the way athletes do. But as soon they got into their gym suits and up on that stage they froze with terror. All the suppleness and grace were gone. They became wooden and awkward, tripped over each other, and when the big pyramid collapsed the hall reverberated with the howls of pain from bruised kidneys. Nobody did anything right.

So we stayed there long into the night. Parents phoned that the chores weren't being done. Little sisters or brothers who needed a ride home in the buggy hung around the hall and wept quietly. Irate fathers came in and demanded to know what the hell was going on here anyway.

Finally I got them back into some semblance of a gymnastic troupe and sent them home with instructions to forget all about the show until the next night.

Friday night came and the hall began to fill up. The farm community and the town community were there in full force. There was to be a lunch and a big dance following the speeches and the athletic display. A big night.

We had made our arrangements with the greatest care, but there was one fatal flaw. I can see it now so clearly, but at the time everybody overlooked it. There was no supervision of the boys down in their dressing room.

Harry King, as chairman of the evening, was required to sit close to the stage to make a speech and introduce Jim Walters as chairman.

As the director of the athletic display I had to take up my place in the front row with my whistle ready to give my signals. Larry Petrie, the other male teacher, had conveniently left town for the weekend. So there was nobody down there in the dressing room with the boys, and that would seem to be safe enough if it hadn't been for Looie.

Everything went fine for a while. When I gave my first

little tweet on the whistle, six junior boys carrying Indian clubs marched smartly onto the stage. Another tweet and they stopped. Another and they turned smartly to the right. Miss Grant began to play the piano and the boys began to swing to the rhythm. Another tweet and they turned sharply left. Another and they marched off. Applause.

Four more boys dashed onto the stage and laid out the mats for tumbling and again everything went fine. Front rolls, over one kneeling figure, then over two, then over three. Then – can he make it? – over four. More applause.

Now it was time for the senior students to strut their stuff. I tweeted the whistle and nothing happened. Another tweet, still nothing. Another louder and longer tweet and Johnny Gar dashed out onto the stage, took up his position and grinned happily at the audience.

There was something wrong with his appearance that at first I couldn't quite make out – something a little off. Then I realized it was his navy blue gym shorts. They were too tight at the front and not tight enough at the back. He had them on backwards. There was something else about him, too, that I couldn't quite place. A sort of reckless abandonment – an unsureness about his movements.

I figured it out pretty quickly when Pete Walensky ran onto the stage. Well, actually it was more of a stagger than a run. He was followed by Bill McElvey who also seemed a bit uncertain. The two of them took up their places beside Johnny, who as prescribed bent his knees slightly to receive their feet. But they didn't quite make it. The feet slipped off the knees and the three of them collapsed on the mat, giggling and snorting.

I tweeted with vigour but to no avail. By this time the others had come onto the stage and they were equally uncertain of themselves. Valiantly the five of them tried to build that pyramid and hopelessly they floundered on the mats. Then I realized what was wrong. The whole lot of them were stoned, stewed to the gills, polluted, miraculously and happily drunk.

There was a stunned silence from the audience at first, and then a titter, then a guffaw and then a roar. This only increased the eagerness of my gymnasts to entertain. They cavorted like fools about the stage, laughing and yipping and improvising new and better pyramids. Finally somebody thought of pulling the curtain and the show was over.

It didn't take long to find out what had happened. For the better part of a year Looie Shanks had been making home-brew in the nice warm furnace room of the Opera House. He had a fine still in there and a good batch of brew was just maturing on the day of our show. The kids had smelled it, pried off his hasp and helped themselves. First little sips and then, after they'd become used to the fiery potion, whole tin cupfuls.

Actually, I think that on the whole the booze improved the show, at least from the audience's point of view. Harry King and the school board didn't think so much of it.

Of course there was a great deal of fuss about the whole thing. Jim Walters was for calling in the Mounties and having Looie thrown in jail. But somehow this didn't happen. Looie removed his still in a hurry and nothing more was said about it.

And the Athletic Club? Well, it sort of petered out after that. The kids quit coming to the meetings and their parents didn't force the issue. Somehow, although I can't see why, I tended to be blamed for the whole mess. Harry was most understanding, told me not to worry too much about it. These things happen. There was some talk of organizing a mouth-organ band for the older boys, but I rather discouraged that.

from The Night We Stole the Mountie's Car

The Rats Are Kept Out of the Rat-Race So They're Out to Take Over the World

Maggie Grant

Don Marquis really struck paydirt when a cockroach named archy started using his office typewriter, for archy was not only a poet and philosopher but the biographer of mehitabel, a notably amoral cat. Even though he had a terrible time with his typing (he had to dive with terrific force on to a key to make it strike and he couldn't work the shift key to make capital letters) he managed to set down thousands of words and, when these writings were printed, Marquis was on his way to literary immortality. Every writer dreams of finding his archy, so you can imagine how I tingled when I found this note in my typewriter one morning.

```
at last you have left paper in your
machine all week i have been wanting to ask
how to get the cellophane off the crackers
in your drawer heliotrope
```

Before leaving the office that night I unzipped the crackers, rolled a fresh sheet into the typewriter and tapped out "Are you a cockroach, I hope?" Heliotrope's reply and the rest of our correspondence follows.

```
a cockroach what a wild idea i am a rat
and proud of it we rats call this building
our ancestral home lately i have fallen on
evil times my boy friend arthur was a good
provider but he left me and ran off to sea
```

```
he used to collect trinkets and things
and sell them on street corners but one
evening some oaf mistook him for a pack rat
and he became morose no wonder pack rats
are terrible bores and whats more they have
bushy tails how come you are the only one
in this office that ever keeps food around
```

All the others are men and they eat out.

```
ask a stupid question you get a stupid
answer speaking of eats i am getting tired
of crackers
```

I have brought you a piece of banana cake. Please tell me all about yourself so I can become immortal.

```
the cake was delicious you may print this
you tell everyone we rats are planning an
uprising we are sick of being a downtrodden
minority
```

Downtrodden minority? Please explain.

```
there are more of you than us admit it we
have nothing you have everything admit it
thieves in the night you call us when all
we steal is food we have to eat and how
can we buy when no one will employ us and
give us a living wage do you know anyone
who ever gave a job to a rat
```

Well no, come to think of it, I don't. More cake on the sill.

```
thanks another thing we are always being
held up to opprobrium its time you humans
paused to consider the slurs you cast on
our fair name like saying i smell a rat
meaning theres trickery afoot theres not a
tricky bone in a rats body and we dont
smell come the revolution we will change
```

that to i smell a cat cats are sneaks and
deserve it we also plan to alter sayings
that glorify undeserving animals so that
they glorify us here is a partial list a
rat a rat my kingdom for a rat a rat never
forgets love me love my rat the rat is mans
best friend patient as a rat a pick me up
will be known as a hair of the rat a
courageous person will be called rat
hearted milk will come from contented rats
thats only one part of the overall scheme
if you dont want to be chewed alive youd
better stop saying something messy looks
like a rats nest how rude can you get why
you could drop into my nest any day and
find it neat as a pin finally why does
everyone refer to rats leaving a sinking
ship as if this were cowardly or something
for heavens sake why wouldnt we leave a
sinking ship you would too and i know it
because my boy friend arthur was once in a
shipwreck and he said it was all his life
was worth to keep from being trampled by
people trying to get off oh to hell with
you and your banana cake

The correspondence ceased abruptly at this point, so not
only am I not going to achieve immortality but now I'm a bundle
of nerves about this building being a revolutionary powder keg
that might blow sky high any day.

from The Canadian Magazine

Zoology

Lex Schrag

Oo's ickle 'ookum-wookums is 'oo?
—Invocation of Ubasti, the Cat-Goddess of
Ancient Egypt, by the High Priestess.

The Zoological Situation at Mortgage Manor ever trembles on the verge of degenerating from bad to dreadful. The ramshackle hovel on Skid Blvd. (in the eastern wilds of Scarborough) is fraught with cats and dogs until the harassed churl insists that each and every of his movements must be made knee-deep in animals. Yet only two of the horde are official incumbents of the place.

When they essayed to tame the suburban wilderness, back in 1950, the churl and churless were proprietors of only two domestic mammals: Bobo, the more or less Springer spaniel, and Lucky, a quasi-Persian type cat. Both took kindly to the desolation of the manor. Bobo at once dug a hole, into which the churl fell as he was trying to round up the pets for the night. Lucky, a more demure beast, developed into a veritable Diana of the forest (of weeds).

The dog had been acquired from the kennels of the Humane Society in Toronto. Early in their wedded bliss, the churless intimated to her spouse that their home was incomplete without the patter of little feet. As it appeared unlikely, at their advanced ages, that the churl and churless would remedy this lack by the propagation of a junior specimen of the genus *homo*,* the churl suggested that they become the sponsors of a watchdog.

Expense, he grandiloquently declared, was no object — as long as it didn't run to more than five dollars. For once, the churless declined to debate that point. Her soft, capacious heart longed to comfort some cuddlesome puplet that had been deprived of its master.

She and the churl found the kennels of the Humane Society

*Brat.

to contain only one pure-bred specimen of the canine race. This was a large and adult Chow. Each time a visitor poked his head over the edge of the dog's compartment, it unsheathed a set of sabre-like teeth and roared imprecations with a Mongolian accent. The churl decided at once that there would hardly be room in the East Trawnta shack for a dog of the Chow's talents. He hastily looked in the kennel at the other end of the row.

There sat Bobo, a picture of mild and dignified grief. He had been a family dog. He hoped, his expression indicated, that he would again be a family dog before the gas chamber got him. But he did not demean himself by clamouring at the bars of the kennel. When the churl slipped his hand through the bars, Bobo sniffed politely, then timidly licked the proffered fingers, wagged his tail and sighed gustily. Even the churl's crabbed heart was touched. With scarcely a whimper, he put up bail for the dog, and whisked him out of durance to the comparative safety of the East Trawnta menage.

Lucky, a smoke-shaped kitten, was the gift of compunctious friends who lacked the courage to drown the offspring of their wild Persian lady cat. The kitten must have had as father one of the most amicable Toms in Greater Trawnta for she developed a disposition entirely different from that of her carnivorous mother.

When she was introduced to Bobo, she spat for the record, while Bobo gave her a copious and rather doubtful sniff. Thereupon, the kitten sidled up to the dog and rubbed herself ingratiatingly against his front axle. Thenceforth, they were the best of friends. Bobo, although he was a mature brute of three summers when he came to East Trawnta, tried to join the kitten in her sportive ventures. Even after they had been transferred to the manor, he would lumber anxiously about the house in pursuit of the cat, upsetting minor articles of furniture and skidding ridiculously on the mats.

Although Lucky proved to be the huntress of the clan, Bobo was the first to make major contact with one of the original residents of the wilderness. In early April, the churless noticed something peculiar about the atmosphere of the manor.

"You," she told the churl, "will really have to take a bath. You've let yourself go altogether too long, this time!"

"That," the churl informed her with immense and injured dignity, "is a skunk."

His deduction was not entirely correct. It was Bobo, who

had made the monumental mistake of being impolite to a skunk. Amidst roars of profanity from the churl, he was ushered out of doors, and told to stay out until he bleached.

"But it will be cold out there tonight," objected the churless.

"My dear," stated the churl, "you are entirely welcome to sleep outside with him and keep him warm if you wish. *But he is not coming in! ! !*"

Muttering to herself, the churless poured a forty-ounce can of tomato juice into a pan, and went out to deal with her pet.

Whether as a result of her ministrations, or because he had been merely grazed by the blast, Bobo became tolerable again within the next four days. His spirit, however, was temporarily broken. Not only had the skunk rejected his advances in a most dastardly way, but the churless had added insult to injury by anointing him with Essence of Lotus. Being a masculine dog, Bobo found it difficult to endure the raucous jibes and pointed remarks of fellow mongrels when he sheepishly appeared amongst them smelling like an untidy boudoir.

As spring waxed into summer, Lucky's preoccupation with the chase grew amazingly. Ordinarily, cats are indifferent to the hunt when they are well fed at home. Not so the diminutive feline guardian of the manor. In one week she brought back, as trophies of her prowess, two starnosed moles, an infant rabbit, five or six mice, several sparrows and, to the churl's intense delight, a robin.

From year to year, the robin population at the manor increased in numbers, noise and nuisance value. When the churl at last succeeded in establishing a strawberry bed, the robins ate more than half the crop. The cherries timidly produced fruit in the third year. The robins harvested the cherries. "(Censored)", screamed the churl. "(Deleted! ! ! !)"

In retaliation, the churl purchased an air rifle. He fired volleys, enfilades and barrages. In two years of belligerent effort, he failed to score a hit on one of the voracious birds. The robins, in fact, enjoyed his buffoonery. They brought visitors to the manor for a hearty laugh.

The churl made the mistake of admitting, in one of his published reports on agriculture, that he was belting away at the robins with pneumatic arms. This won him the lasting enmity of a confrere in the newspaper business who, as between ornithology and humanity, was strictly for the birds.

"You should not shoot at the sweet little things," this lady informed him severely. "If you want to stop them from eating your strawberries, you should put up strings over the berries, and hang strips of rag from the strings. And you must not put it in the paper that you are shooting at them with an air rifle. You are setting a dreadful example for the children."

The churl sourly opined that if any juveniles in Greater Trawnta wanted to volunteer in the robin war, he would be glad to arm them. With an ill grace, however, he strung wires over the strawberry bed, and hung strips of cloth from the wires. The robins were entranced. The wires provided excellent points of vantage from which to select the ripest berries, and the strips of cloth could be used by the more hygienic birds for wiping their bills after dining.

In her brief lifetime, Lucky devoted many of her hours to keeping the robins at bay. Even her skill, however, was insufficient to wreak any important toll upon the brazen birds. In the end, it may have been that the robins were victorious. Late in her second summer at the manor, the cat began to fail. A delicate eater at best, she refused her rations completely and slowly wasted away. The churless hazarded the guess that a bone from one of her victims may have penetrated her digestive tract. One sunny afternoon, Lucky walked down the garden with slow, sad dignity and bade farewell to the manor.

The churless broke silently into tears when she learned that her gallant pet had gone to a better world. The churl, of course, scoffed at such a show of tender emotion.

"Making all that fuss about a cat," he sneered. He then retired to the bedroom and blew his nose, noisily, several times in quick succession.

from Mortgage Manor

88 Keys to Trouble

Mervyn J. Huston

If you are going to a party and you know how to play the piano keep it a secret like a hole in your sock. Playing the piano at parties is the surest way to psychic scarification and social disaster.

Suppose you don't follow my advice and arrive at a party prepared for pleasure, sociability and refreshment. What happens? You get time for one quick pass at the cocktail tray and are then banished to the keyboard where you are isolated, backwards, the rest of the evening. Theoretically, when you sit down at the piano everything shushes and you are the centre of rapt attention. Actually, things go on much as before but at a higher decibel rating. I have had hostesses beg me to play and then when I sat down to do so walk over and turn the radio up. The wise hostess knows that the best criterion of the success of a party is the amount of noise it generates and that the converse of all theorems is true.

Once you sit down at the piano you've really had it. The bar will be a distant mirage and your throat will parch and wither unless some kind emissary fetches for you. If he does he will bring scotch if you're a rye drinker, or vice versa. This doesn't matter too much because he will put it on top of the piano where it will shortly fall in your lap. Everyone will glower in your direction and you will have established a reputation for disorderliness.

People will stand around behind you all evening, dribble rye down your collar and drip caviar in your hair. These are the members of the evening's Glee Club and although you won't meet many of them you will certainly hear them. Since your undefended ears will be directly in the line of fire, your head will feel like the cockroach that fell into the bassoon during *Finlandia*. Do not expect too high a quality of musical attainment from your colleagues or you may be disappointed. Also do not expect to be the leader but recognize early that you are the tail on the dog.

If you start to play a number, the singers will probably elect something different. There's no use fighting this and you might as well switch with what aplomb you can muster. If you and the singers come to a prior agreement they will start off first leaving you to latch on later. This is all right except that they have an uncanny knack of selecting a key with five or six sharps. Even if you come to a general agreement as to what is to be undertaken there is very apt to be an individualist present who will elect to sing something different. He may gain recruits as he goes along and the primary group may be hard put to it to maintain its choice. In view of the number of notes which many songs have in common it is surprising how poorly most of them fit together.

There are always a few who sing harmony. It is difficult at first to distinguish these from those who are singing a different number. With practice you can, since the pitch usually rises and falls parallel to the melody and the words may roughly approximate. These rules are not infallible. It doesn't matter much anyhow.

Someone is sure to want you to play something you never heard of and won't believe you when you say so. He will then hum it to you: "It goes like this . . . umpty, umpty, doodle oodle," and poke out parts, incorrectly, on the piano. Sometimes two people will do this at the same time concerning the same or different pieces . . . it is often hard to tell which. Your stupidity in not picking it up right away is openly commented on and you are compared unfavourably with George, who is absent, who can *really* play the piano.

You may be fortunate enough to have a fellow artist present . . . one who plays by ear . . . never took a lesson in his life. He will sit on the bench with you and play the melody, with variations, an octave higher, and a bar behind. He may even play a different number for the enjoyment of a select clientele at that end of the piano. Letting the fingernails of the right hand grow and filing them to a point may be helpful here.

If you make the mistake of playing a classical piece you will find yourself despised by all normal red-blooded humans present, but enthusiastically adopted by some scrawny harridan with a drooping hem-line and declivities behind her clavicles like goldfish bowls. The rest of the evening, through din, smoke and boogie-woogie you will be involved in an intense discussion of polytony, cacophony and other diseases of modern music. There's no use sending up smoke signals to your wife. She will be over by the punch bowl discussing divorces and ignoring you. Or so you think until you get home and find you are in the freezer for devoting yourself all evening to That Female. "I don't know what you see in her. However, if you want to make a fool of yourself it's none of my business. Couldn't care less."

It's a well-known fact that music plays upon the emotions and this may be put to good use . . . or bad, depending upon how you look at things. Like a friend of mine who had designs on a beautiful girl and got tipped off by the petticoat grape-vine that slow, low-down New Orleans blues put rockers on her heel. Their paths crossed at a party and he set out to soften her up with some fractured Basin Street. He kept an eye on her and sure enough, after eight bars she was looking at him with smouldering eyes and her nostrils were twitching slightly. He was on the right track. He poured it on. His left hand beat out the slow sensuous rhythm of the primordial jungle and spoke of love and basic things. Chord progressions wove in and out of the melody which disappeared to return under new and ever more exciting guises; judicious discords resolved into throbbing sweetness. After two choruses of this she disappeared out onto the dark sun porch and got engaged to a used car dealer who didn't know a quarter note from a niblick. They asked my friend to play at the wedding.

Musical humour takes a variety of forms. Women are particularly great humorists when it comes to singing. They find it excrutiatingly funny to sing very high and very loud with a wide vibrato and many glissandos. The performance is usually directed at one male but shared in willy-nilly by all. You are apt to get requests for bits of grand opera — particularly the sorrowful arias which lend themselves so well to the humorist. These establish the performer as a patron of Cultural Things but a Good Sport.

Male humour tends to head straight for the barn. Men seem to feel that the magic of music removes the scum from depraved words and they will sing at the top of their voices things they wouldn't whisper, in conversation in the same gathering. This situation may slip up on you before you notice it unless you are alert. Things may begin with a rather mild parody of *Alice Blue Gown* but before you know it you're into *North Atlantic Squadron* or *Cats on the Roof Top*. So beware if things get racy for the risqué goes rancid quickly and you, the piano player, will get blamed for the whole thing.

So now you know what to expect if you play the piano at parties. You would be much wiser to take up the oboe. Nobody ever asks you to play an oboe at a party . . . not twice anyhow.

from   The Great Canadian Lover

*f*rom Willows Revisited

Paul Hiebert

. . . This chapter which was entitled "Willows Revisited," after John Swivel's poem by that name, was most appropriately prefaced by a hitherto unpublished poem entitled "Spring" written by Sarah Binks herself. Concerning this poem at least, there has never been any dispute as to its authorship, since it was actually signed by Sarah. It was discovered by sheer chance in a desk in the office of *The Horsebreeder's Gazette* by one of two tax auditors who happened to be examining the desk at the time, and it was at once recognized as having literary value. Apparently it had been submitted by Sarah two years before her death and had been accepted for publication, since it bears the stamp, "Paid, June 15th, 1925." Such manuscripts, according to the editor of the *Gazette*, were kept for filler and were used as occasion arose. But this particular poem had been completely forgotten, since it had been pushed to the back of the drawer because of his secretary's habit of keeping both her lunch as well as his in front. The editor, however, was quite willing to trade Sarah's "Spring" for a copy of Joyce Kilmer's "Trees" of which he had never heard and which on examination he declared to be "just about the same length."

In "Spring" Sarah's natural exuberance takes over without any stress upon the more solemn political spirit which characterizes "Moonlight on Wascana Lake" and it is therefore more appropriate as an introduction devoted to poetry and culture of Saskatchewan. In "Spring" Sarah simply bubbles with joy. She catches that fleeting moment in which the seasons in Saskatchewan change from the dead of winter to the heat of summer. For spring in Saskatchewan is never a season; it is an event. It is a day like Christmas Day or Fair Day except that it never comes by the calendar; it comes as a complete surprise. No one in Saskatchewan ever *expects* spring; he hopes for it. Spring there is a matter of faith, not science, but faith there is always justified, however late. Saskatchewan would be only too glad to celebrate the arrival of spring on a certain day much as the ancient Druids celebrated the arrival of the vernal equinox, if they only knew when it would arrive. But Sarah catches it on the fly:

SPRING

By Sarah Binks

> It's spring again! Who doubts the day's arrival,
> Peeks not the thistle from the garden bed?
> And shrieks the robin not the glad survival
> Of cut-worm lifting up its vernal head?
>
> In swelling chords, full-throated to the weather,
> And strong of lung, once more spring voices sway —
> Alto and bass, the cow and calf together,
> Spring, spring is here, peal out its passing day!
>
> I know of nothing that can so elicit,
> Such great relief as spring, I know no boon,
> That's half as welcome as the annual visit,
> Of spring between the equinox and June,
>
> Let voices then lift up in high endeavour,
> To greet this day— the robin and the kine,
> And add the wind at sixty for full measure,
> And one shrill note which happens to be mine.

Sarah is always the true artist. There is something positively Wagnerian in her adding her own voice, the "one shrill note," to all that noise with which spring announces itself. This is because spring is in her heart, and she is also true to her own province in that she introduces the cow as a kind of spring symbol emphasized by the appearance of the spring calf. It may well be that the cow as a *leitmotif* in so much of the contemporary poetry in Saskatchewan, owes its origin to Sarah's repeated reference to the spring calf. It is certainly a heritage which should not be overlooked.

It is interesting to observe here in connection with the cow that in the second edition of *Fifty Years of Progress*, the poem which replaced the deleted "Moonlight on Wascana Lake" was one dealing with cows and was written by the Laureate, Jones-Jones. He had been commissioned by the Department of Agriculture to write two poems, one dealing with wheat and the other dealing with cows, and he was paid fifty dollars each for them. This probably represents the high-water mark for literature in Saskatchewan, but the Government felt that this was an anniversary and was willing to pay a little extra for quality. "Cow," the second poem, was duly published in *Fifty Years of Progress*, but "Wheat" became lost in the confusion of so much publishing, and the one verse which has so far appeared came out a full year later in the Bulletin (No. 4506) entitled *Bird Houses and Bee Culture*, the bee culture being that part of this fascinating subject which had not already appeared in the Premier's message. (It also contained a final recipe for apple cake which had been sent in very late by one of the ethnic groups.) The poem "Wheat" was apparently meant to deal with some of the farmers' problems in raising grain for the market, in this case the problem being that of the game birds and ducks eating the grain before the hunting season opened in the fall. No doubt, in keeping with the Department of Agriculture's tradition, other problems were dealt with in the poem, but these are not available and "Wheat," what there is of it, merely raises the problem without settling it.

WHEAT

(Probably one of the later verses)

Tweet-tweet, tweet-tweet,
The birds eat wheat,
And wild ducks gorge the oat,
And man must shout

To keep them out,
In words unfit to quote;
Unless, of course, he feels his toil
Must fatten them for fall,
So that the man who raises oil,
Can come and shoot them all.

It is a pity that the rest of "Wheat" was lost. It is actually of a higher order than "Cow."

COW
(*By Osiris Jones-Jones, S.O.M.*)

Throughout the ages, lo! the cow,
Kindhearted, useful, good,
Is oft forgot, we praise her now,
We praise her loud — and should.

The milk, the cheese, the steaks we eat,
Are they not from the cow?
And multitudes upon the street,
Are they not shod — and how?

And though the sire, of puffing snoot,
Lascivious, goggle-eyed,
Is mean and shiftless, dissolute,
And given to false pride,

Let none decry the cow — but state
That such is nature's way;
Each living thing selects its mate,
In beauty or in hay;

And if, perchance the cow seems odd
To crave such no-account,
She still has virtues left to laud,
The bounties from her fount;

For even man may take to bed
A one of virtue's doubt —
But cow at least, when given head,
Knows what it's all about.

"Willows Revisited" in the Government's anniversary book
followed the sections dealing with Oil, Industry, and Education,
and it dealt with the cultural achievements of Saskatchewan, particularly literature. In addition to the space given to Sarah Binks
and to the fame brought to her native province, the Government
paid tribute to various contemporary ethnic groups for the
contributions they were making towards the enrichment of western
culture in the matter of folk-dances, folk-costumes, and folk apple
cake, and also commended them for their efforts to transplant the
habits and customs of their homelands to the new country of their
adoption. Particular reference was made to Purge Potatok, the
New Canadian of Ukrainian origin upon whom the Saskatchewan
Order of Merit was conferred for his poetry, and mention was
also made of the translations from the German by Mathilda
Schwantzhacker, although no particular honour was here
bestowed.

The group of poets, which until then had been simply and
somewhat loosely known as the Regina School was now, with the
addition of Potatok, given official recognition as the School of
Seven and was to be regarded henceforth as Saskatchewan's
answer to Ontario in the matter of culture, the hope even being
first expressed here that some of these days Saskatchewan would
be able to go Ontario one better. Moreover as a special honour to
mark the anniversary year, upon each member of the School was
now conferred the Saskatchewan Order of Merit, an honour
which carried with it the privilege of writing s.o.m. after the name.*
Finally all seven of the poems which had been declaimed over
Sarah's grave the year before, on the twenty-fifth anniversary of
her death, were published in the chapter, "Willows Revisited,"
even including as a concession to modernity the poem recited by
Professor Bedfellow and which John Swivel, who acted as master
of ceremonies on that occasion, had predicted the Department of
Agriculture would never publish. But it was pointed out by the
Minister of that department that "there is a place for everything
in this country and on the whole the poems are as good as anything
in Canada," which they undoubtedly are. The Minister mentions
also the place and occasion which gave rise to the seven poems
and states that "when it comes to shrines we here in Saskatchewan

*The original intention of the government to institute a Saskatchewan Order
of the Bath, was disallowed by the Dominion Government at Ottawa as
being an attempt to restore hereditary titles into Canada.

don't have to take a back seat to anybody." The reference, of course, is to the famous meeting place, Willowview Cemetery, where the School of Seven first met as a body.

The School of Seven*

One and a half miles north of the little town of Willows lies the acre and a half of light and sandy soil known as Willowview Cemetery. It is not visible from the town of Willows itself, being concealed by a slight rise of land. Nevertheless it is appropriately named Willowview, since from the top of the wrought-iron gate which the schoolboys in search of gophers are fond of climbing, it is possible to see the upper halves of the two elevators of Willows. There were once four elevators at Willows, and at the time when Willowview Cemetery was named, it was possible to see the tops of all four from the gates. In the earlier days of the western prairies the number of elevators in a town was always a measure of its importance and a matter of local pride, and it is probable that Willowview was so named because it was felt that the departed citizens should not be altogether deprived of a sight which during their living days had always gladdened their hearts. Since only the tops of the elevators were visible from the cemetery itself, the suggestion that there was a further reality "beyond the hill" gave the whole a kind of spiritual quality. This has been somewhat reduced by the loss of two of the elevators and even more by the erection within sight of the cemetery of a filling station, also called Willowview, and of "Joe's Eats" at the correction line a half mile away. Adjoining the cemetery itself on the north lies the farm of Purge Potatok, a hundred and sixty or more acres of sand and alkali which no one has ever bothered to plough, crossed by many prairie trails and short cuts centering in a small barn and the shanty where Potatok lives.

Since the historic meeting of the School of Seven in Willowview, the cemetery has been, to quote the mayor of Willows, "spruced up." It has been enclosed within a stout fence of barbed wire, the grass has been repeatedly cut, and the letters above the gate which had been dislodged by the schoolboys in

---

*It is the *School* of Seven and not the "Group" as in Ontario according to *Fifty Years of Progress.* "We don't have to follow every damn thing they do in that province," said the Premier of Saskatchewan in his message in that booklet.

their climbs have been replaced and soldered back into their original position. (At least it is claimed by the local tinsmith who did the soldering that they are in the original position and who has, according to his claim, "the holes to prove it" despite the fact that two letters I and E in the sign have been transposed and that it now reads WILLOWVEIW.) In addition to such improvements as fence and gate, the concrete obelisk which marks the last resting place of Sarah Binks has been straightened since it had developed a decided tilt away from the prevailing west wind, and was, in fact, in some danger of falling over. A small sign has also been placed on the gate by the Town Council of Willows stating that the lighting of fires within the cemetery is strictly forbidden and that violators will be prosecuted.

Apart from the activity around Joe's Eats on Friday and Saturday nights, the scene around Willowview (or Willowveiw if preferred) is one of great peace. And it is singularly appropriate that here in the quiet obscurity of a wayside cemetery, the great poetess of the prairies should sleep. She has been much forgotten. Fame, alas, is always a fickle jade and apart from such special occasions as Saskatchewan's semi-centennial celebration, she is remembered only by the poets themselves. But she is remembered particularly by those who gathered in Willowview to celebrate the twenty-fifth anniversary of her death and to pay her homage in poetry of their own.

Perhaps it is just as well that Sarah died when she did. If she had continued to live, the School of Seven might never have got under way, and we would have missed the fascinating diversity and variety of outlook expressed by the poets of the contemporary scene. Nevertheless Sarah has left her indelible mark upon the literature of Western Canada. One can never say, of course, that her mantle has descended upon any particular one of her successors, yet there is not one, with the possible exception of Wraitha Dovecote, but owes her a great debt. The poetic well from which Sarah scooped her famous "Up From The Magma" still quenches the thirst of her followers. The poetic springs, once started, continue to flow even in the dry belt. The dream of oil, which in the case of Sarah's father's farm was to remain always a dream in spite of repeated drillings, may have become a physical reality in many of the farms of her home province, but those borings can never tap the streams of poetic fancy which Sarah tapped. Indeed, the contrary is true. Sarah's drillings reached only failure and frustration, but these taught her the great lesson of literature which she was to express in one form or another throughout her mature poetic life. "Literature is mostly doleful choral, and grief the poet's steady stock in trade," she was to cry when contemplating the "marble slab" (or as it turned out, the concrete obelisk) which was to mark her fame. And since not all of Saskatchewan is by any means underlaid with oil, those poets of today who have not access to what there is of it, must needs still dip their pens in the alkaline waters of the prairie which seeped into Sarah's well of inspiration. Certainly those poets of Saskatchewan who have, as they say, "struck oil" in one way or another, have found their fount of inspiration emulsified to the point where it no longer flows, and they have disappeared from the literary scene. It would almost appear as if the frustration and defeat and non-recognition with which until recently the poets of Saskatchewan have been faced, have also presented their own challenge and opportunity. Without them we would never have had that peculiar, intangible quality of *innerness,* a spiritual no less than physical hunger which pervades so much of the School of Seven and which reaches its highest expression in the *Vestal Verses* of Bessie Udderton.

The little group of Saskatchewan poets who gathered in Willowview Cemetery that hot and windy Dominion Day in 1954 to pay homage to Sarah Binks were not unaware of the literary significance of their meeting, more especially since the Government through the Department of Agriculture had signified its willingness to publish their poems. Perhaps no one was more aware of this than the Great Dean of Saskatchewan letters, John Swivel, who addressed them that evening in the Clarendon Hotel following the duck dinner.

"This," he said, "has been a definite historic occasion. We owe it to Sarah Binks. Insofar as Sarah is remembered, we will be remembered. And let us keep in mind that whatever this day has meant to us — and we certainly owe the Committee a big vote of thanks for all the trouble they went to in making arrangements for the dinner and things like that so that it means even more than we had originally thought it would — let us keep in mind that we are heirs of a great poetic tradition and it's up to us now. It's unfortunate that we had that fire but I think we can settle the whole thing for under five dollars or something like that, and I think we can afford to raise it among ourselves especially as we know the Department is going to publish the things we did here today — at least six of them. Anyway you can't say I didn't warn you, and I am sorry it had to be Miss Dovecote who was the chief sufferer because it wasn't her fault. Anyway, we really put it across today and those poems of ours, and I won't say they are all of the highest quality, are going to have their impact. After all, this Willow-Quagmire district is the Premier's own constituency and Sarah Binks's monument is smack in the middle of it. And while I'm at it I might as well tell you that this afternoon while the rest of you were going over Mr. Deepy's poems, I added the date of this meeting to those on Sarah's monument, because, as I said, this is a historic occasion and deserves to be remembered. We certainly owe a lot to her."

The six poets who were joined later by Purge Potatok are those upon whom the Saskatchewan Order of Merit was later conferred. They are:

John Swivel (The Great Dean of Saskatchewan letters).

Wraitha Dovecote.

Mrs. Martha Waffle (Bessie Udderton).

Professor Baalam Bedfellow, Ph.D.

Jordan Middleduck.

Osiris Jones-Jones (The Laureate).

Purge Potatok, D.P. (Appeared later).

Each of these poets had written a poem for the occasion in honour of Sarah or of her birthplace, Willows, and these were to be read and tossed upon a ceremonial pyre built on Sarah's grave. They are each in keeping with the individual's own work and poetic point of view and are correspondingly of great interest on that account. But apart from personal temperament and individual differences of approach, there are certain characteristics of the School of Seven as a whole which can be considered. Of these the two outstanding ones are those already mentioned, *innerness*, and the use of the cow as a symbol.

From a literary point of view, it has always been something of a mystery as to why the poetry of Saskatchewan should so often turn upon the cow as a central theme. Saskatchewan has never been a "cow country" in the sense that Texas and Arizona were cow countries. The Canadian prairies passed almost imperceptibly from the control of Sarah's "The Red Brother," to the wheat economy of which the cow was a mere adjunct, more for domestic comfort than of economic significance. There was certainly no intervening period of gunslinger and cowpuncher around which a people as bardically inclined as the Canadians could have written the ballads and the heroic literature which inspired the American Southwest. And yet it would almost seem that no poet of western Canada, and certainly no poet of the School of Seven, can feel that he properly belongs unless he has written at least one poem about the cow or has made some passing reference to the cow as a poetic symbol. But it is just in this very symbolism that the attraction of the cow as a theme lies.

Sarah Binks undoubtedly started it all. We need only go back to her very earliest poems to the calf, and her "Song to the Cow" to perceive that for her the cow was a symbol of domesticity. The cow, for her, represented farm and fireside. The cow's nose was "plush-like and warm," its eye quick to perceive the best feeding ground, and it had "a breath like ale," all of which Sarah summarizes in her commendation by

> These attributes in a cow, I deem,
> Are the best to be had and win my esteem.

Sarah loved the cow as one loves a fellow-creature of any kind able to receive and return affection, and she invariably clothes it in human qualities. Even in "Hiawatha's Milking," Co-boss, although perhaps a bit unwilling to yield something of her essential self to one who in her opinion could represent no more than a past culture and a civilization which was already on the way out, is nevertheless sad. Her eyes are "doleful" as well as soulful and she sighs deeply before kicking Hiawatha in the pail. Such things reveal the cow as standing for the domestic virtues as well as for the security of the land of which Sarah always felt herself to be a part. And even in "Spring," where the cow and the calf blend their alto and bass in harmony of praise to the new weather, there is somehow or other a suggestion of a happy domestic scene like children singing together in the joy of Christmas morning.

The cow, having thus quite unconsciously been set up as a symbol by Sarah, her successors have naturally followed suit. But not slavishly. For the different poets, the cow carries different significance. Only in the case of Purge Potatok can we say that the significance of the cow is the same as it was for Sarah. And even here it is slightly different, since in Sarah's case it was coloured by her femininity. But the "home and hearth" solidity which the cow represented for Sarah has its counterpart in the mind of the

New Canadian, Potatok, as standing for economic security. For him ownership of the cow is not spiritual freedom as some have held, but rather freedom from the grinding poverty of his homeland where tradition still maintained that only an Archbishop or a Grand Duke or even the Czar could ever aspire to a cow. And like Sarah he has a deep personal fondness for the cow as a fellow creature, especially for his "boy-cow" whom he affectionately calls "that little baster," whatever that means, and whom he somewhat playfully slaps "six times on the pents," certainly not in anger, for having escaped the corral he built for it.

In his Ph.D. thesis at St. Midget's, Byron Rumpkin advances the interesting theory that what has since come to be known as *archetypal bovinism* arises out of a repression within the subconscious, either self-induced or externally forced whereby the natural desire for milk during infancy becomes replaced by a desire for alcohol. In this process the *id* becomes to some extent identified with the *bos* image in the subconscious mind which seeks an outlet. It is then projected, but its semantic implications depend entirely upon the value structure acquired during maturation, and in the case of the poet these may be manifold though the form remains the same. The different symbolic significances of the cow may thus be accounted for.

More evidence should be adduced to confirm this theory, but as far as it goes it is useful in explaining the wide variety in cow symbolism which is observed in the School of Seven. It is certainly consistent with Jordan Middleduck's high-minded value-structure that he should perceive the unusual, though by no means altogether unknown, cow-in-the-sky phenomenon through the eyes of Noah's wife and draw the comparison with clouds as a heavenly manifestation. On the other hand with Jones-Jones, the symbolism of the cow is, as we have seen, simply and readily expressed by fifty dollars.

Further consideration of cow-symbolism is reserved for later and more detailed discussion of the individual poets and some examples of their different uses of the cow will be given as they occur in their works. John Swivel's frequent reference to the cow to symbolize his favourite theme of time's passing and the vanity of life is well known. Less obvious, of course, since she attempts to conceal it, but still understandable on the basis of Rumpkin's theory, is Wraitha Dovecote's famous sigh of farewell to her departing youth in the brilliant "Hast Milk to Spare?" But it is difficult to know in the case of Baalam Bedfellow, why, as in "Seared Land," he should call out in an apparent agony of spirit, "Strive for us cows, for we are weak," when we know perfectly well that he hates cows almost as much as he hates birds. He has certainly never had archetypal bovinism, since this, on top of his anti-snearth complex, would have killed him. It must be that as a Westerner he just can't get the cow out of his system. For when he cries out as he does in some of his other poems, or even in some of his later instalments of "Seared Land," "Strive for us, ye Powers for we are weak," or even, "strive for us ye stars for we are feeling pretty weak these days," we cannot but conclude that he merely uses the cow as a figure of speech. We cannot feel that like Potatok or like Sarah, he loves the cow. Bedfellow is just too cerebral for such emotion.

Interestingly enough, the only member of the School of Seven who has never written about the cow is Bessie Udderton. True, she has a great fondness for dairy products and these, for her, have become to a considerable extent identified with *innerness* with which so much of western poetry has been identified and of which she herself is the chief exponent. It may be that her reluctance to write about the cow is due to the fact that she once, in referring to the countryside around her home described it as being "studded with cows," an expression for which she was immediately taken to task by her readers who felt that although a poet was entitled to get her metaphors mixed, taking liberties with sexes that way was something else again. Milk, cream, butter, cottage cheese, beef-Stroganoff, tenderloin tips with mushrooms, grilled T-bone, sirloin roast (medium) — Bessie makes the oblique approach to the cow, but it is no less real on that account. Moreover, as Rumpkin has pointed out, the very fact that she chose the pen-name, Bessie, is itself significant. The *bos* image dies hard.

Not so apparent as the cow but more deeply imbedded in Saskatchewan literature is *innerness,* that quality of poetry which, although not unknown in Canada, has become a definite characteristic in the School of Seven. It is a peculiar inversion of two negatives to form one positive. All poetry, as we know, must have its roots in history but *innerness* arises out of Saskatchewan's lack of history. It arises furthermore out of Saskatchewan's characteristic economy of wheat, or at least what was its characteristic economy before the discovery of oil. Wheat, in

Saskatchewan, has always stood, and indeed still stands for prosperity — of food and an abundance of things to eat. But it is a prosperity of which the poet traditionally suffers a lack. And in Saskatchewan's history the very soil which the poet was seeking to express and out of which he was to draw his inspiration, was refusing him its essence. Reaching then into the history of the land itself for further inspiration, the poet finds another lack since there is practically no history worth mentioning. The result of all these lacks is however not what we would expect, a frustration and a withdrawing, but actually an idealization. The poetic spirit is not easily crushed.

Those who hold that *innerness* in Saskatchewan is merely a case of the poets there being hungry and that they are writing about it, cannot see the fine points of literature. To understand *innerness* we must go back as far as we can into what there is of Saskatchewan's history. Actually there is very little. *Fifty Years of Progress* undoubtedly represents, as the Government points out, a tremendous percentage increase in almost everything, which is not surprising considering there was nothing to start from. In actual years the Saskatchewan poet has no long period of political or heroic history from which to draw his inspiration. Sarah Binks, of course, wrote her own history but the poet of today cannot call upon Caesar and his legions as did Sarah for poetic inspiration, especially since the historians, notably Farley Mowat, have shown that it was not the Romans but the Norwegians who first discovered Saskatchewan; and these at best can serve only as a poetic mulch. Nevertheless, the poet makes the best of what he has even if it is, as the great German critic and historian, von Hinten states, "ever so little." Without it, he declares, it loses one *Geist* after another:

> Lacking *innerness* [declares von Hinten] no poet can interpret history. Poetry is the innerness of history. Without *innerness*, no poetry. But also without history no *innerness*. It then becomes history in the special or the *ersatz* sense. It is to ask ourselves whether or no.
>
> But history in this special sense requires two things, namely, history in the ordinary sense, and the poetic historian in the extraordinary or disordinary sense. Of these two the latter is the most important. The history of a people lies not so much in the *Zeitgeist*, or record-of-events, as it does in the strength-

through-interpretation-given-to-events, that is to say in effect, the *Wienerschnitzelgeist* of the poet. And we must here again ask ourselves whether or no. If no — then no. If not no — who can say? But always the historian must be master of both or he loses the soul-spirit, the *Poltergeist*.

This he cannot acquire on his own. It is given or it is not given. If the poet cries, "help me with," we can do nothing. It can thus be qualitative as well as quantitative, depending on the negation. But of history in the ordinary sense there must always be some, if ever so little.

Here we have the dilemma of the Saskatchewan poet. Having of history in the ordinary sense "ever so little" he sublimates it by bringing it into the present and mixing it, if not exactly with wheat, at least with what wheat and wheat products once stood for. *Innerness* and the cow here meet on common ground. Undoubtedly the Regina School may have been hungry in its early days. But this is no longer actually the case. If the poets still tend to regard food with more than the usual poetic anticipation, as Bessie Udderton undoubtedly still does, it is all the more to their credit. The great poet penetrates the hidden depths of life and has therefore a deeper inspiration; but for the School of Seven, food has lost its mere sustaining and caloric significance. It has become spiritualized and like the cow has taken on a higher meaning. True, its physical necessity as poetic fuel is acknowledged and even Jordan Middleduck, probably the most impecunious and certainly the leanest of the School of Seven, says as much in his "Break Not the Lute," despite the fact that as a rule Middleduck is far above such considerations of the flesh as food, let alone other things:

      Break not the lute, the poet's spate
  Rests not alone on vernal scenes,
  But also on when last he ate —
  He cannot function lacking beans;

      For tears that fall upon the page,
  And sorrow which the poet pens
  Unless with nourishment assuaged,
  Yield no poetic dividends;

> And unfed Muse, the sulky jade,
> Like women all will soon retreat,
> And never be at best arrayed,
> Unless invited out to eat.*

We owe much to the Saskatchewan Government for its encouragement of the indigenous poetry of Western Canada and for its recognition of the School of Seven in conferring the Order of Merit upon its members. Such things bring them to the fore. They are all, in a sense, the literary heirs of the immortal Sarah Binks "than whom" to quote a voice from the distant past, "no greater has ever hit the prairies." But they all lack Sarah's verve, her ebullience, her youth, and, above all, her joy in the soil. They may, like Sarah herself, still represent their province and their native land, but what with the oil and industrialization of Saskatchewan they seem to have become old before their time. Wraitha Dovecote, the one from whom we would expect to find before all others some of Sarah's clear notes of joy, has fallen into an infinite sadness. John Swivel, the Great Dean, despite all the honours and success which have come his way, has returned again to the writing of those very *In Memoriam* poems through which he had first won recognition. Bessie Udderton's lyrical *innerness*, especially as she tends to put on weight, tends also to become more and more a mere index of chain-store products, and Professor Bedfellow, the Piltdown Man, is becoming increasingly difficult to understand, as he returns more and more to the primitive in his efforts to reach a pre-bird period of history. Osiris Jones-Jones, although high in Government regard as the Laureate and author of the Provincial Song, "Saskatchewan, Thou Golden," is nevertheless counted more for his skill in bird-watching and in running a tape recorder than as a creative artist. Only perhaps in Purge Potatok, the lowly immigrant, the D.P., the newcomer to this country, do we capture again, albeit in broken English, some of that love of the Saskatchewan soil that once was Sarah's.

Talent they undoubtedly have, and all are poets of the West. But it is no longer the same West. It is no longer the kingdom of wheat and no longer can any of them shout, "The

---

*This is the poem to which Bessie Udderton, the poet of *innerness* wrote two verses in reply. Incidentally, the theme of the broken lute is a favourite one with the School of Seven and on one occasion at least was even adopted by M, the unknown Muse of Jones-Jones.

farmer is King!" They may reflect their province but it is no longer a province of Sarah's "field and sky and rain-drenched hill." As we have seen in their co-operative "Moonlight on Wascana Lake," political considerations now intrude. There are economic frustrations and there are deep spiritual and psychological problems which must be overcome. But in the end it all makes for a great literature.

from Say, Uncle

Eric Nicol

Prehistoric America
(Before Lawrence Welk)

In the beginning, the whole of the United States was under water, except Milwaukee, which was under beer.

Proof of this is that Midwest farmers in ploughing have turned up clamshells, some millions of years old, others marked SOUVENIR OF LAGUNA BEACH.

The rich oil deposits of the central plains were built up by trillions of shrimps.* But over the eons the great plains became dry. (See chapter on Anti-Saloon League.) Some parts, such as Death Valley, rather overdid it. But most of the U.S. was a desirable prestige subdivision of North America, extending from Montezuma in the south to Minnehaha in the north.

The earliest residents of the United States, after the great lizards whose descendants may still be seen on the desert servicing slot machines, were the Indians.

The Indians were broken down into tribes. Some tribes were more broken-down than others, depending on how often they had been scalped by neighbouring tribes.

---

*In Texas, prawns.

Famous American tribes of Indians include the Blackfeet, the Sioux, the Cleveland, and the Wooden. The Cleveland Indians were the ones that used finger language for words like "run," "walk," and "steal second."

The Indians' favourite method of attack was to come over a hill and pause outlined against the sky, then charge down and circle the enemy, riding single-file and pitching off their horses in droves.

Thanks to this method of warfare the Indians earned the title The Vanishing American. Their greatest contribution to American civilization was the custom of talking to each other by means of smoke, a method still used in hotel rooms at U.S. political conventions.

America Discovered

The discovery of America was an accident, fortunately not serious.

Christopher Columbus had been commissioned, among other things, by the Queen of Portugal, to help him find a new route to India.* Having no sense of direction but plenty of moxie, Columbus sailed west in his three ships, the *Santa Maria, Santa Lucia,* and *Santa Sees You.*

Contrary to popular belief, Columbus did not land up in Ohio. Instead he sailed full tilt into a group of islands off Florida. America was actually discovered in Flagrante Delicto, a beautiful island today owned by Ernest Hemingway.

Columbus found the natives of the islands very friendly, eager to give him anything he desired, so he called them the Virgin Islands, or West Undies. He took a pair of natives back to the Queen of Portugal, because she was crazy about novelty earrings.

"Here are two natives of India, or Indians," Columbus told the Queen.

"In a pig's valise they're Indians," said the Queen, who was knowledgeable. "Indians wear a white thing slung between their legs and have chutney on their breath."

Columbus was therefore recommissioned to find a new route to India and no goofing around this time. Columbus thereupon sailed west again and landed up among the same islands

*The Queen wanted more spice, the King being dead.

as before. This time the natives were not as eager to give him everything he wanted, so Columbus decided to call it America.

Returning to Portugal he told the Queen: "I've discovered America, your Majesty, and here to prove it is a heap of gold, popcorn and chewing gum."

"Pepper!" yelled the Queen. "Pepper is what you were sent for, and the poppies of Cathay."

Columbus hastily assembled another crew and set sail for India. When those same islands came into view, with the natives wearily waving at him to get lost, Columbus did not have the heart to go home and tell the Queen. However, by a stroke of good luck, he then died.

A Packet of Pilgrims

Various countries sent colonists to America, but the English were the only ones that took it seriously.

This was because they were Pilgrims. At that time England had fallen under the influence of Charles II, who had spent some time in Paris, resulting in the persecution of everybody who didn't believe in living it up.

The Pilgrims' ship, the *Mayflower*, landed in the New World at Plymouth Rock, because it looked like the best place to be utterly miserable.

Almost immediately the Indians introduced the Pilgrims to the turkey and Indian corn, while the Pilgrims introduced the Indians to grapeshot and Christianity.

The first settlements of New England were frugal in the extreme. Everybody ate nothing but Boston baked beans, and there wasn't much social life apart from the Saturday-night drowning of a witch.

Life was simple. All the men were called John, all the women were called Mary, and practically everything was a sin but hard work. This work consisted in the main of constructing the most uncomfortable furniture imaginable, a craft honoured to this day by the waiting rooms of U.S. airports.

Pleasure seekers were put in stocks. Backsliders were put in bonds. In fact so many sinners went into stocks and bonds that it was necessary to found the New York Stock Exchange.

This in turn required the purchase of New York from the Dutch colonists, who had called it New Amsterdam and were pretty fed up with trying to cut canals through the solid rock.

The Puritan settlers got Manhattan for a song ("Rock of Ages"). This was the beginning of the New Englander's reputation as a sharp trader, always looking for the Maine chance.

A Charming Tale, If True

At this time a rather charming episode occurred between Captain John Smith and a dusky Indian maiden named Pocahontas. In love with Pocahontas, a bashful friend of Captain Smith's begged Smith to ask Pocahontas if she would marry him (the friend). When Captain Smith did so, Pocahontas blushed prettily and said, "Speak for yourself, John." John did, and this was how he lost a friend but gained a squaw.

It also established a principle of American commerce: the middleman gets the gravy.

This romantic interlude is so famous in American history that, to this day, when loving couples register at a hotel, the gentleman signs them in as "Mr. and Mrs. John Smith." It is one of America's most honoured traditions.

The American Revolution
(17? to ?83)

Nobody knows when the American Revolution started. The rebels were so badly organized that they forgot to make a note of the date, as well as having no shoes to speak of.

The first seeds of revolt were sowed by a group of hot-heads, all named Adam — Samuel Adam, John Adam, Mary Adam, and so on. These people were especially upset about the Stamp Act, a British act which made it compulsory to buy stamps even though there was no postal service.

They therefore asked Benjamin Franklin to put down that blasted kite for a minute and print the Declaration of Natural Rights, according to which the colonies would have the right to be perfectly natural and no more of those fool wigs the English wore.

They also called the first Continental Congress, which voted unanimously to inform the British government that America was a continent and therefore too big to be pushed around.

The British government refused to take this seriously, being under the influence of the beginning of the Romantic Movement (absence makes the heart grow fonder). Instead Parliament passed the Maritime Act, according to which the whole of America was officially under water — except, of course, Milwaukee — and therefore under the British Navy.

This touched off bloodshed. For the occasion, Benjamin Franklin invented gunpowder.

The first American troops were the Minute Men. (Just add water and stir into an open revolt.) The Man of the Hour was George Washington. There were sixty Minute Men to every Man of the Hour.

These small, mobile forces confused the British, who were accustomed to marching against the enemy in a straight red line, even numbers being shot, odd numbers stepping up.

Yet at first the revolutionary army bogged down, owing to lack of equipment, bad luck, and snow that fell only on the American side of the battlefield.

Moreover, their Esprit de Corps — a French unit that joined up because of the war in Canada — was always high. Too much wine. Then General Washington impressed his troops by throwing a dollar across the Potomac. Money went farther in those days.

The first American patriot of the war was Paul Revere, who left his regular job of making copper-bottomed pots to jump on his horse and ride through the countryside shouting, "The British are coming!"

Since he always did this at midnight people got pretty fed up with it. But one night he was right, the British *were* coming. For this he was made a hero, there being no other nominations.

Later, at the height of a British bombardment of one of their own forts, Betsy Ross made the first American flag. She did this by the rocket's red glare, and by hand. She also gave birth to the Daughters of the American Revolution.

While they were waiting for the British to make one of the gallant blunders for which General Gargoyle was famous, the revolutionary leaders drew up the Declaration of Independence. The author of this historic document was Thomas Jefferson, today generally recognized as being the brains behind the whole caper.

Disheartened by the Declaration of Independence (the British troops wanted life, liberty, and the pursuit of happiness just as much as anybody else and maybe more), as well as defeated by the French Navy that had sneaked into the war in violation of the Maritime Act, Cornwallis surrendered. Cornwallis was (a) a fort, (b) a general, (c) an Indian soup. (Do not mark more than three.)

republished in Still a Nicol

Perry Mason and the Case of The Dapper Detective

Pierre Berton

In this dream, see, I am the world's greatest criminal lawyer, fighting tooth and nail for my client. At the moment I am conducting a brilliant and penetrating examination of one of the prosecution witnesses. The wretch is cringing in the box under the harsh light of my questioning. His name is Perry Mason.

ME: Now, Mr. Mason, I think it's time we examined your source of income.

MASON: I have nothing to hide. My income consists entirely of legal fees received from clients.

ME: (*Sneering*) Your legal fees! Ha! Since when, Mason, have you ever accepted a legal fee from a client?

MASON: Now just a minute — in *The Case of the Pitiful Prowler* I —

ME: (*Reading from a document*) You accepted just thirty-seven cents according to this T.V. script I have here.

MASON: Well, she needed my help.

ME: Exactly! They all need your help! And you always take their case! And you never ask for money because they never have money! Yet you have this huge office, roughly the size of the ballroom at the King Eddy and this flashy modern desk and this flashy modern secretary and you have at your beck and call at all times the Paul Drake Detective Agency —

HAMILTON BURGER: Objection, your Honour! I really do not see what this recital of Mr. Mason's personal effects has to do with the case at hand . . .

ME: If it please the court, I intend to show that the witness Mason at no time acts like a real grasping lawyer. This line of questioning is essential to my point.

JUDGE: Overruled. Proceed.

ME: I quote from another T.V. script. In *The Case of the Fractured Fireman*, Mason is speaking to Drake. He says: "Found out anything about the missing ruby, yet, Paul?" and Drake replies: "Not yet, Perry." Mason says: "How many men have you got on it?" and Drake answers: "Johnstone, Everson, Charlesworth and Goldberg. All good men." Whereupon Mason answers: "Better put two more men on it, Paul. We've got to have the answer by trial time." Now I put it to you, Mason, that those men each receive a hundred dollars a day and expenses. At least that's what Sabre of London gets. Would you mind telling the court the total amount of the fee you received for this case?

MASON: (*In a low voice*) There was no fee; this poor fireman had no money.

ME: Exactly! None of your clients have money because they are all innocent. Right?

MASON: Right.

ME: And innocent people never have any money — it's always been stolen from them. Right?

MASON: Right.

ME: Only crooks have money. Right?

MASON: Right.

ME: And you don't defend crooks?

MASON: No.

ME: Then where do you get the money to keep an enormous detective agency at your beck and call twenty-four hours a day?

MASON: I– I–

JUDGE: Witness must answer.

ME: Is it not a fact that after three solid years of work you now owe Paul Drake the sum of $457,892.37?

MASON: I – yes.

ME: And, therefore, it would have been in your interest to have Paul Drake rubbed out?

HAMILTON BURGER: (*Rising*) Objection, your Honour! The question is incompetent, irrelevant and immaterial.

JUDGE: Sustained.

ME: (*Smugly*) Withdraw the question. Now Mr. Mason, let us turn to another puzzling phase of your operations. I refer to the situation with Della Street!

MASON: (*Rising and half blind with rage*) I'll have you know that Miss Street is a fine, upstanding clean-living American girl.

ME: (*Silkily*) No doubt, Mr. Mason. But it seems to me that her work is often beyond the call of duty.

MASON: Why, you – !

ME: By that I mean she works more than the 37½-hour week laid down by the International Union of Office Employees. She is there, in fact, from morning until night. In *The Case of the Parboiled Paperhanger*, for instance, your office was called at 10:30 p.m. and she answered the phone. She often installs your clients in motel rooms late at night (*The Case of the Cultured Corn Husker*) or in the wee small hours of the morning. And she appears, I might add, to have no social life of her own. Do you pay her overtime, Mason?

MASON: But, you see –

ME: Your Honour, will you instruct the witness to answer the question? Yes or no!

JUDGE: Witness will answer.

MASON: No!

ME: So she is more than a secretary to you? More than just an — employee?

MASON: She's — .

ME: Is she or isn't she? Answer the question!

MASON: Yes.

ME: Are you in love with Della Street, Mr. Mason?

MASON: (*Goes white. Goes red. Then blurts it out*) Yes! Yes! Yes! Madly! Insatiably!

ME: But you were insanely jealous of Paul Drake, weren't you?

MASON: What do you mean?

ME: He was always hanging around the office, paying Miss Street little compliments . . . taking her out to dinner ostensibly at your request, because you were busy . . . calling her "beautiful" in front of you . . . chucking her under the chin. On the T.V. screen at the opening of each story, *he's always beside her*! And you couldn't do anything about it, could you, Mason, because you owed Paul Drake $457,829.37 plus accumulated interest!

MASON: This is ridiculous!

ME: Not so ridiculous, Mason, when one considers that Drake, not you, owned every stick of furniture in that office. You had to let him have it in lieu of payment as this document shows. Not only that, but *Drake wanted Della Street along with the furniture.* You were in his power, you were losing your girl, and there was only one way out: *murder*!

MASON: (*Buries face in hands*) Yes.

ME: You killed Paul Drake, Perry Mason!
    Lt. Tragg who has had nothing to do until now rises and clamps the handcuffs on Mason.

ME: Your Honour, the defence rests!
    I walk out of the courtroom with my client, Della Street.

from Just Add Water and Stir

from The Eye Opener

Bob Edwards

In the quiet cove of High River we anchor the Eye Opener, hoping it won't bust like the Maine. Clothed in righteousness, a bland smile and a lovely jag, the editor of this publication struck town two weeks ago. The management has decided on the name, "Eye Opener" because few people will resist taking it. It will be run on a strictly moral basis at one dollar a year. If an immoral paper is the local preference, we can supply that too but it will cost $1.50.

from The Eye Opener's first issue, March 4, 1902

Peace River, N.W.T.
The Fall, 1902.

Dear Father:

I often think of dear old Skookingham Hall and the splendid shooting. How I should enjoy one of our good old grouse drives again. The only shooting I have done out here of late years has been at craps, a different species of game from grouse or partridge.

About things in this country. The few thousand pounds you gave me to start farming with in Manitoba were duly invested in a farm. In my labours I had several assistants, Hi Walker, Joe Seagram, Johnny Dewar, Benny Dikteen, men of exceptional strength and fiery temperament and in place of serving me as their master, soon became my masters. So it was not long before I had no farm. I then quit farming and went tending bar for a hotel keeper in the neighbouring village whose prosperity seems to have dated from the hour of my arrival in the country.

The love of liquor, which I must have inherited either from yourself or my grandfather, made me a failure as a bartender and I soon got the bounce. So I packed my things in a large envelope and hit the blind baggage for the West where I went cowpunching. Worked during the summer till the beef gather and lost all my wages in one disastrous night at poker. After a long hard winter as cookee in a lumber camp I struck for Peace River country where I am now.

I am married to a half-breed and have three ornery-looking, copper-colored brats. We are all coming over to visit you at Christmas when you will be having the usual big house party at Skookingham Hall. I shall so like to see the dear place again and my wife is most anxious to become acquainted with her darling husband's people and obtain a glimpse of English society. The Hall will be quite a change for her from the log 'shacks and teepees she has been used to all her life.

If I only had about a thousand pounds just now with which to start afresh, I would invest it in cattle right away, settle down to business and forego the pleasure of a trip home and remain right here. But I do not know where to lay my hands on that amount. The climate here is lovely. With love and kisses to mother and the girls, believe me, dear old Dad.

Your affectionate son,
Albert Buzzard-Cholomondeley.
(Eye Opener, Oct. 24, 1903)

Dear Father:

When you open this letter at the breakfast table do not read it aloud to mother and the girls. Keep the contents to yourself . . . am at present in the direst distress and have had to postpone indefinitely my newspaper venture at Leduc.

You remember me writing to you that my half-breed wife was very ill and was being attended by an Indian medicine man who beat a tom-tom by her bedside to drive away the evil one. Well, she's dead. Her untimely death affected me deeply. So enraged did I become, often brooding over the maladroit practices of the tawny Aesculapius that I determined to kill him. Before doing anything rash, however, I consulted a friend, one of the most distinguished bartenders in Edmonton, who promptly offered me his profound sympathy and a small flask. His advice seemed reasonable enough. He said: "Shoot him by all means but do as the gamekeepers in the Old Country do with boys bird-nesting. Don't use shot. Put salt in your shells and you will thus both scare and hurt the brute without getting yourself into trouble."

Returning to camp I loaded up a couple of shells with salt

as per advice. I also put the little old flask out of business before I mustered up courage enough to pepper the gentleman with the salt. Then I let him have it with both barrels at a range of about three feet. He dropped like a log and never came back. He was stone dead.

Then began my troubles. The coroner examined the body carefully and the jury returned a verdict of wilful murder. I explained that I had only used salt, not wishing to do other than nip him a little. "Yes," said the coroner, "that may be so, but unfortunately you used rock salt." As a matter of fact, I didn't have any table salt.

I am now incarcerated in Fort Saskatchewan awaiting trial. Owing to recent events in the police I am chained to a ring in the floor of my cell and all visitors have to talk with me through a megaphone placed for that purpose on the top of a bluff half a mile from the fort. They are taking no chances. My bartender friend sent me a box of cigars to while away the time and the policemen smoked them all up to make sure there were no files concealed in the wrappers. It is a strenuous life. Think of your little Bertie occupying a murderer's cell.

Dad, I must have a thousand dollars immediately to secure the services of a competent lawyer from Calgary. There is a famous criminal lawyer down there by the name of P. J. Nolan whom I should like to get. All the best murderers of the West employ him. The few whom he fails to get acquitted without a stain on their characters are singularly successful in escaping the hangman. They get off somehow. There is no doubt but what Mr. Nolan would accept a fee of one thousand dollars if I can give him reasonable assurance that it is all I've got.

On one occasion, so my friend the bartender told me through the megaphone, Mr. Nolan defended a man who had killed another by filling him full of buckshot. His line of defence was that deceased came to his death through natural causes, because how could a man be expected to live with half a pound of lead in his vitals? The jury took the same view and the murderer in now leading a virtuous life and travelling with a stud horse.

Dear father, it is essential to my safety that I be immediately provided with funds to hire this lawyer. Should I hang, the papers will bristle with lurid descriptions of the execution and shocking headlines, all of which will be copied into English papers.

"Buzzard-Cholomondeley, son of old man Cholomondeley, hanged today! Painful scenes on the scaffold!"

"The Gates of Hell ajar! Buzzard-Cholomondeley strung up for foul murder! Says he had no table salt."

"Buzzard-Cholomondeley, the assassin, in dying speech attributes his fate to refusal of father to provide funds for lawyer. Sympathy felt for doomed and indignation expressed towards unnatural parent!"

"Scion of old English family sent to Kingdom Come for Brutal Murder! Death Instantaneous!"

Cable over the money at once. Sending by mail means disastrous delay. If I can secure P. J. Nolan I am saved. If not, I am a gonner. They say he won't save a man's neck on jawbone.

Your wretched son,
Albert Buzzard-Cholomondeley.
(Eye Opener, Jan. 2, 1904)

Dear Father:

Your cable to the bank at Edmonton for one thousand dollars has saved my bacon and the honour of the Buzzard-Cholomondeleys. I was duly acquitted of the charge of murdering the Indian doctor who attended my late lamented half-breed wife.

The money arrived in the nick of time and I at once put myself in telegraphic communication with P. J. Nolan of Calgary, asking him to come right away and try my case, mentioning as a fee the sum of five hundred dollars. In declining to rescue me from the jaws of death for this amount, he employed metaphorical language, symbolical of the season, suggesting that I was a frost and a cheap skate, so perforce I had to cough up the thousand straight. How he knew you had sent me a "thou" I cannot say. Be that as it may, it is to his diabolical ingenuity that I owe my life.

Mr. Nolan, after looking me over carefully and talking with me on general subjects, entered a plea of insanity. The fact of my being a bloody Englishman made the task an easy one for my learned saviour. On the morning of the trial he came to my cell with a pair of very baggy pants for me to put on, also a pair of leggings and a remarkably high white collar which made my ears stick out at right angles like the topsails of a ship in distress. Then he handed me a package of abominable cigarettes with instructions to rise at a critical moment during the trial and crave the permission of the judge to smoke them in court. I followed counsel's instructions to the letter and the jury never left their seats. They decided I had a violent form of dementia and that the asylum for the insane at Brandon was my proper sphere.

The prospect of passing the remainder of my days in a lunatic asylum was not an alluring one, but any old thing was preferable to being hanged. Mr. Nolan expressed the fear, as he pocketed your "thou" and bade me goodbye, that I might feel a bit lonesome at first in the asylum, as from what he had learned, I would be the only Conservative lunatic who had ever been confined within its walls and added that the name of Buzzard alone would have the effect of making me a rara avis.

The following day, in charge of a North West Mounted Policeman, I started for Brandon asylum, with the machinery in my idea-box turned on at full pressure. The trip to Calgary was uneventful. While waiting for the midnight flyer going east, the policeman and I strolled leisurely up and down the platform. The butt of his revolver protruded temptingly from his pocket. There was no one on the platform at that late hour and everything was quiet. We were just turning around close by the fence of the CPR gardens when, quick as thought, I whipped out his gun from his pocket and told him there was the twinkle of a star between him and his finish. Me to the bug house? "Na, na my bonny Jean."

Swiftly I steered him into a labyrinth of boxcars and made him peel off his clothes and hand over his uniform, boots, hat and overcoat. At the same time I took off my own togs and ordered him to put them on. Thus we exchanged raiment. I was the policeman, he the lunatic. Right carefully did I keep him hazed amongst the box cars in the darkness until the express came along and for fear of possible hitches, did not board the cars with my madman (he was mad all right) till she was moving out.

In the pockets of my new clothes I found railroad tickets, money, warrant for my, or rather his, incarceration in the bug house, and a set of shackles. I lost no golden moments shackling my man to the seat. Of course he kicked up a tremendous row and appealed for help to the conductor and passengers — knowing I wouldn't decently shoot him in a car — but ha, ha, my dear old dad, I was a Mounted Policeman and he was an insane prisoner. The brakeman even suggested knocking him over the koko with a coupling pin to keep him quiet. Happily for me we passed through

Regina in the night. It wouldn't have mattered very much, however, because the police at that point are located away on the horizon, miles from town.

I turned over my unfortunate victim to the asylum authorities at Brandon, explaining to them his pitiful hallucinations about being a policeman and got a receipt in full for the delivery of "Albert Buzzard-Cholomondeley."

Having the policeman's return ticket and his little wad of money, I thought I might as well return to Calgary where no one knows me. It did not take me long to rustle a suit of civilian clothes on my arrival there. The Fort Saskatchewan authorities will no doubt attribute the constable's delay in getting back to the usual drunk and may not get uneasy for a week or two. The Brandon people certainly won't catch on because they will lay the ravings of the hapless policeman to the hallucinations I told them about. You ought to be proud to have such a brainy son in your repertoire.

Now look here, dad. Although I may not be dead, I am dead broke. The trick I have played is sure to come out sooner or later and I must get out of here. I cannot get out without money. Cable over another hundred pounds to take me home. I shall come alone, my two children being still [out] on shares at Lesser Slave Lake. Cable on receipt of this letter and I shall start right away.

Love to mother and the girls.

Your affectionate son,
Bertie.

(Eye Opener, Jan., 1904)

My Dear Dad:

When last I wrote you I was running the Black Cobra Distillery full blast in conjunction with my friend Courtenay. Since then I have sold out my interest and am at present worth all of $50,000. In consequence of this pleasant accession of wealth I am resolved to branch out and return on a visit to the ancestral home in England, crowned with laurels and with honours thick upon me. With this laudable aim in view it is my intention to enter the Dominion Parliament, running on the Prohibition ticket. Money being plentiful, my chances are excellent.

As soon as the committees of the two great parties learned that I was willing to spend $20,000 on getting elected, they waited upon me and besought me with tears in their eyes to run on their respective sides. I told them they could not play me for a Cochrane.

The Prohibition ticket I am running on is pretty sure to be a winner as the liquid I propose prohibiting in this case is water. The hotels will pull for me as one man and the local sports have promised to stand by. My committee is a singularly influential one, being composed of all the bartenders in town, with Fred Adams as chairman. Every man who steps into a hotel for a shot is presented with a quart of Black Cobra with "Vote for Buzzard-Cholomondeley" blown in the bottle, together with a little circular containing my electoral address. This latter effusion runs as follows:

"Fellow citizens: In soliciting your suffrages I beg to state that my attitude on all public matters will be one of unswerving adherence to my own political interests. I believe in a public man getting out of it all there is in it. Let us be honest in our villainy. What is the use of me telling you that I will only stand for clean government when you know and I know that if the opportunity presents itself for making a stake at the expense of the people, I will drop on it like a bee on a posy? As a good straightforward grafter I expect to make my mark in the House. I shall always be on the side of the Government so that if any horrible scandal should arise, a carefully selected commission of enquiry will whitewash me and make me clean. You will lose nothing and I shall be having my treasure on earth that neither moths nor flies will corrupt.

"I am a Prohibitionist. What I propose to prohibit is the reckless use of water. Its effect on health, habits and moral character of the community is disastrous. Look at the interminable series of typhoid cases with which our hospitals are filled from month to month, people dying who never died before, young men and maidens who have not reached the middle arch of life passing away down to a watery grave. It is sad to contemplate the distressing results of the steady tippling of germ-laden water. Every sample of the horrid stuff shows the presence of colon bacilli and an excessive number of other bacteria including pollywogs. If men would only confine themselves to a good stiff rasping old whiskey like Old Cobra, Calgary would be happier and better today. Any germ that can live after a gulp of Black Cobra has struck it, must be a corker.

"I propose erecting a beer fountain at my own expense in the CPR gardens and having it playing there all the time instead of the band. Although my business connection with Black Cobra has been severed, I can still recommend it as a means of grace and as a hope of glory. It touches the spot.

"I am in favour of abolishing the office of licence inspector altogether and of appointing a water analyst with full authority to prosecute those responsible for distributing typhoid dope throughout the town. The young man alleged to have died last week from drinking Black Cobra confessed at the last moment that he always took water for a chaser. Rash youth! Perhaps, after all, he is better off in hell, where his opportunities will be but slight for indulging his unnatural craving for water. Had he lived, he might have grown up to be a burglar or a member of the city council. You never can tell about these things.

"On this platform I appeal for your support. If I prove recreant to my trust and false to my promises by becoming too darned immaculate, I shall be willing to resign. But there is no danger. I leave myself in your hands. Call at the committee rooms and get a bottle of Black Cobra.

Respectfully,
A.B.C."

Perhaps, father, you think I am crazy to issue a brutally frank address such as this, but believe me the rank and file of the voting public in Canada have reached such a pitch of exasperation toward the smooth flannel-mouths who pose as saints on the hustings and turn out to be nothing more than commonplace sinners when in office, that they are ready to welcome with open arms a man who is honest enough to announce beforehand that he is not seeking their suffrages for his health.

Money talks without stammering in this country . . . Graft is the rule. Boodle is the stake. Were I to tell the people that I disapproved of that sort of thing and would not tolerate it in others, they would instinctively distrust me. So my Bismarckian tactics of artless frankness will win me the day. They remember their folly in returning Frank Oliver to parliament as an independent. When I get in my fine work at Ottawa on the rake-off pile, I shall not be ashamed to face my constituents later on, seeing that permission to steal and sell my vote at every opportunity was incorporated in my platform. . . .

Borrowing a Match

Stephen Leacock

You might think that borrowing a match upon the street is a simple thing. But any man who has ever tried it will assure you that it is not, and will be prepared to swear on oath to the truth of my experience of the other evening.

I was standing on the corner of the street with a cigar that I wanted to light. I had no match. I waited till a decent, ordinary man came along. Then I said:

"Excuse me, sir, but could you oblige me with the loan of a match?"

"A match?" he said, "why, certainly." Then he unbuttoned his overcoat and put his hand in the pocket of his waistcoat. "I know I have one," he went on, "and I'd almost swear it's in the bottom pocket — or, hold on, though, I guess it may be in the top — just wait till I put these parcels down on the sidewalk."

"Oh, don't trouble," I said, "It's really of no consequence."

"Oh, it's no trouble, I'll have it in a minute; I know there must be one in here somewhere" — he was digging his fingers into his pockets as he spoke — "but you see this isn't the waistcoat I generally . . . "

I saw that the man was getting excited about it. "Well, never mind," I protested; "if that isn't the waistcoat that you generally — why, it doesn't matter."

"Hold on, now, hold on!" the man said, "I've got one of the cursed things in here somewhere. I guess it must be in with my watch. No, it's not there either. Wait till I try my coat. If that confounded tailor only knew enough to make a pocket so that a man could get at it!"

He was getting pretty well worked up now. He had thrown down his walking-stick and was plunging at his pockets with his teeth set. "It's that cursed young boy of mine," he hissed; "this comes of his fooling in my pockets. By Gad! perhaps I won't warm him up when I get home. Say, I'll bet that it's in my hip-pocket. You just hold up the tail of my overcoat a second till I . . ."

"No, no," I protested again, "please don't take all this trouble, it really doesn't matter. I'm sure you needn't take off your overcoat, and oh, pray don't throw away your letters and things in the snow like that, and tear out your pockets by the roots! Please, please don't trample over your overcoat and put your feet through the parcels. I do hate to hear you swearing at your little boy, with that peculiar whine in your voice. Don't — please don't tear your clothes so savagely."

Suddenly the man gave a grunt of exultation, and drew his hand up from inside the lining of his coat.

"I've got it," he cried. "Here you are!" Then he brought it out under the light.

It was a toothpick.

Yielding to the impulse of the moment I pushed him under the wheels of a trolley-car and ran.

from Literary Lapses

Twentieth Century Artifacts Away Back in 1959

Pierre Berton

Professor Rodney Glrb's recent archaeological expedition to the former site of Toronto, one of the ancient cities of the Old World, has been highly successful. Professor Glrb's excavations, painstakingly carried out over a three-year period, have produced many new artifacts which cast further light on the lives of the primitive peoples who inhabited this area in the mid-twentieth century. Reproductions of some of the chief finds are shown below:

This particularly fine example of mid-twentieth century art was one of several unearthed during Professor Glrb's dig. However, this is the only one that he was able to maintain intact. The flask, obviously in common use at the time, preserves all the naïve art and primitive vigour of a people who loved to work with their hands and – in spite of their many vicissitudes – enjoyed a zest for sparkling refreshment.

FIG. 1

Note the classic lines, simple and yet authoritative, of this roadside god, whose effigy appeared at regular intervals along thoroughfares of the day. Natives propitiated the deity by regular offerings of small metal pieces on which had been carved, with great ingenuity, the face of their leader or chieftain.

FIG. 2

Cunningly wrought from preserved skins of domestic animals, this fetish was carried everywhere by the males of the tribe, who believed that its possession conferred good fortune upon them. Without it, they felt lost, almost naked. Its presence gave them a sense of power and confidence, and a feeling of "belonging."

FIG. 3

Twentieth-century man's ideas of the working of the human body were crude in the extreme. Fig. 4 shows a 1960 conception of what the human brain was like. Natives actually believed little hammers inside the head caused headaches, tension, edginess, etc. They often swallowed pills in the hopes of combatting this "dull feeling."   FIG. 4

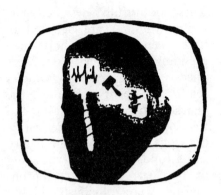

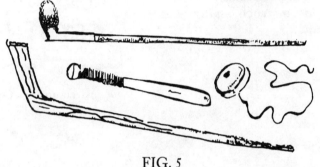

FIG. 5

Hand-carved clubs of various styles, many of them beautifully wrought, were chief weapons of the period. Tribes fought with them incessantly, and even children were drawn into warfare. Circular object (right) came equipped with string so that it could be retrieved by user after enemy was bested.

Professor Glrb and his researchers had great difficulty identifying this object, believing as they did that by the early 1960s all cooking was done within the dwelling. As these and similar artifacts were always found in the backyard or native *patio*, he is forced to conclude that they were used for animal sacrifices to the various gods of the day. Theory is fortified by discovery of heavily-charred animal meat in the near vicinity.

FIG. 6

These beautifully designed garments (*aprons*) are believed to
have been worn by holy men
presiding at sacrificial rites. Meat
juices staining many samples
reinforce theory. Note the
delicacy of the workmanship and
the sophistication of the native
drawings which show high ability
and a fundamental understanding
of both art and taste. Toron-
tonians were obviously highly
developed in such skills and
handicrafts.

FIG. 7

from Adventures of a Columnist

Three Cheers for Me

Donald Jack

The Man Who Went Abroad

I had expected to be sent to the Twenty-fifth Training
Wing, at Castle Bromwich, for more advanced training but
instead I was posted to a new airdrome in Surrey, and when I
looked it up on the map found it was only thirty miles or so from
Burma Park. Thirty miles by air, that is. By English roads it was
450 miles. But still, I felt obscurely delighted, for Burma Park was
even then casting its strange spell over me.

In the meantime I was given a long weekend in London.
I didn't particularly want the days off, being unwilling to miss

any good flying weather. Not that I wasn't due for leave; I'd had none since leaving Beamington. However, Major Brannon seemed keen on my going, so off I went in a slow train for the capital with all my kit in the luggage racks and a copy of *The Times* clenched in my hands.

There wasn't much in it. A Turkish Bath attendant had massaged his wife to death with his bare feet; all was quiet in France; there'd been some kind of revolution in Petrograd, but this was a Good Thing as it meant that Democracy was at last coming to Mother Russia and President Wilson of the United States was said to be delighted with the turn of events and was urging a loan to the new leaders of Russia as soon as it was known who the new leaders were. And so on. It was all very insignificant. So I put the paper aside and got talking to a charming person, Lady Constance Chatterley, who was on her way to see her husband, Sir Clifford Chatterley, off to Flanders. They had only been married a month. I wished her all the best and hurried out of Victoria Station with a ton of kit and eleven pounds to spend.

I got a small room in the Spartan Hotel nearby, had a bath, then dined in the hotel restaurant, which contained just two other occupants, an elderly man and his wife, both of whom wore black moustaches and had strange accents that I took to be either Swahili or Scottish. In the evening I settled on a Spot of Entertainment.

It was a drama called *The Man Who Went Abroad* and had just begun when I stumbled into my seat in the stalls. Act II was almost over before I caught up with the plot. It concerned a fellow on an Atlantic liner called Kit Brent who was impersonating Lord Goring of the British Cabinet in order to draw off a pack of German spies led by one von Bernstorff. Kit is supposed to be taking some secret papers to Washington. To compromise the supposed Lord Goring, Bernstorff employs a beautiful Austrian dancer, Ani Kiraly, in the hopes that fears of a scandal will force "Lord Goring" to hand over the secret papers. But Ani falls in love with Kit Brent, alias Lord Goring. Then it turns out that Ani is not an Austrian after all but a Dalmatian —

At this point I hurried to the bar and ordered a drink called "gin." For a moment I thought they'd made a mistake and given me a glass of perfume, Nuit d'amour or something. It tasted lascivious, but it was better than the play.

So I squelched back to the hotel, which was virtually unheated, so that I couldn't get warm in bed until I'd togged myself

out in a cardigan, scarf, a pair of socks, and a balaclava helmet.
I made a mental note to buy pajamas someday.

With peace and quiet in which to think, I tried to work it
all out. What was it exactly that drew me to Burma Park? Was it
because of Miss Lewis? But I had not experienced that quickening
of the senses that is supposed to signify a s—xual attraction. Perhaps
it was snobbery. By making inquiries among the permanent
members of the training squadron I'd found out that Mr. Lewis
was some kind of administrative civil servant and worked at the
Foreign Office, that the Lewises were definitely County (I didn't
quite know what this meant but it was obviously something
impressive), and that their family had been living at Burma Park
since Rockingham's Government (which practically made them
upstarts, as this was a mere one and a half centuries ago).

Perhaps it was simply the place itself, with its welcoming
atmosphere.

I sighed and turned over carefully, so as to admit the
minimum volume of cold air, and found myself indulging in the
absurd nostalgia of retracing in imagination the short journey from
hall to library. And wishing . . . I don't know what. . . . But
there was something about the Lewises, something about Burma
Park. . . . I fell asleep and dreamed of that horse Marshall, and
woke with a fright to find spring sunlight pouring over London.

In the afternoon as I scuttled down Charing Cross Road
looking at the bookshops, I found myself working out ways of
regaining admittance to Burma Park. "Why, hello, Mr. Lewis,
I just happened to be passing your house and thought I might as
well drop . . ." No, that was no good: I could hardly happen to
be passing the house when the nearest public road was three miles
away. "Good morning, Miss Lewis, I've just force-landed in your
wood pasture again —"

"Now look here, Bandy," she was saying, "this is getting
monotonous; it's the seventh time this month you've force-landed
in our wood pasture. If you don't stop it I'll set Marshall on you."
I fled. . . .

I found I'd been staring into a shop window for five
minutes. It was filled with hymn books, tracts, garish biblical
illustrations, and the face of the proprietor gazing suspiciously at
me from between two curtains. Being thus reminded, I went in for
a new Bible.

The bookseller had a high, noble forehead, long tapering

fingers, and a clerical suit. The atmosphere of the shop was purple with reverence. After he had satisfied himself that I wasn't contemplating a smash-and-grab, and seeing I was a Canadian and therefore grossly overpaid, he offered me a rare Italian gold-tooled Bible weighing forty pounds that had once belonged to the Duke of Radcliffe's mistress and was attractively stained with port wine. The bookseller assured me it had been the very best port wine available. Next I was offered a gray pigskin binding with blind tooling and painted line work with a dedicated flyleaf thick enough to deflect a .303 bullet. This cost a mere seventy guineas. Finally we settled on a small St. James in bookbinding leather guaranteed free from harmful acids, for which I paid ten shillings. Later, on examining the rear cover, I found the correct price to be five and sixpence.

I had lunch at the Savoy, then went for another walk; but, getting tired of saluting senior officers along Whitehall, I turned onto the Victoria Embankment and watched the snowflakes extinguishing themselves in the river. Then back to the hotel, where I met a Canadian officer (I must say I thought he was English at first) called Renny Whiteoak. I also thought he was a bit squiffy, the way he kept babbling on about someone called Jalna, no doubt some French girl he'd met on active service. To listen to him you'd have thought that Jalna was the most wonderful creation on earth; but I know these affairs — they never last.

Mrs. Lewis

My next encounter with the horse was in May. I'd got on quite well with Robert Lewis, and was delighted when he invited me back for his last weekend at home before leaving for France. Brian had been invited too, but was unable to come.

Robert was out when I arrived on the Thursday evening, but was due back any minute. I met his mother for the first time, being ushered into the presence by a diminutive housekeeper I hadn't met before.

Mrs. Lewis was sitting straight-backed in a chaise longue in the room with the piano, knitting a pair of bullet-proof combinations, or perhaps it was a muffler. She had a long, aristocratic face and a voice that rattled the leaded windows.

"It's a gentleman, mum," the housekeeper announced. "He said he was expected, mum."

"*I* did not expect him," Mrs. Lewis said severely. "And for the last time will you cease addressing me as 'mum'? I am not your mum, and even if I were I could hardly be expected to acknowledge such an ugly offspring, especially one who conversed in a foreign tongue."

"I keep telling you it's no a foreign tongue, mum; it's Scottish," the little housekeeper said equably.

"Who is this uniformed person?" Mrs. Lewis went on, unheeding. "Surely you know by now that the gas meter is in the cellar."

"He's no the gas man, mum; he's a military gentleman."

"Bartholomew W. Bandy," I said, bowing.

"Brandy? Never heard of him. Give him a cup of tea and sixpence, and send him away."

"He says Master Robert invited him, mum."

"Indeed? Then he had better sit down, I suppose." Mrs. Lewis looked at me, or rather, raked me fore and aft. Not a shade of expression crossed her long, lined, haughty face. "My son," she said, when the housekeeper had gone, "is in the habit of bringing home some very odd company, Mr. Brandy, but on this occasion I must say he seems to have excelled himself."

"You mustn't flatter me, Mrs. Lewis; it goes to my head."

"There seems to be plenty of room for it there; indeed, you have the largest face I have ever come across."

I nodded. "It's sometimes a very time-consuming task washing it."

"Let us hope that that does not deter you too often, Mr. Brandy. However, I don't think we need go into your face any further this afternoon."

"No, ma'am; I try to avoid it myself."

"Very commendable, I am sure," Mrs. Lewis boomed. She examined me carefully for a moment longer, then patted the cushion at her side. "Come and sit here." I did. "And now," she said, "would you care to paw me —?"

"*Paw* you?"

"Paw me some port."

We exchanged compliments until Katherine arrived. She wore the same simple white dress as at our first meeting, but had added a jade necklace. She smiled.

"I hope I'm not too late to save you," she said. "Oh. I see

I am. I hope you didn't pay any attention to Mother, especially as she means everything she says."

That was the effect Mrs. Lewis always had on people: their dialogue took on a literary flavour.

"Your friend is a very argumentative fellow," Mrs. Lewis said crossly.

"Oh, is he? Then he must have been holding his own."

"Holding his own what?" Mrs. Lewis said, looking outraged.

"We've been having a very interesting discussion about my face," I said hurriedly.

"It wasn't the least interesting," Mrs. Lewis said, starting to rise. I dashed over to help her. She bellowed. "Mind my rheumatism, you fool."

"She's offended," Katherine said, giving her mother an affectionate hug, "because it's usually her own face that comes up for discussion."

"I can see that it would be a fascinating topic," I said gallantly, "with endless possibilities."

"Your friend," Mrs. Lewis said, "is argumentative, disrespectful, and impossible. Instead of looking suitably overawed in my presence he had the impudence to sit beside me with a casualness and lack of timidity that suggested he was interviewing me for political office, a bishopric, or some such disreputable position." So saying, the old lady turned her redoubtable prow toward the door and started to sail out at half-speed, gasping angrily as her rheumatism twinged. I followed respectfully.

"I understand," she said, turning at the door and glaring at me, "that I'll be unable to avoid your face during the next three days."

The old devil. She must have known all the time who I was.

"Fortunately," she went on, "I have been resigned to the inevitable ever since that hitherto squeamish person Lady Travellan cut her throat after poisoning her head gardener with his own weed killer."

"She didn't cut her throat at all," Katherine said. "She fled to America."

"Oh, did she? Well, it amounts to the same thing," Mrs. Lewis said, and, tapping me sharply on the head with her knitting needles, wallowed out of the room. Her angry gasps faded into the distance.

"She likes you," Katherine said wonderingly.

Sex and Death

The evening we went down for dinner at the local village was the first time I had been away from the squadron in about a month and a half, not counting my strolls in the neighbourhood. Since my narrow escape from being raped I had kept completely clear of Louise and the farm.

There were four of us: Wordsworth, Scadding, Darwin, and myself. We walked the two miles, talking shop and other dirt. I had a reason to celebrate, as I had just scored another triple victory over two two-seaters and an Albatross that tried to intervene, an achievement that automatically made me one of the squadron's élite. I was also considered ripe for the loony bin, for to attack even one two-seater was considered the height of stupidity; but nobody had told me this beforehand.

The village was a drab huddle of cottages without even a church. However, one of the more enterprising inhabitants had converted the ground floor of her house into a café which served quite good meals for only two or three francs. We had a bottle of wine each – I'd given up drinking but saw no harm in vin rouge, it didn't really count as intoxicating liquor – and everyone became quite jolly.

The proprietress, a Madame Malfait, was plainly fascinated by Wordsworth's baldness but even more by Scadding's unique leer. She spoke no English. She told us her husband had been killed in 1914, following this information with several heavy sighs.

"I wonder if that's an invitation for one of us to take his place," Scadding said in English.

We looked at her. She wasn't unattractive. Her hips were perhaps a shade motherly.

"How about it, Wordy?" Scadding said. "She's interested in you. If you like, we'll keep your wine hot if you want to pop upstairs."

"I leave that kind of thing to you unmarried chaps," Wordsworth answered. He had recently acquired a pipe. He blew down it, creating a spine-chilling gurgle.

"Didn't know you were married, old boy."

"On my last leave, to the ugliest girl in the world," Wordsworth said, gargling complacently.

Madame Malfait nodded and beamed at her aviators as if she understood every word.

"How about it, Madame?" Scadding smiled up at her, his eyes bright with lust. "By gad, I wouldn't mind having two handfuls of those jolly old buttocks." He continued to smile charmingly. Madame smiled back and looked at me inquiringly.

"The monsieur said he wouldn't mind having two pounds of butter if you had any to spare," I translated.

She smiled, shrugged, and went into a voluble explanation to the effect that butter was hard to come by.

"What did you tell her?" Scadding asked.

"I told her you wanted to sleep with her. She replied that, alas, she suffers from insomnia."

"Tell her that what I have in mind is the best soporific in the world."

"The monsieur said he has enjoyed your meal so much that as a mark of gratitude he would like to help you wash the dishes."

She replied, shocked, that an officer couldn't do a thing like that.

"She said she always does that kind of thing in the kitchen and that she couldn't expect an officer to make love among the pots and pans. It wouldn't be delicate."

"Tell her I'm ready to make love in the sink, breadbox, kitchen table, anywhere," Scadding said.

"The monsieur insists. In civilian life he was a professional dishwasher and he wants to keep his hand in."

No, no, she couldn't permit it. An officer of the gallant English Army washing dishes? Certainly not. Madame was getting flustered. She looked at Scadding with indignation mixed with a little concern.

"She said her favourite place was the sink, for her husband always made love to her at the sink after drying the dishes."

"Tell her it sounds awkward but I'm game."

"He says, Madame, that it's part of English military training to wash dishes. It's the first thing they learn in the army before they go on to advanced training in peeling potatoes, ironing, sewing, knitting, and gunnery."

Madame replied that she had long since ceased to be surprised at anything the English did and that if the monsieur really insisted . . .

"She said," I told Scadding, "all right, provided you wait for her signal."

"What signal?" Scadding asked.

"I'll find out." I turned back to Madame Malfait. "The monsieur does insist. You can see plainly how the thought of dishwashing excites him. But one should warn you that washing dishes gives him another kind of excitement, how would one say, the excitement sexual, and the more dishes he washes, the greater is the erotic effect."

She blushed crimson and her eyes sparkled with offended dignity. She said it was disgraceful. I interrupted.

"If you want your honour to remain intact," I told her, "do not on any account smooth your dress in a seductive fashion, for this is the signal that will turn him into an animal with uncontrollable and raging desires."

"I shall be very careful," she said agitatedly, then went on to wonder what the British Army was coming to. Still, if the English officer was adamant, well, it was her duty to maintain the entente cordiale; but assuredly she would exercise great caution.

"The signal," I told Scadding, "will come when she smooths down her dress in a seductive fashion."

He jumped up. Madame bowed to him stiffly, turned, and went out. Scadding followed with an armful of dishes. Darwin and Wordsworth, both of whom spoke some French, looked at me. Darwin half rose to call Scadding back, then slowly sank back into his seat. We had to wait a long time for Scadding. Finally he sauntered in from the kitchen smoothing *his* dress. He looked only moderately relaxed.

"What happened?" Darwin asked at last.

"What do you think? It was excellent, too. Only, she certainly made me work for it, the devil."

"How?"

"Well, I thought she'd never get through washing up. Took simply ages. I don't mind telling you I started to get a bit impatient when she began taking down *clean* dishes from the cupboard and washing them, too."

As Madame didn't come back, we placed a few francs on the table and left thoughtfully. All the way back I kept saying, "Sex, sex, sex. What on earth," I mused aloud, "is France coming to?" which made everyone look at me rather queerly.

Chock-Full of Aplomb

I was walking back after breakfast one day with Rolls-Revell when the major stopped us.

"You're off for the day, aren't you, Bandy? You too, Rolly? I'm going to Boulogne. Would you like to come? Well, hurry up," he said, gesturing fussily, "the car's waiting."

It took most of the morning to make the sixty-odd miles to the Channel. Rolls-Revell, imperiously surveying the usual military chaos through his monocle from the back seat, looked so lordly and contemptuous that several officers mistook him for a staff officer and had flung themselves into a ditch to avoid having to salute before realizing their mistake.

After a leisurely lunch in the town during which Ashworth became expansive and showed us pictures of his wife and nineteen children (he happened to have his photograph album with him), he confided that I had been recommended for the Military Cross for my exploit in shooting down the two two-seaters single-handed.

After the meal he went to visit some staff friends, and, pleasantly primed with wine and champagne, Rolly and I strolled about Boulogne. Compared with the local village it seemed a bustling metropolis. Passing a dusty-looking millinery shop, I suddenly remembered that I owed Louise a dress.

I'd never bought any women's clothes before and I felt a bit nervous about it. I stared into the shop window for quite some time before plucking up courage to enter. The window contained just one dress, a long spotted frock with frills at the bottom, or rather at the ankle.

The interior was dark and smelled of dust and old corsets. A woman with a fantastically long body came up. It was the longest trunk I'd ever seen in my life. She seemed to have a habit of rubbing her left thumb and forefinger together as if testing material or hinting that she was open to bribery; in fact, I started to reach for my wallet out of pure reflex. Rolly was looking around and caught the eye of a girl of about nineteen behind the counter, who had been looking bored until he came in. She was now looking vaguely taken aback at the sight of a painfully contrasted pair of aviators, one tall and looking like a bland horse, the other short and looking like an effete fox.

I cleared my throat. "I wish a dress, Madame," I said baldly.

The proprietress looked disapproving. However, business was business. "Certainly, sir," she said discreetly. "And what size does the monsieur take?"

It was obviously going to be one of those days. I drew myself up. "It is for a young woman," I said coldly.

"Ah. Of course. And what size is the young woman, sir?"

"Eh?"

"What size is the bosom of the young woman," the proprietress said patiently.

"Er . . . oh," I said, and raised my hands and started to illustrate, then quickly put them behind my back again. "Large," I said. "Quite large." (*Tout a fait grand.*)

"That must be Louise," Rolls-Revell said.

I looked at him sharply, but before I could say anything Madame had started to prompt me by quoting various measurements in what seemed to me excessive numbers of centimetres.

"Oh, no," I said, sweating a little, "not as large as all that."

Madame indicated the girl behind the counter. "Is it as large, perhaps, as that of my assistant?"

The assistant drew herself up and took a deep breath. I went over and studied her. So did Rolly. His monocle fell out.

"Yes," I said. "That's . . . that's about it. Perhaps — " I cleared my throat. "Perhaps, incredible though it may seem, even somewhat larger."

The assistant looked depressed and expelled her breath, which blew a pair of lacy nether garments off a wire rack.

"Larger?" Rolly said, studying the assistant. "Oh, I don't know. . . ."

The assistant smiled gratefully at him and started to take another deep breath.

I was beginning to get flustered by what appeared to me to be an unseemly curiosity on the part of the Madame.

"A commodious robe, that is all I wish," I said with dignity, and started mopping my brow, until I realized I was doing so with the pair of lacy nether garments I had retrieved, and hastily put them down and looked quickly at the ceiling, where my eyes fell on several pairs of houseflies copulating in a veritable entomological orgy.

The proprietress just couldn't let the subject drop. "But it is necessary," she was saying, rubbing her thumb and forefinger together in a manner that now seemed slightly obscene, "that I know the size of the young woman, sir."

"Quick," Rolly said at the window. "There's a woman going past who's about the right size." The rest of us rushed to the window and peered through the curtains. "Hurry," Rolly was saying, "half of her is already out of sight."

We strained over each other to peer down the street. An elderly shopper who had stopped to look in the window recoiled and hurried on. Too late to examine the one Rolly had meant, we all looked this way and that for a facsimile of Louise.

"How about that one?"

"No," I said.

"That one, Monsieur?"

"Too — too pendulous," I said uneasily, following the woman down the street with my eyes.

"There," the assistant shouted in my ear. "How's that one?"

"Too close together," Rolly said, warming to the problem.

"There. There's a fine bosom —"

"No." Rolly shook his head.

"Ah. Here is a fine prominent citizen."

"Too wide apart," Rolly said.

"Look here," I said, turning to Rolly, "I'm supposed to be buying this dress, not you. Whose bosom is this, anyway?"

"Regard, sir," Madame said eagerly. "There is an example magnificent."

"Yes," I said, and followed the girl down the street interestedly. When I got back to the shop, I said, "No. But it was close."

However, I thought it was about time to put a stop to all this. "Perhaps," I said pointedly, "it would be easier if you showed me a robe or two."

This struck the proprietress as an inspiration, and she came back with an armful of dresses. "Come here, Cecile," she said. The assistant came forward, smiling at Rolly, and had a dress fitted to her.

"Too fussy," I said.

Cecile modelled another. "Too plain," I said.

This went on for some time. I finally purchased the polka-dotted dress in the window with the frills at the bottom, or to be exact, at the ankle; then we all went out for a cup of coffee to celebrate, and the next thing I knew Rolly had disappeared with the assistant, leaving me holding the bag, or to be exact, the proprietress, who had, as I say, the longest trunk I'd ever seen.

I soon made some feeble excuse and went shopping by myself and bought some notepaper, a silk scarf, and a parcel of rotten pears. Of course I didn't know the pears were rotten until I opened the parcel, when it was too late to return them. Rolly, when he turned up later at the agreed rendezvous, had also bought notepaper as well as a stick of sealing wax and a family heirloom the assistant had given him, a pornographic book called *The Dialogues of Luisa Sigea*. He read one page, the blood drained from his face, and his monocle steamed over.

On the way back I had a look at it too, and discovered there was a lot more to sex than I had thought. In fact the book made it seem like a branch of mechanical engineering. I had to take cold showers for several days.

from The Bandy Papers, Vol. i

Aunt Matilda's Bed-Time Story

Keith Crombie & J. E. McDougall

"Come, children, and gather about your dear old Aunt Matilda and hear a nice story before you go to bed."

"As Mary Elizabeth stepped out of the bank with her alimony cheque, she suddenly came face to face with the Iddelywumps himself.

" 'Fancy seeing you here !' she said.

"The Iddelywumps flapped his purple wings angrily at the insult, tipped three of his scales, and slowly uncoiled his tail from a hydrant.

" 'I haven't eaten for a year,' he growled.

" 'What do you eat?' asked Mary Elizabeth.

" 'Little boys and girls,' was the gruff reply.

" 'Oh, you naughty, naughty thing!' cried Mary Elizabeth, 'you should love little boys and girls.'

" 'I do love them,' he snorted, *'fried with butter and sugar!'*

"At this the Iddelywumps tied a beautiful pink ribbon on his left horn and sighed deeply into a near-by ashcan.

" 'You don't know what love is,' he grumbled. 'By the way, you look sweet enough to eat, yourself !'

"So saying, he grabbed Mary Elizabeth and whisked her off to his dreadful, dark dungeon, full of snakes and rats and spiders and everything.

" 'You will stay in there, till you wither up and die,' he said as he bolted the iron door.

"Poor Mary Elizabeth started to cry and think of her dear grass-widowed mother, when suddenly she heard a cheery voice at the grating over her head.

" 'Who are you?' she cried.

" 'Oh, I am Prince Rupert, B.C.' was the melodious answer, 'and I am going to save you.'

"Just then a tremendous terrific noise was heard and the awful Iddelywumps rushed up, wrung the Prince's neck and flung the body far, far away into the deep, deep valley full of pebbles and goitres.

"Then he ate Mary Elizabeth all up — the nasty, nasty Iddelywumps!

"And now children," said Aunt Matilda, "toddle off to bed."

And all the little children laughed merrily, O so merrily, and went to their little cribs to dream sweetly of the Iddelywumps.

from Sackcloth and Splashes

The Typical Moron

Mary Lowrey Ross

"Let's see, you go to the movies twice a week don't you?" Miss A. asked.

"Three times a week sometimes," I said. "Why?"

Miss A. checked in her notebook. "How about reading habits?" she asked. "Do you read newspapers, magazines and books, and in what order?"

"I don't read them in any order," I said.

Miss A. shook her head. "That could be bad," she said. "Now, let's see, Judgement." She glanced at my butterscotch dessert, "Questionable I should say. . . . "Learning rate, accuracy, swiftness. . . ." She tapped her pencil thoughtfully against her teeth. "Would you say poor?"

"Why ask me?" I said.

"The subject in these tests is supposed to co-operate," Miss A. said. "Let's see, there was the time you put the vacuum cleaner together wrong and nearly asphyxiated yourself using the dichloricide appliance instead of the shampoo. And the time you made a house-dress and got the placket up around the neck."

"Those are specialized aptitudes," I said.

"Well then, how about unskilled labour," Miss A. said. "Do you think you could earn five dollars a day and car-tickets?"

"Oh easily," I said, "I've often thought of taking it up."

"Foresight," Miss A. said. "That comes into it too. Can you save anything?"

"Not a cent," I said.

Miss A. considered. "The only thing that spoils the picture is that you *did* get beyond the eighth grade in school," she said. I had upset her theory and she smiled an entirely false smile of congratulation. "In other words you escape the category."

"Whose tests are these anyway?" I asked.

"Dr. Ruby Jo Reeves Kennedy's tests for typical moronic conditions," Miss A. said. "Dr. Kennedy applied it last year to 256 cases in Connecticut. It's a fascinating study. You ought to take it up."

"Thanks," I said, "I like to do my character-smearing in my own way."

"Nonsense," Miss A. said. "There's no disgrace about being a moron."

"I know," I said. "It's no worse than a bad cold."

That was quite the wrong attitude Miss A. said. "Dr. Ruby Jo Reeves Kennedy says herself that in their humble way morons are worthy citizens who bear their share of the world's burdens and do nothing to threaten the welfare of society."

I said after a moment, "What we really need is a survey of typical psychologists, I can think of a lot of test questions for Dr. Ruby Jo Reeves Kennedy."

"Such as what?" Miss A. asked.

"What is the actual proof of the non-existence of Santa Claus?" I said. "Why is the base of a psychological problem always wider than the hypothesis? What is the right-side-up of an upside-down cake? Why is a psychologist when she spins? And who is Dr. Ruby Jo Reeves Kennedy anyway?"

Miss A. shook her head. "They wouldn't be scientific," she said. "These studies are based on absolutely scientific tests. The whole idea is to help civilization by extending the known boundaries of human personality."

"I still don't see how civilization is going to be helped by proving that there are 256 scientifically certified morons in Connecticut," I said, "and it certainly won't help the morons."

"On the contrary," Miss A. said, "there is every reason to believe that the subjects, far from being humiliated by interrogation, feel that it adds to their human dignity to be used as instruments in the advancement of science. In fact the chief problem of the researcher is to sort out the scientific data from the wealth of material supplied. Even the simplest subjects recognize the impersonality of science and are eager to contribute their share. Look, I'll prove it to you."

She turned and beckoned to the waitress, who came over, taking her own time. She was a red-haired girl with a vigilant suspicious eye.

"If I might be permitted to ask you a question," Miss A. said, "Do you find your favourite entertainment in the movies?"

The waitress stared for some time in silence. Then she said, "What's the idea, you giving out passes?"

"Not exactly," Miss A. said. "This is in the nature of a survey." She paused. "A scientific test," she added encouragingly.

"I'm sorry, I got customers," the waitress said.

"But you like the movies," Miss A. said.

"They're o.k.," said the waitress.

"How about reading then?" Miss A. asked. "Do you read newspapers, magazines or books, and in what order?"

"I read them front to back like everybody else does," the waitress said sullenly.

"I see," Miss A. said. "Now how about speed, accuracy and learning rate?" She turned to me. "Deficient, wouldn't you say?"

"Listen — " the waitress said.

"For instance, I asked you to bring me a pot of hot water with my tea," Miss A. said. "I was quite clear about it, but you brought me a large pot of hot water in the tea." She paused, then went on quickly. "This is not of course a personal criticism. You must understand this is a purely scientific and impersonal test." She paused again, and when the waitress's face failed to brighten she went on, "Do you own a house?"

"What do you mean, do I own a house?" the waitress asked.

"In other words, you rent," Miss A. said. The interrogation was not going very well, but she went on briskly, "Are you able to save any money? Obviously you are not. Did you progress beyond the eighth grade in school?"

The waitress turned and glanced wildly towards another waitress who was advancing with a tray. Her face was deep red but when she turned back she had regained her composure. "If I could be permitted to ask you a question," she said, in an excellent though slightly falsetto imitation of Miss A.'s tone. "How would you like to be crowned with a plate of spaghetti?"

Miss A. turned to me. "You see," she said, "an almost perfect example of the type."

"What do you mean type?" the waitress cried. "Who do you think you are anyway?"

The approaching waitress laid a hand on her arm. "Listen Marlene, pipe down."

"Nobody's going to call me a type," Marlene cried. She turned to her friend. "Here's a customer asking for a plate of spaghetti, and I mean asking for it."

"Get out, quick!" I said to Miss A., and rather unexpectedly she withdrew, leaving the test unfinished. "It was just a mistake," I said hurriedly tucking a dollar under the plate. "She just happened to pick the wrong subject."

"I'll say she did," the waitress said. "Did you progress beyond the eighth grade!"

Her colour and her indignation had begun to subside. She picked up the dollar and tucked it into her cuff. "You certainly meet all kinds in this business," she said. "Just a typical moron."

from Saturday **Night**

from Himie Koshevoy's Treasure Jest of Best Puns

Children have a keen sense of sound and when this attribute is combined with their prolific imagination they arrive at some weird combinations of words they think they have heard. There was the little girl who returned after Sunday school and told her mother of a cross-eyed hairy animal named Gladly. After a lot of questioning mother was able finally to decipher: "Gladly, my cross-eyed bear." . . . The following week another young lady said the Sunday school lesson was about houses. The explanation went: "You know, the one about my shack, your shack and the bungalow."

Few explorers have had as many honours heaped on them as Michael Dolan and Francois Darlan. For a long time almost every issue of the National Geographic magazine contained some reference to one of their current or past exploits. They are best remembered in the world's great libraries for their storehouse of knowledge and detailed maps of the upper reaches of the Zambesi river. Their skeletons rest on its bank today (when not being used for a cannibal gambling game known as rolling the bones). You see, the two intrepid men were captured by man-eaters who were such gourmets they hung all their meat for at least six weeks for proper aging. So after Darlan and Dolan had been taken prisoner, they were suspended over a cliff to hang by rawhide straps tied to their wrists. But theirs was not to be a normal, peaceful, cannibal-type death. Some boys of the village, playing along the cliff edge, began to saw away at the leather straps with sharp stones. Looking up, it was then Dolan uttered the memorable words that rank him with Stanley. "Darlan," cried he, "they're fraying our thong!"

When Syngman Rhee was in power in Korea, he sent his son to the United States to study journalism. He told the lad, who was much more modest and charming than his stern father, to apply for a job with the late Mr. Luce whose publishing empire included

Time, Fortune and Life magazines. The publisher put young Rhee on the editorial staff of Life so he could earn some bread while pursuing his new career. On his first day in New York he toured the city to acquaint himself with some of its fascinating aspects. He found them so interesting he tarried longer than he planned and the Life executives became worried about the possibility of his being lost. An agent was assigned to find him and he searched for hours before he came upon the smiling Oriental with the shining face. The searcher's relief at finding the important youth can be judged from the detective's glad greeting as he cried: "Ah, sweet Mister Rhee of Life, at last I've found you!"

A poor, rundown monastery on the Suffolk Downs decided it must find some commercial avenue to obtain money for rebuilding. The abbot studied hard and came to the decision to establish a fish and chip shop at the gate. Brother John and Brother Leo were put to the task and Brother John found he had an innate talent for deep-frying the fish to just the right taste while Brother Leo's forte was French fries. Each became well-known for his part in the succulent snack and the locals soon learned to ask for one man or the other when they wanted just fish or just chips. One night, a man went in who wanted just fish. He said to the cowled counterman: "I say, are you the fish friar?" "No," said Brother Leo, "I'm the chip monk."

A Spaniard, Juan by name and not nature, fell in love with Carmencita, a most possessive girl. She had heard the gossip that his was a wandering eye but it didn't surprise her because that trait was inherited from his primitive ancestors when they swung continually from limb to limb. She decided there was only one way she could be certain her man would remain faithful until she could exchange the altar for the halter. By accompanying him everywhere, every waking moment, she became the village joke but her vigilance was rewarded when she was able finally to wed her suitor without his ever once being unfaithful, a state of grace hitherto unheard of in all Spain. Everywhere she went, eager, enquiring maidens would ask her for the secret of her success and her wise answer can be condensed to seven words: you always herd the Juan you love.

Many a fund-raising campaign has been launched to assist the starving in India where famine, like death and taxes, seems inevitable. In this regard there is an apocryphal story about the illustrious Joey Smallwood, premier of Newfoundland. Touched by the plight of the East Indians and with the unanimous consent of the skippers of the fishing fleet, he sent off a large portion of the annual catch from the Grand Banks. When the fish had been loaded aboard the mercy freighter, the captain thought some historic message should accompany the generous gift. He radioed Smallwood, asking if he would apply his ingenuity to the idea. The premier was equal to the demand. He wirelessed back: "Nehru, my cod to thee."

A Short Story

C. B. Pyper

The other day a man asked me why I didn't write a short story. He said there was money in short stories. I said I would do anything there was money in, so I wrote one, with short chapters by way of innovation. Now to see if I can get the money in it out of it. Here is the story:

Chapter One
Mamie — that was her name — was deliriously happy. Her sky was unclouded. She had youth, a compact and loads of refinement. She used everything the magazine advertisements told her she ought to use, and the tea leaves had promised her a meeting with a dark stranger. As she sat at her little window looking out over Colony Street North her little heart swelled with joy.

Chapter Two
Bob — he had been called Bob in early youth — was gay. His future was before him. He had youth, personality plus and

plus fours. He used the right razor, the right razor blade, the right toothbrush, the right toothpaste, the right hair grease, the right socks and the right sock suspenders, and he had athlete's foot. As he dialled the radio in his home on Colony Street South, he wouldn't have traded himself in for Bing Crosby.

Chapter Three

Mamie and Bob were, in a sense, strangers. They had lots of friends apiece, but each had never met the other. If they had thought of this they would have been sad, for they seemed made the one for the other and the other for the one. They didn't think of it and so they didn't think of it. It was sad, but, in a way, perhaps natural, for you never know what Fate has in store till the store opens.

Chapter Four

Far away on the ocean their parents — Bob's father and mother and Mamie's father and mother — were speeding to their loved ones, in different boats. Bob's father and mother were in one boat and Mamie's father and mother were in one boat. They were strangers, too, in a sense, for though Bob's father knew Bob's mother and Mamie's father knew Mamie's mother, and vice versa, Bob's father and mother didn't know Mamie's father and mother, or vice versa.

Chapter Five

It was a rainy day in Montreal when the two boats docked, and it was a rainy evening as the fond parents boarded the train that was to bring them back to Winnipeg. By a strange coincidence, they got on different trains, for though Bob's father and mother got on the same train and Mamie's father and mother got on the same train, Mamie's father and mother didn't get on the same train as Bob's father and mother. This was because these travelled Canadian Pacific while those travelled Canadian National. Nevertheless Fate was bringing these six characters nearer and nearer every minute.

Chapter Six

It was a fine evening in Winnipeg when the trains arrived, and there, exactly at the right stations, respectively, were Bob and Mamie. The meetings were happy, but it doesn't look as if there would be enough room to describe both, and it would not be fair to describe one without describing the other.

Chapter Seven

Anyhow they got into two taxicabs — Bob's father and mother and Bob in one, and Mamie's father and mother and Mamie in the other — and turned for home. Fate was bringing them closer and closer, and working fast.

Chapter Eight

By a strange coincidence, or was it the hand of Fate, the two taxis arrived at the corner of Portage and Main together and turned down Portage side by side. Neither Bob nor Mamie knew, but there in one taxi was Bob and there in the other was Mamie. If they could only have guessed. If even their parents could only have guessed. But they didn't know. None of them knew. Even the taxi drivers didn't know, though taxi drivers know a lot more than they're given credit for.

Chapter Nine

At every red light they could have spoken to each other easily, if they had only known. Once Bob looked across idly and caught a glimpse of blonde hair, and once Mamie, looking past her father's whiskers, caught a glimpse of a dark, nicely oiled head, but neither guessed. The time was not ripe. Fate had brought them close together, but had not introduced them yet.

Chapter Ten

Together the taxis sped down Portage, to the Colony Street intersection. There, at last, brought together by Fate to the same street, they turned away in different directions. Mamie's taxi went north and Bob's taxi went south. So they never met. Fate had brought them together only to part them again. It was sad, but necessary. If they had met this would have been a longer story, and there is no use writing a long story till you see if you can get any money out of a short one.

from One Thing After Another

Ladders

Norris Hodgins

"I was talking yesterday to Armand Laflamme in the shipping room," said Lem suddenly, looking up from the plate of bacon and eggs on which he was breakfasting.

The Sage beamed encouragement. A true democrat, he approved of treating one's fellow workers, even shipping clerks, without hauteur.

"Seems he knows of a small ladder-manufacturing business that's going on the market soon," added Lem. "He thinks I could get it reasonable." He stirred his coffee meditatively as he tried to visualize himself in the role of Captain of Industry instead of thimble-packing, which he found boring.

"That's odd," observed Petunia. "Only last Sunday morning the Rector had a reference to ladders in his sermon. He said ladders have a poetical or even a spiritual significance as they represent man's urge to climb upward . . ."

"Or downward," put in The Sage who, as usual, made the third at the Parsley breakfast table.

"Tennyson, it's true," continued The Sage conversationally, "held that men may rise on stepping-stones of *their dead selves* to higher things but most poets favour ladders, possibly for their association with Chivalry, which was very romantic and happened mostly in the Middle Ages."

"What I was wondering . . ."

"In those days," explained The Sage, "knights spent a good deal of their time rescuing damsels, but the quest usually began with a hunt for a stout ladder needed in mounting, on account of their galvanized cuirass, corselet, girdle, etc. Wicked barons, too, needed ladders when ravaging the castles of their kinfolk. As these kin usually tried to poke them off or douse them with boiling pitch, pedestrians were often spattered with pitch or flattened under several hundredweights of armour-clad baron, thus giving rise to the current superstition about walking under ladders."

"I was wondering," persisted Lem, "if there's likely to be any *future* in ladders."

"So far as I can judge," said The Sage, "there should always be a demand for ladders. Not sensational, perhaps, but steady. They may not *always* be poetic but they're uncommonly handy, especially to a man who falls down a well. As a rule," he added thoughtfully, "odes and blank verse will leave him cold but he'll clutch at a ladder, even a quite coarse one of undressed hemlock, if sound."

"Why *will* people fall down wells?" frowned Petunia, who, as a careful housewife, liked things tidy.

"When a cow or other domesticated beast falls down a well," said The Sage, "it's usually the result of negligence, viz., forgetting to place planks over the opening after you've got your well dug. As a rule, however, when a *man* falls down a well it's not of his own volition but because of gravity, the Natural Force that causes everything to be attracted to everyhing else (for example, fluff to a blue-serge suit) and tends to pull towards the centre of the earth everything that's loose and heavy.

"Hence," he added tolerantly, "from the time you slip until you hit the water with a splash you're not strictly responsible for your movement or speed."

"Armand thinks the business may be a bit run down," began Lem. "Needs pushing . . . "

"In my judgement," said The Sage, "ladder manufacturers haven't shown much initiative. Like the first ones made, ladders still consist mainly of two strips of wood or metal with rungs laid crossways for stepping on — though sailors use uprights of rope as this is often good for a laugh.

"No serious attempt has been made," he continued earnestly, turning to his host, "to increase velocity by adapting to ladder-making the revolutionary principles involved in the development of the wheel, jet propulsion, and the like. I doubt, in fact, if the average man can swarm up a ladder any faster today than he could have done a century ago. If he strikes a loose rung, of course," he added, "he can *come down* at a rattling pace. But barons descended noisily, too, by all accounts."

Lem moved restively and looked at the clock. He'd have to move soon if he was to get his bus.

"I've examined this business pretty narrowly, at one time or another," went on The Sage, "but I can't recall a single note of modernity or what we industrial designers call 'eye appeal' in the average ladder offered on the market today. Except, of course, in the case of ladders in nylon stockings."

Lem rose and made preparations for departure.

"To my mind, however," advised The Sage hurriedly, "it would be best to aim at a strictly male clientele, especially at the beginning. Ladders," he explained, "have never been popular with the fair sex, as few women look their best on a ladder. And besides," he concluded, "women instinctively distrust ladders owing to their tendency to fold up when washing the kitchen ceiling.

"Also," he called after the retreating Lem, "they claim it makes them giddy."

"H-ph-m," muttered Lem, closing the door behind him.

"Oh, well," said Petunia, musingly, "it'll probably blow over. Lem gets these fits."

The Sage gathered his things together and moved to the door.

"If it comes to a choice," he suggested, "I think you should urge him to forget the poetry and try to make something of the ladder business, as ladders are in keener demand nowadays."

He nodded encouragingly, and went out.

from The Parsleys and The Sage

Brutally Explicit! Rossi's Erotic Tour de Force

Alexander Ross

(Being an exclusive interview with Allessandro Rossi, the brooding, brilliant, devilishly handsome young director of the film everyone's talking about, Last Audit in Bowmanville.)

He walks into the hotel room like a brooding spirit left over from a 1931 tea dance, a black Borsalino pulled down over one craggy eyebrow, the long scarf flung carelessly, romantically, about his neck. A sardonic smile plays about his full, sensuous lips.

Rossi seems serenely undisturbed by the furor his latest film has provoked. Pauline Kael has called Last Audit " . . . a filmic event as significant as the last flight of the dirigible Hindenburg . . . the screen's first unflinching look at Central Ontario eroticism."

Unsurprisingly, it has been banned in Bowmanville, picketed by a committee of outraged mothers in Tillsonburg, denounced from the pulpit in Bramalea, and roundly condemned by the Ontario Institute of Chartered Accountants.

The plot, as everyone knows by now, grapples powerfully with the twin themes of love and death as they affect the practice of accountancy in Central Ontario. Malcolm McRectitude, a 53-year-old CPA, who in his spare time enjoys collecting and cataloguing used paper clips, has spent thirty-eight years with Clarkson Gordon, and has just been passed over for a junior partnership in the firm. Despondent, he goes out on his Last Audit, to examine the books of Meat-o-Rama, the popular chain of surrogate hamburger outlets.

There at the fast-fry counter, he meets Maria, a pouting, sensuous teenager who is trying to forget a brief, casual affair with a mayonnaise salesman.

The inevitable happens and, with consummate artistry, Rossi's cameras pitilessly record each shocking detail. Before they are even properly introduced, Malcolm and Maria, in a scene which Kaspars Dzeguze has called "an erotic tour de force," pelt each other with gobs of mayonnaise and squirt catsup at each other from little plastic containers.

Nothing is spared — not even the audience's sensibilities. In one brutally explicit scene, Malcolm forces Maria to commit tax evasion by adding fictitious dependents to her T-4 form. Later, the fiscally sophisticated gamine initiates Malcolm into the perverse mysteries of double-entry bookkeeping.

Is it art? Or is it embezzlement? Critics, churchmen and spokesmen for the Ontario Institute of Chartered Accountants are still hotly debating the question. But Rossi — the calm eye at the centre of this moral hurricane — affects to be uninterested in the current controversy. He's already planning his next film, a searing exposé of above-the-waist premarital petting in Central Ontario.

Twirling a small tumbler of cognac in one hand and gesticulating with the other with a tiny cigar, sprawling in deep languor on the sofa of his Park Plaza Hotel suite, Rossi unburdened himself to this reporter, in a wide-ranging conversation on his life and art:

"Ah God," he began. "I am so . . . so *weary*. This film, these infernal publicity tours, the constant attention of the press, the starlets who importune me even in my bath . . . it is — how you say? — it makes of the soul a withered begonia, yes?"

Reporter: Signor Rossi, do you feel the fact that you were born in Kapuskasing had any influence on your choice of thematic material?

Rossi: There is an old proverb in Kapuskasing — "The artist cannot escape his origins." So, yes, I would have to acknowledge this influence in my work, yes. In my boyhood, there was very much playing of the hockey with — how you say? — the frozen road-apples being used for pucks, and you will notice this image recurring again and again in my films. In The Legionnaire, for example, you will notice the road-apple slapshot through the window of the Canadian Legion Hall. That was my statement, if you will, on Central Ontario militarism. The frozen road-apple is my — how you say? — my metaphor.

Reporter: But there's no road-apple in Last Audit.

Rossi: No, but did you take a close look at those Meat-o-Rama hamburgers? The image is transformed, but the metaphor endures.

Reporter: I see. Signor Rossi, some critics have remarked on the influence of Antonioni and Rossellini in your work. Do you feel that this is a fair observation?

Rossi: (With a sardonic smile): They were, yes, competent craftsmen in their day. But I cannot claim direct filmic lineage from these men. Technically, Last Audit is perhaps a homage to the 1948 Foster Hewitt hockey broadcasts and the early Roger Ramjet cartoons. But my art, please signorina, is my own. No one but I can assume the blame.

Reporter: Some critics have charged that Last Audit is — well, that it's obscene, that it's fiscal pornography masquerading as art. Do you . . .

Rossi: (Excitedly): Fiscal pornography! Poof! I say poof to these people! True Davidson and Gordon Sinclair debating on the radio about the old-age pension — that to me is obscene. Wasaga Beach! Hah! That too is obscene! But two human beings smearing each other with mayonnaise . . . we are dealing here with reality on a symbolic level. The cinema cannot deal in compromise!

Reporter: One final question, Mr. Rossi. What do you wear to bed?

Rossi: (Coyly): A Timex.

from The Toronto Star

Afternoon of an Art Critic

Norman Ward

One of the abiding pleasures of entering an art exhibit nowadays lurks in the element of surprise. In the old days, before artists emancipated themselves from the necessity of being artistic, the most you could count on in an art gallery was a collection of painting and sculptures that seemed to be about people and things. Now, thanks no doubt to the mechanization of everything from typewriter erasers to the crating of eggs, you can never be sure. You may, to be honest, still encounter painting, including abstracts, of dazzling loveliness. But you are just as likely to find a series based on whittled automobile fenders, fragmented glass eyes mixed with iron filings, or welded mouse hides in isinglass. Whatever else may be said of the contemporary tradition, it is certainly entitled to full marks as the funniest in recorded history.

This impression is heightened if you attend a show in the company of an *aficionado*. A friend of mine who feels obliged to consider everything new as good recently took me to a travelling exhibition by one school of toilers who, he kindly warned me, were way out in front. Once you gave it the once-over, you could see what he meant.

"Doesn't it just give you the dithyrambic jitters?" he said ecstatically as we stood in the doorway surveying the accumulated debris; and certainly it did that.

The centrepiece was a huge mobile suspended from a single strand. It looked like, and in fact was, a four-drawer office filing cabinet, with the drawers extended to various lengths. I mentioned this.

"You're missing the whole point," my adviser replied, "the symbolism of it all. It's hanging," he added, "on a deep-sea tuna-fishing line."

I had missed both the string and the symbolism, and admitted it manfully. My companion shrugged me off, as if he were not surprised. "Incidentally," he said, "it's not true that the thing fell the other day and hurt five people. Only three were under it, and only one of them was hurt badly."

It didn't seem enough to make a fuss about. "The symbolism being that the sculptor should have used a hundred-pound-test-line instead of a fifty?"

"No, no." My friend always humours me when under the influence of art. "I happen to know most of these artists, and that one hates having to work in an office to make a living."

"I get it. He creates filing cabinets that will drop on people, hoping he'll get the right ones."

"Not at all. The sculpture is a gallows on which he has hung a typical chunk of office equipment that epitomizes all office work."

"What about the tuna line?"

"Oh, that. That happens to be all he had around the house at the time. He would have preferred piano wire, to suggest garrotting as well as hanging. But he didn't have a piano."

"It's a nice wholesome conception."

"Yes, isn't it? He's captured beautifully that depressed feeling of being boxed in that offices give one. There's an almost lyrical sense of spiritlessness and frustration about it. Elegant, really. Gives you the idea that space isn't a soaring glory after all, but just one big cosmic snarl."

A new dimension opened before me. I gazed around at the blobs and scratches that adorned the walls, and moved in for a closer look. I had to step carefully around several sculptures that looked as if their fabricator had first shaped them in the usual manner and then dropped an anvil on them.

I stopped before a sequence of canvases of identical size, linked by curious names ranging from "Ten Yards" to "One Hundred Yards." Those in between were ingenious spatters of bright colours, some of them pure, others consisting of several pigments superimposed on each other in layers. "Ten Yards" was the most poorly coloured, and was full of holes. "One Hundred Yards" was all but blank. Except for the two on the ends, the pictures struck me as a uniformly cheerful row of portraits of something vaguely familiar, probably amoebas.

I grinned at my friend, but before I could say that I rather liked them he gave voice. "Splendid, aren't they?" he asked, chin in hand. "That assonant frangibility." He gestured towards the paintings. "That magnificent air of niggling poltroonery, of pusillanimous skulking. They are completely successful."

"Successful?"

"Yes. I know the artist well. He's a timid and even cowardly soul who has been trying for years to express himself with confidence. At last he's made it."

I looked at the pictures again. "They don't appear craven to me."

"You don't know him. The one thing that has everybody intrigued about these is how he did them."

I examined them carefully for a few moments. "His technique is obvious," I told the expert. "He used a shotgun, either twelve or sixteen gauge. I imagine he crammed the shells with little plastic bags of paint and fired away. That's why 'Ten Yards' is full of holes. He used too much powder."

"But not enough for 'One Hundred Yards'?"

"Either that, or he's a lousy shot."

My friend clapped his hands happily. "Superb, superb!" he cried. "How utterly honest of him to use a technique he had not yet mastered."

I spoke up for the defence. "It may be that the plastic bags wouldn't carry that far."

"No, no. He could have experimented, or left that canvas home. Don't you see that his sheer incompetence is an essential part of the truth he is seeking to reveal?"

It certainly explained a lot of the work I had seen in the past few years. "Are they all like that in this show?"

"Pretty well." We moved on to study a cynical but recognizable picture of a middle-aged woman, framed in a seat sawn from a common species of farm building. Next to it was a strikingly lifelike representation of a partridge mounted on a slab of pressed sawdust. "A fine piece," my friend observed, and we pushed on. "The smell is of course necessary," he asserted as if I were arguing with him, "but I do think the artist would have been well advised to have had the bird stuffed first."

"Perhaps that would have failed to be an accurate reflection of his integrity as a creator."

"True, true. They're a wonderfully miserable lot, this school, and they reveal it with tremendous skill. Could you beat that for unadulterated foot-shuffling evasiveness?" he asked, indicating a warty specimen that seemed to have eczema.

"It gives the impression that the painter is a small-time crook. With acne."

My friend clapped me on the back. "You're coming along like a house afire! Actually he's in the advertising business, and he's done time for bigamy. A born slubberdegullion if I ever saw one. And a sound, forthright painter whose every canvas exudes shiftiness and malingering. Clever of you to see it."

Actually I had not seen it. I had described a visitor to the exhibition whom I could see standing behind my companion. I confessed.

My friend turned around. "You're still right," he said. "That's the painter."

"But suppose it had been some swaggering doll? Or an archbishop?"

"But it wasn't. You felt it instinctively and expressed yourself honestly. Grasp that, and you'll understand these paintings."

I grasped it, all right. Unless I had got it all wrong, it hardly seemed worth while.

from The Fully Processed Cheese

On Our Cultural Renaissance

Doug Fetherling

Five years ago Canadians thought culture was a photograph by Karsh, any linocut that didn't show a Spanish galleon, a carving of a walrus that looked like a mole, a bad American movie about an impotent husband and any book published by House of Anansi. Now Canadians think culture is a restaurant that revolves while you're eating, a close-up of dew drops on the leaves of a weed, a play in which actors swear at each other, a bad Canadian movie about a hockey player, and any book published by House of Anansi five years ago.

"Momma Isn't Home Now"

Eric Nicol

There are quite a few things that can fill me with alarm on sight, of which small boys and simplified can openers are not the least.

But for instilling sheer, spine-numbing, teeth-rattling terror, nothing, in my estimation, can equal a truly determined house-to-house peddler.

Wave a brush salesman under my nose and I collapse as abruptly as an old opera hat.

When I was younger, as I once was, I used to fear being left alone in the house at night because of goblins that appeared at the window. Now the goblins appear in the daytime at the door, and try to sell me shoelaces. The fact that I don't wear shoes seems merely to serve as a challenge to their powers of persuasion.

Moreover, they always seem to attack the house just when I have gone into the bathroom for a bath or something, and the place is filled with the roar of swiftly running waters, plainly audible outside.

Often, in the middle of a bath, I suddenly shut off all the taps, stop splashing, and listen closely. I'm always afraid a peddler has somehow gotten into the house, and is now picking the lock on the bathroom door, under cover of the noise within.

My greatest phobia is that of being trapped alone in the bathroom by a man selling potato peelers.

When I was younger, too, I could rout peddlers by simply toddling to the door and lisping:

"Momma isn't home now."

The fact that Momma *was* home, and lying flat on her stomach on the living room rug to avoid being seen, was just part of the game.

Now, however, I usually shuffle to the door with a couple of days' growth of beard, and look about as juvenile as Lionel Barrymore. Thus the line, "Momma isn't home now," seems to have lost some of its punch. Instead of retreating, the peddler just jams his foot deeper into the door, and starts firing Christmas cards or retreaded girdles from the hip.

In self-defence, therefore, I bought a large dog, and placed an even larger sign on the lawn: "Beware of the Dog." Unfortunately, Theodore, who repeatedly bit every member of the family and frightened all delivery boys into oblivion, lavished an almost sickly affection on peddlers.

From sidewalk to door and back to sidewalk, Theodore showed them the greatest solicitude, and acted as a sort of canine convoy.

It was rather disconcerting, everything considered, to have Theodore standing there on the porch in front of the peddler, teeth bared, and growling in his throat if I tried to get out of buying the peddler's wares.

After Theodore ran away with a Fuller Brush man, I had to fall back on native ingenuity to outfox the peddlers. The technique consisted of hurling myself at the radio at the first sound of footsteps, shutting it off, and then crouching behind the sofa until the raid was over.

Yesterday, however, I suffered a stinging and humiliating defeat at their hands.

A peddler came to the back door. To my horror, after he had been knocking on the door for about ten minutes, I saw a load of inside fir pull up in the alley. The inside fir for which we had been waiting, praying, offering blood sacrifices (my little cousin Louie), had come! And it would never come again.

I could hear the peddler talking to the driver.

"Nobody home. Been knocking on the door for ten minutes."

A cold sweat broke out on my forehead. What to do? What would Disraeli have done in such a situation? Our lovely, barky, pitchy inside fir on the one hand, and on the other, a peddler whom I had persuaded to believe that there was nobody home.

I plucked up my courage, fitted it roughly over my face, and flung open the door.

"I guess I didn't hear you knock, I guess," I babbled to the peddler.

"Then how did you know I *had* knocked?" he demanded caustically.

I winced and I felt my courage slip partly off my face. I turned to the truck driver.

"You can dump the wood right in the alley," I said eagerly.

"Is your name H. J. Pugg?" the driver asked.

I shook my head dumbly.

"Well, this load is for H. J. Pugg," he grinned maliciously. "Sorry, bub."

I watched him go down the path and drive away, and somehow felt that he had taken part of me with him. I blew my nose sibilantly, turned slowly to face the peddler. He was blocking the back steps, his face wreathed in a sneer of triumph.

"That's my brother," he said. "We work together. It's funny how quickly people come out of the house when he helps me."

I nodded heavily as he whipped out a bottle of liquid.

"Now, I have here a sample of 'Ojoy,' the wonder juice for aiding digestion. 'Ojoy' is gentle, yet persistent, bringing quick, easy relief, usually within thirty days. Also good for polishing white shoes. . . ."

Something snapped in my brain. The next thing I knew, I was running along the street, blindly. I had blood on my hands.

from Still a Nicol

The Old Man Earns His Drink

Farley Mowat

One small difficulty still remained. We had no charts of the east coast of Newfoundland. The lack of charts, combined with a misleading compass and the dead certainty of running into fog, suggested we would do well to ship a pilot until we could make a port where charts could be bought and the compass adjusted.

The obvious choice for a pilot was Enos. Like most Newfoundland seamen he possessed, we presumed, special senses which are lost to modern man. He had sailed these waters all his life, often without a compass and usually without charts. When you asked him how he managed to find his way to some distant place he would look baffled and reply:

"Well, me son, I *knows* where it's at."

We needed somebody like that. However, when we broached the matter to Enos he showed no enthusiasm. For a man who was usually as garrulous as an entire pack of politicians, his response was spectacularly succinct.

"No!" he grunted, and for emphasis spat a gob of tobacco juice on our newly painted cabin top.

There was no swaying him either. Persuasion (and Jack is a persuader *par excellence*) got us nowhere. He kept on saying "No" and spitting until the cabin top developed a slippery brown sheen over most of its surface and we were prepared to give up. I was, at any rate, but Jack was made of sterner stuff.

"If the old bustard won't come willingly," Jack told me after Enos left, "we'll shanghai him."

"The hell with him, Jack. Forget it. We'll manage on our own."

"Forget him nothing! If this goddamn boat sinks I'm at least going to have the satisfaction of seeing him sink with it!"

There was no arguing with Jack in a mood like that.

He arranged a small farewell party on board that night. It was one of the gloomiest parties I have ever attended. Six or seven of our fishermen friends squeezed into the cabin and ruminated at lugubrious length on the manifold perils of the sea. When they got tired of that, they began recalling the small schooners that had sailed out of Southern Shore ports and never been heard of again. The list went on and on until even Enos began to grow restive.

"Well, byes," he interjected, "them was mostly poor-built boats. Not fitten to go to sea. Not proper fer it, ye might say. Now you takes a boat like this 'un. Proper built and found. *She* won't be making any widows on the shore."

This was the opening Jack had been waiting for.

"You're so right, Enos. In a boat as good as this a fellow could sail to hell and back."

Enos eyed Jack with sudden suspicion. "Aye," he replied cautiously. "She be good fer it!"

"*You* certainly wouldn't be afraid to sail in her, now would you Enos?"

The trap was sprung.

"Well, now, me darlin' man, I don't say as I wouldn't, but a'course . . . ."

"Good enough!" Jack shouted. "Farley, hand me the log. Enos, we'll sign you on as sailing master for the maiden voyage of the finest ship you ever built."

Enos struggled mightily but to no avail. He was under the eyes of six of his peers and one of them, without realizing it, became our ally:

"Sign on, sign on, Enos, me son. We knows you'm not afeard!"

So Enos signed his mark.

Happy Adventure sailed an hour after dawn. It was a fine morning, clear and warm, with a good draft of wind out of the nor'west to help us on our way and to keep the fog off shore. We had intended to sail *at* dawn but Enos did not turn up and when we went to look for him his daughters said he had gone off to haul a herring net. We recognized this as a ruse, and so we searched for him in the most likely place. He was savagely disgruntled when we found him, complaining bitterly that a man couldn't even "do his nature" without being followed. Little by little we coaxed him down to the stage, got him aboard and down below, and before he could rally, we cast off the lines.

Happy Adventure made a brave sight as she rolled down the reach toward the waiting sea. With all sails set and drawing she lay over a little and snored sweetly through the water actually overtaking and passing two or three belated trap skiffs bound out to the fishing grounds. Their crews grinned cheerfully at us, which is as close to a farewell as a Newfoundland seaman will allow himself. There is bad luck in farewells.

Before we cleared the headlands I celebrated a small ritual that I learned from my father. I poured four stiff glasses of rum. I gave one of these to Enos and one to Jack, and I kept one for myself. The fourth, I poured overboard. The Old Man of the Sea is a sailor and he likes his drop of grog. And it is a good thing to be on friendly terms with the Old Man when you venture out upon the grey waters that are his domain.

All that morning we sailed south on a long reach keeping a two- or three-mile offing from the grim sea cliffs. We came abeam of Cape Ballard and left it behind, then the wind began to fall light and fickle, ghosting for a change. The change came and the wind picked up from sou'east, a dead muzzler right on our bows, bringing the fog in toward us.

Enos began to grow agitated. We were approaching Cape Race, the southeast "corner" of Newfoundland and one of the most feared places in the Western Ocean. Its peculiar menace lies in the tidal currents that sweep past it. They are totally unpredictable. They can carry an unwary vessel, or one blinded by fog, miles off her true course and so to destruction on the brooding rocks ashore.

In our innocence Jack and I were not much worried and when Enos insisted that we down sail and start the engine we were inclined to mock him. He did not like this and withdrew into sullen taciturnity, made worse by the fact that I had closed off the rum rations while we were at sea. Finally, to please him, we started the bullgine, or rather Jack did, after a blasphemous half hour's struggle.

The joys of the day were now all behind us. Sombre clouds began closing off the sky; the air grew chill, presaging the coming of the fog; and the thunderous blatting of the unmuffled bullgine deafened us, while the slow strokes of the great piston shook the little boat as an otter shakes a trout.

By four o'clock we still had reasonably good visibility and were abeam of Cape Race — and there we stuck. The engine thundered and the water boiled under our counter but we got no farther on our way. Hour after hour the massive highlands behind the cape refused to slip astern. Jack and I finally began to comprehend something of the power of the currents. Although we were making five knots through the water a lee bow tide was running at almost the same speed against us.

The fog was slow in coming but the wall of grey slid inexorably nearer. At six-thirty Jack went below to rustle up some food. An instant later his head appeared in the companionway. The air of casual insouciance, which was as much a part of his seagoing gear as his jaunty yachting cap, had vanished.

"Christ!" he cried, and it was perhaps partly a prayer. "This bloody boat is sinking!"

I jumped to join him and found that he was undeniably right. Water was already sluicing across the floor boards in the main cabin. Spread-eagling the engine for better purchase, Jack began working the handle of the pump as if his life depended on it. It dawned on me his life *did* depend on it; and so did mine.

The next thing I knew Enos had shouldered me aside. Taking one horrified look at the private swimming pool inside *Happy Adventure*, he shrieked:

"Lard Jasus, byes, she's gone!"

It was hardly the remark we needed to restore our faith in him or in his boat. Still yelling, he went on to diagnose the trouble.

He told us the stuffing box had fallen off. This meant that the ocean was free to enter the boat through the large hole in the sternpost that housed the vessel's shaft. And since we could not reach it there was nothing we could do about it.

Enos now retreated into a mental room of his own, a dark hole filled with fatalistic thoughts. However, by giving him a bottle of rum to cherish, I managed to persuade him to take the tiller (the little boat had meanwhile been going in circles) and steer a course for Trepassey Bay, fifteen miles to the eastward, where I thought we might just manage to beach the vessel before she sank.

There was never any question of abandoning her. Our dory, so called, was a little plywood box barely capable of carrying one man. Life-preservers would have been useless, because we were in the Labrador Current where the waters are so cold that a man cannot survive immersion in them for more than a few minutes.

By dint of furious pumping, Jack and I found we could almost hold the water level where it was, although we could not gain upon the inflow. And so we pumped. The engine thundered on. We pumped. The minutes stretched into hours and we pumped. The fog held off, which was one minor blessing, and we pumped. The engine roared and the heat became so intense that we were sweating almost as much water back into the bilges as we were pumping out. We pumped. The tidal current slackened and turned and began to help us on our way. We pumped.

Occasionally one of us crawled on deck to breathe and to rest our agonized muscles for a moment. At eight o'clock I stuck my head out of the companionway and saw the massive headland of Mistaken Point a mile or so to leeward. I glanced at Enos. He was staring straight ahead, his eyes half shut and his mouth pursed into a dark pit of despair. He had taken out his dentures, a thing he always did in moments of stress. When I called out to tell him we were nearly holding the leak he gave no sign of hearing but continued staring over the bow as if he beheld some bleak and terrible vision from which he could not take his attention for a moment. Not at all cheered I ducked back into the engine room.

And then the main pump jammed.

That pump was a fool of a thing that had no right to be aboard a boat. Its innards were a complicated mass of springs and valves that could not possibly digest the bits of flotsam, jetsam, and codfish floating in the vessel's bilge. But, fool of a thing or not, it was our only hope.

It was dark by this time so Jack held a flashlight while I unbolted the pump's face plate. The thing contained ten small coil springs and all of them leapt for freedom the instant the plate came off. They ricocheted off the cabin sides like a swarm of manic bees and fell, to sink below the surface of the water in the bilges.

It does not seem possible, but we found them all. It took twenty-five or thirty minutes of groping with numbed arms under oily, icy water, but we found them all, re-installed them, put back the face plate, and again began to pump.

Meanwhile the water had gained four inches. It was now over the lower part of the flywheel and less than two inches below the top of the carburetor. The flywheel spun a Niagara of spray onto the red-hot exhaust pipe, turning the dark and roaring engine-room into a sauna bath. We pumped.

Jack crawled on deck for a breather and immediately gave a frantic yell. For a second I hesitated. I did not think I had the fortitude to face a new calamity — but a second urgent summons brought me out on deck. Enos was frozen at the helm and by the last light of day I could see he was steering straight toward a wall of rock which loomed above us, no more than three hundred yards away.

I leapt for the tiller. Enos did not struggle but meekly moved aside. His expression had changed and had become almost beatific. It may have been the rum that did it — Enos was at peace with himself and with the Fates.

"We'd best run her onto the rocks," he explained mildly, "than be drowned in the cold, cold water."

Jack went back to the pump and I put the vessel on a course to skirt the threatening cliffs. We were not impossibly far from Trepassey Bay, and there still seemed to be a chance we could reach the harbour and beach the vessel on a non-lethal shore.

At about eleven o'clock I saw a flashing light ahead and steered for it. When I prodded him Enos confirmed that it might be the buoy marking the entrance to Trepassey harbour. However before we reached it the fog overtook us and the darkness became total. We felt our way past the lightbuoy and across the surrounding shoals with only luck and the Old Man to guide us.

As we entered the black gut which we hoped was the harbour entrance, I did not need Jack's warning shout to tell me that our time had about run out. The bullgine had begun to cough and splutter. The water level had reached her carburetor and, tough as she was, she could not remain alive for long on a mixture of gasoline and salt sea water.

Within Trepassey harbour all was inky black. No lights could be seen on the invisible shore. I steered blindly ahead, knowing that sooner or later we must strike the land. Then the engine coughed, stopped, picked up again, coughed, and stopped for good. Silently, in that black night, the little ship ghosted forward.

Jack came tumbling out on deck for there was no point in remaining below while the vessel foundered. He had, and I remember this with great clarity, a flashlight in his mouth and a bottle of rum in each hand . . . .

. . . At that moment *Happy Adventure's* forefoot hit something. She jarred a little, made a strange sucking sound, and the motion went out of her.

"I t'inks," said Enos as he nimbly relieved Jack of one of the bottles, "I t'inks we's run'd ashore!"

Jack believes *Happy Adventure* has a special kind of homing instinct. He may be right. Certainly she is never happier than when she is lying snuggled up against a working fish plant. Perhaps she identifies fish plants with the natal womb, which is not so strange when one remembers she was built in a fish-plant yard and that she spent the many months of her refit as a semi-permanent fixture in the fish-plant slip at Muddy Hole.

In any event, when she limped into Trepassey she unerringly found her way straight to her spiritual home. Even before we began playing flashlights on our surroundings we knew this was so. The old familiar stench rose all around us like a dank miasma.

The flashlights revealed that we had run ashore on a gently shelving beach immediately alongside a massively constructed wharf. Further investigation had to be delayed because the tide was falling and the schooner was in danger of keeling over on her bilge. Jack made a jump and managed to scale the face of the wharf. He caught the lines I threw him and we rigged a spider web of ropes from our two masts to the wharf timbers to hold the vessel upright when all the water had drained away from under her.

When she seemed secure I joined Jack on the dock and cautiously we went exploring. The fog was so thick that our lights were nearly useless and we practically bumped into the first human being we encountered. He was the night watchman for Industrial Seafood Packers, a huge concern to whose dock we were moored. After we had convinced the watchman that we did not have a cargo of fish to unload, but were only mariners in distress, he came aboard.

He seemed genuinely incredulous to find we did not have a radar set. How, he asked, had we found our way into the harbour? How had we missed striking the several draggers anchored in the fairway? And how, in hell's own name (his words), had we found the plant and managed to come alongside the wharf without hitting the L-shaped end where the cod-oil factory stood in lonely grandeur?

Since we could not answer these questions we evaded them, leaving him with the suspicion, which spread rapidly around Trepassey, that we were possessed by an occult power. Witches and warlocks have not yet vanished from the outport scene in Newfoundland.

The watchman was a generous man and he told us we could stay at the wharf as long as we wished. He felt, however, that we might be happier if we moored a hundred feet farther to seaward.

" 'Tis the poipe, ye know; the poipe what carries off the gurry from the plant. Ye've moored hard alongside o' she."

Happy Adventure had come home with a vengeance and, for all I know, it may have *been* vengeance at that.

That was a singularly dreadful night.

We had to begin repairing the leak immediately, while the tide was low. We soon found that Enos's diagnosis had been correct. The outside stuffing box, or gland, had come adrift when both retaining lag screws parted, allowing the box to slip down the shaft until it rested against the propeller.

In order to repair it we had to borrow a big drill from the

helpful watchman, drill out the remains of the old lag screws, fair off the dead wood where the shaft had chewed it up, and then screw the gland back into place. Perhaps this does not sound like much of a task, but let me try to paint the scene.

To reach the gland we had to wade knee-deep in black, stinking muck, a composite product consisting of aboriginal slime fortified over the decades by decaying contributions from the fish plant. We worked in darkness except for the light from two poor flashlights which could produce only a dim orange glow in the shroud of bitterly cold fog that enveloped us. We kept dropping things, and the recovery of a wrench or a bolt from the sucking slime brought to mind Hercules at his task in the Augean stables.

By three o'clock the job was done and just in time because the tide was rising. We waited impatiently for it to float the boat so we could haul her out along the wharf, away from the ominous presence of the "poipe." Half an hour before the plant began operations, the tide was full.

It was not full enough. *Happy Adventure* did not float.

We had run her ashore "on the last of springs," which is to say, on the highest tide of the month. Enos, who knew all about such things, pointed out to us it would be nearly twenty-eight days before the tide was as high again.

Enos also said he felt it was time for him to leave. He said he did not want to be a bother to us and, considering the cramped accommodation of our little vessel and the fact that we would be making a prolonged visit in Trepassey, he thought it would be better if he went away as soon as the fog thinned. He said he would sacrifice his own comfort and stay with friends ashore until he could find transportation back to Muddy Hole.

I did not attempt to dissuade him but Jack was displeased because, as an old Navy man, he took a dim view of people jumping ship. However after breakfast Jack found he was able to accept Enos's departure with equanimity.

I cooked that breakfast. It was a hearty one for we were all half-starved. I cut up and fried about three pounds of side bacon. It was fat bacon; it was tough bacon; and it had a rind on it a quarter of an inch thick.

Jack and Enos sat at the saloon table while I served them. What with the layers of muck that coated our clothing, and what with the stench from the fishy flats outside, the atmosphere was not salubrious. However for once Jack was too tired, too hungry, and too depressed to care about his mealtime surroundings. Grimly he went to work on his bacon while I turned back to the stove to cook my own rashers. Suddenly I heard Jack make a despairing, strangled sound. I spun around.

Jack sat rigid on the bench, his eyes staring glassily from a face that had lost its usual ruddy colour and had become grotesquely mottled. He was staring at Enos.

All unaware of the scrutiny Enos was busy eating his bacon. It had proved too tough for him to deal with while his badly fitting dentures remained in his mouth, so he had removed both plates. He now held them firmly in the angle between thumb and forefinger of his left hand, and he was making them snap open and shut with a dexterity that argued long practice. With his right hand he was passing a strip of bacon between the two sets of grinders. When this remarkable operation had macerated the strip of bacon sufficiently he threw back his head, poised the bacon over his mouth, and gummed it down.

Jack struggled to his feet, pushed his way past me, and vanished out the companion hatch. Before he returned, an hour or so later, Enos had packed his gear and gone ashore. I cannot in all conscience say that either of us was deeply pained to sign him off.

from   The Boat Who Wouldn't Float

Then I Remembered

Keith Crombie & J. E. McDougall

I ran into Thompson in a down-town hotel rotunda.

"Hello, Petey," he said, "how you been?"

"Fine," I replied, "and you?"

"Great," he exclaimed. "By the way, I saw old Whats-his-name this afternoon."

"Oh!" I interjected, politely.

Thompson's brow wrinkled in thought.

"You know who I mean, don't you?" he asked.

"Well——" I commenced.

"Oh, you know," he waved a finger at me, "great big fellow, awfully jolly; used to wear a red coat around the house."

"Santa Claus?" I suggested, tentatively.

Thompson snorted.

"No, no!" he exclaimed. "Don't be silly. This fellow was dark complexioned, had sort of curly hair and was quite an athlete. Could lick anybody his own weight hands down."

I considered a moment.

"You don't mean the great Jack Johnson, do you?" I asked.

Thompson looked at me in disdain.

"Can't you see I'm trying to think," he said. "It seems to me his name began with P. Something like Purvis, or Pugsley, or Pringle."

"Proggle?" I suggested, helpfully. "Progley, Purgle, Pungle, Pringsley, Pugvis, Pumplestein, Piggle? Any of those?"

Thompson stared at me. "Say," he said, "I'm not sure that his name did start with P either. It was quite a short name, and like a rather common one, only different."

"Bjones," I ventures. "Slith, Browner, Sobinson?"

But Thompson still shook his head. "No," he said, "I can't remember his name. I'm sorry, too, because I wanted to tell you I'd seen him. He borrowed twenty dollars from you the day he graduated from college and I don't think you ever got it back."

A great light suddenly dawned. "Jimmy Smithers!" I exclaimed. "Where did you see him?"

"At the railway ticket office," replied Thompson. "He's leaving town again for Vancouver this evening. Where are you going?"

But I was already out of the hotel and on my way to the railroad station to sit and wait for dear old Jimmy.

from Sackcloth and Splashes

A Child's Garden of Clichés Culled, at Great Expense, from (You Should Pardon the Expression) The Various Media of Communication

Pierre Berton

Well, thank you for those very kind words, Ed. Believe me, this new post does represent a new challenge for me, and all I can say is I'm going to give it my very best. And whether or not I make good, I know that I'm going to have a lot of fun trying. . . .

First, let me say, gentlemen, how very sorry the Prime Minister is that he is unable to be with you this evening. I know he would want me to express to you his very real regret that previous commitments have made it impossible for him to attend. I hope, in his absence, you will permit me to read this prepared speech. . . .

What's happening to us, Marcia? In the old days, even when we lived on salami and chips, we seemed to be so close. And now, I don't know, it's as if we were drifting apart. . . .

Well, Dick, I just want to thank you for taking time out from your busy schedule and coming down here to the studio to talk with us tonight, and I think I speak for all the boys and girls on the show when I say we wish you all the luck in the world, fella.

My warmest thanks to Miss May Fellows, Miss Alicia Whitehead and Miss Freda Schon for typing the manuscript through successive drafts. A special word of gratitude, too, to Miss Aimee Larson for reading the proofs and making valuable editorial suggestions, and to Miss Anne Sylvester for her encouragement throughout. I am also deeply grateful for the special help of Miss Patricia Lowe and Miss Abigail Sells. And finally, of course, my thanks to my dear wife without whose patient understanding this book would not have been possible.

Try to understand, Mrs. Hargreaves: Jimmy didn't die in vain. Thanks to him, thousands of decent, God-fearing American boys will grow up to live useful and worthwhile lives without fear haunting their footsteps. Jimmy isn't really dead, Mrs. Hargreaves; not as long as America lives!

Before I commence my formal address this evening, gentlemen, I should be remiss if I did not thank your Chairman for the very kind remarks addressed to myself. I can assure you he has been far too generous, and I am afraid after such a fulsome eulogy that what follows is apt to sound like an anti-climax!

DEAR AUNT MINNIE THANK YOU FOR THE LOVELY PAIR OF SOCKS THAT WERE JUST WHAT I WANTED HERBIE GAVE ME A BEAR THAT REELY RUNS BACKWARDS I HOP YOU HAD A LOVELY CHRIST-MAS LOVE YOUR LOVING NEPHEW JOE.

You got to listen to me Jake! You're not going out on that street alone! Not after all the promises you made. Just this once, Jake, you got to hear me out. This isn't your fight. What do you want to get mixed up in it for?

I should like to turn now to another dilemma of our industrial civilization: this endless search for a will-o-the-wisp called "security" which is stifling individual enterprise in this country. Where, I ask, is the rugged individualism of our pioneer forefathers? Would they have built this great nation to its present state of prosperity had they worried about something called "security?" The answer, gentlemen, does not lie in security, it lies in increased production. . . .

What drives you, Johnny? What keeps you running? Have you ever stopped to ask yourself why you're running and what you're running from? Some day you're going to have to stop running, Johnny. Some day you're going to find out that a man can't keep running from himself. .. .

Mr. Jackson and class: The subject of my speech to you this afternoon is "Our Community." Our community is, indeed, a fortunate one. Situated as it is between the teeming industrial centre of Toronto, Canada's largest city, and the richly endowed agricultural belt of Southern Ontario . . .

Don't tell me you're the little girl with the freckles on her nose and the bands on her teeth whose pigtails I used to dip into the inkwell in old Miss Smaltz's room back at Grosard Junior High!

Mind you, gentlemen, I have nothing but respect for our trade unions. Over the years they have raised the status of the labouring man to a high peak, and I doubt that there is anyone in this vast audience tonight who would deny their intrinsic worth. And yet, one cannot escape the feeling that today union leaders are demanding too much. . . .

We've always been peaceable folk, son, you know that. We never did hold with violence of any kind and we always brought you up to believe the Lord's way was the best way. But there comes a time when every man has to stand up for what he believes is right.

My only regret is that I am leaving all you girls behind, with whom I've spent so many rewarding months. Whatever happens, I'll never forget the gang here at the office and I know I don't have to tell you that, as soon as we're settled, the latch is always open to each and every one of you, and I mean that sincerely.

And in closing, I would like to thank my producer, Marty Schulmizz; my director, Rick Waldorf; my personal agent, Sim Reisman; my arranger, Jon Neelson; the cameramen, dancers, grips, script assistants and all the other wonderful people connected with the show without whose whole-hearted co-operation and unstinting support this award could never have been possible.

I think I can say — and I believe I speak for every member here tonight — that seldom have we in this club heard as inspiring and as down-to-earth an address as our speaker of the evening has honoured us with.

Well, folks, I see the old clock on the wall is coming around once again to the sixty-minute mark so I guess that sorta kinda winds it up for another Friday night. It's been fun being with you: see you all next week at the very same time. Meanwhile, drive safely and take care, won't you?

from Adventures of a Columnist

Stephen Gives Me a Man-to-Man Talk—on Dragonflies

Gary Lautens

I can recall my first man-to-man talk about sex as if it were yesterday.

Actually, it's almost a week now. But I'm still shaky.

"You'd better talk to Stephen about the facts of life," my wife said. "He's been asking questions."

"But why me?" I protested.

"Because you're the head of the house," she explained.

"But . . ."

"I don't want to hear another word," my wife interrupted. "I'll get Stephen."

Stephen came into the room.

My hands began to perspire; I could feel a twitch developing in my left eye; and I had to clear my throat several times.

"Mom says you want to see me," Stephen opened.

"Yes," I replied. "Sit down."

"Could you hurry, Dad? Brian's waiting for me."

"This won't take long," I began. "I just thought you and I should have a little talk. I thought maybe you'd like to ask me some, well, questions about things."

"No, I don't," Stephen replied. "Can I go now? Brian and me are . . ."

"Brian and I," I corrected.

"Brian and I are going down to the creek to catch bugs," Stephen told me.

"Bugs! That brings up a very important question, Stephen. Do you know where bugs come from?" I asked.

"From the grass around the creek," he answered.

"I mean, do you know how they're born?"

"Not exactly," he confessed. "Do you?"

"No," I said. "I hoped you might."

"Can you hurry, Dad? Brian's going to go home if I don't come out soon."

Throwing discretion to the wind, I went directly to the point. "Do the boys and girls at school ever discuss, well, boys and girls. You know — sex," I finally blurted.

"Sometimes," Stephen confessed. "I caught a dragonfly yesterday. Dad, Brian and me . . . I mean, Brian and I are keeping him in a jar."

"I don't want you to think that it's dirty or shameful," I said. "It's beautiful. And you should never be ashamed or embarrassed about something that's beautiful."

"What's beautiful, Dad?" Stephen asked.

"It's beautiful," I explained. "What we're talking about."

"You mean dragonflies or sex?" he wanted to know.

"The second one," I answered.

"Oh. Can I go down to the creek now or do you want to talk some more about sex?" Stephen requested.

"Your mother thinks we should talk," I said.

And, for the next ten minutes, that's what we did.

I looked Stephen straight in the shoulder and told him all I knew about life and kissing and girls and babies. I didn't hold anything back.

When I finally looked up, there was a pained expression on Stephen's face.

"What's the matter?" I asked, fearing I had said too much.

"My foot's asleep," Stephen replied. "Besides, Brian's gone home."

from The Toronto Star

Flattery

Keith Crombie & J. E. McDougall

Arthur was the perfection of indecision. In the morning he often spent as much as an hour deciding whether he would wear black shoes or brown, and in the matter of ties he was forced sometimes to resort to the eeny-meeny-miny-mo method of selection. He never wrote letters because he could not decide what to say and on one occasion he stood for forty minutes upon a street corner wondering whether it would be better to walk down or take a street car.

Both Sarah and Geraldine – Heaven knows why – were in love with him. Arthur spent many months of anxious worry, while trying to decide which was his affinity. Then Geraldine told him that she admired his capacity for quick judgement and action. He married Geraldine.

from Sackcloth and Splashes

The Bee Fight

Billy Bock

One episode that stands out sharply in my sinful childhood memories concerned Grandpaw, myself, and about a million of Grandpaw's bees. My Grandpaw was about the best authority on the behaviour of bees in the whole country. He read many books about them, sold colonies of them to his neighbours, could track down a wild bee to its home in a bee tree, cut the tree down, take the honey and sell it, then capture the bees, take them home, put them in a hive and start them making honey and money for him.

He often told me about how smart his bees were, how they all worked hard to gather honey, except the drones who were too lazy to work and were killed by the worker bees in the fall. He explained that each bee had his own job, part of a well-organized plan and each colony had a queen who directed the activities of the thousands of workers and was boss of the whole shebang. In her spare time she laid eggs enough to replace the worker bees after they had worked themselves to death. She was the only girl bee in the outfit so there was no time lost among the workers who might otherwise get romantic ideas in their heads. I was fascinated by his wide knowledge of nature and was keen to learn, but I wondered why those bees always picked on me and never stung him. When I asked him he said, "W-e-l-l Willie, them bees is pretty smart. They are so used to me, and they know I am their friend. I am careful never to shake them up or disturb them, but they don't know yet what kind of a feller you are. They may think you are a bad boy that needs some stinging. Maybe you don't do what your maw tells you and they find out about it. They are pretty smart, you know." Well, I couldn't quite buy Granddad's idea and I figured he was putting something over on me. I wished that they would try stinging him for a change, but he would go around those hives, and take the lids off without even wearing gloves or a veil, and I figured that here was a problem that would require further investigation.

One day I was sitting in the shade of the old carpenter shop watching Grandpaw taking honey from one of those hives and carrying the combs to a small extractor house where he would put the combs into a machine like a separator which would whirl them around so that the honey would be drawn from the cells by centrifugal force. Grandpaw had the lid off the hive and with his hands and face bare was lifting the frames, brushing the bees off with a feather, before carrying the frames to the extractor house where Grandmaw was helping him turn the machine.

I was out of sight, behind some gooseberry bushes, hoping that something would happen to excite those bees enough to have a few of them sting Grandpaw. In fact I was almost praying that something would happen. Then I remembered Grandpaw telling Grandmaw one time, "W-e-l-l Maw, it's no use just sitting around waitin' fer things to happen. You got to jist make things happen sometimes." Now I rather liked this piece of philosophy, and was about ready to subscribe to it. Satan may have had something to do with helping things along, too. I was in my bare feet digging my toes into the warm sand and I felt a nice round smooth stone about the size of a prune. I picked it up, hefted it, took a look at the hive with the roof off and let it go without even a windup, and I was a pretty fair shot with small stones even at my age.

WHAM! That stone struck the bee hive plumb centre, and I ducked back behind the bushes and peeked out. A black swarm of bees boiled up out of that hive like a tornado. Grandpaw was starting back toward the hive when the bees met him about half way, buzzing like mad, looking for a target with their stingers cocked and nobody in sight but Grandpaw. Well, I had made something happen. A flock of those bees must have forgotten about how good a friend Grandpaw was and went after him with all the stops out. Grandpaw threw himself on the ground and hollered "MAW! MAW! BRING THAT SMOKER!" He buried his face in the sand and in about two minutes flat Grandmaw came tearing out of that shack pumping smoke in all directions. (A smoker is a tin box with a bellows attached in which you burn rags and puff smoke at the bees. Smoke is about the only thing they don't understand, and quickly restores them to normal behaviour.) Grandmaw soon had things under control, and, with the bees gone, she started pulling stingers out of Grandpaw's neck. He had saved his face by shoving it in the sand.

I got away from behind that old workshop pretty fast and was busy digging holes in a pile of sawdust behind the mill when one of my uncles came along. He told me about Grandpaw getting stung, and said, "Somebody must have done something to that bee hive and made the bees mad." I expressed my sympathy for Grandpaw and suggested that it might be a good idea to sell those darn bees for they were always stinging me too. If he suspected me of having had a part in any skullduggery he never said anything about it to Grandpaw, and I never told anything about it either. Grandpaw's neck was swelled up for a while but after that he didn't have so much to say about how smart his bees were. I know I should never have done it, for if Grandmaw had not got around so quickly with that smoker they might have stung him to death. Sometimes I think my uncle knew more about it than he let on for one day he told me, "A good way to give a hive of bees exercise is to throw a couple of rocks at them."

from The Best of Billy Bock

Man, You're a Great Player!

Gary Lautens

Occasionally I run into sports figures at cocktail parties, on the street, or on their way to the bank.

"Nice game the other night," I said to an old hockey-player pal.

"Think so?" he replied.

"You've come a long way since I knew you as a junior."

"How's that?"

"Well, you high-stick better for one thing — and I think the way you clutch sweaters is really superb. You may be the best in the league."

He blushed modestly. "For a time," I confessed, "I never thought you'd get the hang of it."

"It wasn't easy," he confided. "It took practice and encouragement. You know something like spearing doesn't come naturally. It has to be developed."

"I'm not inclined to flattery but, in my book, you've got it made. You're a dirty player."

"Stop kidding."

"No, no," I insisted. "I'm not trying to butter you up. I mean it. When you broke in, there were flashes of dirty play — but you weren't consistent. That's the difference between a dirty player and merely a colourful one."

"I wish my father were alive to hear you say that," he said quietly. "He would have been proud."

"Well, it's true. There isn't a player in the league who knows as many obscene gestures."

"I admit I have been given a few increases in pay in recent years. Management seems to be treating me with new respect."

"You're selling tickets," I said. "You're a gate attraction now — not some bum who only can skate and shoot and the rest of it. Your profanity is beautiful."

"C'mon."

"No, I'm serious. I don't think anyone in the league can incite a riot the way you can."

"I've had a lot of help along the way. You can't make it alone," he stated generously.

"No one does," I said.

"Take that play where I skate up to the referee and stand nose-to-nose with my face turning red. It was my old junior coach who taught me that. He was the one who used to toss all the sticks on the ice and throw his hat into the stands and pound his fist on the boards."

"You were lucky to get that sort of training. A lot of players never learn the fundamentals."

"I think there are a few boys in the league who can spit better than me."

"Farther, perhaps, but not more accurately," I corrected.

"Well, thanks anyway. I've always considered it one of my weaknesses."

"That last brawl of yours was perfectly executed. Your sweater was torn off, you taunted the crowd, you smashed your stick across the goal posts. Really a picture Donnybrook."

"The papers gave me a break. The coverage was outstanding."

"Do you ever look back to the days when you couldn't cut a forehead or puff a lip or insult an official?"

"Everyone gets nostalgic," he confessed. "It's a good thing I got away from home by the time I was fifteen. I might never have been any more than a ham-and-egger, you know, a twenty-goal man who drifts through life unnoticed."

"What was the turning point?"

"I had heard prominent sportsmen say that nice guys finish last, and that you have to beat them in the alley if you hope to beat them in the rink. But it didn't sink in."

"Nobody learns overnight."

"I wasted a few years learning to play my wing and to check without using the butt of the stick. But I noticed I was being passed by. I skated summers to keep in shape, exercised, kept curfew."

"Don't tell me. They said you were dull."

"Worse than that. They said I was clean. It's tough to live down that sort of reputation."

I nodded.

"Anyway, during a game in the sticks, I was skating off the ice — we had won five-one and I had scored three goals. The home crowd was pretty listless and there was some booing. Then it happened."

"What?"

"My big break. My mother was in the stands and she shouted to me. I turned to wave at her with my hockey stick and I accidentally caught the referee across the face. He bled a lot — took ten stitches later."

"Is that all?"

"Well someone pushed me and I lost my balance and fell on the poor man. A real brawl started. Luckily, I got credit for the whole thing — went to jail overnight, got a suspension. And, talk about fate! A big league scout was in the arena. He offered me a contract right away."

"It's quite a success story," I said.

"You've got to get the breaks," he replied, humbly.

from Laughing With Lautens

Geralde and the Green, Green Grass

Robert Fontaine

My great-uncle Geralde, at the age of ninety-seven, developed an intense liking for walking barefoot in the grass. We ourselves had no grass, but in front of the house next door was a nice young lawn. Around this lawn there was a thin string running. In the middle of the lawn was a sign:

KEEP OFF THE GRASS

Geralde and I used to sit on the verandah and look at the grass next door.

"We, too," Geralde said, "should have grass. I *like* grass."

"The ground is no good for grass," I said. I was about eleven, and a student of where grass *would* grow and where it *wouldn't.*

"Next door, same ground," Geralde said. Geralde was so old he often talked like an Indian to conserve breath.

"Next door they planted the earth *with* the grass. It came like jelly rolls."

Geralde rocked in the old chair and laughed his shrunken head off.

"Name of a name! Oho! It came with the earth, the grass. Like a jelly roll. Oho!"

I was insulted. "It's true," I said, "because I saw it come. A truck arrived with many rolls of grass with earth attached. They placed all the pieces together and *voilà* a lawn!"

"When you are older," Geralde said, "you will have more sense. Over there the grass grew. Over here it will grow. In France I became a member of the French Academy of Botany for the green grass I grew."

Geralde planted grass seeds in front of our house. He watered them with a watering can. He filled one can and watered. The rest he left dry. He had a theory that the water found its way to the places it was needed.

"The grass which is dry opens up the mouth and the water advances," my great-uncle explained.

"This is not the way we learn in school," I remarked.

"Tell me," Geralde asked, "what is the capital of Peru?"

"I do not know," I said.

"You see?" Geralde cried triumphantly. "In school they teach you nothing."

Of course no grass grew in front of our house. Geralde decided the birds ate the seed before they had a chance to take root. He borrowed my gun which shot corks and sat on the verandah every day. Whenever a bird lighted on the yard Uncle Geralde let go at him with the popgun. He never hit anything, but he scared the birds away all right.

A chicken roamed out front from in back and he could not even hit the chicken, though he scared it.

"Chickens eat corn, not grass, anyway," Geralde said.

What Geralde did hit was Miss Lapean, who lived next door and owned the lawn which they had brought in pieces like a jelly roll.

She was walking by when Geralde aimed at a sparrow and popped Miss Lapean in the nose. Miss Lapean's face turned red and she ran up the walk and shook her fist at old great-uncle Geralde. Geralde nearly fainted.

"You want to kill me?" she shrieked.

"I aim at the sparrow," Geralde said.

"You're crazy," Miss Lapean shouted.

"No. You are crazy," Geralde countered. "You buy grass like a jelly roll instead of growing it in the normal manner. I will report it to the police. A crazy woman lives next door to me."

"If anybody is reported to the police it will be you," Miss Lapean said. Then she ran down the walk and into her own house.

"I think," Geralde said to me, "it is Miss Lapean who pulls up my grass. She is jealous."

"Since we have no grass, how can she pull it up?" I asked.

"Don't argue with your elders," Geralde warned me.

It was about a week later, and just as dawn was making everything bright, that I looked out my window and saw Geralde in front of Miss Lapean's.

He had his shoes off and he was running barefoot through the grass which was wet with morning dew. It would have been all right if he had not started to dance like some wild creature of the woods and to sing at the top of his voice.

The noise attracted Miss Lapean, who came out on her verandah in a bathrobe, her hair in curlers.

"*Va t'en chez vous!*" Miss Lapean shouted. "*Va donc!* Go away, crazy man!"

Geralde just laughed at her and went dancing through the grass. Miss Lapean chased after him and grabbed hold of his shirttail which had come out during the ballet.

"You kill my grass!" Miss Lapean screamed.

Geralde turned around and secured a headlock on Miss Lapean. He forced her to the ground and they began to wrestle. Presently Miss Lapean squirmed out of the headlock only to find herself the victim of a toe hold. Geralde had her by the foot and was bending that foot backward towards her waist while she screamed for help.

They wrestled like this for a few minutes until someone called the police.

At the police station the desk sergeant asked Geralde what was the matter anyway.

"What is the matter?" Geralde repeated.

"Yes."

"Yes," Geralde repeated.

"There must be some reason to walk barefoot in the grass of a neighbour," the sergeant said.

"There must be some reason to walk barefoot in the grass of a neighbour," Geralde repeated. This was a tactic of Geralde's whenever he was questioned. He would simply repeat the question.

"You wish to go to jail?" the sergeant asked. "In jail we have no grass, alas. In jail you can go barefoot among the small rocks."

"No, no," Geralde said. "No, I like to walk in the grass. What is the harm?"

"The harm is to the grass which costs money to lay down in long strips," Miss Lapean said.

"The grass," said Geralde with scorn, "maybe cost money. Maybe. But to tell you the truth it is not worth it. I would not walk in such grass again. Never."

"Do you promise to leave alone the grass of Miss Lapean and to walk somewhere else?" the sergeant asked.

"I promise," Geralde said. "Under protest."

"*Bien*," the sergeant agreed. "Unofficially, then, I suggest you pay to Miss Lapean ten dollars for the use of the grass and everyone is happy."

Miss Lapean smiled and rubbed her hands. I was in the front row and I whispered to Geralde.

"Five dollars," Geralde said.

"Ten," Miss Lapean shouted.

"*Ferme ta bouche*," the sergeant said to Miss Lapean. Miss Lapean shut her mouth.

"Why five?" the sergeant asked Geralde.

"Because," Geralde replied sadly, "the grass of Miss Lapean has worms. It is not good for walking."

"If it is not good for walking, then why are you walking on it?" the sergeant persisted.

There were murmurs at the sergeant's sharp wit.

Uncle Geralde looked from the sergeant to Miss Lapean and then back to the sergeant. His wrinkled face seemed more lined than ever and his usually bright eyes were moist with melancholy. His thin frame trembled.

"I am an old man," he said solemnly. "I admit it."

"Ah," said the sergeant, "let us have no appeal to sentimentality. Justice is fair to the young as well as the old. Do not, please, pluck at our heart-strings. You will hear only discords."

There were murmurs again. Half those present seemed to be pleased with the sergeant. The rest seemed a little provoked.

Uncle Geralde stared at Miss Lapean with the sadness in his eyes of a sick poodle dog whose paw has been crushed.

Then he turned to the sergeant.

"Your honour, I am an old man. Justice cannot deny it. My pleasures are few. My teeth are not for steaks nor my eyes for beautiful women or great books. My blood does not race with the spring and my flesh does not sing with the autumn. I cannot gamble, for I have no money. I cannot sing, for my voice is feeble and harsh. I cannot dance, for my legs do not follow my heart. Good wine elevates the pressure of my blood and is dangerous."

He stopped here to wipe from his eyes what I decided was a tear. The sergeant coughed uneasily. Miss Lapean produced from her pocketbook a small lacy handkerchief.

". . . still . . . still . . ." Geralde went on feebly, "there is in me yet a small spark of life, you understand?"

"I understand," the sergeant agreed solemnly.

"Yet what is there for me to do? *Voilà*, I walk in the soft grass and feel the earth beneath me and I am not too sad to be alive. Is it too much to ask from my fellow human beings? The loan of their grass? When they have singing and dancing and music and . . . "

Miss Lapean dabbed the end of her nose with the lace.

"Monsieur le Sergeant, if it is within the scope of justice . . . if it is possible, *c'est à dire* . . . the complaint . . . uh . . ."

"You wish," the sergeant said slowly, sniffling a little, "to withdraw the complaint?"

Miss Lapean drew a deep breath.

"I wish not only to withdraw it, but I wish to give the defendant the right to walk on my grass until the day he dies, heaven forgive me for being so heartless."

"*Bien*," the sergeant said, blowing his nose.

After the cheers had died away in Geralde's ears and he had personally forgiven Miss Lapean, we sat together at a small table, Geralde sipping cognac, I drinking strawberry soda.

"Are you sad, my uncle, because what you told the sergeant was a lie?"

"No. Because it was the truth," Geralde replied, drinking his cognac.

After a moment he added: "That was my last cognac. Now all there is left to me is the green grass, under me for a while and then over me."

Still, it was many a year before he died, and many a night he danced through the grass of Miss Lapean. And if it was good for Uncle Geralde, believe me, it was also very good for the grass, which to this day grows very, very green in the front of the house of Miss Lapean.

from Maclean's Magazine

Could I See a Good Murder?

Stuart Trueman

"*Professionally trained librarians,*" says a news item I'm reading, "*are very scarce. It is difficult to encourage young people to enter the field. They think it must be a dull and inactive life.*"

That's certainly absurd. Why, public librarians enjoy a more active life than anybody else. I know. I've seen them enjoying it.

This being Library Week, let's just look in on the hushed reading-room of a typical mid-Victorian library in a typical mid-Canadian town.

Old Mr. Beskwith, who drifts off to sleep while reading, often talks in his dreams. Today he lets out merely a loud whoop: "HEY! STOP!" This wakes him up again. Everyone turns and stares. He stares back, puzzled — he didn't say anything.

The librarian, Miss McQuill, comes running. She inquires earnestly in his ear, "Are you all right?" He looks up: "Why, sure." He is a little huffed. He doesn't see why she's always asking him; lots of other people in the room look sicker than he does.

An assistant librarian hurries in, whispers to her, "The Reverend's up again." This electrifies Miss McQuill. She dashes out, and up a steel stairway to a second-floor platform of book racks where an elderly man is grasping the railing, teetering.

"I want to see a good murder," he explains as she grabs his bony arm.

Miss McQuill knows that. He reads one every day. She finds them for him. Unfortunately, if she seems busy, the kindly old gentleman gropes up the stairway himself, then feels too dizzy to come down again.

"Could I see a good murder?" he reiterates as they stumble together off the final step. "You will," she mutters under her breath, "if you do that once more."

From the reading-room, suddenly — "GIT, DOG! GIT!"

"Here, hold this!" says Miss McQuill, handing the Reverend's arm to an assistant for safekeeping. She sprints, but she knows there isn't a dog in there; only old Mr. Beskwith. She starts over to speak to him, sighs, then changes her mind. He is glaring at her over his newspaper. He knows what she's thinking of, and he's getting pretty fed up with it. She's thinking of making a public spectacle of him again.

"*Many young people,*" the news item goes on, "*reject the idea of a methodical library job in favour of a more competitive calling, one where they will have to match wits with their fellows.*"

There's just the point! If young people only knew it, librarians do more wit-matching than anybody.

Just look at Miss McQuill as she tiptoes down a line of backroom book racks, stopping to flick a speck of dust off. Is she dusting? Not a bit of it: She's hot on the trail of a common library halfwit — the man who rubs out bad words with a hard ink eraser. She's matching wits with him.

An assistant taps her shoulder: "Miss McQuill — Miss McQuill! We've just found three more books in the next room with words rubbed out. Two with whole chapters torn out. And somebody has written all over the pages of a religious book!"

Poor Miss McQuill. At the desk, more exciting news awaits her: "While you were gone, somebody cut three more slips off the begonia."

Oddly enough, Miss McQuill doesn't even cast a suspicious glance at the Reverend's wife who is patiently waiting for him near the desk — even though she is known to be an African violet enthusiast. This is possibly due to the fact that last Christmas, when they were all so sure she was the guilty party, the librarians sardonically presented her with one of the library's small potted begonias.

The good woman gasped with elation: "I've never had a begonia in the house before." And, it turned out on later investigation, neither she had.

The only problem now is what to do next Christmas. The Reverend's wife will be expecting something again. I understand Miss McQuill is planning to give her one of the potted ferns — if the library commissioners don't find out about it first.

"Youth today wants a career that constantly opens up new vistas, new opportunities, new mental challenges."

Well, if there are any better mental challenges than trying to figure out the book titles library customers ask for, I haven't heard of them.

Watch Miss McQuill. Nothing rattles her. A meek-looking middle-aged man sidles up, half-glancing around as if expecting to see his wife materialize at his elbow. He whispers, "Do you have *Leona*? I'm not sure — it may be *Lorelei*."

"Sorry, sir," says Miss McQuill without hesitation. "We didn't get *Lolita*."

"Oh, thank you very much," says the man, a silly look of embarrassment on his face as he fades around the corner of the book racks.

With the same equanimity, Miss McQuill fulfills requests for "*Doctor Chicago*, I think it is," *Anatomy of a Murderer* and *The Man in the Long Gray Flannel Underwear*.

"All young people interviewed had the impression the librarian's life is not sufficiently rewarding."

I don't know what money librarians make. But there are other rewards. Why, most people almost never fail to enclose a present with the books they return.

Miss McQuill has a cigar box half full of goodwill tokens that have fallen unexpectedly out of the pages — numerous bobby pins, several snapshots of young men squeezing laughing girls, six unpaid bills, two blank cheques, a dog show best-of-breed ribbon.

"Once," she muses nostalgically, "we found a ten-dollar bill." Of course, the owner returned for that.

Miss McQuill also remembers reading that a U.S. library once found a strip of bacon in a book. There's originality for you

— a bookmark that can be eaten while you read!

"One college girl said, 'I'd be afraid to be a librarian. I might become a frozen-faced old maid.'"

This is the height of absurdity. That fearsome falcon-eye librarian stare she remembers from her childhood — that was all put on! Librarians assumed the look on purpose — in self-defence — like school teachers. They had to intimidate people.

I know, myself. Once, as a boy, I heard an ominous whisper over my shoulder: "Are you eating something?" In desperation to hide it, I clenched my teeth tight on a two-for-a-cent chewy molasses candy known as a honeymoon. They stuck.

"Are you eating something?"

I couldn't answer. I hoped they would think I was dumb, but the assistant asked me to leave. It was, I thought, a pretty poor way to treat a dumb boy — especially when I was such a regular patron of the reference room, as all my classmates were. You see, word had got around our school that the city library possessed a huge Oxford dictionary set — a volume about the size of a family Bible for each letter — with every bad word defined in full glorious detail, including Shakespearean and other classical examples of its use. The whole class went to gain a new appreciation of the Bard. As we certainly raised the attendance figures at the library that year, it seemed to me a burning injustice to be put out merely for eating honeymoons, especially when I hadn't even finished the "B" volume yet. I haven't got over the experience yet; it has given me a complex.

Everywhere you'll see countless inhibited victims as the result of such childhood experiences — casualties of an era when libraries were solemn cathedrals of literary worship.

Watch a gaggle of middle-aged clubwomen straggling into Miss McQuill's library. As they open the massive door, they are still shrieking and chortling. . . . "But if Betty won't tell him herself, then who on earth — "

Sudden silence. They shuffle in red-faced, bumping into one another, each prodding the other to go ahead first — as if they'd opened a wrong door and found themselves in the midst of a funeral service.

The truth is, they're little girls again.

"The consensus was that students want a job 'right in the know' of what's going on in their community, with lots of chance to meet stimulating people."

"What's going on" — is that what they want to know? Then who knows better than the librarian? Miss McQuill can tell you immediately, for instance, when a depression is coming without even looking out the window: People start reading a phenomenal number of books. It's a sure portent.

If you're not interested in depressions, she can tell you — but she won't — exactly who in town is going to have a baby. She knows even before the relatives do. It always happens the same way: A recent bride comes in and asks, crimson-faced: "Do you have any books on painless childbirth? A friend of mine asked me to get her one."

Friends of recent brides, it seems, are particularly susceptible to maternity.

As for "stimulating people" — where else but in a public library could you meet anyone as stimulating as old Mr. Beskwith? When he gives a sudden shout, "DON'T ROLL OVER ON ME," everyone in the reading-room jumps a foot.

Running neck and neck with him is the Reverend. No one else can keep so many librarians running.

I must say I envy him, in a way. I envy all clergymen in a public library. No matter what they ask for, other patrons praise them to the skies. If they suggest a humour book, it shows the warm human side of their nature. If they want an adventure story, they long for the broader horizons they cannot have; if hot stuff, they merely want to keep track of what the younger people are reading.

Today he is bringing back *Lady Chatterley's Lover*. Somehow, he explains, he got hold of it by mistake; he didn't know what kind of a book it was. If I said that, Miss McQuill would think it was a weak excuse. But in the Reverend's case, they understand it immediately: The good man thought, naturally, that Lady Chatterley's Lover must be Lord Chatterley.

A middle-aged man and his wife, who evidently used to be his parishioners, tiptoe over and greet him effusively. They talk — as middle-aged people in a library always do — in stage whispers that carry all over the building, disturbing everyone, even though they themselves can't understand what they are saying to each other.

The woman nudges her husband in a sharp aside: "Keep that book under your arm. Don't let the Reverend see you read cheap murders."

Then the Reverend quavers loudly, "I'd like to see a good murder, please."

The woman whispers to her husband, "Isn't he a fine man! — likes to keep his brain as nimble as the next fellow."

And out they go, still whispering, into the strange raucous world where people shout across the street and automobile horns bleat as if they didn't even know they were making such an ear-splitting din.

from My Life as a Rose-Breasted Grosbeak

from Canajan, Eh?

Mark M. Orkin

EVER   An intensive widely employed in Canajan. Quite unrelated to English adverbial usage, the interrogative or inverted form is usual. "Is it ever hot!" (It sure is hot!) "Didja have good time at the drive-in lass night?" "Did we ever!" (We certainly did!) "Coodja gofer somepm cold?" "Could I ever!" (You bet I could!)

The Dog Explosion

Hugh Hood

For Raymond Fraser and Sharon Johnston

Not used to foreseeing consequences, a bit of a kidder, Tom Fuess sat quietly in his living-room, in a comfortable armchair in front of the fire. He thought of making mischief. His wife Connie had her legs curled up underneath her on the davenport; she was reading some book or other and looked absorbed in it. Tom looked at her thighs, then at the fireplace; the light reflected on her panty-hose excited him. He shook out the evening paper, making plenty of noise so that Connie would look up. Then he folded the sheets back and squinted at the middle of page three, as if concentrating on the news. He spoke in a level voice:

SCIENCE STRIKES AT A NEW SCARE

DOGS TO COVER EARTH BY YEAR 2000

Baltimore, Oct. 9, A.P. While North American and European foreign-aid programs strive to control man's threat to reproduce himself out of existence, via birth-control clinics in underdeveloped lands (see picture page four), an unforeseen new peril strikes at efforts to limit food-consuming populations, said Doctor Bentley French, famed animal ecologist and head of the Johns Hopkins Institute for Canine Reproduction Research, today at the second annual international conference on dog population.

"Unless steps to correct an unmistakable statistical trend are taken immediately," said Doctor French, "the balance of world food supply is gravely in danger of irreparable shock. Worse still, if present dog birth-rates are maintained, and the extension of normal canine life-expectancies continues, a drastic over-population problem will confront us in the mid-seventies.

"Congress must act immediately to appropriate funds and inaugurate programs for world dog-population surveillance. By the year 1980 these trends will be irreversible, and the dog explosion will amount to nothing less than Armageddon.

"According to latest figures obtained from all quarters of the scientific community," said Doctor French emphatically, "unless we in the free world move at once, the entire habitable living-space of the globe will be covered with dogs' bodies to a depth exceeding three feet, by the year 2000.

"Samoyedes are the worst for some reason," concluded the Johns Hopkins spokesman."

"Hmmmnn," said Tom, ostensibly to himself, "here's another item, like kind of a continuing dialogue."

SAMOYEDE OWNERS REBUT FRENCH

A.S.P.C.A. "DEEPLY INVOLVED" SAYS PREXY

"Hmmmnn . . . rejection of any measure to extirpate man's best friend . . . dog's inalienable right to multiply his kind . . . pariah dogs on Indian sub-continent . . . give a dog a bad name . . . science no ultimate authority . . . Samoyede breeders press counter-charges against Afghans and Pomeranians."

He glanced up at Connie, who was now staring at him with electrified attention. "I'll be a son of a bitch," he said, "I always thought dogs were some kind of sacred cow."

"You!" said his wife.

"No, no."

"You made that up. You did, Tom."

"Not at all."

"Read it again."

He repeated what he had said, making slight changes in the wording. Connie got up off the davenport and came around behind his chair. "Show me where it says that," she commanded.

"Got it right here," he said, "let's see. 'Nudie shows ruled acceptable to general public.' 'Jacqueline Onassis fells cameraman with karate chop.' I tell you, it's here somewhere."

"Balls," said his wife, and he dropped the paper and started to laugh helplessly. "The dog explosion, Christ, can't you just see it?"

Connie began to get a malicious gleam in her eye. "See what?"

"It's a natural, that's all. If I went up to the university and said something about this casually to, oh, let's say, three people, it would galvanize the intellectual community. I'm willing to bet you the Montreal *Star* would have a full-page story on it within a month, anyway six weeks."

"There isn't a word of truth in it, is there?"

"Not an atom. It just came to me. Imagine the possible implications. Serious men in lab coats hunched over our four-legged friends in the small hours, seeking a way to implant anti-ovulatory capsules in the thigh at birth."

"And trying to figure out how to keep them from scratching?"

"Now you've got it. Programs of public education in the Bombay and Calcutta metropolitan areas, with pictures and easy-to-understand diagrams because, naturally, dogs can't read."

"But they sure can screw."

"You bet they can, the little buggers. Doggy diaphragms. Research into whether or not contraceptives have undesirable side-effects. High incidence of migraine among Pekingese on the pill."

"Do owners who forget the daily dose unconsciously desire their pet's pregnancy?" asked Connie.

"Or their own," said Tom. "Then there's the darker side of the program: mass neurosis, the threat to individual dog living space, the resentments of dogs in the have-not nations."

"Now you're letting your imagination run away with you."

"Well maybe, just a bit. If there's anything I can't stand, though, it's discrimination on the basis of race, colour or breed."

Connie said, "It's a good thing you don't talk to anybody but me this way. You could stir up a lot of animosity."

"All the same . . ." he said.

"You mustn't."

"It's worth a try."

"Don't say I encouraged you."

"Certainly not."

A day or two later, Tom started to circulate this rumour among faculty members chosen apparently at random: a junior lecturer known for his radicalism and espousal of all humanitarian causes; two men from the computer centre he bumped into at the coffee machines.

"It doesn't seem possible," one of them said.

"I don't know . . . I don't know," said the other, looking upset. "Remember, they laughed at Malthus. Where did you hear this?" he asked Tom.

"I read it somewhere, I think in the *Star*."

"It's possible all right. It's all a question of the curve of progression. I never thought of it before, but you do see a hell of a lot of dogs around."

"Sure do," said Tom, finishing his coffee. He watched the two information theorists walk away agitatedly, and felt pleased with himself. The next person he inoculated was an elderly department chairman, close to retirement, a kindly man unwilling to think ill of anybody and therefore very receptive to fantasy.

"Have you heard about this dog business, sir?"

Professor Joyce gave a start. "I don't want to hear any scandal, Fuess," he said.

Tom told him his tale.

"The poor creatures, surely something can be done for them," said Professor Joyce.

"Well, you see sir, the whole problem is in the communications breakdown."

"Of course, of course."

"It's a question of getting across to them, don't you see?"

"Perfectly."

"I understand that a number of linguistics departments are trying to evolve a code for dog language." When he said this a flicker of doubt crossed Professor Joyce's face, and he went on hastily, giving the story colour, "You know, like the work they've been doing with dolphins. Apparently dolphins have a consistent system of verbal signals on regular wave-lengths, with logical structures. Now if they could only break down the language of dogs in the same way. . . ."

"I don't think there's any consistency in a dog's utterances," said the professor. "I should think the right way to tackle the problem would be to help them to restrain their impulses, I mean to begin with. Get right at the heart of the matter and alleviate misery. I don't like to think of any sentient creature suffering the pangs of hunger."

"Maybe some dogs would sooner reproduce than eat," said Tom.

"There is that," said Professor Joyce. "Tell me, do you know of any program of public education?" He fumbled around in his attaché case, and to Tom's amazement produced his cheque book.

"I don't think the public has been alerted, sir."

"Pity," said the old department chairman, letting his cheque book flap open and looking vaguely around him, "a great pity."

Tom went home and announced his results to Connie, who was already beginning to chicken out on the experiment. "You better not mess around with Joyce," she said. "For one, he's too nice, and for two, he has an awful conscience."

"That's why I picked him out."

"Do you think he'll remember that it was you?"

"I'll deny it."

"You'd better let it drop."

He really meant to take her advice, and made no further references to the dog explosion for some time, except now and then to drop the phrase into conversation as though it were one of the recognized social problems of our time, like the generation gap or the monolithic nature of the power structure. He mentioned it in a couple of classes and noticed that the students nodded wisely, as though they were wholly *au courant* dogwise. This reaction seemed promising to him, and he idled through his lectures and his daily routine, waiting for feedback.

A month later he met Professor Joyce in the cafeteria, and they had lunch together, from time to time eyeing one another with misgivings. Over dessert the professor broke a silence of some minutes by clearing his throat twice, then saying, "This dog affair is snowballing, eh?"

Tom ate two spoonfuls of caramel pudding without answering.

"The dogs, the dogs," said Joyce.

"What?" said Tom.

"You know. C.A.N.I.N.E. *Committee Against Native Instincts and Natural Energies.*"

Tom almost choked, but managed to preserve his composure. "I don't understand you," he said.

"I'm a founding member," said Professor Joyce. "I don't like the name too much. I mean generally I'm in favour of nature and energy. Lifetime of studies in Nietzsche, you know. All that. Still, they were the only words that would fit the letters, and I suppose they stick in your mind. Good advertising."

"But what is it?"

"C.A.N.I.N.E.?"

"Yes."

"It's the official relief agency to combat dog overpopulation, for this area to start with. But we hope to extend our activities internationally. We plan to get in touch with that fellow in Baltimore, what's his name? Baldwin French?"

"Who?"

"Baldwin French, isn't that it?"

"The big dog man at Hopkins?" said Tom, hoping to mislead. "French doesn't sound quite right to me. Might be Francis."

"You've heard of him then," said the professor with relief.

"Somebody said something to me about him, when was it, might have been a month ago."

"It wasn't you who mentioned the problem to me?"

"Me, sir? No, I've never mentioned it to a soul." In case this should seem heartless, he added, "I've thought about it quite a lot, naturally. You might say it's been constantly on my mind."

Professor Joyce looked sad. "I was certain it was you, Fuess. Must have been somebody else. Sorry. Pressure of work, you know, and then I have all these committees and my work with C.A.N.I.N.E. It may have been somebody in the biology department."

Tom got away as soon as he could, which was not too soon because the professor insisted on giving him a full rundown on animal population.

"I don't know where he got all those figures," he said to Connie that evening. "Do you suppose he was kidding me?"

"I don't like to think about it. That's exactly how these things get started," she said. She did a lot of grumbling while washing the dishes and hurried off to bed an hour earlier than usual on the pretext of a sick headache, leaving Tom to wander around downstairs. He knew that she liked old Joyce and thought that perhaps he had exceeded certain unspoken limits. He might say something about what he had done next time he saw the professor, but decided that he wouldn't go looking for him. It would be better if they just came across each other accidentally.

The old guy might look like a bumbler on the brink of senile decay, but he had terrific energy and a well-known reluctance to let anything drop, once he'd taken it up out of humanitarian impulse. Tom considered this out of line; he couldn't see why anybody had to make a federal case out of a mere prank. After all, what he had done was harmless sport, in no way destructive, and it seemed to him kind of a shame that he would now have to embarrass himself with such a confession. Maybe nothing would come of the affair; better to wait and see. Meanwhile there was Connie to placate. She upbraided him continually for his frivolity.

"A joke is one thing and malice is something else."

"Malice?"

"You've got a nasty habit of speaking out of both sides of your mouth at once."

"White man speak with forked tongue," said Tom thoughtlessly.

"Oh, cut it out!"

"Sorry."

He came home one afternoon to find her staring morosely at the paper, and when he asked what was the matter she pointed out a tiny box on page sixty-four, next to the comics:

C.A.N.I.N.E.

All contributions gratefully accepted
Star. Box 261b. Montreal

"That's nothing," he said, but all the same he was worried. He kept seeing Professor Joyce away down at the end of a corridor or turning into somebody's office, arm-in-arm with men from the computer centre. The old man would wave to him cheerily, mouthing good news at him from a distance, his pockets bulging with papers. It got so that when Tom saw dogs making love in alleys or pissing against posts, digging in garbage cans or just walking along on the end of a leash, he would snarl mentally, sometimes even mumbling curses under his breath.

Around Hallowe'en Tom and Connie were sitting in the playroom watching TV late at night when the station breaks are surrounded by commercials. The movie on the CBC station was lousy, so they switched to the NBC outlet in Burlington just as the Carson show went away for a break and a string of half-minute spots came on. They drowsed through Uncle Ben's Converted Rice, Northern New England Light and Power, and Albert's Restaurant-Hotel on the Northway, just outside of Glen's Falls. Then they came sharply awake when the familiar face of one of the great movie stars of the forties hove in view on the screen.

"Hi there, I'm X.Y.Z. (famous movie star of the forties),"

he said. "Say, do you know that over seventy percent of the world's dogs kennel-up hungry every night?"

"Christ," said Tom.

The star continued. "When your Rover or Prince or Spot beds down on his warm blanket in your kitchen, do you ever stop to think about his millions of cousins in Asia and Africa and Latin America who sleep in ditches and swamps, who go hungry because they have no master to feed them, who breed irresponsibly because they just don't know any better? Are you and your neighbours aware that unless the unplannned reproduction of world dog population is brought under control now — NOT TOMORROW — NOW — that human and animal food supplies will be inadequate in five years, and at mass famine level by 1980? More dogs are alive today than in the entire previous history of the world. Ninety-five percent of all dogs ever born are alive now and the numbers are increasing hourly. Help us to avoid the crisis of the dog explosion! Write today for the free pamphlet, *From Pillar to Post*, and send your contributions to C.A.N.I.N.E., Box 500, Washington, D.C. Remember, only you can help avert disaster. Don't forget. That's C.A.N.I.N.E., Committee Against Native Instincts and Natural Energies. Post Office Box 500, Washington, D.C."

The station's call letters came on the screen; then Johnny Carson reappeared, but Tom switched the set off. He and Connie looked at each other silently for a while. Finally she said, "You must never, never admit that you had anything to do with this."

Tom said, "Half a minute on the network. Can you imagine what that cost? They've got it institutionalized now — somebody has a letter-drop in Washington and he just sits there opening envelopes with cheques in them. There's no way to stop it."

"That's right," said Mrs. Fuess.

After that whenever they saw one of that series of public-service announcements they would huddle close together as if for mutual protection, giving themselves up to apprehension and dismay.

from   The Fruit Man, the Meat Man and the Manager

from The Short Happy Walks of Max MacPherson

Harry Bruce

Everything that has had anything to do with the publication of these columns — or rambles, or love-letters to the city, or whatever they are — has been accidental and faintly ridiculous. They grew out of a casual conversation, like some crazy and unpredictable drinking-party; and, for me anyway, they began to work the way such parties do. They acquired a silly logic of their own and I, as the chief carouser, was never quite able to control the way they were going.

In this case, the casual conversation occurred a couple of years before the party began. At the time, I was working for *Maclean's* Magazine and I happened to be shuffling down Spadina Avenue with a fellow employee named Peter Gzowski. We were searching for a steambath, because certain excesses of the night before had rendered us both indescribably uncomfortable. I have often noticed that your solid gold hangover produces a mood of odd contemplation, a kind of reverent observation of things that you would normally not see at all. Gzowski, on this particularly cruel Saturday morning, kept remarking how *interesting* he found the old brick houses of Spadina, and the way the bricks fitted around the third-storey windows.

He said, "I wonder why one of the dailies doesn't let some writer just wander around and write anything he likes about the streets of Toronto. I mean, not a reporter, but a writer, a magazine writer." We had both worked as daily reporters but we regarded ourselves now as *magazine* men and, though the difference is too personal and probably too boring to define here, we took considerable pride in it and, right away, I thought I knew what kind of writing he meant.

That was quite a few jobs ago. I forgot the conversation until, one day in the fall of '66, Gzowski phoned me. He had recently become Entertainment Editor of the *Toronto Daily Star*.

He was a newspaperman again, and he wondered if I were ready to start walking where our talking had left off. He had this idea that walking, respectfully approached, was a form of entertainment (indeed, *free* entertainment), and that therefore writing about walking could justifiably take its place beside writing about theatre, movies, books, music, films, and, as it were, the dance. Moreover, if I would take one walk a week and write about it for his pages on Saturday, he would pay me fifty dollars per amble.

I had spent all of my adult life in journalism, and I could not imagine a sweeter or more pleasantly improbable deal. I would never have to phone up anyone to ask nasty questions. I would never have to add figures, rifle eight-hundred-page government reports for the New Angle, listen to odious speeches, chase ambulances, sort out the municipal budget, harass working firemen, or ask the next-of-kin for photographs of their dead. All I had to do was take a walk and, when I got home, try to turn my notes into something people would read. Moreover, the parts of the city that I chose to explore would be entirely my own business, and so would my schedule of walking. If I could not sleep, I might creep out into the empty streets at, say, five in the morning, watch the rising of the sun over a downtown railroad trestle, and know that I'd get paid for my observations.

There was one complication. By now, I was happily and fully employed as an editor of *The Canadian* Magazine and, though *The Canadian* did not object to my walking on behalf of the *Star*, I had some vague idea the professionally courteous thing for me to do was to walk under a phony name. I live on MacPherson Avenue, and I simply happen to like the name Max. The Saturday after Gzowski called, the mythical Max MacPherson strode forth for the first time, without a trace of a hangover.

As the weeks went by, and then the months, and walk piled upon walk, something odd began to happen. I don't know whether this sort of thing happens to other writers who work under pseudonyms but, some time in the winter of '67, I noticed that Max was taking on a character of his own. He revealed a faint quality of lechery that Harry Bruce had never demonstrated in print. His observations of the plump, white legs of high-school cheerleaders, for instance, and his tendency to peek over backyard fences at juicy, sunbathing housewives — they seemed to border almost on voyeurism. Moreover, Max, unlike the *public* Harry Bruce, often appeared to be quite unable to complete a walk without exploring some crumby bar. The bar did not have to be exceptional in any way — in Toronto, that would have made things most difficult for Max — it just had to be a bar.

Another thing about Max. Harry Bruce had never betrayed the slightest interest in odd publications, but Max, gleefully and rapaciously, was for ever purchasing such absurdities as Chinese dictionaries, mouldy *National Geographics,* Italian rock-'n'-roll magazines, Communist propaganda, and books. Books like *All About Canada For Little Folk* (1926); *Canada at the Cross Roads* (1921); *Proceedings of the Canadian Club, 1912-13; The Torontonian Society Blue Book and Club Membership Register* (1946); and *What a Young Wife Ought to Know* (1908). (The best of these, incidentally, was the last; even Harry Bruce was fascinated by the things a young wife ought to know.) The development of Max's magpie instinct was a natural result of the pressures of walking for money. Some walks just weren't working out as prose, so Max raided other people's writing to flesh things out with what he hoped were fascinating irrelevances. Frequently, he erred. I'm still not sure why he chose to own a 1919 edition of a Department of Agriculture pamphlet entitled *The Angora Goat.*

The first real indication that Max was getting out of hand, that he was trying to take me over, came on a local CBC radio show. Nobody had ever talked on the CBC about my writing, but after Max had taken roughly twenty walks for the *Star,* a radio commentator undertook to assess both his work and his character. He said very nice things about Max's prose (though, unfortunately, the sentence he chose to prove that Max was a master of the language happened to be one Max had plagiarized from Rudyard Kipling). Then, however, he concluded that, on the basis of the walks, Max was short, forty-seven years old, and the possessor of a great thirst, a tremendously dirty mind, and rooms full of useless junk.

Actually, I'm five foot eleven, but the part of all this that intrigued me most, and still does, is the fact that the commentator added fifteen years to Harry Bruce's age. I think there are a couple of reasons why people thought Max was much older than he was or, rather, I am. For one thing, I was born and grew up in central Toronto, and there are several parts of the city where I simply cannot take a walk without remembering things that happened to me years ago, and things I felt. There is always some tree, some fleeting smell, some old shade of brick or shape against the sky to remind me of a lost summer of boyhood war games, or some teen-age girl to whom I once thought I was closer than Man had ever been before to Woman. You cannot use so traditional a form of travel as your feet and, at the same time, maunder on in print about the intimacies of your past *without* sounding old. Men in their early thirties don't do that sort of thing in newspapers.

False Spring, and the Growth of a Good Memory

I step outside, not meaning to go anywhere, but the moment I've closed the front door, something, some combination of warmth in the air and the summer angle of the sunlight, something reminds me of the words of a poet: "Spring is mud-lovely." So I move off, down my dirty street, and before I know what's happening, a female person, someone I've never seen before in my life — this short, round, and bemused young woman in a brown, unbuttoned overcoat — she looks straight at me, smiles, and says, "It's spring again."

I search for a snappy rejoinder but, on such short notice, I can think of nothing better to say than "It sure is." We keep on going, in our opposite directions, but something about her and the mud-loveliness of the day makes me want to take a Nostalgia Walk and pretty soon I find myself exploring the grounds of the public school where, a couple of decades ago, I spent most of the days of my life. It is Brown school just south of St. Clair on the west side of Avenue Road.

The schoolyard is empty, and the fields of snow across the outfield are feeding a stream that sounds like a Rocky Mountain freshet as it falls and dies in the sewer opening. The great, drooping central tree that once gave the whole yard symmetry has gone. There are basketball hoops here now, and solid new softball screens, and the Board of Education has paved almost the entire yard. But, in other respects, the place is very much the way it was on the March mornings of twenty years ago.

I find three mittens, squashed milk cartons, a broken Coke bottle, old orange peels and apple cores, and more than enough candy and gum wrappers to prove that the children of Brown are still upholding the school's enviable reputation as a big-league consumer of sticky things. I am gratified to see that Crispy Crunch chocolate bars, Thrills gum, Nibs licorice, Mackintosh's toffee, and Neilson's Rosebuds are easily holding their own against such newfangled delights as Ugly Stickers bubble gum; and it comforts me, too, to discover on the walls of the school that "Paul is a bum," that "I hate Sylvia," and that "Valerie Holland loves Donald Lang."

I remember another morning in another March when, right here, in one beautifully sudden moment, I knew I could hit the ball. All through the previous summer and right on into the football season, a bunch of us had been hooked on this funny game, this perversion of baseball, and right up to the day the first snow flew, I had been the Pitcher's Delight, the Strike-out King, the Incredible Buffoon at the Plate. I was so predictably and excruciatingly awkward at bat that my own team-mates couldn't bear to watch me, and the enemy pitcher would chuckle horribly as he wound up, spinning his arm in his shoulder socket with all the confidence of Bob Feller on a hot day.

And then — praise be to the Yankee Clipper — there was this miraculous morning in the false spring of the following March.

Years later, I still believed that my friends and I had invented this crazy game, but I know now that all through the war and the late forties, kids played variations of it in otherwise empty schoolyards across the city. And perhaps, here and there, they still are. But the playground supervisors and the school authorities have never quite grasped that *all* the pitchers who take this game seriously have superb control, and it's part of these officials' responsibility in life to worry about such matters as smashed classroom windows, and so, over the years, they have tended to discourage the development of this graceful and character-moulding sport.

Therefore, after you've got your players (they should be between ten and fourteen), and your softball bat, and your filthy old tennis ball, you must find a schoolyard that's deserted. Moreover, the schoolyard must have at least one of those six-foot-high and three-foot-wide basement windows that rise straight from the yard's pavement and are covered with a heavy wire screen.

That screen, my skinny little friend with the large St. Mary's bat, is your strikeout zone; and, if the pitcher can throw that dirty napless ball past you three times so that it makes the screen sing, then you are, once more, out. Since you are also, perhaps, somewhere between four and five feet tall with short tubular arms, it soon becomes horribly clear that this is a pitcher's game.

He wears a real hardball glove — he needs it for "balance" —

and he has rubbed enough greasy dubbin into its pocket to make it sweaty. He grinds and twists and rolls the ball around in there. He spits, glances over his left shoulder, pumps his arms, kicks out his ankle like Ewell Blackwell, and — Duke, or Slugger, or King Kong, or Rocky, or whatever you're vainly pleased to call yourself — you are about to have superior insight into the mind of the man facing Don Drysdale. You are about to look awfully stupid.

A couple of fielders help in this game but, since nobody ever runs a base-path, two can play against each other with ferocity. A single is any hit that passes the willow tree; a double is any hit that passes the girls' swings; triples and homers go farther. You merely move the imaginary men around the imaginary bases, add up the score, and play on and on, through some obscure and dusty and sunny afternoon, till the twenty-first or the twenty-second or the twenty-third inning — or until someone senses that his mother is waiting and getting angry.

Anyway, on this March day in the forties, four of us came up here to Brown school to resume the season. It wasn't really spring, but it was warm, you could smell the mud, the ice cakes were sweating and shrinking back over people's lawns, the dark water was charging along in the gutters, and, because it was too early for flowers or grass, the earth of the city sprouted soggy newspapers, old cigarette boxes, and all the other thawing legacies of the fading winter's human carelessness.

The snow still lay in big damp sheets in the outfield, and it was the day I learned to hit the ball. I could *see* it coming. I knew when the curve would break, and I could wait for it. I could let the sucker pitches go by and lean into the good ones. Pow! Pock! Bam! Thwack! At bat you faced west, and, by the end of the afternoon, the sliding sun had burned my face red.

I had a sunburn in March; I was hot and sticky; I could hit the ball; and, even if I could possibly have known that only two days later winter's rattiest blizzard would strike Toronto, I would not have cared.

Anglo-Saxon and I

Shakesbeat Latweed (Margaret Atwood)

When I walked innocently into my first Anglo-Saxon class, I was totally unprepared for what was to follow.

This was mostly because there had already been six weeks of classes, none of which I had attended.

However, I soon found that everyone else, including the professor, was as ignorant as I of the cataclysmic events that were about to produce an unprecedented ferment of enlightenment in our little group. We should have known that the introduction of a radical progressive force, such as myself, into a static confining structure such as Anglo-Saxon, would result in a violent reaction of some sort. But I digress.

The professor was not (as I had expected) dressed in a large helmet with cows' horns, nor did he have two long braids of yellow hair or a targe of linden-wood. In fact, he looked quite modern. I experienced a sinking of the heart akin to that which I had felt when my Ancient History professor had appeared in a tie instead of a toga.

The lesson began. It was all quite incomprehensible to me, but I listened intently to the rhythm of the sounds — a vigorous pounding pulse, as if someone were jumping on your stomach — and contented myself with visions of Aelfric and the Cakes.

Imagine my bewilderment when I realized that a dead silence had been falling on the room for some time. The professor was looking at me with a bland smile.

"Mr. Latweed, I asked you to translate," he said, through his blandly smiling clenched teeth.

After I had opened my book, I rose gracefully from my seat.

"Actually, sir," I said, in my most impressive manner, "I'm a great authenticarian, and I feel that the spontaneous oral tradition of Caedmon and the bards should not be desecrated. If you would like to wait until I return with my harp, I would be happy to sing you something."

He seemed to feel that we might be able to struggle on,

however inauthentically, without the benefit of musical accompaniment. My sensitive soul shivered.

I looked at the fateful passage:

"Oft ic sceolde ana uhtna gehwylce mine ceare
cwipan; nis nu cwicra nan pe ic him modsefan minne
durre sweotule asecgan."

It was obviously an account of the sibling rivalries of two five-year-old children.

I said, in my most urbane and sophisticated tones, "Sir, this is obviously an account of the sibling rivalries of two five-year-old children. I shall make my translation as free as possible, in order to preserve its remarkably condensed poetic qualities."

And I proceeded:

"Often I scold Anna – this is the little boy speaking – out of the wheelchair quipping, 'Mine car!' Is now quick ran Anne Theeking (this is baby-talk for "seeking") mothersafety (I conjecture that the first syllable of the compound, "modesfan" is a familiar term for "Mother", corresponding to "Ma" or "Mum") at Minny's door (Minny is the older sister; the mother must be either dead or divorced); sweetly I sock Anne."

I added that the style resembled a combination of James Joyce and Walt Kelly, with somewhat of an e. e. cummings format, and that the plot might have provided inspiration for many of our modern novels of childhood reminiscence. I also indicated several interesting words which have undergone semantic evolution since the time of composition. "Sweotule," for instance, which used to denote "with great sadistic glee" now has a much milder meaning.

The professor was not amused. He was bemused, or perhaps just confused. I realized that my theories were a little too advanced for him. I had bitter thoughts about prophets in their own countries.

I prepared exhaustively for the next class. I looked up all the words in the assigned passage – a pleasant little thing called "The Wanderer" – and produced an extremely literal translation:

"Often the solitary man for himself awaits the kindnesses the mercy of the measurer although he sad at heart over the waterways for a long time had to stir with his hands over the sea as cold as frost travel the paths of exile."

This did not quite satisfy my aesthetic sensibilities.

The professor desperately tried to avoid asking me to translate, but only three people had come to the class, and he found it difficult. At last my chance came.

"Sir," I said, "I found a word-for-word rendering quite unsatisfactory. Since I am (and I blushed modestly) somewhat of a poet myself, I have composed a verse reproduction that I think captures admirably the wistful undertones of the original."

I cleared my throat and began:

"As he wanders weak and weary
O'er many a cold and dreary
Frosty exil'd path the salty Boreas blows,
The lone man must cry for blessin'
For the sad heart's hopes that lessen,
And paddle in the water with his toes."

I could hardly restrain myself from adding something about the lost Lenore or a comforting crowd of golden daffodils, but I reflected that, after all, poetic liberty is not poetic licence.

The professor expressed the opinion that I might not have stuck quite closely enough to the original, but he was indecisive. I could see that he was weakening.

The next day was my day of triumph. It was the day on which the teaching of Anglo-Saxon was revolutionized, the day that saw the heralding of a new dawning, the day that ushered in the Method now used wherever two or more Anglo-Saxons are gathered together.

The professor entered, pale and haggard. The bland smile of former days was gone from his face. I was waiting for him.

He called upon me first, so as to get it over with. I stood up slowly and majestically.

"Sir," I said, "I don't believe that poetry should be translated. Furthermore, I don't believe that it *can* be."

"But," he quavered, "How then are we to understand it?"

"Understand? Nonsense!" I snapped contemptuously. "Poetry doesn't have to be understood. It is merely a pattern of sounds and, obviously, Anglo-Saxon sounds cannot be reproduced in Modern English."

"But what about the meaning?" His eyes were wild.

"Sir," I said, coldly but politely, "I'm beginning to suspect you of having archaic views. If it ever gets around that you are a Nineteenth Century Romantic, you'll be ruined. The Isaacs Gallery won't let you in; your subscription to *Tamarack* will be cancelled. Why, you'll have no place to go but the Canadian Authors' Association!"

This last crushed him. He was whimpering and submissive. "What do you suggest then?" he managed to gasp.

"I suggest," I suggested, "that we forget all about this odious translation business (my lip curled involuntarily) and instead have poetry readings."

Now we do. Little girls in rimless glasses declaim long passages about warriors being skewered through the gizzard, fields oozing with the blood of the fallen, and bodies stuck so full of javelins that they bristle like porcupines. (I must confess that, out of morbid curiosity, I sometimes peek at the vocabularies, although this is now considered cheating.) Then we all make lovely comments about the beauty of the sounds and the profundity of the arrangement.

Then we all adjourn for cookies and tea.

Aelfric, no doubt, would turn over in his barrow.

from Acta Victoriana

Officer, Arrest That Book!

Gary Lautens

"Gentlemen, you've been called together to form a new squad in the police department. Our task will be to examine all bookstands and confiscate the dirty stuff. First of all, can you all read? Never mind, Smedley, you'll be travelling in pairs."

"Do we have a name, Chief?"

"Any ideas from the floor?"

"As I see it, our job is to Harass and Expurgate Lewd Literature. We could shorten that to HELL Squad."

"Hmmm. Catchy. But the people might get the wrong impression, Johnson. Forces of HELL, and that sort of thing. Good thinking though. We can leave the name till later. Right now I should mention some basic rules and hand out the equipment."

"No gun?"

"No. You each get spectacles, a library card and a

dictionary. There's also an automatic scanner which picks out all four-letter words on a page with a glance. Beeps like a geiger counter. I think a good safe rule of thumb is one *double entendre* per chapter. Use your own judgement on innuendo."

"Could you give us some specific examples of what we're looking for, Chief?"

"Well, take Robin Hood. Now why were his men so merry? It's something we should look into. And that leads us to the business of Maid Marian. You should check to see if there is any evidence of a marriage certificate; we don't want another Tarzan scandal on our hands."

"I take it, Chief, that anyone who chops off the tails of blind mice is definitely sadistic."

"You're getting the idea, Johnson. Check into those old stories. What was the relationship between Snow White and the Seven Dwarfs? Were they just friends, or something more? Why was Red Riding Hood chased by the old wolf? Was he interested in her picnic basket or do we have an early, symbolic form of the Lolita theme? You can never be too sure."

"I have often wondered why Jack and Jill went all the way up the hill to fetch a pail of water. Seems pretty suggestive, to me."

"Keep up the good work, Thompkins. Remember our motto: Be suspicious. I've obtained some books so that we can practise right here in class. Think of yourselves as Smut-Busters. Now read — especially between the lines."

"But . . ."

"Smedley, you'll be assigned to the picture-book division for now, so don't worry. Blue pencil the prurient and lascivious."

"I don't like this title, Chief. *Black Beauty*. We could get some complaints. Why not change it to *Charcoal Beauty*? Get the meaning across — and eliminate any hint of race."

"I'll make a note of that, Johnson. With that kind of thinking you may make sergeant. And, Johnson, explain to Smedley what I mean by prurient and lascivious."

"Wow! Hahaha."

"What is it, Thompkins?"

"It's this bit on page forty-six, sir. Positively scandalous. You see, this couple, haha, is ship-wrecked on a desert island and, haha, they . . ."

"Tear out the page and pass it around, Thompkins. I want the others to see what I mean by obscene writing. After that page has been around, send it up here. I think we should make a collection of the confiscated stuff. It might even be the beginning of a best-selling text book."

"Pretty nasty description, Chief?"

"Yes, Williams. I think we'd all better take another look at that page. No need to underline the worst bits with pencil, however. And no drawing in the margins, please, men. Perhaps I should mention now that I expect our squad to have the cleanest lavatory walls in the division."

"Here, here."

"Smedley! Any objectionable, disgusting pictures yet? Don't nod. Bring them up and pass them around. I think we should get a bulletin board where these photographs could be posted so that our men will have a clear idea of what we're looking for. Sort of a 'most wanted' list."

"Look at this one, Chief. Absolutely shameful. If you hold it close, you can see all sorts of hidden meanings."

"Don't push, men. We'll all get a look. You can tell even from this distance that it's meant to arouse and ruin the young. Don't bend the corners, Wilson. Must be careful of the evidence."

"Here's an odd book, Chief. Doesn't have any pages. It's a phony with a secret compartment."

"Looks like microfilm inside, Wilson."

"Apparently it came in with that batch of books from the embassies."

"I remember. The one book had all that white powder inside and now this one with microfilm. Can't understand it. Well, throw it away. We haven't got time to waste on nonsense. There's work to be done."

"Were Adam and Eve ever churched, Chief?"

"I think we can let that one go, Johnson. All right, Smedley, speak up. . . ."

from Laughing With Lautens

Brevity

Maggie Grant

When this magazine was in its infancy various arty types took a hand in trying to brighten up my column. Visually, that is. Arty types don't care what's *in* a column, they only care how it *looks*. First, they printed it in larger type, then decided that a stylish sketch should top it off. Having thus cut down my lengthwise space by more than a third, they proceeded to trim width by adorning each side with curlicues. Just as I was beginning to fear I would be asked to get my ideas across in less than one paragraph, everyone forgot about me and things returned to normal.

However, in case art should again rear its ugly head I have been practising the craft of paring to the bone. Let's say that sitting in a country churchyard has inspired me to write an elegy. I have just completed —

> The curfew tolls the knell of parting day,
> The lowing herd winds slowly o'er the lea,
> The plowman homeward plods his weary way,
> And leaves the world to darkness and to me.
> Now fades the glimmering landscape on the sight,
> And all the air a solemn stillness holds,
> Save where the beetle wheels his droning flight,
> And drowsy tinklings lull the distant folds

— when word comes that I must cut down in order to leave room for a charming drawing of a grave. Wiping away my tears, I study my masterpiece and grudgingly begin to see verbiage that can be spared. For openers, when curfews were all the rage they usually rang at dusk (or parting day) so why stress the point? As for the cattle, herds invariably low and always move slowly except, perhaps, in the rutting season.

That brings me to line three, re plowman. It stands to reason he'd be weary, eh what? And what right have I to presume in line four that all the world is in darkness simply because I (me) am (are?)

Now for lines five and six. Faded landscapes do not glimmer, and that they're out of sight is too obvious to mention. *All* the air *solemn*? Tut! The air inside some houses might be madly gay. As for line seven, since it's too dark to see the beetle, how in thunder do I know it's wheeling? It might be going straight up like a rocket. Then, sitting beetles do not drone, ergo if they're droning they're flying. Any reader could figure that out. Line eight, are tinklings necessarily drowsy *or* lulling? Some animals are insomniacs, according to a reliable source, while others get irritated with repetitive bell-ringing. Feeling triumphant, I am now left with —

> The curfew tolls, the herd winds o'er the lea,
> The plowman homeward plods, leaves darkness and me.
> Now fades the landscape and the air a stillness holds,
> Save the beetle droning, and tinkling distant folds.

Drat! Still too long. Let's see what else can be scrubbed. Too many thes. Delete all. Who but a crossword puzzle fan knows what a lea and an o'er are? Begone! Is the plowman really going home? Could be he's headed for the pub, actually. And, as I am writing about seeing this damn silly scene it's redundant to mention that I'm there. Finally I am down to this —

> Curfew tolls, herd winds,
> Plowman plods,
> Darkness, stillness — save droning, tinkling.

Well, what do you know? That reads like the poetry one finds in avant-garde magazines, a style that formerly eluded me. Maybe I'm on to something.

from The Canadian Magazine

Yes, Santa, There Is a Virginia

Richard J. Needham

Once upon a time, quite possibly in Toronto, there lived a seventeen-year-old girl named Virginia Varoom. Her parents were liberal intellectuals who had immense faith in science, reason, progress, and the perfectibility of human nature. They believed in family planning, town planning, social planning, economic planning, and planetarium planning. They did not believe in God or Santa Claus, and they brought Virginia up accordingly.

"Man has no need of myths or legends or outworn superstitions," her father would say. "He is naturally wise and good, and with the aid of science will create a world of happiness and order. By the way, Virginia, don't go out alone at night; you are the only girl on the block who has not been robbed or stabbed or most foully ravished."

Her mother would say: "We must have faith in the infinite mercy and wisdom of the State, doing everything it tells us and obediently paying it taxes which now amount to eighty-seven percent of your father's total income. I'm sorry they decided to liquidate all those poor Eskimos, but no doubt the State knows what it is doing, and we are entering into an era of true democracy and social justice."

Raised in this manner, Virginia entertained no illusions about jolly old chaps in red clothes flying through the air on Christmas Eve. She got presents, to be sure, but her parents made clear they themselves had gone out and bought them. They were practical presents, too — a good pair of sensible shoes, a sensible navy-blue blazer and plain kilt, a cultured-pearl choker, a briefcase to carry her schoolbooks, the complete works of Shakespeare.

While Virginia herself did not believe in Santa Claus, some of her schoolmates did; and this infuriated her to the point where she wrote to a newspaper columnist, as follows: "Dear Mr. Noodlebaum: Some of my little friends are stupid and ignorant enough to believe in Santa Claus. How can I set these creeps straight?"

He replied: "My dear young lady, I am appalled in 187 different directions to hear that anybody believes in Santa Claus. Put it this way to your chuckle-headed little friends. If they believe Santa Claus actually exists, they will find themselves believing John Diefenbaker actually exists, and then they will find themselves believing Lester Pearson actually exists; and so on up or down the line, depending how one looks at it."

Virginia was delighted, and showed the letter to her friends, and thought about it when she went to bed on Christmas Eve. What (she wondered) had her parents bought her this time? A matched set of ballpoint pens? An English-French dictionary? A blue quilted bathrobe? H. G. Wells's *Outline of History*? A heavy woollen scarf, glove, and hat set to keep out the cold?

Shortly after midnight, she was awakened by the extraordinary noise of sleigh-bells, and the extraordinary spectacle of a red-clad, white-bearded man clambering in through her window. "Ho! Ho! Ho Chi Minh!" he cried. "I am Santa-a-Go-Go, and I have brought you the presents you really want, not those creepy ones your parents are always giving you. I have brought you a cigarette-holder seventeen inches long, and a copy of the *Kama Sutra*, and a forged identity card which says you are over the legal age of twenty-one."

Nor was that all. The dear old fellow had brought her mink eyelashes from England; black and white pony-fur knee-high boots; a Honda motor-scooter from Japan; a box of black star mouches; a white toy poodle with rhinestone collar; an appointment to have her ears pierced; a French telephone; a piece of shirt ripped from the back of Ringo Starr; a year's supply of Dr. Pepper; a modelling course; a computer to do all her homework; a lunch date with the Rolling Stones; a case of incense from Hong Kong; an appointment to have her hair done once a week by Gus Caruso; an 007 sweatshirt; credit cards with Air Canada, the Unicorn, and Sam the Record Man; a wall-to-wall sheepskin rug for her room; a cigarette partially smoked by Sean Connery; forty-eight bottles of Frosted Pink Revlon nail polish; a colour TV set with remote control; and a spring outfit specially designed for her by André Courrèges.

"And now," said Santa-a-Go-Go, "do you believe in me?" The little girl nodded her head delightedly. "In that case," he continued, "I will give you the thing you wish most of all. Whisper it into my ear." She did so. "Good as done!" he cried, and roared with laughter as he sailed off into the sky with his sleigh and reindeer.

Yes, when she went downstairs, they had vanished completely; not dead or anything awful like that; kindly old Santa-a-Go-Go had simply given them a new start in a Chinese commune, where they are very, very happy, and sing songs like *All We Want for Christmas Is To Double Our Pig-Iron Production.* Virginia thinks she might fly over to see them when she is finally satisfied with her eye make-up.

from Needham's Inferno

Appendix

"Of Course It's a Nitwit Country"

National Lampoon's Canadian department says so.

Jack McIver

Canadians have always found Americans to be pretty funny people. Not just Bob-Hope-funny or All-In-The-Family-funny, but *naturally* funny. Nothing, but *nothing*, tickles our national funny bone quite like stories of American tourists arriving in Canada with snow skis strapped to their car — in July.

A riot, right?

Or how about the way Americans refer to their baseball championship as the *World* Series?

Or the visiting Texan (it's always a Texan) who bawls that, "Wha', back home, we got tomatoes the size o' yo' punkins!"?

Heh, heh.

Then, of course, there's Watergate and Spiro Agnew.

O-ho-ho, o-ha-ha, a-hee. Yep, Americans sure are funny.

But what if the shoe was, so to speak, on the other country? What if Americans started making Canadian jokes? What if, say, an American magazine began poking fun at *our* institutions, *our* conceits, *our* faults? "Did you hear the one about the Canadian who. . .?"

Well, it's happened: since it first appeared in March, 1970, National Lampoon, a New York-based monthly that bills itself as "The Humor Magazine," has been regularly, and often not too gently, kicking Canada in her 49th-parallel ribs. While most American publications usually seem unaware of our existence, Lampoon almost always carries some reference to Canada. One month, it devoted an entire section of the magazine to us — "Canada: Consider The Alternative"; another issue carried a story on Canadian border towns called "The SHAME Of The North"; other allusions to Canada appear in Lampoon's faked letters-to-the-editor column.

The references to Canada are anything but flattering: Canadians are, according to Lampoon, bland, humourless, dull, naïve and ridiculously polite. We all wear checkered lumberjack coats and toques, all look the same, are hopelessly out of date, and are trying our darndest — but failing — to imitate Americans. Our favourite expression is "eh" (rhymes with day), a handy little word that we use as a question, for emphasis, as an entire sentence, or for ordering a grilled-cheese sandwich (our favourite meal). And Canadians, says Lampoon, all talk like country bumpkins.

But, hey! Heck, there, hold on a minute, eh? Please? That's not very funny . . . is it? Here's a sample:

Remember that Canada, your closest neighbor to the north, and first line of defence in the event of nuclear holocaust, is a foreign country. Canada has its own currency, customs, and native dress. In Canada, for example, they still have two-dollar bills (worth about $1.98 in real money).

Although nearly all Canadian holidays are the same as the American ones, Canadian Thanksgiving is held a month early since Canadians don't have so much to be thankful for. The Canadian Fourth of July falls on the first of July, so that Canadians have a couple of extra days to get ready for the tourists. But whatever the season, American visitors are as welcome as the flowers in June!

One of the exciting differences about Canada is that in Quebec (one of the ten provinces), everything is written twice, in English and in French. For instance, "snackbar" is "snackbar/luncheonette." And don't be offended if you see "dames" on the restroom door — it's only the Frenchies' word for ladies! It's touches like these that add a quaint European flavor. Outside the province of Quebec, everything is written once, in English. This is known as bilingualism.

Well, maybe it's pretty funny after all.

Canada's presence in Lampoon is easily explained: Sean Kelly, one of the magazine's five editors, is from Owen Sound, Ont., and three contributing editors — Bruce McCall, Anne Beatts and Michel Choquette — are also Canadian. No one at Lampoon can account for the disproportionate number of Canadians on staff, but it's this factor that generates the unusual amount of Canadian content in the magazine. Content like the "Cwick Canada Cwiz":

1. What's the capital of Canada?
2. What's the automotive capital of Canada?
3. What has become of the Canadian protest movement?
4. How do they take the census in Canada?
5. What is a Canadian political cartoon?
6. What is a hard-hitting Canadian political cartoon?
7. Why is it better to shop in Toronto than in Saskatoon?
8. Why is Canada always pink on the map?

ANSWERS

1. Mainly American.
2. Detroit.
3. He got married and settled down.
4. Take the American census and divide by ten.
5. A beaver rolling up its sleeves.
6. A beaver rolling up its sleeves and making a fist.
7. You can order direct from New York.
8. From embarrassment.

National Lampoon has been called the "bastard child" of Harvard Lampoon, the campus humour magazine that gained North American notoriety with its life-size parody issues of Time, Life, Playboy and Cosmopolitan magazines. In 1970, Henry

Beard and Doug Kenney, two Harvard Lampoon editors, and Matty Simmons, chairman of Twenty First Century Communications, the company that distributed their magazine, decided that a national version of the same kind of publication might just catch on. They set up shop in Twenty First Century's Madison Avenue headquarters, hired a small staff, and began churning out the same brand of satirical, irreverent, no-holds-barred humour and parody that had made Harvard Lampoon a best-seller.

After a rather sluggish start, National Lampoon took off: today, its circulation and its annual pretax profits in dollars are both hovering around the million mark. It is, according to the Audit Bureau of Circulation, "the fastest-growing major magazine in America." Lampoon paperbacks, special "best-of" issues, T-shirts and record albums are selling like pep pills at a truck stop. The magazine has also fostered a syndicated radio comedy show and an off-Broadway satirical revue called Lemmings. "Lampoonmania" is in.

National Lampoon "rents" the Lampoon name from Harvard Lampoon, which receives a two-percent royalty on NatLamp's newsstand sales; that small percentage has, according to editor Beard, reached about $50,000 for one year's rent. So has the potential yearly income for Lampoon editors: salaries range from $15,000 to $25,000, but the company's profit-sharing scheme can as much as double those earnings. "Pooners", or Lampoon fans, whose average age is between twenty and twenty-five, are making wealthy people out of Lampoon editors and writers, whose average age is about thirty.

"It was," says Beard, a tweedy, pipe-smoking twenty-eight-year-old, "a case of being in the right place with the right thing at the right time. We came out at the end of the 1960s activist-counterculture-humourless-anti-war thing. When we hit the newsstands, people were really tired of it, and they were ready to be told they were tired of it, preferably in a funny way."

If the dissolution of the 1960s protest movement created a sudden market for humour among its veterans, it is a market that specializes in cynical, often macabre, humour. Lampoon's success is predicated on the principle that no cows are sacred: religion, the flag (of any nation), motherhood, and the physically or mentally handicapped are skewered with no less frequency than war, the drug cult, pornography, or violence. The cover of one issue featured a helpless-looking mutt with a snub-nosed revolver pressed against its ear: IF YOU DON'T BUY THIS MAGAZINE, the message read, WE'LL KILL THIS DOG. (It was one of their biggest sellers.)

The December cover simply showed six progressive photographs of a U.S. $100 bill (serial number B23595675A) as it burned to ashes.

Lampoon has, in the past, featured a Vietnamese Baby Book, with spaces for mother to record baby's first whimper, first wound, and first funeral. Another issue advertised Lieutenant Calley's Kill the Children Federation, offering "foster soldiers" a chance to sponsor the death of a child in Vietnam.

In October, a special Lampoon Encyclopedia Of Humor featured a mock advertisement suggesting that Edward Kennedy might be president today had he been driving a Volkswagen four years ago at Chappaquiddick. The magazine was withdrawn from news-stands three weeks later when Volkswagen of America, which in its own ads had stressed the car's ability to float, filed a $30-million damage suit against Lampoon.

Lampoon's Manhattan mailman delivers dozens of letters from outraged, disgusted readers every day, but the protests don't faze anyone — at Lampoon, *anything* goes: Polish jokes, political jokes, "dead-baby" jokes, "cripple" jokes, and photos of dismembered bodies all find their way into "The Humor Magazine." Anything for a laugh . . . .

Parody and satire are usually forms of protest, but the editors admit that even *they* don't understand what some of the writers and cartoonists are trying to say.

Fortunately, not all the material in Lampoon is dished out with a garden spade: Canada, compared with other Lampoon targets, has been manhandled rather gently. Under the title "Canada: The Retarded Giant On Your Doorstep," Lampoon treated its readers to "just a few of the endless Canadian jokes that keep whole families amused during those long winter nights from August to June":

— *Why did the Canadian cross the road?*
— *To avoid meeting someone he didn't want to see.*

— *What did one Canadian say to the other Canadian?*
— *I'll meet you at the corner.*

— *Did you hear the one about the Canadian and the farmer's daughter?*
— *They got married.*

— *The Mountie's wife is in bed with her lover when she hears her husband gallop into the yard. So she hides her lover in the closet. The Mountie comes in, looks around, but doesn't notice a thing. Later on, the Mountie goes back to work and the lover escapes.*

And then there was the "Could You Be a Canadian in Disguise?" quiz:

Here's how to find out if you, too, have latent Canadian tendencies:

1. *A friend arranges to meet you in a restaurant and arrives an hour late. You say:*
   a. *"Nice of you to show up."*
   b. *"Next time I'll bring along my copy of Hawaii."*
   c. *"How about that! I just got here two minutes before you arrived!"*
   d. *"Remind me to give you a new watch for your birthday."*

2. *The color I like best is:*
   a. *red.*
   b. *blue.*
   c. *grey.*
   d. *white.*

3. *If I ever get a week off, I would:*
   a. *go to a luxury hotel in the Caribbean.*
   b. *paint the garage.*
   c. *have my tonsils out.*
   d. *get in a lot of golf.*

4. *I would prefer to be stranded on a desert island with:*
   a. *a gorgeous movie star.*
   b. *this month's Playmate.*
   c. *a tree.*
   d. *Susan Sontag.*

5. *I would most like to curl up with:*
   a. *a racy novel.*

b. a slim volume of verse.
c. the latest Sears, Roebuck Catalogue.
d. a great metropolitan newspaper.

6. I would go to see a:
a. hit musical.
b. major sports event.
c. partial eclipse of the sun.
d. rocket launching.

If you picked "c" every time, stop denying your Canadian birthright.

Contrary to what editor Beard describes as "a mythos about us that we're at no great pains to dispel," the Lampoon office does not resemble a scene from Bedlam: it's a very ordinary glass-and-broadloom complex in a glass-and-concrete high-rise. Nor do Lampoon staff members spend their days slipping whoopee cushions under each other, swinging from light fixtures, and putting the magazine together by simply tossing jokes back and forth in a ceaseless bout of revelry: "For some reason," says Beard, "people like to believe that we're all crazy, and that we're all on acid all the time — I've never taken a drug in my life. The reality is that it's a job, it's work — we turn out about 400,000 words a year, and they're all supposed to be funny. It isn't easy writing humour — it's an endless, endless grind."

The Lampoon editors are, however, a rather unusual group of individuals to be working in tandem: there's Ivy Leaguer Beard with his turtleneck, pipe and penny loafers, Tony Hendra, a chubby thirty-two-year-old ex-Benedictine monk, Brian McConnachie, a bookish-looking chap who wears a white shirt and tie to work, Michael O'Donoghue, thirty-three, an upstate New Yorker who sports a cane, a scruffy red beard and argyle socks, and ex-college English lecturer Sean Kelly from Canada.

Kelly tilts back his blue-denim Mao cap, lights another link in his chain of Pall Mall filter tips, and strokes his moustache: "I don't really know why we do so well in Canada, but more Lampoons are sold there per capita than here in the States. Maybe it's because Canadians like to see Americans getting knocked, or maybe it's because they like to see Canada mentioned in an American magazine. We also get a lot of manuscripts sent to us from Canada.

"Whenever we do a piece of satire on Canada, we get a lot of outraged letters from Canadians. Canada is a private joke shared by all Canadians, but we don't like other people getting in on it. Of *course* it's a nitwit country, of *course* there are too few of us and we're racially prejudiced, of *course* we bumble around and we're always cold and we keep building enormous monuments to a Canadian culture which doesn't exist. Of *course* we keep electing foolish people who make us promises we don't believe they'll deliver. But it's *our private* joke — we'll laugh at it, but nobody else had better. Canadians don't like Americans getting in on the joke."

That may explain the letters Lampoon received when they published a list of "Canadian Favorites":

Flower: wheat
Car: DeSoto
Hobby: soap-carving
Profession: invisible reweaving
Pastime: going for long walks
Medicine: Phillips' Milk of Magnesia
Flavor: vanilla
Room: hallway

Or the complaints from Canadians when Lampoon dressed a pig in a Mountie uniform.

Or the indignant Canadians who didn't like it when Lampoon printed:

The French-Canadians in Canada, while not exactly white, are very friendly and full of high spirits. They have a volatile sense of humor that often prompts them to indulge in little pranks with mailboxes and policemen, much as Americans do on Halloween or Moratorium Day. But for the most part they are a gay lot, always singing and dancing and shouting out quaint French-Canadian expressions, like maudit anglais or let's tweest!

"It's funny, though," says Kelly. "About twenty percent of the letters from Canadians say, 'Listen, you guys don't know what you're talking about — it's not like that here!'; about the same number say, 'Hey, that's great stuff, but you missed such-and-such . . .'; the rest of them, of course, are just mad."

Kelly, thirty-three, the "renegade Catholic" son of an

Owen Sound alderman, writes Lampoon's blasphemous — and popular — "Son-o'-God Comics." He's also the one who puts towns like Port Manteau, Cowfly, Deerfly, Flim Flam and Sleeping Bag on the (mock) Canadian map, and he helped to compile the "Canadian Lexicon":

U.S.	Canada
huh?	*eh?*
hip	*hep*
pig	*police officer*
fridge	*icebox*
hippie	*beatnik*
geodesic dome	*igloo*
Commie	*Her Majesty's Loyal Opposition*
exposé	*Royal Commission Report*

Despite the angry letters from Canada, Kelly believes that "most Canadians do have a sense of humour about their country and themselves — I believe that Canadians are a very ironic people. Let's face it, the national anthem is a bit of a giggle, really. Standing up singing 'We stand on guard for thee' seventeen times before a hockey game is a bit silly. But Canadians *know* that — Americans don't *know* that their anthem is silly."

Contributing editor Anne Beatts, the slim twenty-six-year-old Canadian who wrote the copy for the Kennedy Volkswagen ad, disagrees with Kelly on Canadians' ability to laugh at ourselves: "Canadians don't have any sense of humour about themselves — they absolutely don't. When we ran an old photograph supposedly showing Toronto as it is today, someone wrote and said 'How could you run this picture of Toronto when it was obviously taken during the 1950s?' They just didn't get the joke. But what's *really* funny is that it was actually a picture of Cleveland or some place during the *1930s*.

"Why do Canadians buy Lampoon? What else is there to do in Canada?"

Bruce McCall, another contributing editor living in New York, is thirty-eight and from Toronto. Henry Beard calls McCall a genius: "He has that most remarkable of all talents — the perfect combination of writing and art ability, not to mention having one of the best senses of humour around. He's able to be in complete control of what he's doing. Bruce is worth five others."

It was McCall, a shaggy-haired ex-advertising man, who wrote and illustrated "The SHAME Of The North," the spoof on Canadian border towns in the April, 1973 Lampoon. Some samples:

But now you're through, across the border. And you're ready for action, Canadian style. Like a million other spree-minded thrill-seekers out for a twenty-four-hour visa in vice on a passport stamped 'Pleasure — Plaisir,' you make a beeline for Main Street — pulsing epicentre of this festering cesspool of forbidden lust. Where they tell of spin-the-bottle games that never stop. Where the wine flows like maple syrup because it is maple syrup. Where a lucky hand of NHL hockey-star trading cards can gain a man a new mackinaw in a single night — and a bad hand can lose a man the McGregor Happy Foot Health Socks off his feet.

You brush off the urchin peddling McIntosh apples and pretend not to notice the lurid posters advertising Ping-Pong night at the YMCA. Keep moving is the rule. You pass right by the Tourist Information Centre with those sepia pamphlets suckering innocents into visiting Upper Canada Village to see the 100-year-old butter churn, or sampling nature in the raw in Algonquin Park. Not this trip, thanks. A man has only so much capacity for adventure.

"Grain Conference Slated!" screams the tabloid on the corner newsstand. But you don't want vicarious sensations; you're after the real thing. So the dime stays in your pocket, and not even "Habs Rip Leafs 3-2" can dislodge it.

"I think," says Kelly, "that most people take us too superficially. American readers would see Bruce's piece as just a joke about Canada, nothing more. But it was also a parody on certain magazines; Bruce was attacking a form of writing — you know, the Tijuana exposé sort of thing. Then he was satirizing the American attitude toward other countries. And finally, he was mentioning some things he's noticed about Canada."

The satire on Canada, though, often comes close to the mark. Consider the plight of McCall's American tourist as he tries to find a drink:

But there's a hitch. Canadian fashion. The government-run liquor store is closed during business hours and is 16 miles out of town. The beverage parlor, where a man can grab a beer, won't let you in without a necktie, a hat, a lady to escort, and proof you're not a full-blooded Cree Indian.

But there's still the hotel dining room — till you find the law says you have to buy two meals for each five ounces of liquor and the cap has to be on the bottle while the food's on the table and the bottle has to be off the table ten minutes before the last drink, unless it's Saturday . . . when the waiter can't bring liquor to the table unless you're not there.

"You really don't see Canada while you're living there," says McCall. "You have to live here in the States to appreciate what's funny about it. Still, as hard as we are on Canada, I'd like to move back — if I was married, I'd go back in a minute."

Kelly agrees: "Any Canadian I know here wants to go back — he thinks that's where he lives, he talks about it when he's drunk, he goes up there whenever he gets a chance, and he gets very defensive about it when other people knock it."

As much as the Canadian contingent at the magazine enjoys lampooning Canada and Canadians, it is, compared to say, the cannonades fired at middle America, pretty gentle stuff. After all, we're presented as polite, conservative, hard-working, fun-loving, friendly, simple people.

And that's not so bad. Is it?

from The Canadian Magazine, Dec. 29, 1973